SUBJECTIVITY AND WOMEN'S POETRY IN EARLY MODERN ENGLAND

Combining the approaches of historical scholarship and post-structural, feminist psychoanalytic theory to women's poetry in the late 16th and early 17th-century, *Subjectivity and Women's Poetry in Early Modern England* makes a unique contribution to the field. It is the first full-length study to apply post-Lacanian French psychoanalytic theory exclusively to early modern women's poetry.

The strength of this study is that it merges analysis of socio-political constructions affecting early modern women poets writing in England with the psychoanalytic insights, specific to women as subjects, of post-Lacanian theorists Luce Irigaray, Helen Cixous, Julia Kristeva, and Rosi Braidotti. McGrath employs these psychoanalytic theories of linguistic subjectivity to discuss its production in poetry written by English women in the late 16th and early 17th centuries. Her study offers a way to understand the psychological and material conditions and theoretical strategies of women's writerly opportunities as they were formulated and validated in their own textual testimonies. Because the social and political construction of the female body materially supports the sense of subjectivity which does or does not ease the way to writing, and because the always gendered ideology of literacy most closely impinges on women's writing potential, two chapters accumulate and analyze evidence of women's participation in the cultural construction of their bodies and their reading and writing.

Intensive readings of Isabella Whitney, Elizabeth Cary, and Aemilia Lanyer demonstrate the different means by which these poets, contributing to and immersed in bodily language constructions pertinent to the female writer, inscribed themselves as subjects in their poetic texts. Moving beyond the re-discovery and descriptive analyses of early modern women's texts, McGrath here attains a new level of sophisticated theoretical analysis of Renaissance Englishwomen's poetry.

This book is for

Alison, Felicity, and Emily,

for Nathaniel,

for my parents,

for my students, and

for the women of the New York Society for the Study of Women in the Renaissance.

Subjectivity and Women's Poetry in Early Modern England

'Why on the ridge should she desire to go?'

LYNETTE McGRATH
West Chester University of Pennsylvania, USA

Routledge
Taylor & Francis Group
LONDON AND NEW YORK

First published 2002 by Ashgate Publishing

Reissued 2018 by Routledge
2 Park Square, Milton Park, Abingdon, Oxon OX14 4RN
711 Third Avenue, New York, NY 10017, USA

Routledge is an imprint of the Taylor & Francis Group, an informa business

Publisher's Note
The publisher has gone to great lengths to ensure the quality of this reprint but points out that some imperfections in the original copies may be apparent.

A Library of Congress record exists under LC control number: 2001053621

ISBN 13: 978-1-138-74116-4 (hbk)
ISBN 13: 978-1-138-74115-7 (pbk)
ISBN 13: 978-1-315-18298-8 (ebk)

Typeset in *Times New Roman* by N²productions

Contents

List of Illustrations

Acknowledgments

Early versions of chapters 1 and 3 have been read at conferences of the Group for Early Modern Culture and at a conference on the Canon and Marginality at SUNY, Binghamton.

Early versions of chapters 2 and 4 have been read at NEMLA conferences.

Parts of chapters 2 and 4 were presented to the New York Society for the Study of Women in the Renaissance.

Part of chapter 6 was presented at the first Attending to Women conference and some details from chapter 2 were used in a workshop at the third Attending to Women conference.

Earlier versions of chapter 6 have appeared as essays in *LIT* and *Women's Studies*.

An earlier version of part of chapter 2 has appeared as an essay in *Women's Studies*.

Some details of chapter 4 are used in an essay on 'Isabella Whitney and the Ideologies of Writing and Publication' in *Options for Teaching Early Modern Women Writers*, ed. Margaret Hannay and Susanne Woods, New York: MLA, 2000.

I thank Betty Travitsky, Joan Hartman, Margaret Mikesell, Shari Zimmerman, Barbara Bowen, Irene Dash, Patrick Cullen, Susan O'Malley and all other members of the New York Society for the Study of Women in the Renaissance for their interest in and warm encouragement of my work. I also thank Susanne Woods for her kindness and support. I thank Anne Dzamba and Lori Newcomb for 'bookish' conversation and friendship.

Thanks are also due to West Chester University for grants, released time, a study leave and a sabbatical leave to work on this project.

And I also thank Mary Shelly of the Franklin and Marshall College Library for her patient help with research sources and the editors of Ashgate, especially Erika Gaffney, for their encouragement and support. Thanks are also due to Lawrence Moulder for help with photographic reproductions.

My thanks are due to Scholars' Facsimiles and Reprints for permission to quote from its 1982 facsimile reprint of *A Sweet Nosgay and The Copy of a Letter by Isabella Whitney*, introduced by Richard Panofsky.

Also to the University of California Press for permission to quote from *Elizabeth Cary, Tragedy of Mariam: The Fair Queen of Jewry, with The Lady Falkland: Her Life by One of Her Daughters*. Ed. Barry Weller and Margaret Ferguson. Copyright © 1993, The Regents of the University of California.

Illustration Credits

Jan David's *Duodecim Specula* is reproduced by permission of the Huntington Library, San Marino, California.

Ambrosius Holbein, *Schoolmaster's Signboard*, 1516 (accession nr. 311), distemper on pinewood panel, 55 × 65.5 cm is reproduced with the permission of the Offentliche Kunstsammlung Basel, Kunstmuseum. Photo credit: Oeffentliche Kunstsammlung Basel, Martin Bühler.

Mary Stuart's *impresa* is reproduced with permission of the Victoria and Albert Picture Library.

The following are reproduced by permission of the British Library:

frontispiece to Andreas Vesalius's *De humani corporis fabrica*;
illustration from Jane Sharp's *Midwives Book*;
frontispiece from Richard Brathwait's *The English Gentlewoman*;
illustration from E. Coote's *The English Schoolmaster.*

Also thanks to the British Museum for *Tittle-Tattle; Or the several Branches of Gossipping*. © Copyright The British Museum.

Geffrey Whitney's siren emblem and the title page of *Salve Deus Rex Judaeorum* are reproduced by permission of the Folger Shakespeare Library, Washington, DC.

The portrait of Elizabeth Cary is reproduced by courtesy of W.W. Winter Ltd, Derby, and with the help of Stephanie Wright.

My thanks are due to the Metropolitan Museum of Art, The Cloisters Collection, 1968 for permission to use the image of St John the Evangelist eating the Book of Revelation (68.74.fol.16 V); and to the Metropolitan Museum of Art for permission to reproduce Albrecht Dürer's *Melencolia I.* The Metropolitan Museum of Art, Harris Brisbane Dick Fund, 1943 (43.106.1).

Chapter 1

The Subject in the Margin. Women and Poetry in Early Modern England

> When she hath spacious ground to walk upon,
> Why on the ridge should she desire to go?
> – Elizabeth Cary, *Mariam*, III.iii.221–222

> I believe a unitary self is unnecessary, impossible, and a dangerous illusion. Only multiple subjects can invent ways to struggle against domination that will not merely recreate it.
> – Jane Flax, *Disputed Subjects*, 93

Beginning with the acknowledgment that is also a ritual for scholars of early modern women's writing, I invoke the presence of an early twentieth-century woman musing on her Renaissance foremothers. Lecturing at Newnham and Girton Colleges in 1928, Virginia Woolf asked the question that became a challenge to those who followed her.[1] Why, she wondered, did no woman write 'a word of that extraordinary literature [of the English Renaissance] when every other man, it seemed, was capable of song or sonnet' (43)? Although, Woolf declared, the image of woman burns like a 'beacon in all the works of all the poets from the beginning of time' (44–45), paradoxically 'in real life she could hardly read, could scarcely spell, and was the property of her husband' (46). Because they were prevented from writing their own histories, Woolf believed, 'nothing is known about women before the eighteenth century' (47). A mere glimpse of these women, 'whisking away into the background' (47), was all she could catch.

Thirty to forty years later, Ruth Kelso, Ruth Hughey, Alice Clark and Pearl Hogrefe launched what has by now grown into a full-scale commitment to represent more clearly the situation of women in the early modern period. As a result, the female half of England's population in the sixteenth and seventeenth centuries has acquired many familiar features.[2] Yet, both because the early modern period cared very much less about markers of individual authorship than we do, and also because Woolf's intuition of the hostile response to women's writing was largely accurate, disproportionately few of the documents which have supplied the narrative details of women's lives and social construction in early modern England have come to us endorsed by women themselves.

Current, over-conservative estimates of English women's writing literacy, as distinct from their reading literacy, which was always higher, suggest a rise from 2–6 per cent at the beginning of the sixteenth century to 25–30 per cent at the end of the seventeenth century. Though the percentages for women grew steadily closer to those for men throughout this period, there were always significantly fewer women than men able to write.[3] As Woolf perceived, however, lower levels of writing literacy do not alone account for the comparatively limited number of surviving manuscripts and published texts attributable to women. Even women who could write were often specifically discouraged from imaginative creation, and the achievements of those who resisted this negative pressure were, because of a general social distaste for all publication and a particular disapproval of women's publication, not usually considered sufficiently valuable either to be made public or preserved.[4]

Even so, as extended research interests have encouraged the search for evidence of women's reading and writing, that evidence has presented itself in surprising quantity and quality. We now know that many women *did* contribute to that 'extraordinary' literary output of the sixteenth and seventeenth centuries, and that some accomplished the feat most disapproved of for women, that is, the writing and publication of poetry, the 'songs and sonnets' that Woolf believed to be the peculiar province of men.[5] As knowledge of early modern women's writing has deepened, an important variant of Woolf's still resonant question has broached itself, not asking 'how and why women were silenced' (Ezell, *Writing*, 43), but how and why they wrote. The aspect of this question that has stimulated this study is how women in early modern England who wrote original poetic verse managed to achieve this sophisticated and prohibited literary goal, and more particularly, how they inscribed themselves as psychological subjects in their poetically imaginative writing. The last half-century's contributions from both historians and literary critics have made this modification of Woolf's original question meaningful and the discussion I offer here possible.

Although surviving texts from ethnically and racially marginalized women's groups in early modern England are few,[6] and the number of retrieved documents from women in the lower classes, though growing, is still small, the list of 'middling-sort' and aristocratic and gentlewomen's texts, representing all genres and all possible ranges of literacy and manifesting the subtle gradations of historical privilege inherent in documented and preserved public language, continues to increase. This list includes the dramatic and lyric poetry on which the second half of my study concentrates, but also prose romances, women's petitions to Parliament, anti-male broadsheets, public speeches by middling-sort women, letters from serving maids, diaries, medical handbooks, religious testimonies and travel journals.

The number and variety of women's texts now available establish an essential reading context for early modern women's writing. Prior to the recent intense critical interest, read in a context of male writing those women's texts that *were* known appeared exceptional, and seemed to owe both their origins and their survival to alliance with systems of patriarchy. Because she was Queen of England, for example, Elizabeth Tudor could justifiably make an authorial appearance in public speeches and in some formal poetry. Lady Mary Sidney, as Philip Sidney's sister, could come into print by continuing her brother's projected translation of the Psalms. Margaret More Roper, as the daughter of an admired and devout father, could acquire a writerly foothold in letters addressed to Sir Thomas More and in scholarly translations begun under his direction. These women's texts once seemed merely to imitate male conventions and language or respond to male directives and to be sanctioned by the upper levels of the culture. Their writers' gender at first *appeared* not highly important as a category of analysis, but I emphasize the 'seeming' of these perceptions because recent readings of these apparently conforming women's texts have persuasively argued the centrality of their gendered strategies.[7]

So, although the collection of recovered women's writing is not vast, it is substantial; awareness of its existence has altered our reading of early modern England and all its texts, familiar or newly rediscovered, written by men or by women. Especially in the post-modern critical context which led scholars interested in gender to seek them out in the first place, the richly various and newly accessible women's texts in the early modern period demand that readers now think carefully about the particular psychological and social construction of female writers, who, contrary to the dominant ideological proscriptions of their time and some theoretical assumptions of our own, did in fact inscribe their texts inside a culture which also inscribed them. Readers with feminist sympathies like myself know that a writer's gender matters crucially, always coloring what a consciously partisan reader,[8] speaking on behalf of the woman writer, will discover in a text.

In adopting this point of view, I am not at odds with early modern readers. Gender as a category of writing, of what Michel Foucault calls the 'author-function'[9] ('What is an Author?'), and as a category of reading, or analysis,[10] has asserted its vital importance for readers of early modern England, at least in part because it was of such moment in the literary theories of what we call the English 'Renaissance' itself, and especially in theories of poetry. Philip Sidney's influential *Apology for Poetry* (1595), in particular, assigns the noble manifestations of poetry to men, not women; gendered language underlines this attribution throughout his text: 'Poetry is of all human learning the most ancient and of most fatherly antiquity' (120), 'not being an art of lies, but of true doctrine; not of effeminateness, but of notable stirring of courage, not of abusing man's wit but of strengthening man's wit' (130). It is '*his* sweet charming force' (my emphasis) that 'can do more hurt than any other army of words' (125). Hostile 'poet-whippers,' on the other hand, are like hypochondriacal 'good women, who are often sick, but in faith they cannot tell where' (120). Poetry is only corrupted by 'that honey-flowing matron Eloquence, appareled, or rather disguised, in a courtesan-like painted affectation' (138).

In the literary codes of the sixteenth and seventeenth centuries (as, indeed, before and after),[11] though the muse of poetry may be female, its proper practitioners and expert disciplinarians are male.[12] In fact, although the lurking classical female muse encourages Sidney at one rhetorically useful moment early in his defense to conflate poetry with its female nurse-muse (96), generously and bountifully feeding the suckling male poet with inspiration, the proper poet transforms this inspirational manna away from 'effeminateness,' to the stronger 'man's wit' and thus finally to 'tougher knowledges.' It is the inaccurate, derisory characterizations, produced by the mistaken *enemies* of poetry (from whom Sidney would rescue a nobler, male-infused version), that depict poetry as female – 'the mother of lies,' 'the nurse of abuse, infecting us with many pestilent desires, with a siren's sweetness drawing the mind to the serpent's tale of sinful fancy' (123).

Passing from theory to the practices of reading and writing further confirms the exile of the socially-approved woman from the world of poetry.[13] Juan Luis Vives (1529) forbids women from reading 'songs' and certainly from writing them, and proffers instead as acceptable reading matter the writing samples of 'wise and sad men' (Bk. 1, ch. 5). George Puttenham (1589) worries about the 'poesies and devises of Ladies and Gentlewomen-makers, whom we would not have too precise poets lest with their shrewd wits, when they were married they might become a little too fantastical wives' (*The Art of English Poesie*). On the same grounds, Sir John Harington was amazed that Philip's sister Mary Sidney could have written her poetic *Psalms* because it 'was more then a woman's skill to expresse the sence so right as she hath done in her vearse' (I, 173) and Mary Sidney's niece, Mary Wroth, was publicly chastised as an androgynous 'hermaphrodite'[14] for writing an unfeminine secular sonnet sequence.

Indeed, a woman writing poetry, says Ben Jonson, must, like her classical Sapphic forerunner, publicly enact a 'tribadic lust,' by forcibly raping the female muse and moving outside the control of heterosexuality ('An Epigram on the Court Pucell'). Even if they remain lovers of men, says Thomas Salter, women who learn to be 'connyng and skillful writers of Ditties, Sonnetes, Epigrams, and Ballades' will be 'subtile and shamelesse Lovers' (sig. C1v). Thomas Heywood associates women poets with witchcraft (*Nine Books of Various History*, bk 8). Translation might be acceptable for women; original imaginative writing was reserved for men.[15] 'I like not a female Poetesse at any hand,' says Thomas Powell flatly in 1631. Even so-called 'feminine' rhymes, with their final unstressed syllables, are regarded by Samuel Daniel (1602) as 'fittest' for unserious 'Ditties,' while serious poetry like his own 'Poem of the Civill Warres' employs masculine rhyme (43).

I wish, then, to address the conundrum that lies at the root of all studies of early modern Englishwomen's writing. In a culture so vehemently antagonistic to women's writing, which constructed a woman writing as a social and sexual threat, what made it possible for women to write at all?[16] This book undertakes to answer a more specific version of this question: in a literary culture which emphatically gendered 'poetics' as the domain of men and declared it taboo for women, what social and psychological processes structured some women's writerly subjectivity in such a way as to let them invade even this specially prohibited and heavily guarded territory?

My study focuses on three women, Isabella Whitney, Elizabeth Cary and Aemilia Lanyer, who stepped over the boundaries of gendered and generic constraint that sought to exile them from poetic practice. It also offers a way to understand the psychological and material conditions and theoretical strategies of their out-of-character writerly opportunities as they were validated in their own, and other women's, textual testimonies. Because the social and political construction of the female body tangibly supports the sense of self which does or does not ease the way to writing, and because the always gendered ideology of literacy most closely impinges on women's writing potential, the second and third chapters of this study examine the textual construction of women's bodies and of their literacy from the middle of the sixteenth to the end of the seventeenth century. Some of the texts I refer to precede the publication dates of Whitney, Cary and Lanyer, and some follow. I am not arguing, however, immediate causal influence from the socio-psychological constructions of women's bodies and literacy to the poems of these three, but rather am establishing an ideological and textual atmosphere in which Whitney, Cary and Lanyer, in their different ways, participated. In these chapters, I build what I consider to be an essential backdrop from women's own textual contributions to a process of self-imaging.

Lacking this part of the story, we may, like Woolf, too easily underestimate women's capacity to influence their own cultural roles. Persuaded by the message of the dominant culture, we may find ourselves accepting as determinative the depictions of early modern women as silent, closeted, private persons confined to the boundaried mental and physical spaces of the home. But wishful male prescriptions of women's seclusion, and some women's idealized representations of their conformity to these prescriptions, other women rewrote resistingly and obliquely in poetic codes, as well as more directly in journals and diaries.

To name only a few rewriters of the dominant formulation, Mary Boyle Rich, Lady Grace Mildmay, Anne Halkett and Alice Thornton tell alternative stories of women moving frequently and independently out of their domestic spaces for a variety of purposes, including caring for the health of others, visiting family or attending to economic or business concerns. Many women poets, including Whitney, Cary and Lanyer, as well as others like Mary Wroth, Anne Bradstreet and Katherine Philips, in flights of narrative, dramatic and poetic imagination, journeyed far from their domestic hearths. It is surely not mere coincidence that among the women who wrote poetry in this period, a substantial number also separated themselves, or were separated by circumstance, physically as well as imaginatively, from a conventional domestic environment.

In the second half of this study, I read the poetic texts of three women in order to understand how some women in early modern England both fashioned themselves and were fashioned by their culture as writing subjects – finding their textual power, out of the norm, in the 'literary' forms of poetry and poetic drama. Their strategies are different, not the same, a point that suggests genuine subjectivity, not a dictated re-creation or simplified imitation of permissible roles or sanctioned models. Assuming that the process of writing itself partially constructs 'author function,' I offer a view of what that variable function looks like in the three different cases of Isabella Whitney, Elizabeth Cary and Aemilia Lanyer, where it is specifically represented as female and poetic at the turning point from the sixteenth to the seventeenth century, at the moment of mixed transition and opportunity from oral to print culture, from manuscript to published circulation.

Concerned as I am with the practice of poetry, my attention in this volume is directed to the educationally or socially advantaged women whose circumstances made it possible to write in this genre. Where social position or educational accomplishment provided this incentive, it did not, however, as Margaret Ezell puts it, 'pull whatever fangs these ladies might have dared to show' (*Writing*, 50). Nor did their rank or learning ensure their co-option by patriarchal values. Women in other situations surely found different ways to constitute themselves as subjects of their experience,[17] but for those women who were able to engage in the complex processes of poetic writing, the oblique and formalized practice of poetry was a peculiarly effective means to subjective inscription and of resistance to obliterating objectification.

Women in early modern England, as in other historical moments, were surely neither helpless victims of patriarchal ideology nor exceptional victors over its authority. Like men, who were largely responsible for the design of power, women were required to respond to the demands of power, but they were also able to find a space, insecure though it may have been, within which to encode their resistance to the power that coerced them. In searching for and defining this subjective space as it manifests itself in poetry, I endorse Judith Newton's view that women's history can more profitably be seen as a process of resistant struggle and creative accommodation to social conditions and cultural forms than as a tragic story of inevitable suffering ('Making – and Remaking – History'). This complex process of struggle and accommodation is textually confirmed by early modern women in the two modes examined in the following chapters:

1. in women's own comments on their position within two worlds of male-directed discourse having specific and powerful impact on women's writing subjectivity: literacy, and representations of the female body; and
2. in the poetic texts themselves, including those examined closely here: Isabella Whitney's poetic collections, Elizabeth Cary's *Mariam*, and Aemilia Lanyer's *Salve Deus Rex Judaeorum*.

At this point I need to acknowledge that my approach to early modern women is attended by my own cultural preconceptions. The questions I ask about these women come out of the curiosity I feel about the similarities and differences that exist between them and me. There are, I assume, certain culturally determined responses that many women, regarded as a group or class, are likely to share with each other within a single cultural moment and perhaps even from one historical moment to another. If, as Robert Weimann suggests, a text is a product of its culture and therefore mimetic, it is also a producer of subsequent cultures and therefore affective. When I approach an early modern woman's text, therefore, I do so along the path where that text, acting as producer, has written into my culture familiar signposts pointing to women's ways of perceiving that will help me read the earlier text. I also need to record the recognized differences with all the sympathetic interpretive skills I have at hand, for, of course, the whole 'value of studying the past is (not only) to find someone or something with which to identify' (Ezell, *Writing*, 27).

None of this means that I essentialize women, or that I assume that all women's experiences are the same, or that there is an ontologically identified entity, 'woman,' that can be precisely defined. On the contrary, I am suspicious of such doctrines and I approach the 'reality of women's experience' warily.[18] I agree with Denise Riley that in studying the past, 'both a concentration on and a refusal of the identity of "women" are essential' to feminist reading (1). I choose not to search for an illusory 'authentic' women's voice and self, but still, like Clare Brant and Diane Purkiss, accept the need to 'explore the ways in which women's writings generate and negotiate speaking-positions in discourse' (3). For, as Rosi Braidotti points out, 'although the subject "woman" is not a monolithic essence defined once and for all' (4), one must still *speak* as a woman. To focus on the embodied, speaking, historically situated woman is, in fact, a 'radical rejection of essentialism' (Braidotti, 4).

Furthermore, although indebted to their invaluable work, I am not myself a material, descriptive historian; I rely heavily on informed interpretation and theory as modes of access to textual culture. My method is eclectic, combining feminist, new historicist, psychoanalytic and deconstructionist analyses. I accept that the cultural and linguistic constructions that control what we believe about ourselves are inextricably tied to what we are able to do. I think that the construction of texts through writing and reading is also the most powerful means of constructing events.[19] This being the case, the examination of women's own texts becomes all the more crucial. In this study I privilege texts by women because they enact a particular form of gendered textual negotiation with their culture and with the possibility of linguistic subjectivity; these texts sometimes agree with, but often illuminatingly alter, the partial view of women's cultural potential and positionality inscribed in desirous, angry or authoritarian male constructions. I therefore accept for their strategic usefulness, and with some qualifications, the three conditions listed by Margaret Miles as necessary, not, I would emphasize, for a 'perfect' or 'complete,' but for an adequate, cultural representation of women: 1) 'adequate representation of women must be [I would prefer to say include and privilege] self-representation'; 2) this 'work of self-representation must occur ... in the institutions and arenas in which the discourse that both reflects and shapes society takes place'; and 3) the adequate representation of women requires 'a collective voice' (170–171) – not always in harmony, but still engaged in productive conversation.

In this work, therefore: 1) I have relied heavily on what early modern women's texts have to say about the circumstances that affected their writing; 2) I have allowed this material to form a backdrop against which I place for examination a set of socially institutionalized, because published, examples of women's poetry; and 3) I have been interested in what perhaps can be styled a 'collective voice,' which states the same recurring concerns and offers alternative modes of self-representation arising out of women's frequently congenial, though sometimes disputatious communities. As that anomalous creation, a feminist literary scholar trained in androcentric Australian and American universities in the second half of the twentieth century, I am enthralled by the problem of women's linguistic agency – both my own problem and the problem of other women. But perhaps it is not a problem at all – rather an invitation to understand how women speak through ideological and linguistic systems that seem to prohibit their speech, but do not, in the end, succeed in doing so.

The Subject

The early modern period in England expended much energy both in defining gender ideology and sexual difference[20] and in projecting oppositional and hierarchical difference onto oversimplified gender difference. In this period women were inscribed by the dominant discourse as not only marginal to social and political power but as specifically marginal to the production of public discourse itself. Women's historically restricted access to language in its publicly influential conventions has been seen, especially by recent feminist psychoanalytic theorists, as requiring the invention by women of a different, uniquely female language in which to formulate their own desire. Far from acknowledging this need, Renaissance gender ideology disparagingly equated the eloquent woman with a whore; the woman whose voice was available to a public audience was also seen as a woman whose body was publicly accessible. A popular translation of an Italian text (1615) announces that 'A Maide that hath a lewd tongue in her head, / Worse then if she were found with a Man in bed' (Varchi, 205).

Female 'sexual and corporeal metaphors' were frequently 'embedded in the presentation of texts for the public audience' (Wall, 41) in a process which commodified both texts and women (48). On the one hand, women's sexual desire was seen as voracious and associated with the desire for language and, on the other, women's expressed desire for language was often reconstructed in male formulations as unreasonable sexual desire.[21] A metaphoric conjunction theoretically elaborated in our own time by Luce Irigaray as an indicator of women's power, but deeply entrenched in the ideology of the early modern period as a sign of their fearsome asocial nature, supplied women with two mouths – both hungry. Social and legal prohibitions and ideological formulations were devised to control both: 'Women writers had to stay the threat of a double 'fall' (both sexual and social) when they chose to wander transgressively into the literary marketplace' (Wall 339).

Stephanie Jed goes so far as to argue that the whole humanist project of reviving and interpreting the texts of classical Greece and Rome may be analogized to the humanistic representation of the rape and suicide of Lucrece, that the projects of human (male) liberation, represented by the Roman uprising against Tarquinian tyranny and by the Renaissance humanist defense of the individual, are, in metaphoric terms, founded on the rape and self-silencing of woman. Yet, in spite of this heavy burden of shame and prohibition, clearly meant to be internalized by them as it was by Lucrece, early modern women in significant numbers not only wrote but also brought their writing into print.[22] How, then, did the female writing subject maneuver within the political and linguistic context in which her needs were codified by others to write a desire more explicitly her own?

The answer to this question relies on the development of a contextually and historically credible theory for reading early modern women's construction as writing subjects. In developing such a theory, I have made use of post-structuralist readings of the linguistically produced, de-centered 'subject,' but have not been willing to give up claims to the agency of the female writing subject. Rather, I endorse the need to 'promote a *recovery of the subject* without lapsing into subjectivism' and agree that 'the de-centering of the subject must not be made equivalent to its disappearance' (Giddens 44–45). I recognize that in taking up this position, strung between the two powerful camps of what Linda Alcoff has called cultural and post-structuralist feminism, I leave myself open, on the one hand, to charges of academic disengagement from the 'real' problems of women and, on the other, to charges of humanistic or sentimental essentialism. Nevertheless, I believe, as I hope my readers will come to agree, that achieving an effective *détente* between these two kinds of feminist reading is a necessary and achievable preface to understanding and valuing the accomplishments of women in the past.

The daunting task of reconstructing in the Renaissance what Michel Foucault calls the 'practices of the self' has produced any number of conjectural and sometimes contradictory proposals. Stephen Greenblatt, perhaps most influentially, has argued that the Renaissance sense of self was constructed socially and materially through masks and personae adopted for public occasions (222). On the other hand, Sheila Fisher and Janet Halley suggest that in the early modern period there may still have been operating a deep-seated belief, carried over from the Middle Ages, in an essential unitary self, 'located in and variously called the soul or the heart or mind' – although they add the important proviso that this concept of the self needs to be 'approached sceptically by those seeking the historical self of woman' (2). But H. Marshall Leicester has suggested that already by the fourteenth century, people in England had become 'discursively aware' that 'matters previously held to be established and maintained by God had actually been humanly produced and then ascribed to divine agency' (27), with subsequent erosion of faith in a 'unitary self.'

Anne Ferry has pointed out that 'the Renaissance did not have a vocabulary (words such as "consciousness" or "individual") for depicting an inner self' (39). The word 'selfhood,' says Jonathan Sawday, 'first recorded in the climactic year 1649 ... is anchored, in a theological sense, to an entirely negative set of ideas ... [I]t expressed the inability to govern the self. "Selfhood" was the mark of Satan' ('Self,' 30).

Nevertheless, Deborah Shuger, drawing on evidence from Andrewes, Hooker and Herbert, makes a persuasive case for the existence in Renaissance England of the notion of a double or even multiplex self sometimes modeled on the dual self proposed by Luther's *Zwei-Regimente Lehre* (*Habits of Thought*, 94–95), although the 'boundaries between these ... selves or persons tend themselves to be unstable or permeable' (257). And at least one of those selves, the spiritual or 'pneumatic' self, is more desire than substance: 'It is permeable, hollow, not a "thing" but an emptiness needing to be filled from without – a representation of the self evocative (to the contemporary reader, at least) of the female body. Its lack of sufficiency leaves the pneumatic self open to the crisis of desolation' (267). Shuger extrapolates from this insight a habit of mind that at one and the same time 'tends toward differentiation,' but 'in which distinctions remain blurred and permeable' (13).

Phyllis Mack's analysis of early Quaker women's efforts to release their inner light by destroying or transcending the self denies the value of a coherent, integrated self, at least for her sample of 'visionary women,' and 'turns our modern archaeology of the personality virtually upside down' (136). Elspeth Graham agrees: 'Although an individualist society and culture clearly does emerge from the period, and emphasis on the self in general grows, a *coherent* sense of self does not emerge uniformly ... For women, issues of the indeterminacy of constructions of selfhood are especially pronounced' (213–215). Finally, Patricia Fumerton says: 'During the series of transitional gaps in the late sixteenth and early seventeenth centuries ... historical transition brought about social, political, economic, and other displacements ... that destabilized the self ... and fomented the need for a renegotiation of the meaning of selfhood' (26).

All of these perceptions, leavened with the 'disconcerting recognition' imposed on Greenblatt by the evidence in Renaissance texts that 'identity may not originate in (or be guaranteed by) the fixity, the certainty, of our own body' (218), and Jonathan Sawday's somewhat different view that 'what was "born" in the period was not "selfhood" but the modern idea of "corporeality"' ('Self', 48), encourage the suspicion that perhaps the notion of a coherent, autonomous self,[23] which post-Freudian readers have often taken for granted as typical of all ages but our own, may in fact have had little applicability in early modern England. A carefully applied and contextually adjusted post-structuralist perspective might therefore open the way to a more useful understanding of early modern perceptions of the self and its attendant writerly subjectivity.

As elusive as the generalized sense of the self in the early modern period is, when we acknowledge that the self is gendered, it becomes still more difficult to unearth a sense of self that might have been owned by early modern women and to discover the relation between that sense of self and the role of the writing subject. This is so particularly because the textual articulation of the self depends on the employment by a writing subject of a power-laden discourse which is established before the subject speaks. For an early modern woman, the assumption of the role of writing subject was emphatically inhibited by the dominant social construction of the female self as 'chaste, silent and obedient.' These qualities, if successfully internalized, would make the woman a passive, reactive recipient rather than an active agent of her own writing experience. If accepted as fully definitive, they would ensure women's complete absence from the field of discourse – an absence accepted by many post-structuralist critics and elaborately theorized by Luce Irigaray and Hélène Cixous.

These French theorists have been indispensably helpful in reading women's construction in patriarchy and imaginatively seductive in their proposals for an alternative, 'private, precious' women's language relying on 'imaginary spaces held to lie outside the reign of the phallus' (Kipnis, 160), though they have not, perhaps, adequately accounted for those texts written by women in the past, which mapped out women's constant desire for speech, their long-lasting pleasure in language. Although patriarchal language has inhibited and repressed women's language, inhibition and repression do not amount to total erasure. Theories proposing that women's silence is mandated by their marginal roles are called into question especially by the poetic records of early modern women who often speak from positions other than those allotted them by hegemonic discourse and who maneuver within male-established poetic conventions with a dexterity which imbues those conventions with new potential.

Foucault has claimed that the Renaissance, like the period of classical antiquity which it so much admired and sought to emulate, had not as yet problematized the 'practices of the self,' including the representation of the self as subject, but instead carried over from the Greeks the notion of the individual who designed for himself an 'exact self-mastery' (*History of Sexuality*, vol. 2). However, this claim seems dubious for English culture of the period, as perhaps also for European culture in general, for canonic and non-canonic evidence from the period, and especially evidence from women's texts, suggests something different. Though it is only fairly recently that a specific theoretical language has been devised to discuss it, I doubt that an understanding of the concept of a de-centered, multiplistic subject position is very new. Even if we were able to think of medieval Christian expansion as a ground for a unitary self located in the soul, it is not certain that this rendering of things continued to prevail in the Renaissance (Leicester, 1–31).

In Florio's translation of Montaigne (1603), admired by and, we must suppose, resonant for English readers, we find this revealing comment evoking a confused, disordered self unable to evoke a subject position which can speak 'entirely' and 'with soliditie': 'I have nothing to say entirely, simply, and with soliditie of myselfe without confusion, disorder, blending, mingling' (II.12). Even if it is true that the Western 'centered' subject has implemented as one of its necessary self-defining goals the 'mandate to make the rest of the world its object: of conquest, knowledge, surplus-value' (Kipnis, 158), this position or practice of the self was still being formulated in the early modern period and was hardly as yet a consolidated goal for men any more than it has ever been for women. To quote Katharine Maus's salutary reminder:

' "Subjectivity" is often treated casually as a unified or coherent concept when, in fact, it is a loose and varied collection of assumptions, intuitions, and practices that do not at all logically entail one another and need not appear together at the same cultural moment' (29).

It may be that the early modern *male* subject was beginning to organize a sense of the self as an autonomous, coherent individual coterminous with a sense of the self as subject, able to claim a linguistic place as an 'I,' able to confirm its identity as 'self-same.' But for women this construction seems improbable. Given the ideological proscriptions against the development of women's linguistic power, we cannot reasonably expect to find in early modern women's writing a stable, autonomous, individual female source. A more credible model is the struggling, destabilized subject, unfixed, in process, contesting for power, and itself a site of contestation for power. Precisely at this site of struggle, sometimes a text is located which voices what Patricia Yaeger has described as an 'explosive protest brought about by the "split subject" who simultaneously gives in to and resists the burden of the sociolect' (252), who draws the thread of an 'I' out of the tangle of prevailing and forbidding linguistic codes and conventions. Or, to cite Rosi Braidotti's persuasive image of a 'nomadic' female subject, it can be conceptualized as 'a creative sort of becoming; a performative metaphor that allows for otherwise unlikely encounters and unsuspected sources of interaction of experience and knowledge' (6).

At this stage of my argument, I am compelled to address an understandable feminist suspicion of post-structuralist theories that question the viability of an autonomous subject. One version of this critique has been articulated by Nancy Hartsock:

> Somehow it seems highly suspicious that it is at this moment in history ... that doubt arises in the academy about the nature of the 'subject.' ... Why is it, exactly at the moment when so many of us who have been silenced begin to demand the right to name ourselves, to act as subjects rather than objects of history, that just then the concept of subjecthood becomes 'problematic'? ('Rethinking,' 196)

But Hartsock's concern is fed by her acceptance that women in the past 'have been silenced.' Carol Neely has also worried about the effect of 'denying subjectivity, interiority, identity which is continuous across time' (7). She reasonably raises the question of whether 'the denial of unity, autonomy, and identity in authors [and] subjects [along with other aspects of post-structural theory] ... [has] the effect of putting woman in her customary place, of re-producing patriarchy [so that women's] language and silence continue to serve the newly dominant ideology' (7).

I do not, however, believe that such negative consequences, obviously untenable for feminists, need to be admitted as the necessary end of problematizing the female (and male) subject. 'Overreading' of the kind that Neely herself rightly urges on the feminist critic – another version of what Patrocinio Schweikart calls partisan reading – will instead show that the protection of the notion of a unified and dominant subject, traditionally gendered as male but sought by some feminists as equally feasible for women, has obscured our sense of women's attainments, especially in the past, when the idea of an autonomous subject may not have had the regulatory power over people's imaginations that it has achieved in the twentieth century. This effort to protect for women the possibility of a unified subjectivity suffers from the same disadvantage as the kind of feminism which seeks equality for women with men – that it is doomed to measure its desires and capabilities by a standard which has already proven false to women and has also fallen short of what might have been possible for men. As Kelly Oliver paraphrases Judith Butler's argument in *Gender Trouble*, 'Feminism needs to give up the notion that it requires a unified subject in order to operate effectively' (187). To attempt to protect the role of a full-speaking subject for women in the early modern period may be to protect what had small viability in the period for men or women, but has rather been a fiction more fully elaborated, because more useful and desirable, in subsequent cultures.

On the other hand, demonstrating the split, destabilized subject's power to speak will also affirm that in a system which recognizes all subjects as at least possibly de-centered, as for early modern England appears a reasonable assumption, women can be regarded as differently expert speakers, possessed of subversive talents not previously sufficiently valued. To call into question the unitary stability of the subject, as post-structuralist theory has done, and to apply that observation to early modern England as I wish to do, does not mean that all functions and processes of the female subject must continue to be denied or compared unfavorably with what the male subject has been able to do. Rather it opens the possibility of conceding the expertness of women's literary and linguistic skills even in the early modern period, when an anxious urge toward social order required the discursive implementation of hierarchical social relationships disadvantageous to women.

From texts written by women in the early modern period, we may filter out admittedly problematized or non-coherent, but nevertheless viable, representations of the female writing subject engaged in devising emancipatory strategies to resist and recast the power of male language. These texts, 'never [themselves] a closed system, hermetically sealed, but susceptible to rupture' (Lilley, 88), confirm that it is not only from a unified and coherent sense of self, but also from a split or divided self-inscription, that the textual voice of a writerly subject can emanate. Isabella Whitney's dedication to George Mainwaring apologizes for her imitation and exploitation of the work of a male poet, Hugh Plat, but she allows to speak for itself the fact that she comes to this task having already performed the revolutionary feat of 'authoring' one of the first collections of public poetry by a woman and is now engaged in upgrading poetically Plat's own work. Aemilia Lanyer also draws attention to her own dislodging of gender expectations, at one and the same time boasting and apologizing that her subversively feminist poem presents a spectacle 'seldom seene' – 'a Womans writing of divinest things' (3). This actually less shocking element in her writing, to which Lanyer draws her reader's attention, serves as a rhetorical decoy, diverting the otherwise potentially scandalized reader from those elements which most seriously violate cultural expectations of women's writing – Lanyer's feminist complaint and her choice of poetic genre. Elizabeth Cary also acknowledges in her preface to her translation of Cardinal du Perron (1630) that her

'Sexe can raise noe great expectation of anie thing that shall come from me'; yet, in the same breath she says self-confidently, 'it were a great follie in me, if I would expose to the view of the world, a work of this kinde, except I judged it to want nothing fitt.' Even more radically she clearly asserts her desire for publication: 'I will not make use of that worne-out forme of saying I printed it against my will, mooved by the importunitie of Friends.'

The Countess of Lincoln was only one of many other women who prefaced her perfectly skillful and also revolutionary writing endeavor – in this case a treatise on breast-feeding – with the assertion that, *as a woman*, she should not and could not write, but as Marilyn Luecke says, 'there is no contextual indication that she understands herself to be inadequate to the task' (240). Other examples of this female self-effacement simultaneously conjoined with the exercise of writerly power occur in the prefaces to the widely disparate texts by the prophet Sarah Wight and the poets Anne Bradstreet and Katherine Philips. All three deny the writer's will to publish, but there they are, functioning effectively in their own time and still accessible to ours. Kathryn King points to Jane Barker's 'sense of herself as one who can neither wholly embrace nor wholly free herself of an urge to versify' (554). The beginning of 'A Second EPISTLE. To ... *Mr.* E. S.,' says King, shows 'a mind that knows itself in part through its conflicted experience of the desire to write' (555): her muse's 'great ... cunning in insinuation' imposes itself over her reluctance. More strongly, An Collins, though conventionally asserting that 'Unto the public view of everyone / I did not purpose these my lines to send' (*Divine Songs*, 2), admits her delight in the pleasure of writing poetry: 'To be brief, I became affected to poetry, insomuch that I proceeded to practise the same; and though the helps I had therein were small, yet the thing itself appeared unto me so amiable as that it inflamed my faculties to put forth themselves in a practice so pleasing' ('To the reader,' *Divine Songs*, sig. A1).

Margaret Tyler's dedication of her translation of a Spanish romance is a marvel of verbal self-contortion and conflicted subjectivity; she writes her shrinking, fragile desire or 'inclination' and 'little libertie' in the same space as her 'triall of ... self' whereby she has riskily 'adventured upon a peece of work':

> Not being greatly forward of mine owne inclination ... but forced by the importunity of my friends to make some triall of my selfe in this exercise of translation, I have adventured upon a peece of work, not indeed the most profitablest, as intreating of armes, nor yet altogether fruitlesse, if example may serve, as beeing historicall, but the while, either to bee borne withall for the delight, or not to be refused for the strangenesse: farther I meane not to make boast of my travaille, for the matter was offered, not made choice of, as ther appeared likewise little libertie in my first yeelding.

In an immediately subsequent address *To the Reader*, Tyler forthrightly claims the right of a woman to be the subject of her own writing rather than the object of a man's: 'my perswasion hath bene thus, that it is all one for a woman to pen a storie, as for a man to addresse his storie to a woman' (sig. A. iiii). Such typical prefatory nods to expectations of the writer's gendered ineptitude, appearing in many, perhaps most, women's texts in the period, and almost invariably in their poetic texts, should not, however, be read simplistically as expressing a failure of nerve, or as acceding to the dominant representation of women as inarticulate, for in all cases the text proceeds successfully, sometimes even joyously, on its way.[24]

Yet neither should these ambivalent, self-abnegating disclaimers be read as occurring in the same register as the apparently similar humility trope sometimes employed for rhetorical and paradoxical effect by men. In a famous example, the highly privileged, highly educated, courtly gentleman, Sir Philip Sidney, in the introductory sonnet to *Astrophel and Stella*, bemoans his inability to write, while, in fact, doing so: 'words,' he complains, 'came halting forth, wanting Invention's stay.' Like women's texts in the period, this text's existence belies the writer's assertion of incapacity, but because this is a male text, it expects and builds on a different effect than a female poetic text could hope for. The male writer and his male reader take the male poet's expertness for granted, and his claim to verbal impotence falls into an ironic rhetorical repertoire, premised as it is on the assumed agreement that his poetic incompetence will not and cannot be taken seriously.

On the other hand, when women invoke their gender to assert a sense of doubt about their writing skill, and when they apologize for their temerity in violating the gendered constraints against their writing at all, they are overtly acknowledging their subject positions as multiple and divided. Because they are invoking one of the strongest ideological prohibitions of the time, they and their readers have no choice but to take their disclaimers seriously. But the very texts which represent their writers as split subjects exiled from the privilege of language *because they are female*, at the same moment either explode or slither through that position and through the ideologically constrained prohibitions against the exercise of women's linguistic skill. Viewed in these terms, these texts represent prodigious feats of writerly agency. Women's texts on the margins of discourse in early modern England exemplify in an unexpected way Jacques Derrida's dictum that texts always overflow their intended or sanctioned boundaries: the voices in these texts declare, 'I am a female person who does not know how to write and I am writing; this is a woman's text which cannot "speak" and it is speaking.'

I agree with Patricia Yaeger and Rosi Braidotti, then, that though the subject may be split and gendered female, nevertheless it speaks. Its capacity to do so, in fact, exposes the notion of a centered, coherent subject as a kind of male fiction from which women have always been exiled – or freed. Mary Poovey has argued that repression is an inevitable consequence of attempting to stabilize any concept as a 'self-contained and coherent entity' ('Cultural Criticism: Past and Present,' 619). Barbara Johnson has also suggested that the force of the powerful, historically male desire to 'transform fragmentation into unity' may have been 'provoked by the fact that the primary text it wishes to unify and simplify was written by a woman; unification and signification have been the province of the male; division and self-difference have been the nature of the woman's voice' (214).

Perhaps an attachment to the fiction of a unified subject is also a bondage to the *status quo* – not, therefore, a position of linguistic and psychological power, but a position of linguistic and psychological paralysis: the male subject has defined himself in 'a circularity that knows no end except the return, over and over again, upon itself/himself. The problem is to break down the walls around the (male) one who speaks, sees, thinks, and thereby now confers being upon himself, in a prison of self-sufficiency and a clarity made of the shadows of denial' (Irigaray, *Speculum*, 199). Male language may have begun to create in the early modern period the illusion of a unitary monolithic subject as a tactic of discursive, capitalist and colonialist political power, but this subject was then, as it has been since, insecure because always in danger of falling into disunity, into a failure of coherent identity; in fact, into a condition which for women writing in early modern England – and probably always – is, though variously defined, a wholly familiar and therefore perhaps more expertly negotiated space. Julia Kristeva's proposal, that both poetry and maternity call the unity of the subject into question in a process that makes it possible to say something new within the language inherited from patriarchy, is especially suggestive; she allies poetry with the representation of a distinctively female bodily performance as modes that enforce a recognition of the need to live within the 'flexible, always precarious borders of our subjectivity in order to learn to live within the flexible, always precarious borders of human society' (Oliver, 13).

Female subjectivity is not a stable position, but rather operates in a process of sometimes combative, always off-balance, dialogue with the language which produces it. It has a different coloring from the confidently male style which 'thinks it knows so much' (Kipnis, 157). Any person who writes at all is already operating inside the medium of language which controls the processes of subjectivity. A female person who writes is necessarily deploying a set of signs which have been installed by men and whose decoding is most readily responsive to male psychoanalytic systems of desire and perception. A woman writing has been 'gendered' in a way specific to her sex and she therefore possesses, not the power to install a new language, but a psychoanalytic coding and decoding system of her own that will make of male-constructed language something different from the uses and interpretations of male readers and writers. Because her interpretive mechanisms are different, her use of that other male person's language will invite the intrusion of a whole set of unconscious possibilities normally suppressed in the language by male use, but leaking into the language when it is used by a woman. Female subjectivity thus asserts itself, both because of the writer's gender and the rich and complex potential of language itself, but in an apparently unstable way, not synchronized with male patterns of meaning imposition and retrieval.

Perhaps, as Mary Poovey (*Uneven Developments*) has also suggested, in the very instability of the marginal subject there resides a more likely possibility of action that induces political change. Precisely because it is now possible to see the subject as a process whose operation occurs within a discursively contentious culture, it is also now possible to open up the usage of the term 'subject' to a strategic application not previously allowed, but which will now admit the writing practices of previously marginalized groups.[25] Subjectivity is, after all, not sacrosanct; it is only a dubiously positioned sense from which one may speak and sometimes act on the world, and there is no reason that speech may not effectively emanate from a recognizably unstable as well as from a problematically stable position. Indeed, if the male subject is perceived as theoretically fixed in a dominant and powerful position of coherence and autonomy defined at the expense of the subjugated female other, the female will also be discursively immobilized in that reduced position. If all, however, are destabilized, 'perpetually in the process of construction, thrown into crisis by alterations in language and in the social formation' (Belsey, 50), a small but genuine benefit of linguistic agency may accrue to the destabilized, but now released, female subject. This is, I believe, a strategically apt, theoretical construction of the processes in early modern England which makes it possible to imagine there a writing space for women.

On the margin: conditions

The surviving examples of women's writing from early modern England demonstrate that, even in historical moments when they appear to have had little space in which to speak, women have not been silent; nor have they simply parroted the tale of the patriarch. As Judith Newton says, 'despite women's lesser access to power,' still, 'history is the tale of many voices and forms of power exercised by the weak and marginal as well as by the dominant and strong' ('History as Usual,' 152). Although not every moment in history has furnished equally favorable conditions in which the marginal female subject could gather herself to speak, throughout the sixteenth and seventeenth centuries in England, despite strenuous efforts at control, circumstances slowly grew more encouraging for the production of all kinds of women's texts. Not unified, but publicly contestatory, the structures of cultural power were not so tightly seamed as to prevent the emergence of the marginalized subject.

Because gender identity and the power to speak as a gendered subject are always sanctioned by culturally produced ideologies of gender and power, in a period of ideological disturbance such as existed in England between 1540 and 1700, the illusory stability of the early modern male subject and his compensatory efforts to gain control of the confused categories of gender led in some cases to exactly contrary results, recorded in women's texts. Elizabeth Cary, for example, examining issues of marital oppression, indicated both an awareness of some women's will to push back against the forces of male power and the desire for an alternative adventurous independence. Her heroine, Mariam, says of her husband:

> For he, by barring me from liberty,
> To shun my ranging, taught me first to range. (I.i.25–26).

Surely not accidentally, the connected issues of women's restrained 'libertie' and their desire to 'adventure' or 'range,' applied by Cary to the institution of marriage, are, as we have seen above, also those applied by Margaret Tyler to the enterprise of women's writing. The same context of thought and the same idioms of resistance to external control explicate a woman's bodily role as wife and her linguistic role as writer.

The chorus in Cary's play, defending conventional gender discriminations and lamenting the restlessness of those women who have not wished to abide by them, asks a question that must have bemused many a solid Renaissance citizen:

> When [a woman] hath spacious ground to walk upon,
> Why on the ridge should she desire to go? (III.iii.221–222)

Yet the desire to scale the exhilarating peaks of poetic language proved irresistible to Cary and other women like her who were not willing to stay in the level territory of docile silence or accept the sober writing task considered permissible for women – translation, not as in Margaret Tyler's impertinent case of a Spanish romance, but of the works of 'wise and sad men' (Vives, II.6).

In fact, in this period, we can see that insistent ideological pressure favoring conventional gender delineation existed side by side with what in later centuries would be recognized as a feminist challenge to these very demands. As Margaret King observes: 'Something changed during the Renaissance in women's sense of themselves, even if very little changed ... in their social condition. That change ... culminates in the consciousness put into words by the first feminists of the Renaissance' (238–239). The social instability that intensified the need of the dominant discourse to define itself oppressively against the female other also, then, induced resistance and 'adventuring' in that other. The early modern period in England supports as a viable hypothesis that when social, political and economic disruptions occur in a culture that has defined its power, as culture must, against an oppressed and differentiated other, multiple contentious discourses will come into being as the phantom identity of the oppressive culture breaks apart. In a political climate where dislocation of ideology is the norm, resistance to the structures of power may more readily gather in the ruptures generated by that dislocation.

No more than any other culture was early modern England able to establish, even or especially within the categories of gender, 'univocal and homogeneous fields of meaning' (Benhabib). Early modern England also offers support for the view that ideology is not monolithic, rarely is it non-controversial, and it operates in imaginary as well as concrete registers. It appears in two guises at least – apparently coherent and authentic on the one hand and internally unstable and artificial on the other.[26] Ideological incoherences in the period between 1540 and 1660 were generated and sustained by changes occurring in all sectors of the culture: vast economic changes including long-term inflation; colonial expansion newly dependent on credit and foreign trade; reduced agricultural production; demographic shifts precipitated by rural unemployment but eventually involving all classes and finally ensuring the economic and political centrality of London; religious upheaval and conflict; a rising and increasingly powerful populist voice; disputes over access to literacy and formal education further complicated by the shift from oral to print culture; and, inevitably, unstable gender roles.

Polarized descriptions of any ideology in the period as simply dominant *or* transgressive, or binary categorizations of gender as essentially male *or* female, or of spheres of influence as public and male *or* private and female, when applied to the turmoil of English culture in the sixteenth and seventeenth centuries, must finally be seen as efforts at order imposed by a controlling twentieth-century sensibility which reflect similar distressed efforts in the Renaissance. Reading women's texts, and men's texts in relation to women's, reveals much cultural confusion about where ideological boundaries might be drawn, where gender differences might be established, and where public and private spaces merge or separate. The popular texts generated in the pamphlet wars about the nature of women, beginning in the middle of the sixteenth century with the publication of *The Schoolhouse of Women*, and continuing at least through the next hundred years, offer but one explicit illustration of the open, sometimes humorous, often hostile, contention and evident insecurity that attached to gender issues.[27]

Jonathan Dollimore has argued that in this climate, 'The transvestite and the hermaphrodite: both were disturbing images' (296). Both he and Stephen Orgel point out the implications of transvestism and gender anxiety in the practice of cross-dressing throughout the sixteenth and seventeenth centuries, on-stage and off. Laura Levine shows that many popular tracts denouncing the theater express the fear that wearing women's clothing might erode a man's masculinity and power. Ann Rosalind Jones and Peter Stallybras conclude that 'the Renaissance hermaphrodite suggests that categorical fixity is inevitably unstable' (105); it would not be till the eighteenth century that 'a phantasized biology of the "real"' (106) would replace the Renaissance fetishization of gender. Fears of hermaphroditism and androgyny, and prohibitions against male and female homosexuality, as well as fairly public evidence of these forms of what Foucault calls 'reverse discourses,' appear in both canonic and non-canonic documents in this period.[28] Randolph Trumbach charts the shift, from the seventeenth to the eighteenth century, 'from three sexes to four genders'; in the seventeenth century, 'there were two genders – male and female – but three biological sexes – man, woman, and hermaphrodite' (113). Gender boundaries in this period waver also because some women internalize the dominant constructions of themselves and some men participate in transgressive modes of discourse and behavior.

Similarly, 'public' and 'private' are terms which have value only when placed in relation to, and made dependent on, each other. The private sphere into which women were supposed to be securely relegated appears after all not really private in the sense of an autonomous space outside the range of public affairs or intrusive institutional influence – as in a Woolfian 'room of one's own.' It can be seen also as a publicly constructed domestic sphere that allowed the family unit to function more efficiently in the service of the new capitalist state.[29] In any case, from this 'private,' so-called enclosed world, the testaments of Alice Thornton, Elizabeth Freke, Lady Margaret Hoby, Lady Grace Mildmay, Sarah Chevers and Katherine Evans, not to mention the remarkably peripatetic Celia Fiennes at the end of the seventeenth century, tell us that they, for various personal, religious, medical, social and even journalistic purposes, fairly readily escaped.[30]

Although absolutely oppositional stances between male and female cannot satisfactorily depict the circumstances of gender differences in this period, differences of many kinds were certainly articulated upon gender in the public discourses of the period, including the discourse of religion – that very discourse which was considered safe and appropriate for women and which they therefore exploited, as did Aemilia Lanyer, to resist as well as promote their cultural roles. In particular, the Puritan emphasis on the authority of the individual conscience opened a space for women to speak in public and to establish a primary relation between their sense of self and God, bypassing the earthly patriarchal control over their activities and further complicating the gender distinctions between private female and public male. Anne Wentworth shockingly abandoned her 'hard-hearted yoke-fellow,' at least in part because he 'in a most cruel manner hindered me from performing, seizing and running away with my writings.' She will be reconciled to her 'earthly husband,' she says, 'provided I may have my just and necessary liberty to attend a more than ordinary call and command of God to publish the things which concern the peace of my own soul and the whole nation' (188). God is here invoked as a support for Wentworth's unwomanly writing, against her husband's opposition. In light of such instances of wifely rebellion, it is not surprising that many texts of the period imply worried concern about the troubling problems of establishing boundaries for religious and social roles.[31]

The massive population dislocation precipitated by the economic upheaval consequent on new financial ventures affected and included women, whose ability to support themselves through household crafts was undermined by the takeover of their activities by large centralized concerns. The numbers of women migrating to London from the country as a result of these economic changes (Parker, 101; Travitsky, 'Placing,' 12–13; Dollimore, 119–120), together with insecurities about gender literally acted out at the level of the middling sort in the theaters, but also promoted at the highest social levels by the reign of two female rulers followed by the openly bisexual Stuart court (in which the disguises of the masque were also fashionable), induced apprehension that women might dismantle or confuse dominant institutions of power.[32] This apprehension, insistently and publicly voiced, no doubt led some women to believe enough in their subversive power to find ways to speak it. Popular literary depictions of women's power, says Joy Wiltenburg, may have reinforced that sense of power. She observes trenchantly that 'women need not share the dominant cultural devaluation of their roles' (254).

That dislocations of class were seen by the self-protective dominant class as somehow related to challenges to gender distinctions is apparent in the set of

Sumptuary Laws concerning dress and class passed under Elizabeth and in the edict concerning dress and gender issued by James.[33] These revealingly semiotic attempts to maintain at least visual differentiation of one class from another and one gender from another, by officially designating the kind of clothing that could be worn by each, stand as part of a larger effort to ensure a definitive identity and hierarchized position for those selected groups whose marginalization was required to mark the power of the dominant elite. These efforts surely could not accomplish their intended goals, but by attempting to regulate issues of class and gender through the same outward sign of clothing, they indicate a worried effort to keep both women and the poor in their marginal places. One woman's ironic recognition of this anxiety is recorded in Elizabeth Cary's *Mariam*, published in 1611, where an angry male character predicts total disruption of the known order if women are allowed to challenge male power. Then, he says, fish will graze in the pasture, birds will sink through the air rather than fly, and male rulers will find themselves de-classed to the occupations of women and the poor – spinning and sewing, chopping wood or hauling water (I.vi.425–430). Aemilia Lanyer's *Salve Deus Rex Judaeorum* also sympathetically associates women with the poor because neither has recourse against the law that oppresses both groups (42–43).

On the Margin: Strategies

Because a dominant ideology cannot exercise total control, neither can it tailor its systems of control to meet the exact situation of each member in an oppressed group. Itself fragmented, and adhered to by fragmented persons, ideology has to rely on a system that will be uniform in its treatment of all, rather than particular and individuated in its treatment of each. In fact, the very process of this efficient/inefficient socialization system may entail the inculcation of skills, such as, for example, reading and writing, that make possible resistance to that socialization. In early modern England, such ideological constructs as education and representations of the female body both imprinted women and provoked their discontent; in the negotiation of her mixed response, the split but competently speaking female subject surfaced: 'the simultaneous and complementary processes of socialization, sexualization, and subjectification are also invested with learning and the development of [resistant and subversive] competencies' (Miles, 188). In 'progressively learning how to engage, control, and reap the rewards of the social order' (Miles, 188), early modern women also learned how to deploy recognizable and iterable discursive strategies of 1) communal resistance, and 2) subversively exaggerated 'enactment' of both ideological demands and literary conventions.

Uniform methods of socialization and oppression often produce an affiliating sense of shared experience in members of an oppressed group; when one member comes into contact with another member of the same group and articulates a history of oppression, they may both see that their experiences are similar and affirm each other's response. Many feminist theorists have argued that women in a marginal position in culture may come to a politically strategic sense of their subjectivity in incremental steps in the affirming company of others who share a sense of oppression, but resist the view of themselves as victims. As members of a group, women may therefore see that when they fail to conform to the ideologically prescribed conditions of their oppression, when, in other words, they resist the language of the Father, they are not crazy or sick as, separately, they have often been diagnosed – as frequently in early modern England as at any other time. From a sense of shared experience, a community may come into being in which can be formulated an alternative discourse, not necessarily internally coherent, but defined by its opposition to the dominant systems of power. Where, then, in early modern England, were communities of women able to gather, in which a strategically resistant discourse might be given utterance?

Founded in women's desire to write their own linguistic and bodily potential, loosely or tightly connected female communities came into being, from which derived women's texts that appropriated and constructed women's roles. For example, in women's communities focused on childbirth experiences, known as 'gossips,' a women's medical community existed, within which midwives and women healers formulated, passed on to each other and wrote down information about women's health and specific female ailments.[34] This knowledge, while protected for the use of and shared with other women, as a further tactic of resistance, was often kept secret from male medical practitioners. The shared experience of motherhood also promoted the writing of a new genre of mothers' advice books (Mendelson, *Mental World*, 28; Valerie Wayne and Travitsky, 'The New Mother'). Protestant sectarian women's groups supported women's religious testimonies and prophesyings and brought these into print. The several thousand Quaker women who in 1659 drafted and published *These Several Papers*, a petition to Parliament for changes in laws affecting religious freedom, are a case in point. During the seventeenth century, taking advantage of the prevailing political and religious agitation, groups of women discovered that in collaboration they could make their petitions heard by Parliament and exercise a political power that individually they could not (Otten, 85–93).

From the Pembroke Circle, a writing community including men as well as women and both aristocratic and gentry-class courtly women, there came an astonishing group of women's poetic, dramatic and fictional texts: the first known play written by an Englishwoman, a long 'feminist' poem praising women, a set of psalm translations and, as later descendants, a prose romance and a sonnet sequence.[35] And this connected group of women writers was not unique; Margaret Ezell has emphasized the importance of a number of women poets' manuscript circles in which women produced texts that 'cannot be dismissed as being either private or unpolished' ('Myth,' 589–590; *Writing*, 54).[36]

Finally, there existed a female reading community, the necessary potentially sympathetic audience, in trusting which a woman writer might construct herself as subject.[37] Louise Schleiner suggests that circles in which women read aloud to each

1.1 Scene of Gossips: 'At the Childbed' from *Tittle-Tattle; Or the several Branches of Gossipping*

other produced a 'reading formation' which 'both shaped and was shaped by their gendered self-imaging' (3). Many women writers participated in and relied on a collaborative 'community defined in part by shared values and in part by shared literary languages' (Ezell, *Writing*, 59–60). Judging by the number and variety of works themselves, their modes of production and, most importantly, the specific and direct appeal made by women writers as different as Esther Inglis, Dorothy Leigh, Elizabeth Clinton, Anne Southwell, Anna Trapnel and Mary Astell to particular or general women readers, this readership was clearly larger and more diverse than has yet been recognized. All three of the poets discussed in detail in this book addressed themselves to potential or actual female readers.

Women poets also sometimes conceived of their inspirational muse, patron or dedicatee as a revered or beloved female friend. Margaret Russell serves this role for Lanyer; for Elizabeth Cary it is her sister-in-law. Anne Southwell styles Cecily Ridgway, her 'worthy muse.' Alice Sutcliffe says in her dedication of her *Meditations* to Catherine Villiers, the widowed Duchess of Buckingham, 'you have beene more then a *Mother* to me.' Esther Inglis couples her assertion of her right to display the writing talents given her by God to her sanguine expectation of a sympathetic reading from Lady Magdalen Herbert, solely *because* her work is the work of a woman; partisan reading, it seems, could be expected by early modern women writers from women readers:

> The Bee draweth noght ... huny from the fragrant herbes of the garding for hir self: no more have I payned myself many yearis to burie the talent God has geven me in oblivion – And therefore albeit I be a stranger and no way knowen to your Ladyship yitt have I tane the boldnes to present you with thir few floures that I have collected of Dame Floras blossomes: Trusting your Ladyship will accept heirof ... and the rather because it is the work of a woman. (Scott-Elliott and Yeo, 26, quoted in Kim Walker, 150)

For as long as the voice of a 'conscious,' unified subject operating in the same register as male discourse was being sought for women, it was possible to think that early modern women were not sufficiently aware of their separable authority as women to speak in resistance to the patriarchy. But, recognized as emanating from a multiplistic, sometimes self-contradictory subjectivity, resistant textual strategies can be detected in women's writing which inscribe a self capable of reflexive moments in which the 'I' appears to establish a position in relation to the constructive invasions of patriarchal power. The texts of early modern women writers reveal their perception of women in relation to the central space occupied by men, and their resistance to the overflowing of the male enterprise into the female margin.

While some women undoubtedly internalized patriarchal models of female silence, these women for that very reason did not come into print at all. Some women, also, must have reserved the right to maintain silence as a mask of rebellion. This rebellion could not be known or checked, but the formulaic demand for women to be 'chaste, silent and obedient' was surely intended to muffle the sharp edge even of women's internal register of discontent. Mary Trye openly advertised her intention to remain silent (at least in written terms) on certain 'women's' medical subjects, declaring that she would share her knowledge of these matters with women who came to her in person, but men should not apply (sig. K5). And Elizabeth Cary's poetic and dramatic text records its awareness of the dominant ideology's need to control silent as well as vocal resistance in women; it sums up the social expectations placed on a woman to 'bare herself of power as well as will. / 'Tis not so glorious for her to be free, / As by her proper self restrain'd to be' (*Mariam*, III.iii.218–219).

But all those women whose written texts survive are, at the very scene of writing, positioning themselves in a resistant stance against the dominant patriarchal discourse. For these women, the idea of woman as represented in the dominant codes, while circumscribing what they wrote, at the same time also motivated them to write. They endeavored to register their writerly subjectivity against the training that would have over-determined their modes of speech. Whatever the content of their writing, the act of writing itself is transgressive. 'A feminine text cannot fail to be more than subversive. It is volcanic,' says Helene Cixous ('Laugh,' 292). Or, as Paul Smith puts it, when 'women begin to speak and act from the same ground of cerned subjectivity and identity as men have traditionally enjoyed, a resistance is automatically effected' (137). Women's use of modes of writing that have been designated as characteristically male is not simply an assertion of equality; it 'necessarily comport[s] a threat and a resistance to dominatory structures' (138). The writing of poetry especially provided early modern Englishwomen with just such a site of resistance, especially effective because, as Julia Kristeva argues, poetry, like psychoanalysis, taps into the unconscious and reveals the alterity or difference buried within the dominant discourse. The metaphoric, metonymic obliquity of poetry skirts the linear logic of patriarchal discourse and provides a peculiarly encouraging linguistic environment for the nurturing of female subjectivity. Speaking from the margins in the early modern period, women who wrote poetry produced a language whose emancipatory strategies established a position for themselves in the cultural discourse. This does not mean that for these women there was any experience of *glossolalia*. They did not begin to speak in tongues. They did not produce a new language never before heard. Rather, they wrote an undercover language concealed inside the patriarchal language, working in equivocal and interrogative relation to it, undermining it. To highlight this strategy of linguistic and psychological resistance it will help here to invoke, in order to adapt, Luce Irigaray's metaphor of enactment.

Irigaray proposes that because patriarchal discourse has situated woman *outside* representation, she must either remain silent or 'enact' the male representation of herself. Yet women do not need simply to act obediently in response to male commands; they may exaggeratedly 'enact' roles already imposed on them by male ideological formulations in order to rescue something of their own desire:

> One must assume the feminine role deliberately. Which means already to convert a form of subordination into an affirmation, and thus to begin to thwart it ... To play with mimesis is

> thus, for a woman, to try to recover the place of her exploitation by discourse, without allowing herself to be simply reduced by it. It means to resubmit herself ... to ideas about herself, that are elaborated in/by masculine logic, but so as to make 'visible,' by an effect of playful repetition, what was supposed to remain invisible: the cover-up of a possible operation of the feminine in language. (*This Sex*, 76)

Even if this enactment occurs from a passive position so that the woman loses herself, the tactic may be worthwhile, for her exaggerated or distorted passivity becomes an act of defiance. The example used by Irigaray is the hysteric who mimes or parodies the male representation of her sexuality, thus opening up a space in which her own pleasure can unfold. Similarly, the mystic claims a transported space, beyond the reach of rational control, in which to mime her pleasure.

But wherever a process of exaggerated or mimicked enactment produces behavior that renders women socially alien in the way that women's literary activity did in early modern England, I would argue, as Paul Smith contends with reference to all women's literary activity, that here, too, it offers 'a threat and a resistance to dominatory structures' (138). In cases other than mystical or hysterical abandonment, and especially in linguistic terms that Irigaray herself does not see as available to women, early modern women writers used in their texts just such enacted modes of transgression to rescue some of their own pleasure in writing. They characteristically enact their liberation from male domination by mimicking in their writing the very roles prescribed for them; they assume strategically, evasively and excessively a culturally condoned stance that has been designed for them, but they turn that stance to the possibility of agency.

Their subversive linguistic achievements, however, are not therefore confined to the prophetic abandoned mode of someone like Anna Trapnel, who, Gary Waller says, 'condemned herself to marginality by the distinctive voice of her work, which is that of ecstasy, seeming incoherence, and (a common charge against women writers generally at the time) apparent madness' (253).[38] The range of women's enacted literary agency in early modern England is much wider than this and should include the achievements of women whom Waller believes are too 'closely tied to the dominatory structures of their age' (254) to be disruptive. Trapnel may more overtly deploy linguistic tactics of disruption, but even the most conventional-seeming women writers engage in their own methods of re-enacting subversively the dominant discourse and rewriting the patriarchal desire that they be obedient, chaste and silent.

For example, many sectarian women like Joan Vokins – as well as Anna Trapnel – used their power to prophesy, acknowledged as an appropriately female talent, to critique current male political practice. As Sue Wiseman describes the practice of women prophets in the seventeenth century, they 'both bypass earthly powers and negotiate with them; authority is in speaking, but also in manipulating an audience that was material rather than heavenly' (194). Also, the submissiveness enjoined on women by the dominant religious discourse, says Sara Jayne Steen, was manipulated by Arbella Stuart in a conscious way to her own advantage; her 'creation of a deferential self was an attempt to exploit the patriarchal models and use the language of flattery and obedience as an indirect means of achieving control when overt power was unavailable' (153). Women in poetic as well as prophetic modes regularly enacted their socially authorized roles as religious writers to a subversive and resistant purpose. Mary Sidney's psalm translations offer political comment on the vicissitudes of power by way of metaphors on urban decay (Prescott). Aemilia Lanyer, claiming to write on Christ's Passion, devotes more than two-thirds of her 3,000-line poem to praise of women. An Collins justifies her poetry, 'a fruit most rare, / That is not common with every woman / That fruitful are' (*Divine Songs*, 57) because it is directed to 'the praise of God's most blessed name,' arguing that 'they have no excuse, / Which of ability will make no use' (3). While maneuvering within the powerful discourse of Christianity, which required their obedience to a whole hierarchy of patriarchal figures, these women defined their own terms of obedience.

In another variant of this same strategic tactic, Anna Maria Van Schurman appropriated and expanded for her own purposes the demand for chastity placed on virtuous women. She argued for a gynocentric possibility, hardly useful to the patriarchy but beneficial for women, of a separate celibate and intellectual life beyond the reach of male desire and outside the range of male control. Similarly, Mary Astell proposed a way to discover the self outside the range of male discourse by constructing imaginatively a female monastery in which women 'may get out of that danger which a continual stay in the view of the enemy and the familiarity and unwearied application of the temptation may expose them to, and gain an opportunity to look into themselves, to be acquainted at home and no longer the greatest strangers to their own hearts' (quoted in Goreau, 252).[39] These women might have agreed with Irigaray that 'virgin is one as yet unmarked by them [men] ... Not yet imprinted with their sex, their language. Not yet penetrated, possessed by them' (*This Sex*, 211). They chose to be chaste on their own terms.

Of particular importance to the purpose of this study is the recognition that by the very fact of employing traditional poetic conventions, especially when those conventions had already been discarded by male writers, early modern women poets discovered a method of writerly disguise which enabled them to write within range of the contemporary anxiety about women's poetic writing. By seeming, unoriginally, simply to copy a conventional style, they were at the same time able to embed in unthreateningly familiar genres a subversive content. Isabella Whitney, using the accepted conventions of the aphorism, epistle and complaint, is able to imprint on these conventions the fresh, charming, ironic voice of a countrywoman translated into the sophisticated worlds of London, love and loss. Elizabeth Cary in her closet drama *Mariam* was able to interrogate the issue of marital tyranny and women's space. Mary Wroth in her early seventeenth-century sonnet sequence *Pamphilia to Amphilanthus* bitterly reappraised the whole convention of romantic love from the point of view of a betrayed woman, finally choosing to abandon, as she says, 'the discourse of Venus.' Aemilia Lanyer in *Salve Deus Rex Judaeorum* agrees to work within the religious discourse permitted to women while turning it to the defense and praise of women. And Katherine Philips in the 1640s used the outdated conventions of Neo-platonic love poetry to celebrate loving relationships among women. These women chose not to be silent. Their poetically oblique mimicry enacts a strategy of subversive discourse and becomes a successful means of literary disruption.

In the poetic theories of the Renaissance, poetry was already understood as a discourse of enactment, a means of what Philip Sidney most influentially described as a 'representing, counterfeiting, or figuring forth' (101). Poetry is seen as mimetic, not in the sense of slavish imitation, but as a dramatic process of representation.[40] It allows 'right poets' to represent 'most properly' by borrowing 'nothing of what is, hath been, or shall be,' but ranging, 'only reined with learned discretion, into the divine consideration of what may and should be' (102). The very factors cited by Sidney in defense of poetry made it possible, one might suppose, for the transgressive voices of those women poets not content with 'what is' or 'hath been' to tune Sidney's *mimesis* up a notch to the level of subversive enactment. Sidney's defense undoubtedly addressed itself to male readers and potential male poets who were legatees of the political, social and pedagogical ideologies that would teach them necessary discretion in the practice of poetry. But perhaps, writing poetry on the margins of acceptability, women did not always feel the same responsibility for exercising 'learned discretion' to protect the centers of power from the challenge of their poetic imaginations. So, although the ideology of writing in the Renaissance was designed to deter women from writing, especially from writing poetry, poetry also held open for women enticing possibilities for oblique, transgressive, mimetic expression.

Julia Kristeva has suggested that the use of metaphor and metonymy characterizes women's language, since these devices fall in the feminine semiotic realm of language outside the masculine Symbolic realm. Metaphor and metonymy are also useful to women as means of linguistic sabotage or resistance. They are devices of disguise which in poetry may conceal a subversive message under an innocent-seeming covering term; in early modern women's poetry, already operating in the literary margins, this potential in metaphor and metonymy – the figure, as Jacques Lacan says, of desire – was fully exploited.[41]

Poetry is, in any case, always engaged in enticing language outside the logical language of explicit self-identity which sustains the Law of the Father. Language in poetry does not clearly assert or even take for granted that A always equals A; the 'poetic' A may possibly equal A, but will surely also, or instead, both equal something else and draw attention to its supplementary and/or alternative possibility. Poetry's revelation of language as a process of self-manipulating and playful representation (language which cannot lie because it nothing affirms, as Sidney willingly admits), rather than as the closed vehicle of logical truth, at the same time necessarily reveals the language-dependent poetic subject as unknown to itself, also in process, unable to name itself definitively and autonomously. The implicit threat in poetry to the patriarchal Symbolic order offers sufficient cause for social anxiety even when discreetly and self-protectively deployed by the male poet. In the hands of less self-invested women, poetry is both more dangerous and also more 'natural' to the female subject, always anyway denied autonomy by patriarchy, always cloaked and 'nomadic,' always in process.

The poetic conventions of this period also sanctioned still another form of disguise than that available in metaphor and metonymy – the use of a poetic persona whose voice was not identified with the poet's; autobiographical expression and self-declaration of the kind typical in later centuries was not part of the usual audience expectation of early modern poetry. And a coterie audience was also normal.[42] For all these reasons, while poetry was considered outside the range of women's proper linguistic practice, and while women's access to the poetic codes and conventions that depended on formal classical education was limited, poetry was also a genre with special appeal to a woman writer who might either wish to display unanticipated personal skill and win admiration for herself and her sex, or who wished to encode a message that was critical of the impositions of the dominant culture, while saving herself and her sex from rebuke.

While generally regarded for men as one way to demonstrate the skills of their social privilege, for women, writing poetry usually required a position of some social advantage or some educational accomplishment to enable them to circumvent the prohibitions against this form of female language. It also required a special skill to turn the conventions of poetry to subversive use. When successful, however, it could provide the best available writerly means to interrogate the authoritarian patriarch, to vent frustration or anger and to transmit a consciously or unconsciously generated, conspiratorial textual message to like-minded readers, while concealing its social and political criticism from retribution-minded readers suspicious of women's tongues. It also, of course, offered a space in which playfully to explore the potential for an alternative women's language. Margaret Cavendish even claims that the fancifulness and playfulness of poetry make it a peculiarly appropriate medium for women's expression, who, while independently choosing the colors and fabrics for their dresses and needlework, practise the necessary skills of original choice and pleasing taste to be enacted in poetry, 'for *Fancy* goeth not so much by *Rule, & Method* as by *Choice*' (*Poems and Fancies*, sig. A3).

In conditions that insisted on their silence, then, early modern women poets in England still found ways to speak. Because for people on the margins, there is always a premium on obliquity, these writers cannily employed a tactic of exaggeratedly enacting and therefore defying appropriately female roles to rescue something of their pleasure in writing and to insert themselves into the discourse as writing subjects redefined in their own strategically resistant terms. These oblique, manipulative methods of linguistic re-enactment should not be seen as signs of weakness because they operate in a register different from the masculine; they should rather be credited as women's best means to subjectivity and linguistic power; they are the clever tactics of skillful people on the edges of political power. Furthermore, as I argue in the following chapters, the idioms of poetic – as well as non-poetic – indirection should more importantly be seen as successful, expert, subversive strategies in their own right. In early modern England, as elsewhere, women's 'fall into writing implies transgressive self-assertion for ... access to language and access to self-hood are symbiotic' (Myers, 20). Their language is a language of resistance, negotiation and exaggerated enactment rather than of overt revolution, but it is not for that reason any less definitive of a range of power appropriated by the subject in the margin.

Notes

1 Tina Krontiris invokes Woolf's question in order to emphasize our recently altered understanding of women's literary accomplishments in early modern England (1). Margaret Ezell has argued extensively against the too-easy acceptance in some recent feminist studies of Woolf's assumptions. Other participants in this ritual are Barbara Lewalski, Louise Schleiner and Kim Walker.

2 The project to reinspect early modern women's history and texts is so far-reaching that it is difficult to single out particular contributors, but I have found especially helpful the volumes edited by Clare Brant and Diane Purkiss, Mary Prior, Mary Burke, Jane Donawerth, Linda Dove, Karen Nelson and Mary Beth Rose, and the indispensable work of Elaine Beilin, Margaret Ezell, Betty Hageman, Elaine Hobby, Suzanne Hull, Constance Jordan, Barbara Lewalski, Louise Schleiner, Hilda Smith, Betty Travitsky and Wendy Wall.

3 The most significant studies so far of women's literacy in this period are those by Patricia Crawford, David Cressy and Margaret Spufford.

4 We need to remind ourselves that the modern desire for authorial recognition was not shared by all early modern writers, for many of whom the coterie audience was sufficient. Nevertheless, among women writers there are those like Aemilia Lanyer and Isabella Whitney and, more ambiguously, Elizabeth Cary, who sought a wide audience, patronage or financial return.

5 See Margaret Ezell's eloquent complaints about the acceptance of Woolf's point of view, even in recent anthologies of women's writing, that tend to dismiss the existence and importance of early modern women's texts ('The Myth of Judith Shakespeare' and *Writing Women's Literary History*, chs 1 and 2).

6 Dympna Callaghan and Barbara Bowen have offered valuable ways of reading *Mariam* and *Salve Deus Rex Judaeorum* in these terms.

7 See, for example, Margaret Hannay and Mary Ellen Lamb on Mary Sidney; Elaine Beilin, Betty Travitsky and Leah Marcus on Elizabeth; and Elaine Beilin on Margaret More.

8 Patrocinio Schweikart has used this idea of partisan reading to emphasize the position adopted by feminist critics in reading women's writing: 'Here we see clearly that gender is crucial. The feminist reader takes the part of the woman writer against patriarchal misreadings that trivialize or distort her work' (46).

9 I use this term because it comprehends a consideration of political and social factors that mediate the role of the writer in the production of texts, even though by Foucault the factor of gender receives little attention.

10 I intentionally invoke Joan Scott's crucial essay on 'Gender: A Useful Category of Historical Analysis.'

11 In the nineteenth century, Thackeray refused to print Elizabeth Barrett Browning's 'Lord Walter's Life' because it was about 'unlawful passion' and therefore 'unladylike,' and Robert Southey told Charlotte Bronte that poetry should not be the work of a woman's life.

12 For an interesting analysis of the fluctuating gendering of poetry, cosmetics, nature and art, see Frances Dolan's essay on the face-painting debate.

13 Of course, these restrictions failed to influence some women. Bathsua Makin, for example, attempted to reclaim poetry for women:

> If women have been good poets, men injure them exceedingly to account them giddy-headed gossips, fit only to discourse of their hens, ducks, and geese, and not by any means to be suffered to meddle with arts and tongues, lest by intolerable pride they should run mad. (16)

She cites Anne Bradstreet, Jane Grey, Katherine Philips, Elizabeth Tudor, Arbella Stuart, Mary Sidney and Lord Burghley's daughters as achievers in poetry, and points out that the Muses and Graces, Faith, Hope and Charity, as well as the seven liberal arts, are all iconographically depicted as women because 'women were the inventors of many of these arts, and the promoters of them, and since have studied them and attained to excellency in them' (21).

14 See Josephine Roberts's introduction to Wroth's *Poems* (31–37); for a summary of the controversy between Wroth and Lord Denny, and for their correspondence, see pp. 237–241.

15 John Florio, in what now seems a singularly graceless gesture, dedicated his translation of Montaigne's *Essais* (1603) to six noble women, but felt called upon in his preface to apologize and defend his own momentarily reduced engagement in this 'feminine' activity. Probably, in spite of the female dedicatees, Florio expected that the majority of his readers would be men whose sympathy he hoped for and whose disapproval he may have feared. See also Suzanne Trill's reminder that because translation was central to the humanist enterprise, it also 'formed a significant part of men's education' (199). Yet for men, this was a small part of their writing activity.

16 Gary Waller, in 1985, maintained that studies of Renaissance women should focus on the questions: 'How do oppositional forces speak when the dominant language refuses them words? How are the voices of silence heard?' (245). Waller looks for answers to his questions in the 'fluidities' of someone like Anna Trapnel. While drawing on the post-Lacanian French feminists who supply this perception of women's language, I prefer to modify their theories so as to encompass more consciously sophisticated poetic discourse than Trapnel's visionary speech.

Louise Schleiner has proposed some answers to these questions by using 'concepts from text linguistics, discourse pragmatics, linguistically based psychoanalytic theory, and linguistically informed neo-Marxism, re-tooled for gender study' (xvii).

17 Evidence of working people's experience has been accumulated by, for example, Sandra Clark, John Gillis, Olwen Hufton, Ann Kussmaul, Margaret King and Margaret Spufford.

18 Joan Scott articulates some of my nervousness about this concept in 'The Evidence of Experience,' although the ways in which I depart from her more faithful postmodernism will become clear as my text proceeds.

19 See, for example, J.G.A. Pocock's persuasive development of this view.

20 For a detailed investigation of this pattern, see Sara Grieco's work.

21 See, for instance, the examples in the second chapter of this volume.

22 Of course, as Elaine Hobby has estimated, the whole so-far documented output of women's works between 1649 and 1688 'form[s] less than one percent of the total number of texts published in the period' (*Virtue*, 6). And the percentage in the sixteenth century was even lower. Yet studies like Akiko Kusunoki's show that women's public expression was already the topic for public male protest in the 1620s and 1630s, suggesting an earlier and stronger incidence than has so far been accepted.

23 For a brief account in Freud, see *Civilization and its Discontents*, 12–13.

24 Although Elaine Showalter's notion of the 'double-voiced discourse' in women's writing comes to mind here, early modern women writers are engaged in a process that is rather different and more complex.

25 Gayatri Spivak protects the strategic use of a unified consciousness in subaltern studies for a 'scrupulously visible political interest' (13). My own concern is not to maintain the concept of unified consciousness but rather to protect an equally strategic possibility of discourse for the split subject.

26 For an exemplary articulation of the processes of gender ideology in Victorian England, whose insights inform my own, see Mary Poovey's *Uneven Developments*. For a useful general discussion of the processes of ideology see Althusser. For an interesting use of Habermas's theory of social discourse as an aid to understanding women's writing in early modern England, see Schleiner, ch. 2.

27 For some of the texts, see Henderson and McManus; for an extended analysis of the controversy and its texts, see Woodbridge. Also notice Susan Amussen's comment that 'the existence of the debate is itself evidence of the concern about the gender order' (183), and Joy Wiltenburg's endorsement of the 'widespread unease and uncertainty' (9) about gender relations. Amussen draws her conclusions from a seventeenth-century rural English town and Wiltenburg from the evidence of popular pamphlets printed in England and Germany. The markers and boundaries of sexuality as much as those of gender, as Bruce Smith reminds us, require the recognition that 'sexuality, premodern or otherwise, is a function of ideology, a social construction that varies according to time and place. Different cultures at different moments in history construct sexuality differently' ('Premodern Sexualities,' 318).

28 See Jonathan Dollimore for an interesting analysis of the discourses of homosexuality in this period (106–123; 148–165; 237–240; 284–306). Also see my discussion of evidence of women's homoeroticism in chapter 2 of this volume. Also see Bruce Smith's 'Premodern Sexualities.'

29 See Roger Chartier for an analysis of these relationships between public and private. Also see Helen Wilcox's analysis of a group of autobiographical texts which, she says, reveal 'a range of public roles for Renaissance Englishwomen, while at the same time suggesting the public nature of any ostensibly private aspects of their lives and demonstrating the inseparability of these two spheres. ... [T]hese texts ... deny the validity of an easy classification of the public or the private in Renaissance women's lives' (60).

30 See Alice Friedman's essay on the attractions exerted by London over the domestic hearth of the country estate for Elizabeth Willoughby and, at least before she finally gained control of her northern estates, for Anne Clifford.

31 Deborah Shuger (*Habits*) has argued that the co-existence of apparently self-contradictory 'habits of thought' which induced anxiety about liminality was typical of the period. She draws on Hooker, Andrewes, Herbert and Donne to show this pattern. The same anxious

entertainment of the ambivalent can be seen in many Shakespearean texts, as for example, *The Merchant of Venice* and *Othello*.

32 Also see the work by Peter Clark, Valerie Elliott and David Souden on the shifting population in early modern England, especially the mobility of women.

33 A now well-known letter from John Chamberlain, dated 26 January 1620, reports that King James ordered the clergy 'to inveigh vehemently in their sermons against the insolence of our women and their wearing of broad-brimmed hats, pointed doublets, their hair cut short and shorn, and some of them stilettos or poniards, and such other trinkets of like moment' (II.286–287) – that is, women's assumption of masculine styles of dress.

34 See Adrian Wilson's reconstruction of childbirth communities.

35 See Margaret Hannay's and Mary Ellen Lamb's discussions of this group.

36 Carol Barash's discussion of women's community as a context for Katherine Philips's poetry (55–100) is especially interesting in this regard.

37 See Suzanne Hull's construction of this female literature and audience.

38 See also Diane Purkiss's discussion of 'parodic or subversive reifications of the construction of women' (144) among seventeenth-century women prophets like Elinor Channel.

39 Of course, a world free from the influences of male discourse needed (and needs) to be fictional. For Joan Kinnaird argues that Mary Astell arrived at a 'radical consciousness of self – important to the growth of feminism' (33), through the influence of Descartes's 'insistence on the thinking "I" as the touchstone of all knowledge and even existence' (33). But the fictional imagination, as Renaissance faculty psychology acknowledged and feared, is very powerful.

40 See my reading of Sidney's theory of poetry in my essay on Donne and Sidney; also see Arthur Barker on Sidney's influence on early modern poetic theory and practise.

41 For example, see my readings in chapters 5 and 6 of this volume of Cary's and Lanyer's uses of metaphor.

42 Arthur Marotti's and Louise Schleiner's work in describing both men's and women's coterie culture has been definitive.

2.1 Frontispiece: Andreas Vesalius, *De humani corporis fabrica*

Chapter 2

The Flesh. The Other Body: Women's Physical Images

> To reconceive of women and femininity in terms independent of men and masculinity requires a major reorganization of sexual, linguistic, and socio-symbolic systems, and indeed of desire itself. More specifically, it requires reconceiving the female body as a positivity rather than a lack.
>
> – Elizabeth Grosz, *Sexual Subversions*, 110

Published in 1543, Andreas Vesalius's renowned anatomical treatise, *De humani corporis fabrica*, is introduced by a frontispiece illustration almost as familiar as the text itself; both the text and the illustration were reprinted frequently throughout the sixteenth and seventeenth centuries, often together but sometimes separately as well. In the center of the illustration, on a dissecting table, a woman's naked, partially dissected body lies, surrounded by avid male viewers, her legs splayed open to the reader's gaze. Jonathan Sawday says of this female cadaver that she '*desires* dissection' ('The Fate of Marsyas,' 123);[1] I see, rather, that the medical and textual anatomists inside and outside the dissecting theater have reduced the sexually threatening female body to an eviscerated corpse, taking for granted her complicity in her fate. She is clearly helpless and vulnerable, lying prone, on her back, propped up to expose her body more readily to view. She is the only female in the whole crowd of about a hundred fully-clothed male viewers.[2] Even the cherubim, also naked, but transcendental and pre-pubescent, gaze down upon her from the frame of the etching. Above her hangs a skeleton, a reminder of the next stage of dissolution beyond the dissecting table. The image further reinforces the oppositional relationship, accepted throughout Western history, between the philosophically and scientifically inquiring masculine mind, represented here by the anatomists, and the female body, regarded as the object of biological and medical investigation. Here the body is inert, outside history because dead and female, outside culture because dead, eviscerated and publicly naked. This image offers an aptly representative example of the way in which women's bodies often appear throughout the early modern period – as sexual, fragmented, linked with corruption, and also as fascinating, though reducible, objects of the male gaze – not just in visual depictions, but also in written texts.

Jane Sharp's *Midwives Book*, published in 1671, also contains an illustration of a woman's naked body, much simpler, not so costly to reproduce, and until very recently, much less well-known. In *this* image, the woman's body is alive, alert, erect and powerful. Her shoulders and her limbs are strong. Her face is calm, her curls luxuriant and beautifully coiffed. Poised on top of, not within, her midriff, her pregnancy exists as a possibility, not as an internalized destiny. The baby is curled and enfolded as the symbolic, fertile center of the flower petals that harmoniously surround it – the flowering fetus in the uterine 'field' or 'ground' of which Sharp writes in her text. Between the woman's legs is suspended another flower, a reminder of the Renaissance term for menstruation as the 'flowers,' but also visually decorating and imaginatively perfuming the thus positively valenced genitalia. There are no surrounding voyeurs in this picture. The woman herself is the gazer here, meeting the projected female reader's gaze with mutual, direct and unashamed recognition. She is a subject, not an object.

These visual images were almost certainly not chosen by the male and female writers to illustrate their texts. In fact, they were probably commissioned by the printers with a view to increasing the texts' popularity and saleability. And they thereby attest to a cultural recognition of the differently gendered responses that might be stimulated by representations of the female body; they also acknowledge the need to construct the female body differently, depending on those same different, gendered contexts. Clearly, they demonstrate some awareness that the Vesalian kind of image is not appropriate in a text like Sharp's, written by a woman, on the topic of women's health, and designed for women readers – midwives like Sharp herself.[3] The passage of time between the production of the one and the other text hints at a shift that occurred during those 130 years in the culturally accepted options for the public representation of women's bodies.

All human bodies are constructed in culture, not entirely determined by birth, for the concepts and in part the material facts of our bodies are socially and linguistically produced and can be socially and linguistically changed. Like other cultural objects, 'the body is the product and effect of various systems of training, discipline, and [institutional] construction' (Grosz, *Sexual Subversions*, x). The body functions and takes on meaning by reference to historically situated texts and itself frequently acquires the readable character of a text. It is always an important site of discursive power. Inevitably, then, cultural insecurity about 'normative' social and sexual roles and functions will mark male and female sex differences in sharply differentiated ways, so that 'the inscribed message will be different ... depending on the type of (sexed) materiality to be inscribed' (Grosz, 'Bodies and Knowledges,' 202).

Far from being undermined, these central perceptions of recent feminist theory are confirmed in early modern England, which supplies copious textual evidence of the power of the dominant male discourse to influence the social construction of the female body.[4] Yet, although the opportunity for a woman to 'assert her own

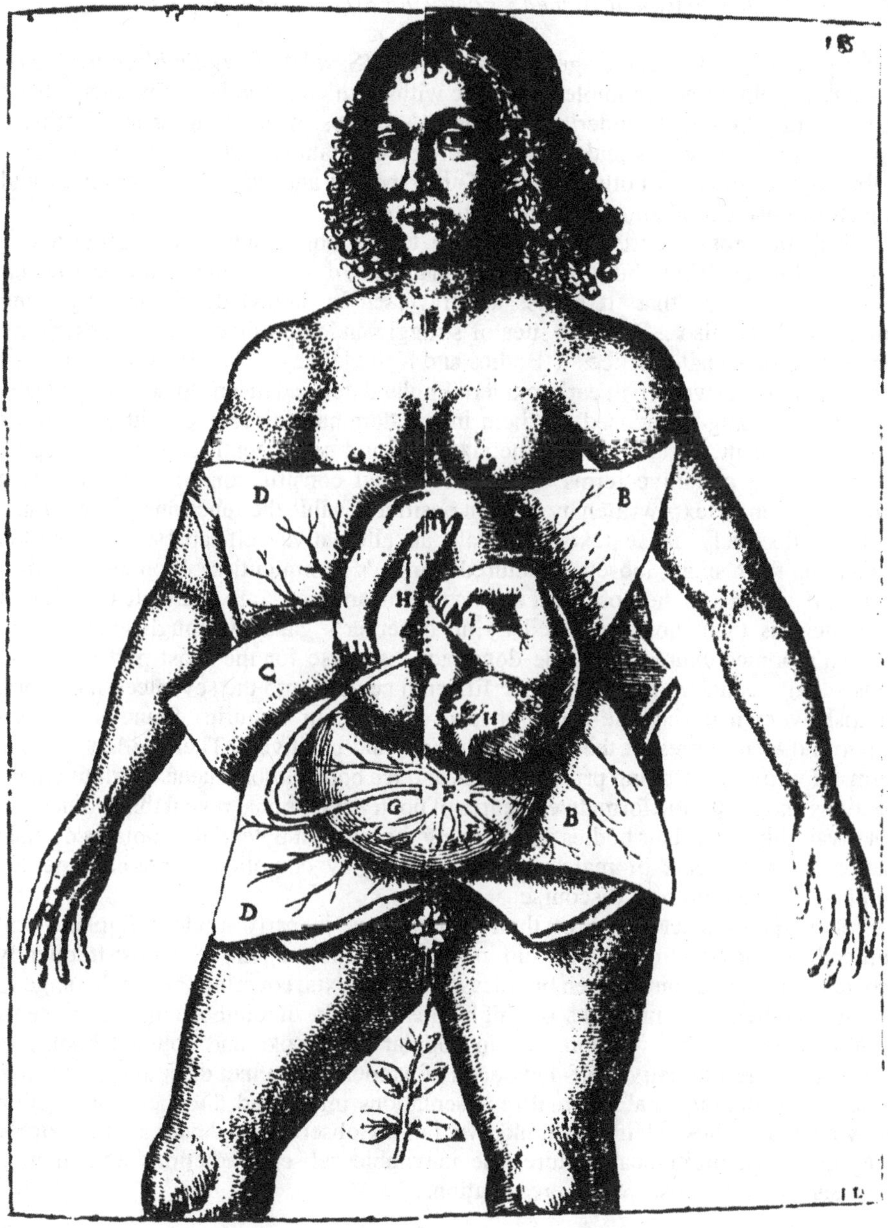

2.2 Frontispiece: Jane Sharp, *Midwives Book*

identity (and body) as a free agent, was unequal' (Sawday, *Body Emblazoned*, 227), this culture supported a complex dialectic within which a number of women's texts disputed the dominant rendering of women's bodies, negotiating spaces both for women's physical selves and for their self-representation, and mediating women's ambiguous position as both subjects of their bodily and writerly experiences and objects of powerful ideological constructions.

Elizabeth Grosz asserts that 'resistance to the imposition of discipline and a potential for revolt' are built into the mechanisms of any regime of power (*Sexual Subversions*, x), so that 'if bodies are traversed by knowledges, meanings, and power, they can also ... become sites of struggle and resistance, actively inscribing themselves on social practices' ('Bodies and Knowledges,' 199). In confirmation of this insight, some women in early modern England devised means to adjust and resist the physical images imposed on them in the dominant discourse. Although some women living in England during the sixteenth and seventeenth centuries accepted the ultimately reductive terms of the patriarchal construction of their bodies, a sizeable group of texts written by women positively value the functions of the female body. Collectively, these texts articulate an alternative self-representation often emanating from small, loosely structured women's communities.[5] Women's lived-in bodies, it appears, in their physical and textual incarnations, are available to different constructions than those provided by an observer's gaze. Although views about women's bodies expressed in the dominant discourse for the most part remained consistently reductive from about the fifteenth century into the seventeenth century, English women during the sixteenth and seventeenth centuries found increasing opportunities to represent themselves publicly and positively. Their widely various forms of writing, including private diaries, advice books, broadsheets, Parliamentary petitions and the public formalized genres of poetry and drama, reveal that women did not invariably view their bodies as achieving their fullest potential as objects of male desire or as breeders of male progeny, that is, by complicitly internalizing the demands of the dominant discourse.

Yet women's inscriptions of their embodiment in early modern England still contend for our attention, as they did in their own times, against the most frequently proclaimed views about women broadcast by male texts, covering the whole range of possible audiences – in works of 'high' literature, in the authoritative documents of law, education and religion, and in popular handbooks and conduct books. In filtering out the alternative self-depictions of women, we cannot discount the ways in which contemporary male textual representations influenced the social production of women's bodies. Neither should we fail to observe, however, in that richly heterogeneous, multivocal culture, the inevitable self-contradictions and internal inconsistencies in those very representations.

The Master's Voice

In the Neoplatonic poetic tradition, which remained influential in England throughout the sixteenth and seventeenth centuries, women were typically presented as silent and chaste objects of male desire. The self-contradictory argument of this poetry both asserted the speaker's seductive desire and proclaimed that the mistress's unviolated body, exemplifying the beauty of a pure soul by resisting seduction, would lead the lover to divine love as a superior displacement of the physical. Despite the idealized elevation of the image of the chaste woman, women's bodies in this poetic tradition, as Nancy Vickers has shown, are typically fragmented and distorted, a 'collection of exquisitely beautiful disassociated objects' (Vickers, 266).[6] This representation disquietingly evokes the common image in the period of the criminally accused and violently abused body, racked, eviscerated and quartered for a public spectacle. It also visually echoes the widely available Vesalian images of anatomical dissection.[7] The female image of sexual desire in male poetry is 'but a twice-removed, scripted rendering of a lost woman' (Vickers, 275). Her absence, objectification and dismemberment also make her an object of repressed violence.[8]

The dissection of, and repressed violence against, the female body, glamorized in male poetry, has an unpoetic parallel in legal and medical records. William Staine, for instance, in 1587 was officially charged with beating his wife 'contrary to all order and reason' (Macdonald, 102). Stephen Rawlins, a regular drinker, beat and abused his wife whenever he drank (Macdonald, 100). A poor widow with two small children, seduced and impregnated by a neighbor already 'infamous for like practices with others,' was abandoned by him, charged with infanticide and sentenced to death (*An Account of the Tryal, Condemnation, and Execution of Mary Goodnenough*, 1; and Otten, 13). An eleven-year-old girl was raped by John Lamb, a physician; sentenced to death, Lamb, protected by the Duke of Buckingham, was pardoned by the King. An angry mob of London citizens, acting outside the law, became the instruments of justice in this case; challenging the royal intervention, in the same year as Buckingham was assassinated, they stoned Lamb to death (*A Brief Description*, 15–21; and Otten, 18).

In marriage contracts, women's bodies were treated as male-owned property, items of patriarchal exchange. A woman's chastity was designated as the property of her husband or father, so that either could sue the wife's or daughter's seducer for damage to his property or theft (Goreau, 9–10; Hill, 249). *The Lawes Resolution of Womens Rights* (1632) sums up the legal inevitability of this view: 'If a Feme covert be ravished, and consent to the ravisher, the husband alone may have an Appeale' (390). A woman's body, over which she had no legal right, essentially decided her legal status. Under the auspices of the law, women's bodies were also made objects of public spectacle, punished on ducking stools, muted and mutated by scolds' bridles, or whipped and 'carted' for supposed or real verbal or sexual transgressions. In the notorious trial of Lord Castlehaven (1631), who had, for his voyeuristic pleasure, arranged the rape of his wife and her twelve-year-old daughter by his servants, and who was subsequently executed for these crimes, Lady Castlehaven's testimony, repeating her husband's self-justification, makes evident the law's consequences for women: he 'told me my body was his, and if I lay with any man with his consent, 'twas not my fault, but his' (*The Trial and Condemnation of Mervin Lord Audley, etc*).[9]

The authoritative ideas that inscribed women's bodies in England in the sixteenth and seventeenth centuries derived largely from patristic sources. Aquinas and Augustine accepted the Aristotelian point of view that while the male was ordained to rational and mental activity, the female was dedicated to the bodily role of reproduction. Although Aquinas permitted a rational soul to woman, her body, he argued, was the sole justification for her creation because of its necessary usefulness in the preservation of the species.[10] In 1599, King James, in his *Basilikon Doron*, was still instructing his son that he should 'neither Marie ... for any accessory cause or worldly respects, a woman unable, either through age, nature, or accident, for procreation of children' (35). Martin Luther, as adamantly, proclaimed of women, 'even if they ... bear themselves out ... this is the purpose for which they exist' (quoted in Ozment, 161). According to this perception, woman is corporeal and reproductive. Yet even in her necessary reproductive role, she is passive, not active, receptive not generative. Her dominance by her body inhibits her moral and mental capabilities (McLaughlin, *passim*); unless closely restrained, women will transform easily to whores. Thomas Overbury's *Characters* (1614) depict a 'Good Woman' as a passive recipient of her husband's directions: 'Shee is much within, and frames outward things to her minde, not her minde to them' (3); yet Overbury also asserts flatly in a following character, 'A Very Whore is a woman' (29) whose 'bodie is the tilted Lees of pleasure,' a 'hie way to the Divell' (28).

This construction of the female body was buttressed by the developing economic emphasis on material property as constitutive of male self and status. And the European colonial enterprise provided a material and metaphoric correlative for the exploitation and commodification by the dominant culture of the female body. A woman in this construction was a useful item which could be traded, manipulated, trained and passed from person to person. Yet the commodification of women's bodies had a darker, even more threatening aspect. The excessive control of her person, the bodily constraints attempted over her coming and going, were inspired by the social anxiety that if her body were unconstrained, lacking a sufficiently rational mind to direct her will, a woman might cause havoc through her unbridled sexuality.

This fear was both excited and challenged at the end of the sixteenth century by the increasing population of vagrant women, displaced from their homes by the commercialization of agriculture (Salgado, *passim*). These masterless, wandering women were seen as likely to disrupt the social order, by seducing men to similar spatial and sexual wanderings (Dollimore, 119; and Parker, 105–106). In other instances, generalized concerns about possible social disruption were specifically displaced onto women's commodified sexual bodies. The proclamation in 1546 ordering the closing of London's brothels (*Tudor Royal Proclamations*, 365–366) was followed in 1603 by an order to demolish large stretches of property in the suburbs of London where the brothels were situated, ostensibly to control the spread of the plague (*Stuart Royal Proclamations*, 47). In both instances, however, the suppression of women's trade in sexuality was also a means of containing other forms of political disorder. J.A. Sharpe says that suppression of sexuality in early modern England was 'one aspect of a wider desire to achieve a disciplined society' (215).

With the loosening of censorship laws in the 1640s, women as well as men took advantage of the prevailing ideological discord to articulate public demands for political and religious rights, yet women's demands continued to be represented by antagonistic men as expressions of their bodies' sexual need. In 1647, a royalist response to women's petitions to Parliament argued that women demanding political rights were really attempting to attract the attention of royalist soldiers (*A Remonstrance of the Shee-Citizens of London*, 18). In 1659, in *The Ladies Remonstrance*, women's demands for religious toleration were derisively answered by the assertion that the religious toleration asked for by women was really 'a demand to be allowed to "lie with man of any colour hair or body shape" ' (quoted in Hobby, 18). Women's bodies were ideologically categorized by men, who installed themselves as the 'heads' or minds of women, reconstructing women's political petitionary claims in terms of sexual objectification. Attached irrevocably to the body, women were nevertheless refused authority over that 'region of all potential contamination' (Jed, 13). Rather, attempts were made to manage women 'through their bodies' (Newman, 6), so that, reduced and objectified to their material bodies, they were perceived as objects of efficient surveillance and control.

Restrictions placed by the dominant ideology on women's sexually threatening bodies dictated a limited, housebound, husband-directed role.[11] Even before marriage, a woman's body was not regarded as under her own control; in male constructions of acceptable female behavior she was directed to refuse her body's pleasures to herself and her ardent wooer for fear that the polluted and infectiously sexual female body might corrupt the male body and rational mind. Although these demands are regularly articulated in the dominant discourse, some women of course exercised a larger degree of sexual freedom: 'women with property, especially widows, were often very active and few females were wholly passive ... The intimacy that we regard as the culmination of a courtship, [members of the peasant and artisan classes, at least] viewed as an inconclusive beginning ... [P]rivate intimacy in and of itself was not proof of any commitment between two persons' (Gillis, 38).[12]

Despite the certainty that some women in all ranks failed to accept its precepts, the dominant representations of early modern England essentialized women as their bodies for two material purposes that are at various moments inconsistent with each other. First, as they are rendered in poetry, to function as objects of desire for male sexual release, and second, as they are directed by the law, religious treatises and conduct books, for use as chaste channels of production for male offspring. The positing of women's bodies in these self-contradictory terms is a symptom and condition of ideological power. Efforts at control over women, attempting to cover all contingencies of resistance, produced inconsistent constructions which in turn justified the further imposition of repressive ideological power. Within this framework, differences of power were firmly articulated on gender.[13]

Although the convention gradually altered during the seventeenth century, as women's literacy increased and women were increasingly identified with domestic affairs, even early handbooks on women's practical household duties of cookery, embroidery and housekeeping were written by men, and marriage guides concerning how to maintain an amicable marriage and how to keep a husband happy, as well as how to keep a wife under control, were written by men and addressed to men. In fact, any male text, literary or legal, which frames the role of women in this period can be seen as a means whereby the male writer and the male reader mutually and 'homosocially' construct *themselves* textually and politically.[14] This homosocial contract, according to Wendy Wall, can also be seen in the bond forged between the male writer and the male reader over the erotically feminized, published book, which, bought and taken home by a male reader, will be thus enclosed and domesticated (205): iconically embodying and 'naming books as women constituted a mutually reinforcing moment of commodification, in which the overt display and objectification of equivalent merchandisable goods policed a woman's cultural standing' (62).

The degree to which all of women's bodily expressions were taken for granted by men as a domain for the exercise of their own power is further evident in the numerous works on cosmetics written by men (for example, Plat, 1602; Wecker, 1660; Jeamson, 1665). While some of these texts discourse moralistically on the deceptions of the painted face, at the same time they provide detailed prescriptions for cosmetic means of female beautification. The audience for these texts is female, but the recipes for cosmetic care are reserved by the male for the sake, one must suppose, of his own material and visual benefit; as Natalie Zemon Davis points out, women's beauty had a political function as an adornment of masculine society and the brilliant courts of Europe (Craveri, 70). Women's use of makeup, styled hair and elaborate dress might also be seen as an effort to conceal their 'selves' from the suspicious and manipulative male gaze, to protect their own self-(mis)representations.[15] Women's ability to manipulate how they seem was regarded as 'monstrous' and unnatural, but because female self-adornment could not be prevented, control over its practice was attempted by male texts on the subject. According to Frances Dolan, although the 'heterogeneous [male] discourse about cosmetics sometimes acknowledges female power, it views that power negatively' (236) and attempts to restrict it.

In texts by Thomas Raynalde (1545), Jacques Guillemeau (1612) and Thomas Vicary (1641) concerning women's reproductive functions, although their audience is purportedly women, there is the curious effect of these writers, too, speaking across their female audience to some unnamed (male) reader, who might be expected to supervise the enactment of their advice. Especially this is evident in the general lack of focus in these texts on women's physical welfare. For instance, Guillemeau comments that frequent childbearing will ruin a woman's beauty, but only as an afterthought does he remind his reader that the woman's health during pregnancy is important, because in the case of the death of the mother, 'the life of the Child is also hazarded' (32). He further advocates purging a woman every month during her pregnancy as a compensation for the absence of the cleansing effects of menstruation – hardly a practice that would benefit pregnant women and one which a 'woman-physician,' Mary Trye, opposed.[16] An obvious example of male intervention in women's physical lives occurs in a work by John Sadler (1636), which offers to instruct women about uterine problems that they are assumed to be too ignorant and too modest to discuss with their physicians (Hull, 201). Sadler fails to acknowledge the useful information about women's health that was regularly circulated among women family members, friends and midwives.

The goals and belief systems of a dominant discourse may be vested in the myth of a consistent, coherent ideology, but in no culture does complete ideological coherence obtain. In early modern England, where ideological disruptions were constant, although the representation of the female as a corruptible, contaminating body was by far the most prevalent, even in male texts this depiction was not consistent. In fact, texts by men which appear relentlessly to suppress women's minds and bodies probably bespeak anxieties about women's perceived power (cf. Wiltenburg, 7–8), even while attempting to suppress points of view which offer a pro-woman challenge. Even so, women's own textual efforts to assert control over their bodies were occasionally paralleled by alternative points of view that seeped into the dominant discourse.

As monasticism closed down in England and a sectarian Protestant challenge was mounted to Catholicism and its patristic foundation, a few more balanced modifications of traditional gender construction began to appear. By and large, women's bodies were still seen as the source of sexual sin, but sectarians in the seventeenth century occasionally undermined and questioned this view, so that sporadically an alternative picture of women's bodies emerged. Quakers, for example, argued against hatred of the body and, like Anabaptists and Ranters, sometimes stripped naked in public – as did Elizabeth Fletcher in Oxford, for example – to testify to this position (Carrol, *passim*; Bauman, ch. 6; Hill, 256–260). Sir Ralph Burgoyne reports another such incident in a letter to Ralph Verney on 28 July 1652:

> On Sunday last sennight a woman in silk being in Whitehall at the sermon, the subject of that discourse being the Resurrection, she perfectly stripped herself of all her apparel, and, as she came into the world from top to toe, she ran into the middle of the congregation, over against the pulpit, and cried, 'Welcome the Resurrection.' ... Some say it was a great piece of self-denial, but for that I shall leave you to judge of. (III.47–48)

The nameless woman's silken clothing, which Burgoyne uses as an identifying class marker, invites a certain respect because of her superior social station; her radical behavior, at least to some observers, though apparently not to Burgoyne, seems a 'piece of self-denial' or self-abandonment in the face of Christ's imminent coming, which might reinforce that respectful response. In some fascinating way, the woman's public exposure of her unclothed body, typically seen as stimulus to and source of corruption, is here seen as at least potentially an admirable abandonment to Christ and purification of the self which *is*, for women, their body.

The public exhibition of the body's declared innocence included women's as well as men's bodies because Quakers, like Familists and Ranters, insisted on the equality of the sexes in the eyes of the Lord and in the world. It is a practice all the more subversive when set beside the more typical reductive analogy found in Mary Fisher's letter to Quakers in Barbados (1657), where she compares ungodly behavior to 'a menstruous cloth ... a shame to be worn' (quoted in Mack, 136). In yet other instances of male textual renderings of the female body as not pestilential, Bishop Hall and John Bunyan argued that female nudity was less seductively provocative than the kind of clothing usually condoned for women by society (Hill, 253). Martin Luther's influential commentary on Genesis (1:27) asserted that 'woman is in no way a botched male, but rather those who accuse her of being such "are themselves monsters and the sons of monsters" for decrying a creature made by God "with the care he might have devoted to his most noble work"' (Maclean, 9). Of course, Luther also accepted without debate that woman was inferior to man (Maclean, 11).

Although men's theological texts supporting the idea of women's equality are few, there is a larger body of material in men's medical texts that treats the woman's body as something other than the source of corruption, so that Ian Maclean suggests 'it is possible to argue that there is a feminist movement in medical spheres' (29). In part, this sensibility derives from the accumulating biological information about the function of male and female organs, so that 'by 1660 ... one sex is no longer thought to be an imperfect and incomplete version of the other. Indeed ... the uterus now evokes admiration and eulogy for its remarkable role in procreation' (Maclean, 33), although women themselves were generally expected to be too modest or ignorant to share this admiration of their own uterine functions. The detailed anatomical studies of Gabriele Fallopio (1561) and the famous dissections of Vesalius probably contributed importantly to the changing view of woman's biology; as a result of these discoveries, women's reproductive systems could be seen as complex and different from the male instead of as similar, but simpler and inferior.

As Hilda Smith (1976) points out, women's health issues were stereotyped in medical texts by their anatomy, so that fevers, vapors, hysteria and general ill health in women were assigned to menstrual and uterine malfunctions. Medical handbooks of the period by men and women alike designate a specifically female disorder called 'suffocation of the mother' or womb. Although including a range of physical problems specific to women, the symptoms of this disease also covered restlessness, raving and hysteria – all also regarded as fundamentally female (Laurence, 'Women's Psychological Disorders,' 210–211).[17] This list of symptoms recalls Luce Irigaray's speculation that women in the past have 'enacted' hysteria to escape from and to rescue their 'mother-matter' and 'prodigality' from patriarchy (*Speculum*, 195). Smith and Maclean also show that the supposed deficiencies of female character and behavior were adduced from their bodies' humors: because women are cold, moist, 'leaky vessels' (Paster, 25), where men are hot and dry, women are less desirous of physical activity and more melancholy, stupider and weaker (Maclean, 29ff).

In medical works generally, written by men or women, more frank discussion of women's sexuality is evident than in any other kind of text. For example, masturbation was frequently recommended as a treatment for the sexual frustration or 'green-sickness' of adolescent girls (Hobby, 2; Winfried Schleiner, 132–140). And, in part to control their socially threatening sexuality, but also for their sexual release, widows are advised by many physicians, including Nicholas Fontaine (1652), following Galen, either to masturbate or to call in a 'skillful midwife' who, with a 'convenient oyntment,' might furnish 'pleasing conflicts' and relieve the widow's sexual tension (Fontaine, 6). Winfried Schleiner has discussed the ethical anxiety and debate generated by this practice among physicians themselves (113–129), whose possible voyeuristic erotic arousal might be categorized as a sin or crime. Focused on the potential moral danger to the attending male physician, the handbooks fail to point out the possibility of pleasurable female-female sexuality as a factor in this treatment.

Current feminist theory has emphasized that women's claims over their own bodies, their right to knowledge about their body and its autonomous pleasures, are essential to the reclamation of the female body from the claims of the state and a necessary means to the development of an alternative women's language and self-inscription. In particular, Luce Irigaray and Hélène Cixous have argued that through reclaiming their pluralistic physical pleasures, including masturbatory and lesbian sexuality, women may begin to shrug off the Law of the Father which forbids their access to the power of language, and may escape their commodification for male pleasure. Early modern medical recommendations that women help each other to sexual release invite speculation that in a culture so dominated by fear of women's heterosexual promiscuity and power, there was likely more female–female sexuality than has so far been recognized.[18] Both Helkiah Crooke's *A Description of the Body of Man* (1615) and Jane Sharp's *Midwives Book* (1671) also discuss in a somewhat off-handed way what both consider the anti-social practices of 'tribadism.'

Of course, Fontaine's recommendation of auto-eroticism and the offices of a 'skilled midwife,' being male-authored, carries its own heavy weight of authoritarian patriarchal intervention. The condescending assumption is that women will be perpetually driven by their bodies' voracious sexual needs while remaining incapable of deciding on their own how to respond to this need. The advice is most commonly directed to widows, a group whose relative bodily and sometimes material independence was seen as posing a significant challenge to efforts to control female sexuality. Widows were perhaps the only group of women who could conduct themselves 'with some legal power' (Travitsky, *Paradise*, 70; King, *Women of the Renaissance*, 57), partly no doubt because they were comparatively free of the requirements exercised over their bodies by the inheritance system. Having fulfilled her sexual and procreative duty, a widow might feel free to reclaim her body and her self.[19] Yet, as well as seeing in Fontaine an unwitting subversion of the totalizing claims of heterosexuality, a modern reader may also recognize a male voice textually asserting its power to permit and orchestrate female sexuality. Fontaine's prescription for women's gynecological disorders is confidently phallocentric: 'married women by lying with their husbands, doe loosen the passages of the seed and so the Courses [menstrual flow] come down more easily thorow them' (5); 'Wives are more healthfull then Widowes, or Virgins, because they are refreshed with the mans seed' (4).

The Subject/Body

Given such appropriative invasion of their bodies by male discourse, and considering especially the insistent essentialization of women as objectified bodies, how were women to claim a sense of themselves as physical and psychological subjects? Early modern women may well have formulated their own version of the question Luce Irigaray addresses to the discourse-owning male: 'Have I ever had a body other than the one which you constructed according to your idea of it? Have I ever experienced a skin other than the one which you wanted me to dwell within?' (*Elemental Passions*, 49).

Even apart from the inhibition of their ability to own and name their own bodies, a system which essentializes women as exchangeable reproductive commodities carries with it other negative relational consequences for women:

> A depersonalization of woman must be seen as a necessary consequence of the assimilation of the male–female relationship into a body–soul relationship, which implies a subject–object relationship between man and woman. The soul–body or subject–object relationship between the self and the 'other,' as visually perceived object, essentially abolishes the 'other' as a 'thou' or a person to be related to with a mutuality due to the meeting of person with person in and through the body. (Ruether, 163)

Although the ideal of Christian companionate marriage as a relationship of spiritual mutuality was increasingly emphasized in Protestant argument from the end of the sixteenth century, it did not satisfactorily do away with this body–soul, subject–object, male–female hierarchical relation because it could not abandon the traditional subordination of women. In any case the individual for whose loneliness Christian marriage was designed as a cure was, first and foremost, male. The 'apt and cheerful conversation of man with woman,' which Milton offers as a definition of companionate marriage in the preface to *The Doctrine and Discipline of Divorce*, was to 'comfort and refresh *him* [italics mine] against the evil of solitary life.' Although a 'good wife' may on the one hand be rhetorically constructed as 'a joint co-partner upon all occasions,' she was still politically an item of patriarchal exchange, an objectified 'blessing given from God to man' (Earle, *Microcosmography*, 248, quoted in Macfarlane, 158).

Yet, persuaded by feminist arguments that it is partly through the body that women may formulate a sense of self, a modern reader will look in early modern Englishwomen's texts for signs that they were able to manipulate positively for themselves the accepted conjunction of the objectified woman's body with the self-interest of the body politic. The connection of the socially constructed body with social ideology establishes the framework within which these textual negotiations need to take place. 'The work of ideology,' as Gail Paster points out, 'includes the social formation of the body because of the "obvious" physical and psychological inseparability of the subject from his/her bodily envelope – no matter how internally divided and self-alienated the subject may be' (4). Still, to what set of ideas did the early modern woman turn when she considered either her right to, or loss of, self?

Renaissance humanism, Lucy Gent and Nigel Llewellyn suggest, endorsed the interiorization of the self, so that the 'body is a rather lowly, albeit necessary, container for the soul or spirit' (5–6). In the arguments of the powerful and popular contemporary theologians William Perkins and John Whitgift, Deborah Shuger discovers the interesting possibility of a double or even multiplex concept of self which allows for private disposition of feeling and public exercise of power; nevertheless, these qualities remain embedded in the 'pneumatic' or spiritual, that is, masculine, self (*Habits of Thought*, 89–105). This typical association of the self with the soul or the mind or the spirit (Ruether, 178; Shuger, 89–105) would have inhibited women's construction of the self insofar as the soul in relation to the body was seen as masculine in relation to the feminine. The gendering of masculine soul and female body feeds into an ideology that would deny women, essentialized as body, access to a legitimate sense of self, unless women were able to work out a strategy which would permit them to invest a positive sense of self in their very physicality.[20] For a woman to discover her language and subjectivity, says Elizabeth Grosz, 'requires reconceiving the female body as a positivity rather than a lack' (*Sexual Subversions*, 110).

Such a move is, in fact, discernible in women's texts, which offer variously: positive valuations by women of their uniquely female biological capacities; resistant efforts by women to withdraw their bodies from male intervention; and more frequently toward the end of the seventeenth century than earlier in the period, an assertive claim by women to authority over the disposition of their bodies.[21] Although women's bodies were represented in contemporary male texts as exchangeable commodities[22] and their role closely identified with the masculine use of their bodies in sex and reproduction, and although the masculine soul, not the female body, was identified with the individual self, the mind or the spirit, this ideological formula did not erase for women all sense of their separate and viable physical selves. More precisely, it may have meant that for women, ontologically essentialized *as* body, a sense of identity was available in a way that is quite familiar to a modern sensibility.[23] As Rosi Braidotti points out, 'The starting point for most feminist redefinitions of subjectivity is a new [non-essentialized] form of materialism, one that develops the notion of corporeal materiality by emphasizing the embodied and therefore sexually differentiated structure of the speaking subject' (3).

Women in early modern England as in most other historical situations seem to have resided in a bodily space where they functioned at one and the same time as both object and subject. Out of this variable, flexible position, they did not achieve – and, as women, could not be expected to achieve – the dubiously attainable Kantian ideal of a transcendental subjectivity. Nor did early modern women (or perhaps any others) arrive at the transcendent presence to the world as subject which Merleau-Ponty sees as vested in the hypothetical lived body which is fortunate enough to exist beyond the range of objectification. They achieved, rather, in common I believe with almost all women and perhaps most men at all stages of history, a kind of limited and divided linguistic power and consciousness of bodily identity which makes possible an effective and interesting, though by no means total, range of textual authority and subjectivity.

Stephen Greenblatt, referring to Freudian theory, and supporting his argument with the example of Martin Guerre, has suggested that a sense of self in the Renaissance was not developed psychosomatically, but in 'communally secured proprietary rights to a name and a place in an increasingly mobile social world' (221). Greenblatt's speculations, though provocative, refer to a male example and probably cannot be applied usefully to women, who did not, unless widows or very wealthy, have ensured legal rights to property, and who were themselves owned or acquired by men as property of the very kind on which the identity described by Greenblatt depended.

Even if Greenblatt is correct that Renaissance men constituted their identity in external property and in masks of social recognition, rather than in bodily terms, as Freud – and Merleau-Ponty – would hold, this theory of identity will not explain the means whereby women established their different sense of subjectivity. It is likely that early modern women came closer to constituting their necessarily multiple and complex identity through the body, but a body perceived as less totalized than male Renaissance constructions allow, and less autonomous, less coherent, more diffuse than Freud sees as necessary for identity, because written out of the patriarchal discourse and waiting for a feminine discourse as the basis for its reconstruction. Again to quote Braidotti: 'Feminist emphasis on embodiment goes hand in hand with a radical rejection of essentialism. In feminist theory, one *speaks* as a woman, although the subject "woman" is not a monolithic essence defined once and for all, but rather the site of multiple, complex, and potentially contradictory sets of experiences' (4).

My interest in women's bodily self-representation inextricably connects with my interest in women's writing. Knowledge of the former, most obviously, depends on the latter. But it is also arguable that one way of arriving at any sense of linguistic subjectivity is through a sense of (always contested) authority over one's material body.[24] Without this authority, we are weakened and inarticulate, for the development of subjectivity may be seen as a consequence of the ways in which the subject perceives and performatively represents its body. Furthermore, the recognition and portrayal of the self either as phallic, powerful, masculine subject or as castrated, uneloquent, female object embodies a too-familiar, oversimplified, cultural dichotomy. Recent feminist theorists have adjusted this polarized cultural projection as well as providing a set of terms to unravel the connection between women's perceptions of their bodies and the access to linguistic power which enables them to define their roles as subjects. Such theorists emphasize the 'situated, specific, embodied nature of the feminist subject while rejecting biological or psychic essentialism' (Braidotti, 99). Both language and the body allow an approach to linguistic agency, to subjectivity. Constraints placed on either or both inhibit either or both as a means to subjectivity. It is possible to understand the expression of one through the knowledge of the other. And the body is, finally, the site of *action*: 'One speaks as a woman in order to empower women, to activate socio-symbolic changes in their condition' (Braidotti, 4).

Therefore, when we notice that during the sixteenth and seventeenth centuries, women in England began to publish their writing and extend the range of their private written records, we might also expect to see that women began to inscribe their textual bodies as sites of power and resistance.[25] The important connection drawn by Luce Irigaray and Rosi Braidotti between 'writing' and 'speaking' and the 'body' does not, however, as Irigaray herself points out, occur spontaneously or without impediment. This relationship is neither 'natural' nor 'essential,' but part of a deliberate and slow construction of the very kind that one observes taking place in England between the middle of the sixteenth and the end of the seventeenth centuries.

In fact, throughout the Renaissance, a worried awareness of the potentially threatening association of women's bodies with language is made manifest in the patriarchal linking of women's two mouths – of literary publication or eloquence with sexual promiscuity (Stallybras, 'Patriarchal Territories').[26] The dominant view is that learning and chastity are not compatible for women, and that publication is on a par with the public use of a woman's body (Jones, 'Surprising Fame,' 76). One among many examples is found in Samuel Rowlands (1603–1617), who asserts that a harlot 'Is noted to be full of words, / And doth the streets frequent' (102). Also, Richard Allestree (1673) warned women that their bodies could be violated with speech: 'Every indecent curiosity, or impure fancy, is a deflowering of the mind, and every the least corruption of them gives some degree of defilement to the body too ... She that listens to any wanton discourse has violated her ears, she that speaks any, her tongue' (148).

But the very essentializing of women as body in order to repress their access to language and writing, while somewhat successful in the short run, actually led in the end to a contrary result. Women's attempt to assert control over their bodies may be seen as an attempt to assert their right to self-expression, indeed to a self which may be expressed by them, and also as an attempt to place themselves in history, for women's bodies are not, in the end, ahistorical or pre-cultural. They are situated and specific and they speak and write and performatively declare themselves.

Throughout the sixteenth and seventeenth centuries, paradoxically (or consequentially), as women became, especially in Puritan ideology, ever more essentialized in physical terms,[27] they were learning to represent themselves as subjects of discourse, in spite of (or because of) their exclusion from the political contract that was at the same time gradually being developed between the modern human subject – subject to and of governance, and the modern body politic – a product of reason, designed to govern and administer the needs of its subjects (Gatens, 61). While there are many examples of women's endorsement of male formulations – as in M. R.'s *The Mothers Counsell* or Dorothy Leigh's *Mothers Blessing* – and of pride in conforming satisfactorily to the terms which produced male approval, it is highly probable that changing circumstances throughout this period of social and political upheaval produced a glimmer of rebellion in women that was, in part, manifest in resistance to the dominant construction of the female body. In fact, M. R.'s Puritan text (1630) itself, even while condemning the mastery of woman's body by desire, frankly acknowledges its pleasurable power: 'There is in every woman two powers, which draw and conduct her: a desire of pleasure bred in the beauty of the body and a good opinion coveting onely good thinges: between these two there is continuall strife' (21). And Valerie Wayne usefully reminds us that 'even the complicity of these authors in women's subordination was undermined by the mode of publication of the advice and the engagement of those women in a public discussion of their own responsibilities' (71). The tension between subject and object positions, between women's desire and patriarchally defined definitions of sexual virtue, undoubtedly opened the space in which any self-construction of women's texts and bodies could occur.

By the end of the seventeenth century, there is ample evidence of women reveling in their license to speak of their sexuality and asserting its power against male sexuality, which is shown as pitifully prone to failure. Aphra Behn's well-known mockery of male impotence in 'The Disappointment' has several less familiar counterparts, as, for example, in the anonymous *Triumphs of Female Wit* (1683), in which the writer insists that women participating in sexual intrigues 'have briskness of parts sufficient to baffle the ablest' of men. The usual plight of woman is a sad one, she contends, 'confined to labor all the day in the kitchen mines of a family, and at night to the ungratifying divertisement of an unperforming husband' (sig. B1). It is impossible to deny that this woman, who, with the other women for whom she speaks, scorns to 'flag [like men] ... in the midst of half-enjoyed pleasure, for want of life to relish, and vigour to finish the innocent enjoyment' (sig. B1), has discovered both physical and linguistic means to assert her sexuality. Not that she has achieved a full 'morphological' restitution of the self, perhaps, but the textual challenges offered by Behn and the *Triumphs of Female Wit* represent a persuasive rhetorical confidence in women's own pleasure, especially when compared to other more restrained sexual or textual voices.[28]

I want now to examine those physical representations of women that were articulated in works addressed by women to an audience of women, in works arising from a community of women, and in private diaries and journals as women speak to themselves. The image of the female body that emerges in women's writing is complex, not simply categorizable, not so much an autonomous, boundaried, clearly definable object, on the model of Freud's psychosomatically bordered self, as an elaborated, blurred self-presentation, an 'I' that emerges tentatively but insistently, admitting the fluidity of subjective spaces and the mobility of boundaries. Its presentation sometimes accedes to patriarchal convention but also frequently represents itself in alternative moves whereby women seek to extricate themselves from patriarchal constructions:

1 in small, loosely-knit women's communities that framed and fostered women's biological gifts, and the construction within those communities of a way of seeing women's bodies that might nourish women's positive self-estimate;
2 in women's efforts to withdraw their bodies from male control, including the tactical use of silence or very restrained expression on certain 'women's' subjects, thus protecting women's lore or secret knowledge; and
3 in women's more assertive, reconstructive efforts to claim authority over their bodies, including the exaggerated 'enactment,' in Luce Irigaray's sense, of chastity and virginity as means of withdrawal from male control.[29]

Writing Bodily Space

In the first place, women found ways to share with each other their distinctively female bodily experiences. The physical accomplishment of childbirth provided an encouraging ground for establishing bonds among them to some extent outside the control of patriarchal surveillance.[30] On 15 August 1599, Margaret Hoby records in her diary that she 'went to awiffe in trauill of child'; as Gail Paster says, 'women in early modern Europe ordinarily gave birth under conditions monitored only by other women' (165). That stereotypically female activity of 'gossip' referred in the seventeenth century to a group of female friends gathered together while one of their number gave birth (*NED*). A probably Elizabethan woodblock, frequently copied, and depicting an early version of a women's space, shows 'fine Gossips' exchanging news 'at the childbed' (*The severall places where you may hear news* and *Tittle-tattle*).

Although we can imagine the conversation during these gatherings included narratives of the then almost universal heroic exploit of giving birth, and although a typical childbirth ceremony has been reconstructed by Adrian Wilson from the fragmentary off-stage testimony of a few husbands (for example, Ralph Josselin), and one or two male observers of midwifery, there are not many surviving examples of women's own recountings of their experiences. Elizabeth Freke, in a diary entry for 2 May 1677, speaks of her 'hard Labour and severall frights' and on 3 June 1675 she records a midwife's successful delivery of a child whom a male physician had declared dead. Even this small degree of candor, as also in Alice Thornton's fuller narration of the events of her pregnancies, is unusual.[31] There *is*, on the other hand, as Wilson points out, some evidence of male hostility and resentment toward the whole collective feminine ritual of birthing and the subsequent lying-in period (82–83), which Natalie Zemon Davis sees as a time when the normal power relations between husband and wife were suspended as the wife was permitted to withhold from her husband her physical and sexual services. At least one male cleric took issue with this time of women's freedom from the sexual claims of marriage and urged women to 'return to their wifely duties immediately after birth' (Wilson, 82). Wilson argues that an attentive reading of these birthing customs reveals women's collective *resistance* to patriarchal authority and 'a striking instance of women's agency' (96).

As producers of children, women were, it is true, bound to the patriarchy by their bodies' breeding functions. A woman's limited control over the frequency of her pregnancies extended the implications of marriage formulas which merged a man and a woman into one legally recognized person and one body over which the man claimed complete jurisdiction. Women nevertheless exchanged self-protective information about 'making a man no better than a eunuch,' practised infanticide (King, *Women of the Renaissance*, 8–11) and procured abortions, with the goal of controlling their fertility (Crawford, 'Construction,' 20; Pollock, 54–58; Laurence, *Women in England*, 63–65).[32] If childless, they also sought to control, with the help of God, their uncooperative bodies, by praying to become pregnant, as Margaret Hoby did on 7 October 1603. They also shared information about how to encourage pregnancy for, as Jane Sharp carefully acknowledges, 'to conceive with child is the earnest desire *if not of all* yet of most women' (93, italics mine). Yet Anne Donne, though herself perhaps illiterate and therefore silent on the matter, could certainly have benefited from fewer pregnancies than the thirteen she endured, and died from, and Alice Thornton, pregnant for the ninth time and more voluble, said she would 'much rather ... not to have been in this condition.' In spite of Lawrence Stone's judgment that contraception was unthinkable before the Enlightenment, Angus McLaren has deduced that methods of birth control, most often in the form of pessaries but also in potions, were attempted in both the sixteenth and seventeenth centuries (141–177).

Even when frequently pregnant, women were not, however, in their own view, necessarily tyrannized by their bodies' reproductive processes. Maternity is inevitably for women an ambiguous function. It testifies concretely that the woman's body is no longer intact, no longer only her own, but also that it is no longer boundaried. Giving birth extends the body's limits, for in pregnancy the body is a container for another body, and the capacity to give birth to a child allows to the body the role of creative territorial expansion because it is able to make and nurture another, not the self. *An Apology for Women* (1620) depicts the pregnant woman approvingly as a 'good Land-Lord to her childe, giving it both house-room and nutriment, when it, like an unruly Tenant, doth grieve and vexe her' (49).

Numerous celebratory comments in women's diaries and letters, affirming the potential of maternity, testify to their joy in giving birth and to their sense of pride and deliverance in having survived this painful and rigorous feat (Crawford, Pollock, Wilson). Alice Thornton, on the birth of her first son and seventh child, expresses palpable, happy relief:

> Almighty God, the wise disposer of all good things, both in heaven and earth ... hath at length had pity on my afflictions, and gave me such a mercy and dear enjoyment to myself and husband, after all his and my several troubles and losses of sons, as I could not hope for or expect; making me a joyful mother of a sweet son, born at full time, after five great trials and hazards of miscarriage when I was with him. (19 September 1662)

The modern reader may pause at that conjunction of the husband's and wife's 'troubles and losses'; the experience of riskily delivering a stillborn or short-lived baby was, after all, physically speaking at least, only the wife's.

Birthing was (and is) a physically dangerous act. Although maternal mortality rates in this period have been placed by recent scholars at about 7 per cent (Schofield), contemporary women themselves did not have access to this after all not so comforting statistic, and Anne Laurence says that 'anecdotal evidence of deaths in childbirth, whether actually giving birth or immediately afterwards, is of a higher mortality than [Schofield] suggests' (*Women in England*, 79). Many, like Alice Thornton and Anne Hulton, came face to face with the deaths of their friends and family in childbirth and feared the same fate for themselves (Crawford, 'Construction,' 22; Laurence, *Women*, 76). And it was not just death that was feared, but that particular slow, tortured exit. Elizabeth Jocelin says that although she had hoped to become pregnant, discovering that she was so, simultaneously confronted her with the possibility of death: 'I no sooner conceived in hope, that I should be made a mother ... but with it entered the consideration of a mothers duty, and shortly after followed the apprehension of danger that might prevent mee from executing that care I so exceedingly desired' (sig. B1); 'Death appearing in this shape, was doubly terrible unto me ... in respect of the painfulness of that kind of Death' (sig. B2).

Some women, Jocelin among them, preparing to give birth, wrote journals or testaments, intended to be read after their demise, as a means of inscribing themselves in the face of the expected death of their bodies. Wendy Wall says that 'these mothers' "wills" ... allowed women to participate in generational transmission and thus to imitate the legal/economic power denied by the culture' (295). Jocelin's testimony is particularly vivid in its evocation of her hesitancy, but equally convincing in its characterization of writing as a replacement of the lost body:

> Yet still I thought there was some good office I might doe for my Childe more than only to bring it forth (though it should please God to take me) ... It came into my mind that death might deprive me of time if I should neglect the present. I knew not what to doe: I thought of writing, but then mine owne weaknes appeared so manifestly, that I was ashamed, and durst not undertake it. But when I could find no other means to expresse my motherly zeale, I encouraged myselfe with these reasons. (sig. B3–4)

In these kinds of works, women like Jocelin instructed their children in how they should conduct themselves when their mother was no longer with them, or petitioned their husbands to take care of their offspring.[33] In a period when a woman's primary expected function was procreative, and when the birthing process was so fraught with risk (Hobby, 185), the fragility and unreliability of her body must have presented a threat to a woman's sense of the self as agent even of this uniquely female act. Yet a self-inscribing challenge to this threat could be issued in the form of a written testament and opportunely justified by engagement with the risky heroism of pregnancy and childbirth. Of these texts Valerie Wayne says that they 'open up spaces for women to remake themselves in alternative ways, and those who read their texts encountered women authors with some desires, commitments, and agency of their own' (71).

Outside of documents recording women's expectations of, and preparation for, death in childbirth, or expressing doting pleasure in the newborn baby, the paucity of women's writing about the actual physical experience of childbirth itself requires some explanation. There exists a reasonable women's commentary on the *concept* of maternity and its associated functions, although as Patricia Crawford wryly remarks, it is 'men [who] had a great deal to say about motherhood,' with the underlying issue being the control of disorderly female sexuality ('Construction,' 6). But there are fewer women's comments on the actual experience of childbearing than on almost any other topic having to do with female sexuality or behavior. A similar, though less profound, reticence of women on the topic of menstruation is noted by William Whateley, though he does not himself feel any inhibition on the topic.[34]

One reason for this silence probably has to do with decorum. Women who were literate and therefore likely to keep written records of their experiences would frequently be of a class that would deem it improper for these specifically women's functions to be publicly discussed. Two accounts where some details about births are recorded – Elizabeth Freke's diary and Alice Thornton's biography – were not intended for publication. Many male physicians and one or two women (Jane Sharp and Sarah Ginnor, for example), wrote treatises on the medical aspects of childbirth, but if Mary Trye's comments on women's diseases in general reflect a prevailing agreement *among women* about what they were unwilling to publicize, women's knowledge about the experience of birth itself must have been still further held secret. In a short postscript to her handbook on women's gynecological health, Trye says: 'The Diseases incident to this Sex are many, and not proper here largely to be discoursed on, therefore I purposely omit them, and shall only say they [women] may have effectual Remedies from me in their infirmities' (sig. K5). Mary Trye's invitation to women to seek her out in person for advice she is not prepared to print is echoed in other midwives' advertisements of their skills (Crawford, 'Printed Advertisements'). Trye's comment not only invokes a rule of decorum but at the same time publicly reveals a purposeful silence inside a female community within which women were willing to share their experiences and help each other, without being prepared to publicize their knowledge. Elizabeth Cellier (1688) says of the art of midwifery that it 'ought to be kept as a secret amongst women as much as possible' (Otten, 208). This closed women's world may be construed as evidence of restriction and repression, but it may equally evidence a conspiratorial sense of female power and agency, as well as resistance to male appropriation of knowledge of women's health, especially given the increasing influence of male midwives and physicians.[35]

It has been argued by Hilda Smith (1976), Audrey Eccles and Ian Maclean that women's midwiving functions were taken over by male midwives and physicians during the seventeenth century, especially in upper-class households, and especially also after the Chamberlen brothers' invention, and control, around 1588, of the design for childbirth forceps. But Linda Pollock and Adrian Wilson have insisted that men did not, therefore, fully replace women's traditional roles in the birth-chamber. Elizabeth Harvey also says that 'women were not actually replaced by men as the primary birth attendants until the eighteenth century' (83); she provides an interesting account of the successful petition brought to the Bishop of London by Mrs Hester Shaw and Mrs Whipp against the Chamberlen brothers' 'unscrupulous and hectoring treatment of midwives' (85–93).

Indeed, even some contemporary male writers, the renowned Nicholas Culpeper (1671) among them, in whatever register of political gesturing, acknowledged the continued control by women of the 'Practical Part' of birthing. Elizabeth Freke, in 1675, says that after she had been in labor four or five days and a male midwife had declared her child dead, 'a good woman midwife' safely delivered a boy (2–3 June 1675). The intensifying conflict over the relative competence of male and female midwives may be read here, but importantly also the endorsement and defense of the skills of a fellow woman by a woman writer. In any case, increased male obstetric activity through the seventeenth century, and women's exclusion by its male practitioners from the developing world of empirical science, do not necessarily imply a generalized sense among women of dissociation from their bodies or loss of control over their bodily lives. There is too much evidence to the contrary available in contemporary women's own texts, as well as in recent research by Patricia Crawford, Dorothy McLaren, Valerie Fildes and Linda Pollock.[36]

The issue of breastfeeding was also a site of contested power over women's bodies. Women needed assertively to claim control of and reconstruct this biological function for purposes useful and pleasurable to themselves; in order to breastfeed their children, women set out to establish that this choice was their right. In spite of strong male clerical insistence in the seventeenth century on women's duty to nurse their children, and a generally held view that nursing was good for the infant, many husbands, most frequently in the upper classes, sought to prevent their wives from nursing their children (Fildes, 101–104; King, *Women of the Renaissance*, 13–14). Wet-nursing was widespread not only among the aristocracy but also among the newly wealthy professional classes (Fildes, 99ff) and even increased during the seventeenth century. While Jacques Guillemeau in 1612 urges women to nurse their children, he acknowledges that they may not be able to 'because their Husbands will not suffer them' (1). The strong-minded Elizabeth Cary did nurse her own children and even, faced with the death of her daughter in childbirth, 'was resolved to have nursed her daughter's child together with her own not yet weaned' (*Life*, 202). Although Elizabeth Clinton, Countess of Lincoln, was herself 'overruled' in her wish to nurse her children 'by another's [surely her husband's] authority' (16), she wrote a tract in which she urged 'every woman ... to nurse her owne childe' (sig. B1). As an aristocrat herself, she acknowledges the class factors at work in deterring women of the upper classes from nursing their children: 'And this unthankfulnesse, and unnaturalnesse is oftner the sinne of the Higher, and the richer sort, then of the meaner, and poorer, except some nice and prowd idle dames, who will imitate their betters' (11).[37] Male resistance to women's nursing may be explained because the nursing function interfered with other domestic duties, because nursing caused scarring and sagging of the breasts (Fildes, 101), because there was a common belief that a nursing mother should refrain from sexual intercourse (Fildes, 107), and because, as Dorothy Maclaren, Audrey Eccles and Valerie Fildes have shown, lactation was suspected by men and known by women to reduce a woman's fertility.

Another possibility that may account for some male objections to women's nursing is the general contemporary male distrust and superstition concerning the mysterious functioning of women's bodies. Something of this feeling, as well perhaps as a son's desire to suppress a daughter's forthright comments about her mother's maternal functions, is evident in a manuscript emendation found in the biography of Elizabeth Cary. The Cary daughter who wrote her mother's *Life* records without embarrassment that her mother was constantly 'either with child or giving suck' (194). Apparently, however, Patrick, one of Cary's sons, found his sister's comment so indecorous that he crossed it through. The difference in the male and female response to this simple record of maternity is revealing, especially as the biographer was a nun. Her empathy with her mother's biology was intuitive, therefore, and not founded in shared experience, but it was still stronger than her brother's.

Maureen Quilligan ('Exit,' *passim*) has illustrated with respect to childbirth that in the sixteenth and seventeenth centuries considerable anxiety attached to the liminal areas where the human and the bestial seemed to meet. If the birth process was seen as at once both miraculous and bestial, the nursing function must have appeared equally ambiguous and disturbing. Kathryn Schwarz suggests that 'the language of rejection, disease, and excess is never far from the maternal breast' (156). A woman's nursing an infant or giving birth would seem to fall into Bakhtin's category of the Renaissance grotesque body which is 'unfinished, outgrows itself, transgresses its own limits' (26). The grotesque as defined by Bakhtin emphasizes those parts of the body 'that are open to the outside world' (26) and it interrogates the ideal of the 'classical' body of the 'finished completed man' which exemplifies the place of class privilege. As Peter Stallybras has suggested, this disjunction between the classical and the grotesque body image is, in the Renaissance, a site not only of class conflict but also of gender conflict. And as Margaret Miles has shown, 'the most concentrated sense of the grotesque comes ... from the figure [of naked] "woman"' (147).

Indeed, the particular quality of women's birthing and nursing functions must have exemplified the grotesque for people made anxious by the intersections of the human and the animal, especially in view of the recommended practice of using a suckling puppy to relieve a woman's over-full breasts (Guillemeau, 18). Cultural unease about breastfeeding must also have been compounded in the sixteenth century by the categorization of colostrum as witch's milk and the belief that syphilis, as well as other diseases and habits, could be transmitted through the nursing process (Adelman, 116–117). In fact, the weight assigned to the nursing issue is demonstrated by the intervention in the discussion by King James I himself, who claimed that he had derived both his Protestantism and his drunkenness from his nurse's milk (Paul, 387–388). In addition, there were probably still some attitudes at work devolving from 'misogynist medieval theology [which] had idealized women who were dissociated from reproductive activity, often through literal or figurative separation from the breast' (Luecke, 241).

Jacqueline Miller has also emphasized the symbolic appropriation in the period by male writers, such as Erasmus, Sidney, Spenser and Milton, of the nursing mother depicted as Muse. Miller supports her argument by reference to the frontispiece of Richard Brathwaite's 1641 edition of *The English Gentleman* and *The English Gentlewoman*, which shows a woman expressing milk from her breasts onto the pages of the book which lies open in her lap. From this construction, it was apparently to be concluded that the Muse-mother's milk will nourish the male writer's work. As Miller has also observed, the image of nursing milk becomes, then, a threat or a challenge to the male writer's ink.

Yet, in the illustration, no intermediary, no male writer, stands between the lactating female Muse and the printed text. Hélène Cixous helps us to see another interpretation here pressing against the more obviously expected one; it is not necessarily that the woman's milk feeds the male book, but that the woman herself may write. She '*expresses*' both milk and herself, even in the midst of male construction and attempted possession of her body; she 'writes with white ink' (Cixous, *Newly Born*, 94). Her body's milk is not accidentally associated with her language. It is 'voice mixed with milk' (93). Certainly, although women's views on this matter seem not usually to have been consulted by the male discussants, some women in early modern England nevertheless adopted the doubly assertive course of insisting, in print, on women's right to nurse their infants, thus reappropriating, in the same gesture, their writing and nursing roles.

The Countess of Lincoln, in her *Nurserie* (1622), asserts that 'it is the expresse ordinance of God that mothers should nurse their owne children ... for by his secret operation, the mothers affection is so knit by natures law to her tender babe, as she findes no power to deny to suckle it'; breast-feeding she describes as 'that which is both natural and comfortable' (2–8). Dorothy Leigh uses the humoral identification of blood and breast milk to invoke the intensity of the mother's love as she nurses her baby: 'Will shee not blesse it every time it sucks on her brests, when shee feeleth the bloud come from her heart to nourish it' (10). In addition, a commonplace

2.3 Frontispiece: Richard Brathwait, *The English Gentlewoman*

image in the period of Christ as a nursing mother, used most frequently by men to represent themselves in the role of the comforted, was deployed by women to cast themselves as privileged to share with Christ the role of comforter (Hobby, 42). In the following poetic excerpt, Elizabeth Hincks (1571) describes the comforting and pleasurable sensation of nursing rather than of being nursed, in order to ally women with God:

> And his seeking thus unto God, is as a sucking Child,
> That seeketh for its Mothers Breast, that is tender and mild.
> And when the Child has sucked its fill, the Breast likewise is eas'd,
> The Child then it is satisfi'd, and Mother also pleas'd. (24)

It is important to emphasize that women in this period probably consciously used lactation as a means of avoiding continuous pregnancy; they were able to deploy one kind of use-value of their bodies to avoid another, less 'comfortable' and pleasurable. The sensuous pleasure of nursing is alluded to in the quotation from Elizabeth Hincks. Alice Thornton found, in nursing her last five children, that breastfeeding was 'personally satisfying' (Beier, 232), and Elizabeth Clinton hints at the same pleasure when she says that Sarah, in nursing Isaac, 'took great comfort and delight therein' (sig. B2). Although it would hardly have been politic for women to dwell insistently and publicly on the pleasurable aspect of nursing, this experience provided them with a source of possible pleasure not participated in by men, and potentially self-revealing.

Advice books that recommend prolonged lactation frequently support their recommendation with the suggestion that nursing will control fertility (Dorothy McLaren, *passim*; Fildes, 108ff). It is impossible to avoid the conclusion that (invariably male) arguments against breastfeeding as well as efforts by women to defend their right to do so must have had some reference, not only to lactation as an exemplification of women's bodily (and perhaps linguistic) power, but to the contraceptive effects of lactation. And Henry Newcome's support of the commonly held belief that nursing should be 'declin'd by great persons for the better securing of succession, by a numerous posterity' (Dorothy McLaren, 24) would seem to clinch the case that here too women were negotiating their right to make decisions about their own bodies outside the demands of patriarchal enterprises. There is evidence enough to show that women's claim to authority over their maternal bodies encouraged them even to violate public strictures against women's writing.[38]

And why should this not be so? It is in describing her pain and joy, her feelings during pregnancy, birth and childrearing, says Julia Kristeva, that a mother may circumvent the patriarchal discourse of science, which is, after all, 'not concerned with the subject, the mother as site of her proceedings,' any more than is the discourse of theology, which 'defines maternity as an impossible elsewhere' (237). Women's language of maternity exists on the margins of patriarchal language. Yet it is sharply inscribed in the pain of Elizabeth Egerton's meditations on the death of her child, aged twenty-one months. It is also heard in the anguish expressed by Mary Carey (1657) when she miscarries a child, combined with the intensity of her joy in her living children and in her love of God: 'So doth my God ... / by my dead formless babe teach me to prize / My living pretty pair, Nat and Bethia, / the children dear.' God is the 'vine' of which she is the 'branch'; God is the 'house' in which she is a 'plant'; from God Carey begs a 'quikning grace.' Carey's metaphoric language of mixed maternal pain and *jouissance* is the kind of language in which, according to Kristeva, a woman may find her subjectivity.[39]

Anne Bradstreet's 'The Author to her Book' metaphorically identifies her poetry, her 'rambling brat,' with a child to which she has given birth, whose training she lovingly undertakes, and for whose discipline or lack thereof she accepts responsibility: 'Yet being mine own, at length affection would / Thy blemishes amend, if so I could.' Margaret Cavendish shows similar maternal pride and anxiety in her work, which she characterizes as her daughter: the world 'may taxe my Indiscretion, being so fond of my Book, as to make it as if it were my Child, and striving to shew her to the World, in hopes Some may like her, although no Beauty to Admire, yet may praise her Behaviour, as not being wanton, nor rude' (*Poems and Fancies*, 1653, sig. A8). In 'An excuse for so much writ upon my Verses,' she writes:

> Condemne me not for making such a coyle
> About my *Book*, it is my *Childe*. (*Poems and Fancies*, sig. A8v)

The authority of the maternal role enhances the authority of the poetic one, even in the strategic, ironic recognition – and dismissal – of the expected social disapproval of women's poetic accomplishments. In these revealing cases, the poet is the mother, the poem is the child, the linguistic subjectivity of the poet overlaps and feeds on the power of the mother. This overt collision of the discourse of poetry with the discourse of maternity reminds us that in Kristeva's formulation, the discourse of maternity, like that of poetry, oscillates between dominant and recessive language, offering a place where dominant representations can be changed. The maternal is a 'unique experience that women can enjoy' as they privilege its language and rewrite its objectified representation in patriarchal discourse (Oliver, 6–9).

The Body in Love

The lessons of negotiation learned by women in claiming textual control over their material and maternal bodies have a parallel manifestation in their composition of love poetry and romance. Women speaking as personae in their own poetic texts tell us that the conventions of romantic love do not enchant *them* to the degree that the male poet would have us believe they affect the absent objects of *his* declamations and seductions. Whether for reasons of modesty prescribed as appropriate for their sex, or to assert their independence from the insistent tradition of male desire, English women poets of this time do not, except self-mockingly, write of themselves in their sexual roles as objects of male desire or as desirous of male lovemaking. For example, Isabella Whitney, one of the earliest English women poets to write about love, to gain a position of rhetorical advantage, contrasts her own sexual virtue with her lover's fickleness; the subject of her poems is not woman's physical passion, but a wry vindication of woman's virtue. The persona in *A Letter ... to her Unconstant Lover* (1567) castigates her unfaithful lover, mockingly alluding to male sonneteers' promises that they will immortalize their lovers in verse; she warns her lover that he will achieve eternal infamous recognition because of his betrayal of her. She has kept *her* body faithful and inviolate, but *he* has gone off to seduce and marry another woman. Some covert criticism of the sexual double standard is clearly at work here, but also an evident rejection of the traditional, languishing female role in romantic love conventions.[40]

In Mary Wroth's sonnet sequence, *Pamphilia to Amphilanthus*, published in 1621, the female speaker invokes the images of female dismemberment, whose sado-erotic role in the male sonnet Nancy Vickers has described, precisely in order to erase them (Donovan (ed.), 107, P41; 109, P44; 111, P48). *Her* body, she implies, still belongs to her, and she doubts that being lover or beloved of a man is an especially desirable prospect for a woman. Her main preoccupation is that her lover should prove constant and that they should share a spiritual love. Pamphilia distrustfully evaluates the varied male representations of love and their possible negative consequences for even the most virtuous woman. And, at the end of the sequence, she rejects the whole discourse of love poetry as deceptive and immature (Donovan (ed.), 126, P75). Resisting the seductions of love language itself, she simultaneously resists the role of the humiliated object of male rejection and finds a voice in a cooler, more calculated register.

At issue here, of course, is the question of desire. In traditional male love poetry, desire is turned to the seduction of the woman's body, thereby testing and undermining the virtue reposing in woman's virginity. But Aemilia Lanyer complains that men, because of *their* lack of virtue, regard women's beauty as an irresistible temptation to lust (59ff). She resistingly rephrases her own desire as a longing for an eroticized and feminized Christ who, loving, understanding and defending women, will help maintain their virtue and allow them autonomous control over their bodies. Lanyer almost certainly was associated with the loosely connected but prolific group of intellectual, writing women (and men) who belonged to the Pembroke Circle, named for Mary Sidney, Countess of Pembroke. Certainly she created textually her own separatist group of women in the cluster of dedications to the *Salve Deus Rex Judaeorum* and in the feminist arguments of the poem.

Other women poets, turning Petrarchan conventions upside down, echoed and confirmed the view that, rather than capitulating to male desire, women could choose to protect their body's autonomy by remaining unmarried. For example, the female persona of the poetic work *Eliza's Babes* (1652) refused to accept the necessity of marriage, declining the option to 'live a slavish life / By being to the world a wife' (31). And, in *The Female Advocate* (1686), Sarah Fyge writes:

Nor do I think there's a necessity
For all to enter Beds, like Noah's beasts
Into his Ark. I would have some releast
From the dear cares of that lawful State. (11)

Jane Barker, in 'A Virgin Life' (1686), 'portrays spinsterhood as a nearly angelic state' (Hobby 160) because it permits 'liberation from "Mens almost omnipotent Amours"' (Barker, 12); marriage is 'organized for the convenience of men' and entails 'for women a loss of liberty and happiness' (Kathryn King, 561). When, towards the end of the seventeenth century, poets like Aphra Behn parodically emulate the male role of lustful lover, they do so with considerable cynicism and wit. Joan Philips (1679) in a narrative poetic sequence describes the onset of love in these irreverent and comical terms:

I felt my Blood run swiftly to my heart,
And a chill trembling seize each outward part:
My Breath grew short, my Pulse did quicker beat,
My Heart did heave, as it wou'd change its Seat:
A faint cold Sweat o're all my Body spread,
A giddy Megrim wheel'd about my head. (7)

In another poem in the same sequence, titled 'Maidenhead,' Philips interrogates the claim of male power over women's bodies by mockingly parodying the voice of the betrayed woman who bewails her lost and wasted virginity after her lover, returning from a voyage to Africa (that other colonized space), marries someone else.

A few women poets directly engage the possibility that the act of writing itself might become a substitute for physical procreativity. Comparing her unmarried and childless state to her sister's life with her husband and children, Whitney (1573) says, 'I to writing fall' (sig. Dii). Anne Bradstreet's poem is the 'brat' for whose birth and manners she alone is responsible. An Collins, in her *Divine Songs* (1653), sounds the same theme:

Yet as a garden is my mind enclosed fast
Being to safety so confined from storm and blast
Apt to produce a fruit most rare,
That is not common with every woman
That fruitful are. (57)

In these instances, women simultaneously seize control of their writing and bodily selves. Suspicion of the value of romantic love for women was not confined to poetry, however. In her autobiographical narration, Margaret Cavendish writes that she 'did dread marriage,' but when she agreed to marry it was because of affection. 'It was not amorous love, I never was infected therewith: it is a disease, or a passion, or both, I only know by relation, not by experience ... But my love was honest and honourable' (*Nature's Pictures*, 375).[41]

Although Alan Macfarlane argues for the prevalence of romantic love for men and women in the early modern period, his evidence comes largely from male texts and such women's texts as he cites I read differently.[42] For example, Macfarlane uses Alice Thornton's comments as evidence of women's feelings of romantic love. Reading carefully the whole of Thornton's biography, however, with its long narrative of perpetual and sickly pregnancies followed by infant deaths, as she sought to produce a male heir, and placing it in the larger generic context of women's diaries and journals, shadows to some degree the assertions of love for her husband. Margaret Hoby, Anne Clifford and Elizabeth Freke also protest their love for their husbands; yet Hoby records that her husband abused her and threw her down the stairs, Clifford tells us that *her* husband bullied her, deprived her of her child and forced her to feed, house and entertain his mistress, and Freke complains that her husband defrauded her of her dowry and subsequent gifts from her father.

The conventions requiring expressions of wifely devotion and marital subordination were very strong. I do not doubt that some wives in this period felt deep affection for their husbands, as is evident in Lady Anne Twisden's letters to her husband, and some young lovers, male and female, longed desirously for each other; it would be peculiar if it were not so. But I remain skeptical about the likely survival of romantic love in the women who found themselves in oppressive and even brutal marriages, and I pay close attention to those murmurs of resistance that challenge the convention of suppressed female speech and the prevailing ideology of hierarchical marriage.

Even though most women accepted marriage as the inevitable disposition of their bodies, from the end of the sixteenth century into the early eighteenth century they tended to marry late in their twenties and, when widowed, remarried less often and less speedily than men (Macfarlane, 216–217; Laurence *Women in England*, 33, 45). Jane Barker and Jane Owen portrayed marriage as entailing a loss of freedom (Crawford, 'Women's Published Writings,' 226–227), and looked forward to the possibility of regaining a certain amount of freedom in widowhood.[43] Some women prophets (Elinor Channel, Anna Trapnel and Jane Lead) regarded marriage as a 'hindrance' to their prophetic work (Purkiss, 157–158). The Countess of Bridgewater saw that, when a husband did not care 'much to be with his wife at home,' the wife, far from lamenting her solitude, might, instead, take the opportunity to 'make her owne happinesse ... as much God's as a virgine' (quoted in Mendelson, 'Stuart Women's Diaries,' 194). Also, Alice Thornton recalls that she 'was soe happy in my condition of a single life, that I loved it above all, haveing the excelent company and example of my mother' (78). One may think here of the mother–daughter connection which Hélène Cixous says must be retained or retrieved from male intervention in order for women to speak as subjects. This association presents itself, not because we should imagine Alice Thornton and her mother creating an autonomous women's space of the kind that Cixous fantasizes, but because Alice Thornton both vehemently articulated her loving valuation of her mother and was also, by early modern standards, a prolific and confidently self-revealing writer, enumerating in vivid narrative sequence the deaths of her sister, her cousin and her mother, her own frequent pregnancies and the births and deaths of her children. After marriage, she was pregnant so often and so uncomfortably that her nostalgia for her single life in her mother's house seems entirely understandable. Similarly, the heroine of Elizabeth Cary's play, *Mariam*, nostalgically looks back on the past 'when virgin freedom left me unrestrain'd' (I.i.72). Both Mariam and another royal woman, Elizabeth I, claimed that they would rather be milkmaids than married and monarchs. 'If I were a milkmaid,' said Elizabeth in an address to Parliament in 1575, 'I would not forsake that poor and single state to match with the greatest monarch' (quoted in Foster, 148; cf. *Mariam*, I.i.58).

And Yet Her Body Is Her Own

Finally, in a crucial move asserting jurisdiction over their bodies, some women overrode the 'male mind'–'female body' dichotomy by insisting on the interconnected functions of women's minds and bodies in intellectual activity, and especially in the act of writing.[44] In *Her Protection for Women* (1589), Jane Anger metaphorically establishes that writing is also speaking the body: 'Shall not Anger stretch the vaines of her braines, the stringes of her fingers, and the lists of her modestie, to answere their [men's] Surfeitings?' (sig. A3). Almost a hundred years later, the author of *The Gentlewoman's Companion* (1675) continued to insist that women's minds and bodies are interconnectedly responsive to the effects of learning: 'Vain man is apt to think we were merely intended for the world's propagation ... but ... had we the same literature, he would find our brains as fruitful as our bodies ... We are debarred from the knowledge of humane learning lest our pregnant wits should rival the towering conceits of our insulting Lords and Masters' (1–2). This argument chastises parents of daughters for letting the 'fertile ground' of their daughters' minds 'lie fallow,' while educating the '*barren* noddles of their sons' (1–2). The language in these passages emphasizes through metaphor that women's minds, far from being non-operative, have been intentionally kept inactive as a means of ensuring that their bodies' breeding functions remain dominant.[45]

Bathsua Makin similarly protested that the emphasis on women's bodies as decorative objects interfered with their capacity to learn, and not only 'adulterate[s] their Bodies; yea, (what is worse) ... defile[s] their Souls. This (like Circes Cup) turns them to Beasts' (22). Margaret Cavendish also, in 1664, takes parents to task for educating their daughters' bodies to dance and sing, while ignoring the education of their minds. 'To teach their Bodies Arts, and not to Instruct their Minds with Understanding ... makes the Body a Courtier, and the Mind a Clown, and oftentimes it makes the Body a Baud, and their Mind a Courtesan, for though the Body procures

Lovers, yet it is the Mind that is the Adulteress' (*Sociable Letters*, 50). Cavendish's argument inverts the usual patriarchal assertions, for she insists that, far from ensuring female chastity, a society that restricts both a woman's mind and body will also encourage both to profligacy and wantonness. Jane Barker's 'A Virgin Life,' says Kathryn King, 'invents for the exemplary spinster a new lineage that transforms the meaning and value of unmarried life' (561); the happy virgin's life is dedicated 'To serve her God, enjoy her Books and friends.' Barker pleads to heaven, 'Suffer me not, to fall into the Pow'rs, / Of Mens almost omnipotent Amours. / But in this happy state, let me remain, / And in chast verse, my chaster thoughts explain' (12–13).

In fact, in pursuit of the intellectual and writing life women seemed to find a means of connecting the body to the mind. It is in adherence to the male construction of the female body as love object, wife or mother that the female mind is erased. It is quite clear that some women recognized the degree to which they needed control of their bodies if they wished to control their minds and pursue an intellectual life. Celibacy was therefore both a choice and a 'performative metaphor' (Braidotti, 6) advocated by some women in this period, though it should not be seen as operating in the same terms as the patriarchal insistence on virginity before marriage and wifely chastity afterwards. At times it is a protest against this very patriarchal attempt to dictate the use of women's bodies. For a woman to deny cultural access to her body, then as now, is also an effort to reclaim the body and to circumvent the dominant male representation.[46] Although the Protestant Reformation rendered the Catholic conventual option unavailable to most Englishwomen, nevertheless some women still chose either a devotional or intellectual life separate from the claims of marriage. They did not choose assertive sexual liberty in relations with men as evidence of their body's freedom for the obvious reason that, without reliable birth control, sexual liberty was a means to the different kind of bondage of illegitimate pregnancy. This inhibition must have been especially persuasive when the double standard held unwed mothers accountable for the sin of their conception and defined adultery as a crime committed only by women, which in 1650 Parliament even attempted to make punishable by death.

The nineteenth-century male-constructed doctrine, familiar to modern feminists, that intellectual activity in a woman would disrupt her reproductive functions, has its predecessor in male arguments in the sixteenth and seventeenth centuries that studying inhibited fertility (Sadler, 121), and that because women were governed by their sexuality, if they wished to safeguard the soul or the mind, they would need to deny their sexuality. It may at first seem surprising to find seventeenth-century women like Anna Maria Van Schurman, Mary Astell and Margaret Cavendish espousing an apparently similar view. On closer inspection, however, an important difference becomes clear. The patriarchal version insists that women's *minds* (if, indeed, they exist at all), should not be taxed, in order that their bodies can function best for breeding. Seventeenth-century *women*, on the other hand, who wrote about this question, reversed and appropriated the dominant claim by arguing that their *bodies* should not be taxed by the sexual duties of marriage and childbearing, in order that their minds might remain free to function well; the productively interlocking relationship of their minds and bodies was possible only if women, not men, retained control over their bodies. Influentially, Anna Maria Van Schurman, known as the Incomparable Virgin, held in 1641, in a Latin text translated into English in 1659 as *The Learned Maid*, that only 'maids (especially during their celibate, or single life) [for the] most part have time to bestow on themselves and so have the most convenience to follow their studies' (Goreau, 166). Bathsua Makin, interestingly and perhaps more radically, flatly asserts that married women, too, should be allowed the pleasures of learning.

What Margaret King suggests of the learned woman in Italy may also have been true for Englishwomen, that 'Chastity was at once expressive ... of [their] defiance of the established natural order and of ... man's attempt to restrain [their] energies' ('Book-Lined Cells,' 78). Constance Jordan agrees that chastity 'could lead to a woman's escape from patriarchal proprictorship' (30).[47] Diane Purkiss shows that 'women prophets were able to revive the positive associations of virginity in order to construct a space for a conditional autonomy' (157), and Theodora Jankowski, writing of Lyly's *Gallathea*, insists that 'Virginity *can* be viewed as a means by which women refuse to be part of the sexual economy, refuse to be defined exclusively in terms of their reproductive capabilities' (267–268).

Slowly, throughout the sixteenth and seventeenth centuries, as a basic line of resistance, some women struggled to withdraw their bodies from male control through various means of acceding to, appropriating and resisting, in short, 'enacting' the primary roles of married chastity and silence prescribed for them by their male protectors. A modern feminist psychoanalytic reading confirms the strategic usefulness of this choice. Chastity, or – in Freud's interpretation – frigidity, 'the refusal of a specifically genital and *orgasmic* sexual pleasure,' is a 'position resistant to the patriarchal requirements of heterosexuality, even if it exacts its price from the woman herself' (Grosz, *Sexual Subversions*, 133). The chaste or frigid woman 'is precisely the woman whose pleasures do not fit neatly into the male-defined structure of physical pleasure' (133–134). Luce Irigaray proposes that, 'A virgin is one as yet unmarked by them [men], for them ... Not yet imprinted by their sex, their language' (*This Sex*, 211).

The implications of this posture for women's writing, theorized by Irigaray and Cixous, were also apparent to seventeenth-century women and men. At least one man confessed that separate female communities of learned and chaste women presented a terrifying possibility of female power: 'The damming up of this vast weight of waters is very dangerous ... To be plain, I'm afraid thus wou'd you deal with us, were your Sex generally confin'd to Nunneries. You'd make a desperate Sally at one time or other, fall upon our Sex when unprepar'd to resist ye, over-run all Mankind, and beat us, as the Amazons did their Neighbours' (*The Challenge Sent by a Young Lady*, 49).[48] The perceived physical threat is made still more disturbing by the dread that nunneries might also, shockingly, encourage women 'to think there was something precious in you ... and again learn to esteem and value that Trifle Woman' (54).

Nevertheless, despite the lack, in England, of the conventual construction of a female community, there can be found several testimonies of women who removed their bodies from patriarchal control to find in other women support, friendship, love and spiritual comfort by which to define themselves in relation to each other.[49] Aemilia Lanyer (1611) places a highly sensual, erotically described and also intensely feminized Christ at the center of a community of women; in this homoeroticized object of their gaze is 'all that ladies can desire' (40). Katherine Evans and Sarah Chevers, two Quaker missionaries, in *A Short Relation of Cruel Sufferings* (1662), record their imprisonment and torture in Malta by the Inquisition and the way in which their relationship, which they liken to a marriage, sustained them and helped them survive to publish their story.[50] When their captors threatened to separate them, they responded in language echoing the marriage service, 'The Lord hath joined us together, and wo be to them that should part us' (13–14). Katherine Philips's poem, 'To My Excellent Lucasia' (1667), celebrates the passionate love of one woman for another:

For thou art all that I can prize,
  My joy, my life, my rest.
Nor bridegrooms' nor crown'd conqu'rors' mirth
  To mine compar'd can be:
They have but pieces of this earth,
  I've all the world in thee.

In 1603, during the court's preparations for James I's move to London, Anne Clifford's cousin Frances Bouchier and Mary Carey came to stay with their aunt at Bagshot, where the thirteen-year-old Anne 'lay all night with my cousin, and Mrs Mary Carey, which was the first beginning of the greatness [closeness] between us,' following which 'I went daily and visited them, and grew daily more inward with my cousin Frances and Mrs Carey' (7). Soon after, in disgrace with her mother, Anne was banished to 'lie in a chamber alone, which I could not endure, but my cousin Frances got the key of my chamber and lay with me which was the first time I loved her so well' (11–12). Fifteen-year-old Mary Boyle writes of the fervent attachment she developed for Elizabeth Killigrew. Married to Mary Boyle's brother before the couple were judged old enough to live together, Elizabeth settled, Mary says, 'in our family (but much more so in my heart).' They became 'chamber-fellows and constant bedfellows; and there grew so great a kindness between us, that she soon had a great and ruling power with me ... enticing me to spend (as she did) time in seeing and reading plays and romances, and in exquisite and curious dressing' (1–17).

These passages describing shared sensuous pleasures and close relationships, suggest that women, like the men discussed by Alan Bray, developed strong, physically and emotionally intimate affiliations with each other 'in the public eye' ('Homosexuality,' 43). 'To be someone's "bedfellow,"' says Bray, 'suggested that one had influence' over the other (42) and an 'equivalent emotional bond' (44) –

an observation that seems to be supported by the 'enticements' in the case of Mary Boyle and Elizabeth Killigrew. The 'female world of love and ritual,' documented by Carroll Smith-Rosenberg in nineteenth-century America, apparently had still earlier manifestations. Perhaps the modern emphasis on individual privacy and the socially emphatic acceptability of heterosexual relationships has broken down a long preceding convention of homosocial, and homoerotic, connection.

As another suggestive example, in 1670 Sarah Davy writes that she was helped to her spiritual conversion, and a sense of her right to narrate it, by a woman whom she loved, who offered her 'sweet refreshments' (21), and with whom Elaine Hobby suggests she may have had a sexual as well as spiritual relationship (70–71). And Margaret Cavendish, in *The Convent of Pleasure*, fictionally (and humorously) constructs an ideal separatist female community in which women love and support each other, satisfying each other's senses as well as their minds. The central character, Lady Happy, asserts that 'Men are only troublers of Women; for they only cross and oppose their sweet delights and peaceable life; they cause their pains, but not their pleasures.' Women 'were mad to live with Men, who make the Female sex their slaves; but I will not be so inslaved, but will live retired from their Company ... my Cloister shall not be a Cloister of restraint, but a place for freedom, not to vex the Senses but to please them' (7).

Most of these more radical escapes from patriarchal control of their bodies were written by women in the second half of the seventeenth century, but their option to write their bodies in this resistant way had been gradually opened for them by other earlier women's texts.[51] By the second half of the seventeenth century, as the quantity of women's writing was rapidly increasing, sexual activity of women with other women was enough acknowledged to be commented on in English medical texts, including Jane Sharp's *1671 Midwives Book* (45). This recognition of 'tribadic' sexuality in a published text written by a woman – and the categorization of it in the same text as something to be kept hidden or 'close' – invite a speculative reading of a subversive female body in this period.[52] The associations drawn in the collective cultural consciousness between women's writing and their sexuality also sometimes hostilely characterized the relationship between a woman writer and her inspirational Muse as operating threateningly outside the control of the heterosexual. In the vituperative 'Epigram on the Court Pucelle,' Ben Jonson represents the woman writer as driven by 'Tribade lust' to 'force a Muse.' Mary Wroth was accused of being a 'Hermaphrodite' because she dared to write. As a writer, a woman entered a world in which both her body and her mind might resist objectified patriarchal inscription and redraw their primary subjective affiliations in relation to women.

In this chapter I have been arguing that, within the ideological context prescribed in early modern England, women's texts show some sense of their potential control over the female body and some consciousness of how to lay a tactical claim to a bodily space. By deploying various writerly strategies of textual resistance, women claimed their bodies, in almost all the ways possible for them. They argued against men's intervention in their physical lives and protected women's lore or secret knowledge about their own health by remaining publicly silent or making only very restrained comments on certain 'women's' subjects. When possible they withdrew from male control their literary, morphological and sometimes maternal selves. They created both the practice and the idea of small women's communities where physical succor, protection and pleasure were available and where they nurtured an image of women's bodies that might support women's self-esteem. And, refusing their bodily essentialization, they nurtured their intellectual lives by mimetically 'enacting' in Luce Irigaray's sense, that is by taking more seriously than intended, and thus appropriating, the requirement of chastity or virginity. That we are able to piece together this story of women's textual and bodily constructions of themselves depends on the fact that in this period some women began to write their own bodies, and thus also found ways to write themselves as agents, as subjects, as selves. For early modern women to write at all is in itself to refuse the imposed patriarchal definition of the female body and begin to speak from another bodily space and of an alternative sense of the self as subject.

Notes

1 For another elaborate and extremely interesting analysis of this illustration, see Sawday *The Body Emblazoned*, 66–72. As Sawday says, 'The image is ... extraordinarily complex in its articulation and its production of numerous rival centres of attention for the viewer' (68). Sawday argues that the ultimate message of the frontispiece is that the world is uterocentric (71), a perception that, if consciously recognized, must have considerably dismayed the male Renaissance audience and reinforced their desire to control and dominate the female body.

2 Sawday sees another possible female viewer on the right side behind one of the columns.

3 G.S. Rousseau assumes that Jane Sharp is a pseudonym for a male author (132). I disagree, especially considering the proliferation of women's texts in the seventeenth century in response to the effort by male midwives to take over the profession.

4 A strong reading of this patriarchal power is to be found in Gail Kern Paster's discussion of Galenic humoral theory, which she argues played into the patriarchal ideology of shame visited upon men's, and especially women's, bodies. I am offering here the counter-narrative to Paster's careful work with male texts on humoral theory, of women's texts which problematize the claims to undiluted power of the patriarchal texts. Similarly, in Jonathan Sawday's brilliant and absorbing study of the influence of the dissected body on the Renaissance imagination (*The Body Emblazoned*), I detect a tendency to accept as total the powerful male construction of women's bodies. Sawday argues that for women 'to escape [the patriarchal] parameters ... was more than could be achieved by any one individual' (229). This may be so, but in small, mutually encouraging groups this escape was nevertheless formulated. Women's textual resistance cannot be dismissed as easily as the Renaissance male may have wished and it should not be dismissed by modern readers succumbing to the persuasions of dominant early modern texts.

5 Although a few of the women's texts I refer to here come from the servant or artisan class, by and large they belong to the 'middling sort' and higher classes, whose social standing

helped them to literacy, who wrote about their physical lives and whose writing is still accessible. For valuable contributions to our understanding of working-class experience see studies by Susan Amussen, Sandra Clark, John Gillis, Olwen Hufton, Margaret King and Margaret Spufford.

6 For an extended discussion of the connections between anatomization of women in verse and on the dissecting table, see Sawday *The Body Emblazoned*, ch. 7. Wendy Wall has argued that even the sonnet collections themselves are 'unified centrally through their transformation from scattered pages into an embodied and singular woman' (61). And Catherine Bates points to George Puttenham's easy recognition that the epithalamion was arguably 'designed to ritualize (even institutionalize) aggressive physical mastery over the female body' (143). Also see Valerie Traub, 'Gendering Mortality in Early Modern Anatomies.'

7 See Francis Barker's use of this connection in his reading of Marvell's 'To His Coy Mistress' (85 ff.) And see also Sawday's discussion of ties between Vesalius and the poetic blazon (*Body Emblazoned*, 192ff). Detailed descriptions of male bodies, whether whole or dismembered, are rare in English poetry. Aemilia Lanyer's lover-like description of a crucified Christ in *Salve Deus Rex Judaeorum* is exceptional. Male poetic descriptions which dwell on the details of male physical beauty are very limited. Shakespeare's sonnets celebrating his male friend's beauty are so weighted with evocative imagery and musings on what may comfortingly be read as the 'universal' human condition that until recently the critical community has been able to avoid a serious reading of a homosexual relationship in these poems. See, however, Pequigney. See also Sawday's *Body*, 201.

8 Although a combination of femaleness and gentility usually protected women from being tortured, examples like Anne Askew reminded the Renaissance observer of the power of the state over the vulnerable body. Jonathan Sawday's *Body Emblazoned* demonstrates how close to the forefront of the Renaissance consciousness was the image of the dissected and shamed body, particularly the female body (ch. 7). Sawday also offers some horrifying accounts of women twice-hanged (220–221). But women's live bodies were also manipulated by the state in particular ways. Female recusants, heretics, sectarians, witches and scolds were abused and humiliated as public spectacles with all of the official forms of torture, but also with gender-specific ducking stools and bridles for scolds and the methods for diagnosing witches which ranged from half-drowning to stabbing with long pins. See Trapnel, 20–26. See also Marianne Hester's study, chs 6–9, and G.S. Rousseau's connection of hysteria with witchcraft.

9 See Cynthia Herrup's riveting study of this trial and its preface and aftermath.

10 Women's singular power to give birth was declared by Paul to be her means to salvation (I Timothy 2:15). This question was debated throughout the seventeenth century, especially by those Protestants who believed in salvation by faith. Labor in childbirth was considered under the heading of 'works' and was therefore debatable as a means to salvation. See Cahn, ch. 2.

11 One can tell, for example, from Lady Anne Clifford's diaries that her husband had extensive jurisdiction over her movements. He was able to remove her child from her as a form of discipline without her having any redress. See especially entries for April and May 1616.

12 The emphasis on virginity at marriage was of greater importance for the propertied and aristocratic classes than for the daughters of the lower classes, where comparatively more sexual freedom before marriage was allowed to women. See Gillis, ch 1. After a

male heir had been produced, however, some married aristocratic women gained an increased degree of sexual freedom. The sexual license for both men and women at the Jacobean court was shocking to many English citizens and provided further fuel for the Parliamentary resistance to royal demands.

13 The clear acknowledgment of sexual difference which permitted this displacement of power onto gender was fully functional much earlier than Thomas Laqueur's estimate of its instantiation in the eighteenth century. Gail Paster also objects to Laqueur's argument that before the eighteenth century 'the boundaries between male and female are of degree and not of kind' (17). And Traub, Kaplan and Callaghan are very clear on this point: 'We thus reject the now prevalent argument, based on the theory of physiological homology between the sexes, that there existed only one gender in early modern culture' (4). Sara Grieco argues that the difference between masculine and feminine was accentuated during the fourteenth and fifteenth centuries in clothing and physical appearance. The straight forms and slender bodices that were common to both men and women in the Middle Ages were exchanged by women in the fourteenth and fifteenth centuries for a more voluptuous, rounded figure. In the Renaissance the whole physical deportment of the body, the woman with a rounded, out-thrust belly, the man with a narrow, defined waist, imaged clear sexual and erotic difference (Hollander 97ff). In fact, a case can credibly be made that the representations of the female body have always imaged extant cultural notions of power and sexual difference.

14 For a discussion of this male homosocial relationship see Eve Kokofsky Sedgwick. Also see Juliet Fleming's discussion of male-authored 'ladies' texts' in early modern England ('The Ladies' Man').

15 See also the discussion of this phenomenon as it related to women's choice of reading and writing matter, in chapter 3 of this volume.

16 Bloodletting was also recommended for almost any menstrual disorder – including excessive bleeding, a case where the possibility of anemia would be further increased (Crawford, 'Attitudes to Menstruation,' 57). The strong-willed Alice Thornton insisted that her physician let her blood during her first pregnancy (117). Audrey Eccles points out that 'erroneous ideas held by the patient were often tactfully complied with' (119). Thornton miscarried and was herself ill for another three months. Although Paster says that 'bloodletting was not normally practiced on pregnant women' (75), Guillemeau's recommendation suggests that it was not as unusual as Paster suggests.

17 Where men experienced similar symptoms, they were said to be suffering from the nobler affliction of melancholy. This is documented in Burton's *Anatomy of Melancholy*, but also see the appendices in Macdonald where he lists the symptoms, age and sex of patients whose records were kept by the seventeenth-century physician Richard Napier. See also Juliana Schiesari's study on the gendering of melancholia in Renaissance literature, and G.S. Rousseau, 138ff.

18 Stuart Clark (110–112) and Alan Bray (*Homosexuality in Renaissance England*, 25) have noted that homosexuality was associated in this period with political and religious heresy and witchcraft and so with fear of social disruption. See also Valerie Traub's essay on the (in)significance of lesbianism in male texts of the period. Also see G.S. Rousseau's commentary on the prescription of female manipulation to orgasm of a female patient 'for the purgation of seed' (113). Winfried Schleiner surveys this practice and its ethical implications, and Katharine Park considers the French sources that consider 'sexual contacts and sexual desires between women' (172).

19 See Anne Clifford's diary, where she makes evident her enjoyment of life as a widow (Travitsky, *Paradise*, 87).

20 In certain circumstances, 'the soul becomes feminine in relation to the divine Logos and lends itself to a sublimated erotic imagery that describes the lovemaking of the virgin Psyche to Christ' (Ruether, 178). This kind of imagery in women's religious works often becomes a metaphoric way of referring to the displaced or 'lost' body.

21 With the decline of humanist enthusiasm for Greek and Roman models of culture, including their relegation of women to the role of chaste motherhood, women began to assert their sexuality. See *The Triumphs of Female Wit*, discussed later in this chapter.

22 This point is especially verified in contemporary divorce laws which, while restrictive enough for men, made absolutely no allowance for women to initiate a divorce. See Turner, ch. 6, Macfarlane and Roderick Phillips.

23 As any number of modern feminist theorists have argued, a Freudian psychosomatic sense of identity cannot apply accurately to women, among other reasons because women's bodies are not irreducible in the sense that Freud assumes is true for men. Women's bodies are constantly used by others, extended and invaded. The whole question of female subjectivity in this period is more extensively discussed in my first chapter.

24 For a complete philosophical connection of the body to subjectivity, see Maurice Merleau-Ponty's argument that subjectivity is located not in the mind or consciousness but in the body. The body, he argues, acts on the world in such a way as to produce the original meaning-giving act (121; 146–147).

25 In her study of seventeenth-century women prophets, Diane Purkiss has argued that 'the visibility of the woman prophet's body was a means by which she negotiated a space within the constraints of seventeenth-century religious discourse, and hence a way for her to threaten established orders and hierarchies' (141).

26 Wendy Wall has convincingly argued that social anxiety about publication was general in the English Renaissance and experienced by, and assigned to, male as well as female writers. Wall acknowledges, however, that this anxiety was coded and differentiated in gendered ways.

27 See, for example, Margaret Olofson Thickstun, 1–36.

28 Luce Irigaray carefully refers to the morphology, not the anatomy, of the female body, to emphasize the meaning assigned to the social body in and by culture (Grosz, *Sexual Subversion*, 111). Her focus on the body is a focus on representation, not on biological determinants.

29 In discussing women prophets, Diane Purkiss also observes a series of what we might call Irigarayan bodily signs – 'parodic or subversive reifications of the structure of women, which by their excess function to open a space for alternative constructions ... [which] enabled women prophets to be heard' (144–145).

30 During the seventeenth century there was a gradual increase in the use of male physicians in upper-class and aristocratic deliveries, but, on the whole, 'women expect[ed] to assist one another with birthing' (Blodgett, 170). See also Elaine Hobby's description of Jane Sharp's *Midwives Book*, 185ff., and L.M. Beier, ch. 8, 'The Character of a Good Woman: Women and Illness,' in *Sufferers and Healers*. As the class and monetary stakes increased, however, so also did male presence and intervention. At the birth of royal children, male witnesses were required, although in the majority of birth-ceremonies, this woman's space remained unviolated. Ralph Josselin, whose diary reveals a man deeply and constantly involved in his wife's affairs, records that although he was usually somewhere in the house

at the time of his children's births, women in addition to the midwife were witnesses at the actual birth scene, being sent for specifically for that purpose (for example, entries for 1642, and for 24 November 1645 and 11 February 1647–8). For an account of the circumstances of delivery and lying-in, see also Anne Laurence, *Women in England*, 75–81.

31 Freke, whose diary is full of unrelieved misery and complaint, was, Harriet Blodgett thinks, not 'entirely sane' (84). Alice Thornton's diary is one of the most generally unconstrained in this whole period.

32 The topic of 'Abortion' appears in Andrew Borde's *Breviary of Helthe* (1547) in an entry in which he acknowledges the ability to induce an abortion, but worries that the means might be used irresponsibly by a 'light woman' if he publishes them in any detail.

33 For example, see Dorothy Leigh, Elizabeth Grymeston and Elizabeth Brooke Jocelin.

34 Jane Sharp's *Midwives Book* denies what 'some [presumably male commentators] say – [that] this [menstrual] blood is venomous'; for 'were the blood venomous it self, it could not remain a full month in the woman's body and not hurt her' (289). Patricia Crawford suggests that women preferred to be private on matters where they wished to avoid male intervention ('Attitudes to Menstruation,' 68ff). William Whateley's discussion of fertility (43–45) warns that a husband should not 'company with his own wife' while she is menstruating. But he acknowledges women's wish that matters of menstruation not be publicly discussed: 'Neither let women think themselves disgraced because I have laid this matter open in plain but modest speeches.' His justification, although he imagines that some of his male readers too may 'take snuff [offense] at this openness,' Whateley sees in the need to protect men from the sin, Biblically forbidden and punishable by death (Leviticus 20:18), of having sex with a menstruating woman.

35 Gail Kern Paster inserts this silence into her reading of 'humoral shame.' Male anatomical texts regularly evince modesty or shame as they introduce discussions of male and female reproductive anatomy, as in Helkiah Crooke's *A Description of the Body of Man*: 'Well, the History of these parts of generation it is our taske in this Booke to describe, over which also we could wish we were able to cast a veile, which it would bee impiety for any man to remoove, who came not with as chaste a heart to reade as wee did to write' (200). Also see Whateley, quoted in the preceding note.

36 Gail Paster suggests that 'treatises on diseases of the womb by male practitioners ... have the effect of making the womb knowable not only to the women who have wombs but also to a variety of men' (175); this 'discourse of knowledge,' Paster concludes, alienated 'women from their own bodies and bodily self-experience' (178 n.). I do not wish to extrapolate from male texts such a broad conclusion about women's response. That women profoundly internalized the directive of male texts on the humoral mechanism of the body to shame and bodily alienation is not so clear to me. Women's own textual narrative of their bodies is not so victimized. Also, Audrey Eccles has argued that a 'marked decline of faith in humoral medicine,' especially in obstetrics, was 'early and clearly demonstrated' (121–122).

37 See Marilyn Luecke's excellent essay on the *Nurserie*.

38 Though our evidence is not the same, this judgment is supported by Patricia Crawford ('Construction'). See also Betty Travitsky on the 'new mother.' And see Karen Nelson's treatment of Elizabeth Cary's *Edward II* as 'exploiting mothers' advice strategies of authorization' (162).

39 Jonathan Sawday reads these lines as struggling toward agency, but finally capitulating to 'God's patriarchal voice internalized' (*The Body Emblazoned*, 228).
40 See Ann Rosalind Jones's reading of Whitney (37–52) and Mary Wroth (141–154) in *The Currency of Eros*, and Wendy Wall's discussion of the same poets (296–310, 330–338).
41 Mary Frances Wack suggests that the malady of lovesickness, considered in the Middle Ages a male disease, in the Renaissance began to be assigned also to women. She wonders whether this is simply a phenomenon of male texts and not evident in women's lives, or 'whether the tightened grip of patriarchy was responsible for a somaticization of women's anger in the form of lovesickness' (175ff).
42 Macfarlane himself admits the likelihood of male bias in his work: 'nearly all of our sources of a personal kind were written by men, and the author of this work [Macfarlane] is a man ... there will be a male bias in the discussion' (48).
43 See Sara Heller Mendelson, 'Stuart Women's Diaries and Occasional Memoirs,' 191–201.
44 Some of this resistance to dualistic thinking derives from northern Christian humanism, but notice that the humanists, on the whole, were concerned with the education of men and did not develop the same arguments for women. Margaret More Roper was regarded by her father and his circle as a phenomenon who was able to achieve something exceptional. The sophisticated and clever exploitation by Elizabeth of the 'Queen's two bodies' as a means of laying claim to political and intellectual power is discussed by Betty Travitsky (Haselkorn and Travitsky, 16–17). However, most of the comments by women asserting the indissoluble connection between their minds and bodies occur toward the end of the seventeenth century, not in the humanist-dominated sixteenth century.
45 Elaine Hobby argues convincingly that this work, usually attributed to Hannah Wolley, was actually a pastiche of some of Wolley's comments from other works, strung together by a hack hired by the publisher. Hobby also supposes an original male author – a conclusion I do not think is persuasive.
46 See Marilyn Frye's discussion of the theory of feminist separatism.
47 In Shakespeare's *Measure for Measure*, Isabella attempts this tactic of withdrawal, but is ultimately forced back under patriarchal control when the Duke marries her.
48 It is difficult to tell from this anonymous work whether these sentiments are those of a male writer or are placed in the mouth of a male by a female writer. In either case, they indicate the subversive power and desires expected of female communities.
49 Here I differ from Valerie Traub's view that the 'discourse of desires and acts that not only can be articulated but correlated with our modern understanding of diverse erotic practices among women ... is not authored by women' (64). I agree, however, that to understand this discourse more clearly in the early modern period, we need to 'crack the code organizing the conceptual categories of [this] earlier culture' (65).
50 Both these women were married and mothers, but this part of their lives was secondary to their joint testimony as Quakers in the world.
51 Elspeth Graham ('Women's Writing and the Self') cites an 'early seventeenth-century' text I have not seen by Dionys Fitzherbert, in which she says Fitzherbert implies 'a resistance to the notion of sexuality in marriage' and an 'uneasy and unconscious erotic, or intensely emotional attachment' to a woman named Mrs H. (224). Citations of the Fitzherbert text are: Ms. E. Mus. 169 and Ms. Bodley 154. See also Theodora Jankowski's speculations about the role of virginity in John Lyly's *Gallathea*: 'This definition of virginity carries encoded within it the notion that strong bonds of friendship and affection existed between women that are *not* acknowledged by patriarchal society or the

patriarchal narrative, and that these bonds might have an erotic component, might grow into woman–woman desire' (268).

52 As we are learning to 'queer' the Renaissance, we should not bypass the implications of female–female physical and affectional closeness, and especially the threat that it represented to a culture determinedly invested in the legislation of heterosexuality and the family as totalizing conditions for the construction of the modern state.

Chapter 3

The Word. Secret Pleasures: Women's Literacy and Learning

> There is, in an initial phase, perhaps only one 'path,' the one historically assigned to the feminine: that of mimicry ... Feminine pleasure has to remain inarticulate in language, in its own language, if it is not to threaten the underpinnings of logical operations. And so what is most strictly forbidden to women today is that they should attempt to express their own pleasure ... For this pleasure is not simply situated in a process of reflection or mimesis.
>
> – Irigaray, *This Sex*, 76–77

> I wisse, al their sport in the park is but a shadow to that plesure that I find in Plato. Alas! Good folk, they never felt what true pleasure meant.
>
> – Lady Jane Grey, quoted in Ascham's *Scholemaster*, 1570, 36

Elizabeth Cary's daughter narrates in her biography of her mother that, in the years before her marriage, Elizabeth was so filled with the desire for, and love of, learning that she stayed up late at night, contrary to her own mother's commands, reading by light from candles she had secretly bought on credit from the household servants. Her mother's antagonism to Elizabeth's learning, in spite of her father's support, who 'loved much to have her read' (*Life*, 188), was sustained after Elizabeth's marriage by her mother-in-law who locked her up, away from her books, and thus unwittingly induced Elizabeth to find an alternative to reading in the even more taboo practice for women of imaginative writing. Despite all efforts to keep her respectably unlettered, Elizabeth autodidactically acquired numerous languages and a considerable education, and not only wrote, but published, several works.

The biography uses the emotive language of passionate and private satisfaction to describe Elizabeth's relationship to her reading and writing activities: she 'loved [reading] much' (186), and wrote 'for her private recreation' (189). The material conditions of women's literacy and learning evoked in the biography also serve as figurative tropes in early modern England for the meaning of women's literacy and education: opposition, in this case maternal, to the value of women's education for its own sake (its pragmatic usefulness not being evident and its social risks obvious); mixed and inconsistent cultural attitudes framing women's learning, apparent here in Elizabeth's parents' divided point of view; and a woman's determined claim to her reading practices and 'recreational' writing and their associated, sometimes solitary, pleasures.

Margaret Spufford cites examples of working-class men engaged in efforts at self-education apparently similar to Cary's. Arise Stevens, though of a social class closer to the servants from whom Elizabeth bought her candles, like her also 'bought candles for the night,' so that he could read his way laboriously through a 'Chronicle ... that showed all the passage in Brittain and Ireland from Noahs Floud to William the Conquerour' (quoted in Spufford, 'First Steps,' 421). Thomas Tryon began his working life at the age of six, spinning and carding, at about age thirteen switched to shepherding and eventually gained enough social power to become the founder of a religious group in London. He attested to the 'vast usefulness of Reading' and exchanged one of two precious sheep he owned for instruction in writing (416). Tryon, like Cary, published several works, including treatises on medicine and education and a piece of *Friendly Advice to the People of the West Indies*. 'Incurable self-improver[s]' like Stevens and Tryon recognized the social and economic power of literacy; their 'desire for information' prevailed over 'the problems of even finding time to absorb it during the working day, or a source of light to read it by at night' (421).

It is tempting to transfer what we understand about the meaning of education and literacy for Tryon and Stevens to what we would like to know about the meaning of education and literacy for women. One might conjure up the romantic image of men and women of all classes throughout England subversively reading by candlelight as they laid the educational foundations to facilitate a shift from their current material and psychological situation to another, more challenging and rewarding. In spite of the parallel visual imagery of night-time reading for Cary and Stevens, however, and the educational self-advancement and emergence into print of Cary and Tryon, the similarities of motivation and consequence were not as profound as they seem. Certainly, the biographical story of Elizabeth Cary and similar narratives of such gentlewomen as the Cooke sisters, Jane Grey, Elizabeth Grymeston and Cary's own daughter-in-law, Lettice – who, like her mother-in-law, read at night 'when she was thought to be in bed' (Duncon, 149, quoted in Fraser, 30) – highlight some women's hunger for reading and writing. But the women in these narratives occupy social and psychological positions very different from Thomas Tryon's and Arise Stevens's.

We are slowly learning more of women from other classes, especially in the mid to late seventeenth century, who acquired literacy in consequence of their training as maidservants for literate households.[1] Louise Schleiner points out that 'the duties of both women-in-waiting and household servant women' in Tudor and Stuart culture included 'reading aloud to their ladies' (3). In Puritan households, literacy seems to have been regarded as a condition ideally attained by all members as the basis of their enhanced spiritual education: 'In accounts of conversion, one sees a close association of maids and their mistresses which may account in part for how the women of the servant classes learned to read and write' (Ezell, *Writing*, 135). Peter Clark cites two moving examples drawn from Canterbury Cathedral records, of non-aristocratic women who also read at night, though without the privilege of solitude, and also encountered opposition to their bookish struggles:

> We hear of Elizabeth Baker, the wife of an Otham yeoman, who one night in 1607 was according to her maid, 'at her book reading as she uses many times to do before she goes to bed.' In another case the witness tells how a Faversham man, Bartholomew Dann, assaulted his wife and 'when she had been reading and leaving her book in some place ... he would catch the book out of her hands and tear it in pieces or otherwise fling it away. ('Ownership,' 97)

Obviously, not all non-aristocratic women and working-class men were illiterate, but for Stevens and Tryon literacy implied an opportunity for movement to a personal and economic autonomy to which few women, of whatever social class, whether literate or not, could aspire.[2]

Cary and her daughter-in-law read at night for reasons different from Stevens's, having to do with restrictions of gender ideology rather than the demands of economically necessary work; the women's reading, unlike the men's, needed to take place in secret. For a working-class man, the acquisition of information and education might be difficult to fit into a long, physically demanding working day, but it held the hope of vocationally applicable and personally beneficial use, not available to Elizabeth Baker or the wife of Bartholomew Dann, and hardly relevant to Elizabeth or Lettice Cary. At a higher level, men's learning had value in the pursuit of careers in the priesthood or ministry, in the law, in education, or the court. For a woman, the 'desire for information' always risked the appearance of frivolity, perhaps of self-indulgence, or, worse, the threat of pleasurable self-inscription.[3]

Both basic literacy and broader education, not unexpectedly then, meant different things for men and women in early modern England. Because 'literacy has been used, in age after age, to solidify the social hierarchy, empower elites, and ensure that people lower in the hierarchy accept the values, norms, and beliefs of the elites' (Gee, 205; Graff, 324), for early modern men the ideologies of literacy and education also implied the expectation and acquisition of material and reputational self-improvement. There is no such accepted trajectory for women. Early modern women's education is sometimes admitted, increasingly in the seventeenth century in middling-sort and mercantile households, as potentially useful to children, servants or ambitious husbands, but it also inspires fear that by abusing their knowledge women will harm men and undermine the social hierarchy.

While the learning of Elizabeth and Mary Tudor, Katherine Parr and Jane Grey was justifiable because of their aristocratic position in the same vocational terms as men's education, Elizabeth Cary's learning, though she was a member of the gentry by birth and an aristocrat by marriage, was still discouraged. Why? Surely for reasons more subtle and deeply embedded in unconscious assumptions about social stability than that her learning was thought to have no immediate practical usefulness. Yet her biography says that even when her pursuit of learning continued to play a disruptive role in her life, incurring the disapproval of her mother and mother-in-law, deflecting her attention from the deportment and self-fashioning expected by her husband and possibly also playing a role in her conversion to Catholicism and final marital rift, Cary persisted. Again, why?

In this chapter I propose that the answers to these questions are embedded in cultural ambivalence concerning the implications of learning for women, including mixed doubts and desires in women themselves, and are especially framed by women's participation in pleasure and privacy as means to subjectivity. While both men and women undoubtedly found a degree of pleasure in learning, cultural discourse weighted women's pleasure with negative concerns not attached to men's. Disapproval of women's education responded to the cultural meaning more than the circumstantial facts of women's education, though each of course affected the other.

Most studies of women's literacy and education in the early modern period have sought to uncover three historical secrets: 1) the nature of women's literacy – the acquisition of what skills marked a shift from the status of *illiterate* to *literate*; 2) the extent of women's literacy and education – how many women could read, write, or more intensively engage with 'learned' texts; and 3) under what circumstances women achieved either or both – whether self-taught, taught by parent or tutor at home, or taught by a teacher in a school.[4] With reference to all three lines of inquiry, scholarly discoveries continue to push toward increased estimates. The currently standard narrative of Englishwomen's literacy during the 200 years between 1500 and 1700 tells a tale of spreading literacy and improving intellectual and writerly status,[5] occurring despite publicly aired, albeit inconsistent, objections to this very advance.

The best-known narrator of this story is still David Cressy, who first provided our most frequently cited evidence. During a prolonged period in the sixteenth and early seventeenth centuries, women's literacy increased slowly and somewhat erratically. Then between 1640 and 1690, Cressy has told us, women's writing literacy rose to as high as 50 per cent. In the fifteenth century in England, 90 per cent of men and 95 per cent of women were illiterate, that is, as Cressy defines this status, unable to sign their names (*Literacy and the Social Order*, 143). By the 1720s, however, Cressy estimates, only 44 per cent of women were still unable to represent themselves by their signatures. Women's illiteracy, as measured by Cressy, was halved between the middle and the end of the seventeenth century.[6]

Supporting this narrative of progress are the numbers cited by Ruth Hughey, Hilda Smith and Patricia Crawford: of the over 600 known titles by seventeenth-century women, more than two-thirds were published in the second half of that century. Although there was a generally rising literacy for both men and women in England throughout the sixteenth and seventeenth centuries, and although men's literacy was always higher than women's, proportionally speaking the rise in women's basic signatory literacy appears to have kept pace with men's from 1540 to 1690. A number of factors apparently contributed: the influence of humanist values and goals, continuing from the sixteenth into the seventeenth centuries, which increased tolerance for some women's education;[7] the developing respectability and patriotic support of the vernacular as a medium of literate education; the increased demand for female servants during the second half of the seventeenth century, opening the opportunity for girls to learn to read in households where the mistress or master assumed the responsibility of teaching their servants to read the Bible; the growth of charity and boarding schools, which encouraged literacy among lower- and middle-class girls, both to increase their market value as servants and to encourage their access to Biblical texts; the influence of Puritan values in seventeenth-century England, which encouraged the spread of Bible reading; and, finally, a developing money-based economy in which a bourgeois woman's literacy skills could benefit her family's fortunes. So at least the summary version of women's acquisition of literate skills and more advanced education would appear to be straightforward and quickly told: their literacy skills and educational levels increased over time; they desired this change and, because of their persistent demands, in spite of some powerful male objections, eventually achieved it.

The construction of this story in its Renaissance, and some modern, versions bears a not accidental similarity to the prevailing historical narrative of women's objectified sexuality and perpetual desire, a connection that, as we know, nagged at the consciousness of early modern men, for whom the eloquent, educated woman bore a worrying kinship to the curious Eve in pursuit of the knowledge of good and evil. Nevertheless, as with all stories interwoven with pleasure and desire, the apparently simple and comforting narrative of linear progress is, after all, not so simple, complicated at the very least by sub-plots and counter-plots of geography, class and social standing. Margaret King, following Sylvia Thrupp, claims that among the merchant class in London as early as 1500, 'if women did not receive quite the same education as men, it appears that "it was quite commonly within their reach"' (173), and Margaret Spufford has questioned Cressy's generalizations about women's literacy progressively rising from minimal levels, because it was always the case that 'small but significant' numbers 'in even the most illiterate social groups ... were able to write their names' ('First Steps in Literacy,' 409).

It is also arguable, because of the suddenness of the jump in women's publication after 1641, when censorship laws were relaxed, that many women, even before that date, must already have achieved some writing proficiency without earlier seeking a public venue for their skill. Not inconsiderable, although not publicly obvious, reading and writing literacy among women seems likely throughout the whole early modern period.[8] Suzanne Hull and Caroline Lucas have deduced broad-based numbers of women readers from the steadily increasing production of printed books clearly intended for an audience of women;[9] by 1694, the *Ladies Dictionary* quite casually advised nursery maids to listen to, and presumably check for accuracy, the reading of the children in their care (Keeble, 191).

As long ago as 1929, J.W. Adamson suggested that 'the absence of the printed word is not decisive evidence of inability to read' (164): '[E]arly printed matter and the later circulation of controversial pamphlets and Biblical translations point to a fairly large number of persons already able to read before the printed supply became available' (168). Adamson cites a document from the Record Office which sets forth a complaint about 'certain maidens who on Ascension Day, 1534, sat in church reciting Matins from an English *Primer*' (169), and he also refers to direct fifteenth-century evidence of letters written by both artisans and women.[10] More recent studies have only confirmed Adamson's earlier judgments.

That the first known use of the word 'illiterate' appears in English in 1556, also suggests a concurrently increasing social recognition of literacy, to set against the institution of the negative verbal marker. Moreover, although the acquisition of writing literacy was postponed beyond the acquisition of reading literacy,[11] and although writing was a skill largely intended for relatively few privileged male students, nevertheless, writing skills, we now confidently believe, proliferated more widely among both men and women of *all* classes than was previously assumed.[12] We may now comfortably extend Adamson's generalization to the conclusion that the absence of the printed word, or even the socially determined exclusion from print of a particular group, is not evidence of an inability to write. This point is reinforced by Juliet Fleming's fascinating argument for the significance of widespread writing with chalk or charcoal, not pen, on walls rather than paper, 'by those (it may have been practically everybody) unconcerned with the extensive circulation and long survival of their *bons mots*' ('Graffiti,' 329).

Finally, Jonathan Goldberg offers a suggestive refinement to reliance on signatory estimates: 'What,' he asks, 'does a signature authenticate when a person can produce multiple versions of the signature in different hands and spellings?' (*Writing Matter*, 242).[13] As Goldberg suggests, prioritizing the signature reproduces (possibly inappropriately) the 'modern notion of what constitutes literacy – the ability to sign the name and thereby to reproduce the individual,' thus 're-marking' and re-making the subject (243). For we are trying here to understand a culture in which the signature was perhaps not always assigned the individuating symbolic value it commands among twentieth-century people, although, to complicate matters still further, Anne Clifford may offer counter-evidence to this assumption, for she thought it important enough to record in her diary on 19 April 1617, that she 'signed 33 letters with my own hand.' If literacy and further learning in any way feed into the process of women's subjective self-inscription, we will need to look for something more than signatory skill to validate that process.

To discover how literacy and further learning were used in women's texts as means of inscribing subjectivity, we need to scrutinize the meaning of early modern women's learning to the culture at large, but particularly to women themselves. This distinction can be thought of in terms of what Sidney Mintz categorizes as '*outside*' meaning and '*inside*' meaning, defined as: '*outside*' – 'the wider social significance of those changes effectuated by institutions and groups whose reach and power transcend both individuals and local[ized] communities' (22); and '*inside*' – the significance imparted by individuals 'to their own acts and the acts of those around them' (23). 'Outside' meaning can be imparted only by those holding the structural or institutional power to do so, that is, with respect to early modern women's changing educational levels, the male educators and pundits who initially defined the conditions within which this change was able to take place as well as its larger social significance. 'Inside' meaning is discovered by those implicated in the changes permitted by the wielders of outside meaning, that is, in this case, the women affected by, experiencing and eventually, as subjects, rewriting the significance of those changes.

When considering women's increased literacy and publication during these 200 years, we additionally need to remember that these phenomena mark even more than, on the one hand, the acquisition of basic reading and writing skills, or, on the other, the generation of a sophisticated means of expression. They mark as well an indoctrination into the whole ideology of literacy, with its multiple ambivalences. Education and literacy, reading and writing, are inevitable sites in culture for tension and conflict over the disposition of power.[14] For male commentators in the early modern period, able to assign institutional significance or 'outside' meaning to the process, educating women meant an opportunity to inculcate in them the cultural terms of their own submission and to implicate them in the preservation of the *status quo*.

There is evidence everywhere of an accepted understanding of this goal, not least in the insistent demands for tight restrictions on the content and nature of women's education. Juan Luis Vives, whose *Instruction of a Christian Woman* (1523) proliferated throughout Europe in forty editions (nine in England), recommended no rhetoric, no romance, no Latin (except for princesses), but instead much wool-weaving, 'sober' cooking, and the reading of many repressive, 'wise and sad men' (43–44). For Richard Brathwaite, the goal of a woman's education was still to 'estrange' her from 'rudeness of breeding' without disrupting her silence or, 'God forbid,' making her 'not be readier to learn than to teach' (320), that is, not to move her from passivity to agency.

Yet, as Henry Giroux has argued, whatever the imposed restrictions, literacy is ultimately 'a rupturing practice that engages questions regarding who writes for what audience in what institutional setting, and with what purpose in mind. Literacy, in this case, becomes a form of ideological critique that makes visible how oppressive and dominating practices mediate between the margins and the center of power' (2). As Vives and Brathwaite surely knew, education may benefit society, but also sow the seeds of insurrection. Attitudes to literacy and its results, both amongst those who already are, and those who are becoming, literate, are often contradictory and the fissures in the contradictions highlight ideological bias (Stuckey, 23).

For women, the loss of marginal, because unlettered, status, in an increasingly literate and print-oriented early modern culture, was a loss of the illiteracy which exiled them, but also perhaps at the same time protected them to some degree from painfully acknowledging their complicity in, and repression by, the codes of misogynist power.[15] Goldberg cites François Furet's and Jacques Ozouf's comments on the double edge of literacy: 'The extension of literacy is not automatically the opening of new domains of freedom and political representation ... Increasing literacy means the increasing inscription of subjects' (*Writing Matter*, 48). The acquisition of literacy may imply the submission 'to be shaped in certain ways' (Hoskins, quoted in Stuckey, 76). Perhaps for early modern women this meant having to engage in the not always liberating rhetoric of contentious and defensive debate; being able to read sobering warnings against their wicked ways might reinforce women's sense of subjection, but being able to write imposed on less fully indoctrinated women the responsibility to reply.

Jane Anger, for example, in 1589, complains that men believe they can attack women with impunity because 'they suppose that there is not one amongst us who can or dare reprove their slanders and false reproaches ... [T]hey think we will not write to reprove their lying lips' (175). But Anger herself mounts her complaint from a sense of injustice, addressing herself to the 'gentlewomen of England,' committing 'your protection and myself to the protection of yourselves' (173). Able to reach a sympathetic audience, women's writing could begin to build a communal response, an 'inside' meaning, encouraging the pleasurable self-inscription of the female subject. It could potentially produce the kind of insurrectionist answering-back offered by Mary Ward (1621). Full of the power of her learning and the authority accrued from teaching her own classes in her self-founded Institute of the Blessed Virgin Mary, in which young girls could 'embrace either the secular or the religious life' (memorandum to Pope Paul V quoted in Fraser 124), she declared: 'For what think you of this word, "but women"? but as if we were in all things inferior to some other creature which I suppose to be a man! Which I dare to be bold to say is a lie' (quoted in King, *Women of the Renaissance*, 112).

Christine de Pizan in *The Book of the City of Ladies*, written in French in the early fifteenth century and translated into English and published in London in 1521,[16] certainly recognized the ambivalent possibilities, embedded in the practice of literacy, of imprisonment in, or liberation from, the demands of dominant ideologies (Stuckey, 77). Describing the process whereby she comes to discover the 'inside' meaning of her reading and writing skills, she begins her tale with a description of herself contentedly alone in her study, 'surrounded by books on all kinds of subjects,' devoting herself to 'literary studies' – as, she says, 'her usual habit' (3). Yet because, or in spite of, her scholarly habits and skills, her story takes a poignant turn, for as she reads, Christine comes to the dismaying recognition that all poets, philosophers and orators appear to 'speak from one and the same mouth' about the vicious behavior of women (4). 'A great unhappiness and sadness welled up in my heart,' she says, 'for I detested myself and the entire feminine sex, as though we were monstrosities in nature' (5).

Only under the instructive auspices of the three allegorical female teachers, Reason, Rectitude and Justice, does Christine come to understand that men have written malicious lies about women, concealing those lies from women themselves in order to reinforce the shared male distrust of women. For instance, Reason tells Christine, 'Some pope – I don't know which one – excommunicated every man who read the [*Secreta Mulierum*] to a woman or gave it to a woman to read' (22). This was done 'so that women would not know about the book and its contents, because the man who wrote it knew that if women read it or heard it read aloud, they would know it was lies, would contradict it, and make fun of it' (22–23).

Christine accepts that it has been uniquely granted to her by God to stand as women's defender (184–185). But when she asks why all the other learned women in history have not refuted male attacks on women, Reason weakly answers that they were engaged in other tasks ordained for them by God. The opening of Christine's own text has supplied another more credible answer – that those women who could read, and who had therefore been initiated into the male denunciation of their sex, without a visitation from the three crowned ladies whose bright faces have shone on Christine (6), might be so entirely convinced of their own monstrosity that they would not dare claim the right to challenge the negative male depiction. In Christine's text, then, we see an uneasy recognition of the damaging power of the male text's 'outside' meaning over the female reader, its self-occluding effect on women who can read but not write and its potentially inhibiting effect even on the woman with writing skills sufficient to engage in a battle against misogynist texts.

It was in facing such unwelcome recognitions forced upon them by their literacy, in negotiating the maze of self-contradictions in their own responses as well as in the 'outside' meanings of their learning, in struggling, without Christine's supernatural aides, to assume the responsibilities of learning and, finally, in claiming the crucial subject-defining pleasures to be drawn out of this complex experience, that women were able to write themselves as literate, learned subjects. Let us, then, now consider the ambivalences in the 'outside' meaning of women's learning to the male pedagogues and adjudicators of women's learning, and compare the intertwined, but differently ambivalent, textual reactions of literate women who assigned 'significance to their own acts [of learning] and the acts of those around them' (Mintz, 23). 'The wider distribution of printing and literacy,' says Frances Dolan, 'was a mixed blessing for women' ('Reading,' 150). Much of the rest of this chapter will be devoted to discussing: 1) the ambivalent response of both men and women to women's immersion in the cultural meanings of literacy; and 2) women's textual testimonies to the ultimately irresistible pleasure of literacy's 'mixed blessing.' A quite surprising number of early modern women's texts comment directly or indirectly on the implications for women of what lay on the other side of the slowly opening doors to women's learning. To understand and reconstruct the processes of women's writerly and poetic subjectivity in early modern England it seems essential to find out what these women's texts have to say about their initiation into textuality, and to acknowledge their so far largely unregarded, but remarkably shrewd and sophisticated, insights.

What May Women Learn? Mixed Blessings, Mixed Messages

Expanding educational opportunities in early modern England were initially advocated by sixteenth-century humanist scholars, who saw literacy and further learning as pre-eminently desirable at least for socially privileged men, and as essential to civilization and social development. That this view continued beyond the lives of the humanists and came to be applied to classes lower on the social scale, is apparent in an example quoted by Cressy: David Brown, a schoolmaster, attempting to drum up trade in 1622 by working on 'parvenu insecurities' about lack of education, claimed, '[I]t is shame both to employ a notary to subscribe for thee in any security, and to want that good token of education which perhaps thine inferior hath' ('Literacy in Context,' 309).

Responses to women's education are more conflicted.[17] Juan Luis Vives believes that education might, in the best-case scenario, contribute to women's virtue, but he cannot quite believe that women's formal book-learning can be made to support the interests of a patriarchal Catholic state. He intends that women should learn from their education to internalize the needs of male society and to monitor their own behavior, but, suspicious of their inner waywardness, he is doubtful about women's capacity to absorb and retain this 'outside' meaning.[18] Though he hopes for the best, his rhetoric reveals that he shares the worries expressed by others, which, while disputing, he also forcefully emphasizes. He describes the benefits of women's education by negation, postponing an acknowledgment of its value to the end of his defense; he too fears that 'woman's thought is swift, and for the most part, unstable' (44): 'I perceive that learned women be suspected of many: as who saith, the subtlety of learning should be a nourishment for the maliciousness of their nature. Verily, I do not allow in a subtle and crafty woman, such learning as should teach her deceit, and teach her no good manners and virtues' (48).

The dominant view concerning women's education was self-protectively mixed, and the terms of the surrounding debate continued largely unresolved after Vives into the seventeenth century. John Shawcross says that 'A work like Daniel Tuvill's *Asylum Veneris or a Sanctuary for Ladies* (1616), which argues that women should have the same access to learning as men, is indeed rare' (164), but Tuvill's attitude was supported even more vehemently in other texts. Cornelius Agrippa's *Pre-Eminence and Nobility of Women* (1542), for example, offers the startling defense that women are superior to men in beauty, virtue, indeed everything, even including those areas normally closed to them in early modern England: philosophy, oratory and poetry.[19] Yet Agrippa conveniently hedges his claims: his examples of women's learning and virtue, deriving from classical history and legend, offer no immediate threat.

Philip Stubbes (1583), at the other end of the spectrum of opinion, believes that the seeds of vice are buried in general and permissive education, including the education of girls: 'remiss liberty in the education of youth ... maketh them so soon whores, strumpets, and bawds' (*Anatomie*, sig. F4 vi–vii). Even fifty years later, Richard Brathwaite still conservatively limits the expectations for a gentlewoman's education.

3.1 From E. Coote's *The English Schoolmaster*

Focused on social skills rather than intellectual pursuits and more attuned to personal discipline than to academic disciplines, 'Her education hath so enabled her as she can converse with you of all places, deliver her judgment conceivingly of most persons, and discourse delightfully of all fashions' (sig. Mm 1). Especially to be guarded against when admitting women to education, according to Thomas Elyot, is the stimulation of the 'wit' which flourishes in women, 'in trymmynge them selfes with praty devyses' (*Defense*, 33), that is, their tendency to frivolity and the pursuit of pleasure, especially as it is typically inscribed in their sensuous love of pretty clothes.

Though not always agreeing about the potential value of women's education, many English educators do accept that the content of women's learning must be strictly controlled, and, to ensure this end, most choose to exclude the two primary markers of boys' education: Latin and rhetoric. In considering the subject matter of an acceptable curriculum for women, they share restrictive opinions similar to those expressed in the early fifteenth-century Italian humanist Leonardo Bruni's letter to Battista Malatesta:

> There are certain disciplines which ... to ascend to the utmost heights of them is not at all admirable. Such are geometry and arithmetic, on which if too much time and energy are expended ... I shall restrain you by force. And I shall do the same in the case of Astronomy, and perhaps also in the case of Rhetoric ... For why exhaust a woman with ... a thousand difficulties of rhetorical art, when she will never see the forum? ... For if a woman throws her arms around while speaking, or if she increases the volume of her speech with greater forcefulness, she will appear threateningly insane and requiring restraint. (11–12)

Bruni, unlike many English educators, does grudgingly permit a woman to learn Latin, but confines its use to the sober reading of Christian writers and serious classical authors like Cicero, Virgil, Livy and Sallust (Grafton and Jardine, 32–33).

Vives is more typical of pedagogues in England: girls should always pray and be taught in the vernacular (Watson, 22). The perceived danger of Latin is that it will connect one source of intellectual pleasure in the act of reading, with that other physical pleasure most feared in women, by granting them access to erotically inflaming texts by such authors as Ovid and Lucian. Nevertheless, in the first decades of the seventeenth century, Lucy Hutchinson, whose father helped her violate Vives's recommendations, learned Latin, Greek and Hebrew, and seems to have come to, and caused, no socially subversive harm by it, developing eventually into an exemplary wife for a grateful husband. While still a young student, she thought it 'no sin to learne or heare wittie songs and amorous sonnetts or poems' (quoted in George, 18). And though when young, 'for my needle, I absolutely hated it' (quoted in Fraser, 136), when older, she balanced necessity against desire, finding a way to translate Lucretius while embroidering, a pen, as it were, in one hand and a needle in the other: 'I turned it into English in a roome where my children practizd the severall quallities they were taught, with their Tutors, & I numbred the sillables of my translation by the threds of the canvas I wrought in, & sett them downe with a pen & inke that stood by me' (dedication to translation of Lucretius, *Kissing the Rod*, 215). Yet, unpersuaded by this impressive example, or others like it, in 1652 Ralph Verney was still warning Dr Denton, 'Let not your young girls learn Latin' (quoted in Emily Lu Pearson, 215), and telling his goddaughter, Nancy Denton:

> I did not think you had been guilty of so much learning as I see you are; and yet it seems you rest unsatisfied or else you would not threaten Latin, Greek, and Hebrew too. Good sweetheart, be not so covetous. Believe me, a Bible (with the Common Prayer) and a good plain catechism in your mother tongue, being well read and practised, is well worth all the rest, and much more suitable to your sex. (74)

Women in command of Latin and Greek 'threaten,' and should feel 'guilty of so much learning.'

Though the attempted exiling of women from classical languages did not produce the hoped-for censoring of their reading, it did lead to a perceptual linking of their educational possibilities with the vernacular. The intended audience of what Juliet Fleming describes as 'arguably the first dictionary of vernacular English' ('Dictionary English,' 175) is indicative: *A Table Alphabeticall, conteyning and teaching the true writing and understanding of hard usuall English wordes, borrowed from the Hebrew, Greeke, Latine, or French &c. With the interpretation therof by plaine English words, gathered for the benefit and helpe of Ladies, Gentlewomen, or other unskilful persons* (1604).[20] Yet Edward Hake, in *A Touchestone for this Time Present* (1574), inveighed even against the corrupting influence of vernacular reading and writing on London maidservants, for, like their classically educated betters, who can go directly to the Latin and Greek sources of eroticism, they too choose for their reading 'amorous bookes, vaine stories, and fonde trifling fancies' (sig. C4). 'Much better were it,' he says, 'they should unlearne that againe which they have alreadie learned, then miserably to abuse it as they doe' (sig. C5). Either a little or a lot of learning in women apparently threatens the 'outside' meaning of their education.[21]

With respect to rhetoric, like Bruni and Vives, Erasmus disapproved of women teachers, for, 'It is unnatural for women to have control over men' (*Devout*, 50).[22] Though Vives thought that a virtuous woman could be a girl's first teacher, and mothers might teach their children the basis of virtue in a domestic circle, in general women should not be officially designated as teachers or taught the skills of rhetoric: 'As for eloquence, I have no great care, nor a woman needeth it not, but she needeth goodness and wisdom' (Watson, 52). Constantly prone to error, 'a woman should not teach, lest when she hath taken a false opinion and belief of any thing, she spread it into the hearers' (Watson, 56). Richard Mulcaster, a comparatively liberal spokesman for women's education, perhaps protecting his own vocational interests, also recommended men, as the best practitioners of teaching skills, to tutor girls (Kelso, 267). In 1609, William Heale's *An Apology for Women* expresses the common concern that women, already naturally too loquacious and domineering, if trained in rhetoric and permitted to preach in public, would soon go much too far and preach in private to their husbands: 'I could never approve those too too holy gospellers, who ... catechize their husbands, citing places, clearing difficulties, and preaching holy sermons too, if the spirit of their devotion move them' (quoted in Kusunoki, 88). And Richard Brathwaite in 1641 warns the English gentlewoman, 'in public consorts to observe rather than discourse. It suits not with her honour for a young woman to be prolocutor' (319).

In spite of this prohibitive atmosphere, Bathsua Makin taught in her father's school and, like Aemilia Lanyer, established a school herself, but in 1673 she still had to overcome the social suspicion of women's involvement in 'masculine' areas of learning and teaching:[23] 'A learned woman is thought to be a comet that bodes mischief whenever it appears. To offer to the world the liberal education of women is to deface the image of God in man. It will make women so high and men so low. Like fire in the housetop, it will set the whole world in a flame' (sig. A2). The lack of uniformity and absoluteness in male pedagogical attitudes toward the content, conditions and acceptability of women's education, inevitably cracked open a space where women could resist and redirect oppressive social dictates concerning their learning. This did not mean, however, that women simply and contrarily embraced the educational goals prohibited them, for their 'pleasure is not simply situated in a process of reflection' (Irigaray, *This Sex*, 77). On the contrary, numerous women's texts give witness to another different set of worries and ambivalences of their own, while maneuvering in the direction of pleasurable agency rather than controlled submission.

Men suspicious of women's learning assume that increased learning and knowledge will compound the natural deficits inherited by women as daughters of Eve: 'towardness,' curiosity and lust. Women defending their educational possibilities, on the other hand, expect that education will intensify their natural virtue and give them the means to refute false assumptions about them. Some women argue boldly that, as daughters of Eve, they are the natural inheritors and monitors of learning. Yet women did not advance into this previously closed space of educational privilege with undiluted confidence, for the choices entailed, as Mary Jacobus points out, have consequences: 'Women's access to discourse involves submission to phallocentricity; ... refusal, on the other hand, risks reinscribing the feminine as yet more marginal' (quoted in Heilbrun, 40–41).

Although some early modern women unequivocally desired education, others were skittish about its implications. What might be the consequences of their initiation into this male territory, they wonder? What are its disadvantages? In spite of Luce Irigaray's warning that 'Feminine pleasure has to remain inarticulate ... in its own language, if it is not to threaten the underpinnings of logical [that is, male] operations' (*This Sex*, 76–77), could women nevertheless find in this male-dominated space a language and learning of their own? Or might they need to sacrifice the skills and characteristic pleasures of women's traditional pursuits, while gaining little from the new? Catherine des Roches, though not English, maintaining like Lucy

3.2 Ambrosius Holbein, ***Signboard of a Schoolmaster***

Hutchinson her hold on both needle and pen, clearly articulates this hesitancy and ambivalence:

> My spindle and my care, I promise you and swear
> To love you forever, and never to exchange
> Your domestic honor for a good which is strange,
> Which, inconstant, wanders, and tends its foolish snare.
> ...
> But, spindle, my dearest, I do not believe
> That, much as I love you, I will come to grief,
> If I do not quite let that good practice dwindle
> Of writing sometimes, if I give you fair share,
> If I write of your merit, my friend and my care,
> And hold in my hand both my pen and my spindle. (Quoted in Sankovitch, 240)

Lucy Hutchinson also displays this tension between intellectual curiosity and social conformity in presenting her translation of Lucretius to the Earl of Anglesea, saying she 'translated it only out of youthfull curiositie, to understand things I heard so much discourse of at second hand, but without the least inclination to propagate any of the wicked pernitious doctrines in it' (sig. F2v, quoted in *Kissing the Rod*, 215).

This ambivalent combination of desire and doubt, then, regularly surfaces in women's construction of the 'inside' meaning of their literacy and more extensive education. It highlights the wish, described by Foucault, to stand 'on the other side of discourse, without having to stand outside it, pondering its particular, fearsome, and even devilish features' ('Discourse,' 215). Read as a group, women's texts reveal not merely gender-appropriate modesty, but also a suspicion that the very acquisition and use of literacy skills may of themselves exact a heavy price from women, for what Margaret Miles has suggested about women's sexualization is also the case with women's advance into literacy, that 'the price women paid for respect and esteem' in this arena of social power was 'significantly greater than that required of males in the same culture' (189).

Particularly with reference to Latin and rhetorical skills (the signs in early modern England of the masculine Symbolic order), and to universities as sites for their instruction (perhaps because these areas of knowledge are particularly withheld), women's responses are mixed, ranging from evident desire for entry into these prohibited spaces, through disapproval of their abuse by men, to denial of their usefulness to women or even their intrinsic worth. Clearly, the number of women who learned Latin testifies to their interest in doing so, as well as to the weakness of the prohibitions that forbade it to them.[24] There are the usually cited sixteenth-century paragons, Margaret More, Jane Grey, Elizabeth and Mary Tudor, the Cooke sisters and Mary Sidney, whose learning was encouraged by their humanist tutors. But, without this tutorial support, Elizabeth Cary evinced a strong enough desire for admission to classical learning to teach herself Latin, Greek and Hebrew. Brilliana Harley was 'well enough educated to tutor her sons in translating "some things out of

Latin into Inglisch"' (George, 194). Elizabeth Grymeston knew Latin and Greek and, Ruth Hughey says, was generally 'interested' in classical learning (77). Thomas Good claims, in the preface to Elizabeth Joceline's *Mother's Legacie*, that she was able 'upon the first rehearsal to repeat above forty lines in English of Latine' (sig. B1). Bathsua Makin, taught by her father, learned Latin in addition to Greek, Hebrew, French, Syriac, Spanish and German. Lucy Hutchinson, with similar paternal instruction, acquired Latin, Greek and Hebrew. Jane Barker 'learnt latin by reading the latin poets' (*Kissing the Rod*, 367). Damaris Masham raised her son Francis according to John Locke's theories of education, learning Latin herself as she taught it to him.[25]

Of course, not all women were able to overcome the barrier between themselves and classical learning. Issues of class or family ideology completely exempted some women from the expectation even of literacy, and certainly of learning Latin and Greek. Claiming that men abuse their educational privileges, the author (probably Judith Drake) of *An Essay in Defence of the Female Sex* (1696) feels her own lack as a point of resentment:

> I freely own to the reader, that I know no other tongue besides my native, except French, in which I am but very moderately skilled ... [W]e are taught only our mother tongue, or perhaps French ... whereas the other sex by means of a more extensive education to the knowledge of the Greek and Roman languages, have a vaster field for their imaginations to rove in, and their capacities thereby enlarged. (Quoted in Goreau, 144)

It is noteworthy that this speaker envies just exactly the pleasure of imaginative play, inspired by the classics, that embodies the very cause of anxiety for those who attempted, even more vehemently after the Restoration, to prohibit women from Latin and Greek. The pseudonymous authors of *The Women's Sharpe Revenge* (1640), Mary Tattlewell and Joan Hit-Him-Home, also resentfully complain about the willingness of fathers to educate their sons in grammar school and university, so that they become 'booklearned,' while

> [women] have not that generous and liberal Education, lest we should be made able to vindicate our own inuries, [but] we are set only to the Needle to prick our fingers, or else to the Wheel to spin a fair thread of our own undoing ... If we be taught to read, they then confine us within the compass of our Mother tongue, and that limit we are not suffered to pass. (313)

In her dedicatory poem to William Drummond's *Poems*, Mary Oxlie complains that 'hoarse encumbrances of household care,' promoting 'discontents,' have disturbed the 'untroubled mind' from which her 'Verses [should] flow,' and impeded her access to the classical Muses from the '*Thessalian Fountaine*.' Adding to this injustice, men who are granted these educational privileges fail to appreciate them. The *Women's Sharpe Revenge*, demanding for women equal educational access, denounces in men exactly the same abuse of classical learning that is usually charged against women: 'And what do they do then? Read the Poets perhaps, out of which, if they can pick out anything maliciously devised or malignantly divulged by some mad Muse, discontented with his coy or disdainful Mistress, then in imitation of them he must devise some passionate Elegy and pitiful "ah-me!" ' (313). Jane Barker also scolds her male friends for undervaluing the world of learning that, because of her gender, she may not even enter. In 'An Invitation to My Friends at Cambridge,' she claims that the very possibility of learning depends on Eve's having shared the fruits of knowledge with Adam; yet women have been punished for Eve's appropriation of the source of knowledge by being denied its fruits, which she sees contained in the 'classical learning reserved for men at the universities' (Kathryn King, 556).

In a vivid mix of analogies, in a letter to Oxford and Cambridge prefaced to *The Philosophical and Physical Opinions*, Margaret Cavendish laments women's absence from institutions of higher learning: '[W]e are become like worms, that only live in the dull earth of ignorance, winding ourselves sometimes out by the help of some refreshing rain of good education, which seldom is given us, for we are kept like birds in cages, to hop up and down in our houses, not suffered to fly abroad' (sig. B2v). Kept in ignorance, exiled from classical learning, women are both birds and worms, complexly and conflictedly, both self-consuming and self-sustaining. Susanna Parr (1659) also bemoans the disadvantage suffered by 'weake women (who are not able to speak for themselves in *Print* ... so well as men, especially Schollers)' (114). *The Gentlewoman's Companion* (1673) amusingly finds a practical advantage to women in learning Latin:

> You will be freed from the fear of rencountering such who make it their business to ransack a new world of words to find out what are long and obscure; not regarding how insignificant they carry a rattling sound with them. Thus these fops of rhetoric, spawns of non-intelligency, will venture the spraining of their tongues, and splay-footing of their own mouths, if they can but cramp a young gentlewoman's intellect. (*Broadview*, 1278)

The writer of *Triumphs of Female Wit* (1683) speaks out plainly for these women's aspirations, declaring bluntly: 'we covet Learning' (4).

Cordoned off from university education, these women complain of what they see as their unjust exile, yet others dispute its attractions and value altogether, not so much for its sour-grape flavor as from their sense of its lack of usefulness to women, and also of its intrinsic deficiencies. Although access to the classics certainly seemed desirable to some, many knew that this learning was incompatible with the marital life to which, lacking conventual and scholarly options, they were almost universally destined. Elizabeth Cary, during the years of her marriage, forgot Latin and Greek for want of use, but she retrieved Hebrew and Latin at the end of her life, after she had separated from her husband and thankfully returned to her studious habits. Damaris Masham acknowledges that 'The improvements of reason ... are rarely any recommendation of them [women] to men' (quoted in Goreau, 30). Having learned Latin and, she says, conveniently forgotten it, the three-times-married Martha

Moulsworth wryly notes in the margin of her book that 'Lattin is not the most marketable mariadge mettall' (5).

Other women's texts, especially in the seventeenth century, dismiss classical languages as mere vanity and rewrite in positive terms women's alliance with what becomes in their 'inside' reconstruction the God-given vernacular. They reconstruct the vernacular as a language that is purer, more useful and more nourishing. Jane Sharp, defending both women's authority as midwives and her own English instruction book (1671), uses the Augustinian distinction between the outer shell and the sweet kernel of knowledge to compare Latin and Greek to English: 'It is not hard words that perform the work, as if none understood the Art that cannot understand Greek. Words are but the shell, that we ofttimes break our teeth with them to come at the kernel, ... but to have the same in our mother tongue would save us a great deal of needless labour' (4). Women's role in relation to each other's desire to learn is to be helpful, plain and brief, to find a language suitable to their needs and pleasures, and not to engage in linguistic posturing:

> I have as briefly and as plainly as I could, laid down a description of the parts of generation of both sexes, purposely to use language as a help, not hindrance, omitting hard names, that I might have no cause to enlarge my work, by giving you the meaning of them where there is no need, unless it be for such persons who desire rather to know Words than Things. (80)

Elizabeth Clinton, half a century earlier (1622), expressed a similar goal, choosing to 'leave the larger, and learneder discourse hereof unto men of art, and learning; only I speake of so much as I reade and know in my owne experience; which, if any of my sexe and condition do receave good by, I am glad' (11–12). And eighty years after Clinton, the writer of *The Female Advocate* (1700) sounded a variation on the same theme, rejecting Latin and Greek as inappropriate to 'solid' learning, because contaminated by Babel's confusion of tongues: 'I shall not brag that I understand a little Greek and Latin (language being only the effect of confusion), having made some attempt to look into the more solid parts of learning' (quoted in Goreau, 152). Margaret Cavendish, also, though obviously longing for more formal education, congratulates herself on her escape from the often accompanying pedantry: 'I was not bred in an University or Free-school, to Learn the Art of Words. ... I leave the Formal, or Worditive part to Fools' (preface, *Sociable Letters*, quoted in Hilda Smith, *Reason's Disciples*, 94). These women remove themselves from the oppressive implications of enclosure inside the artificially learned, formal and 'privileged' masculine language and turn to the intimate and affiliative, more accessible, vernacular as a better means of communication for the feminine. They would likely agree with Chantal Chawaf that 'in order to reconnect the book with the body and with pleasure, we must disintellectualize writing' (177).

Although Latin-learned men could take advantage of 'benefit of clergy' that enabled them, whether clergy or not, to escape hanging by reading in Latin a prescribed verse from the Scriptures (Dolan, 'Reading,' 145–146), women who could read Latin were not granted this privilege. Anne Askew, however, cleverly exploited her lack of university education to avoid an accusatory question designed to trap her into heresy, which she tells her inquisitor he must answer himself: 'He sayd, it was agaynst the ordre of scoles, that he whych asked the questyon, shuld answer it. I tolde hym, I was but a woman, and knewe not the course of scoles' (34).

In many cases, admission to university education for women was not even a pertinent issue. Elizabeth Cary was brilliantly self-taught, and so earned the right to disparage, in the dedication to her translation of *The Reply to the Most Illustrious Cardinall of Perron* (1630), the limited learning of university-trained men: 'I will not make use of that worne-out forme of saying I printed it against my will, mooved by the importunitie of Friends. I was mooved to it by my beleefe that it might make those English that understood not French, whereof there are many even in our universities, read Perron' (sig. C2). From a different vantage point, Aemilia Lanyer in her *Salve Deus Rex Judaeorum* reorients her supposed 'want of knowledge' and 'slender skill' to a different kind of women's language. Her lack of access to the masculine Symbolic is reconstructed as a benefit; rejecting men's 'learned' discourse, she is able more effectively to locate her defense and praise of women entirely outside male scholarship in the more congenial, maternally instructive realm of Nature, 'That goodly Creature, Mother of Perfection' (10):

> Not that I Learning to myself assume,
> Or that I would compare with any man:
> But as they are Scholers, and by Art do write,
> So Nature yeelds my Soule a sad delight. (9–10)

Like the poet Jane Barker, Lanyer sees learning and knowledge as belonging by first claim to women, through their inheritance from Eve, but stolen from them by men: 'Yet Men will boast of Knowledge, which he tooke / From Eves faire hand, as from a learned Booke' (86). Though she praises the higher reaches of learning in other women, Lanyer's poetry, designed to speak to women, manages very well without, returning to uncorrupted Nature as its encouraging and forgiving maternal Muse and the source of its 'delight.'

Yet another poet, Isabella Whitney, finds that learned books, while 'masing' her 'muse,' induce in her only a 'brused brayne.' She turns therefore to the sensuous pleasures of Hugh Plat's vernacular literary garden to find inspiration for her own book of poetry.[26] An Collins (1653) similarly comments poetically on the limitations of a scholarly education, which may fail to educate morally and instead foster vanity:

> Learning is sure an excellent thing,
> From whence all arts and sciences spring,
> Yet it is not from vanity free,
> For many great scholars profane often be. (41)

Wittily, Collins turns against scholarly men the accusation of profanity that men feared women would derive from a classical education.

For the traditional women's profession of midwifery, male scholarly accomplishments are as irrelevant as they are for women's marital roles and their poetry. Jane Sharp says that some may erroneously think that midwifery should be left to men, 'who are bred up in Universities [and] Schools of Learning' (2), but the Bible establishes a superior precedent for 'Midwives to the perpetual honour of the female Sex,' and not 'so much as one word concerning Men-Midwives mentioned there' (3).

Puritan women and men find a justification for their suspicion of universities in the Biblical injunction that 'Except ye become as a little child, ye shall not enter the kingdom of heaven.' Yet for women, excluded by their gender from the university, these denunciations carry a more personal resonance. Anna Trapnel (1654) foresees Christ's Second Coming, when any amount of 'Deep speech gathered up and fetcht from both *Cambridge* and *Oxford* Universities shal not affright the Lords flock,' not even 'deep subtile speeches, though they be brought forth with a Latine tongue, and in Greek expressions' (55). Similarly, Anne Gargill (1656) warns, 'The Son of righteousness ... will burn up your schools of learning, and ... your Libraries of Books' (30). Mary Cary's prophetic threat of the demise of the universities (1651) also contains the promise of class as well as educational and gender revolution in its wake: 'not onely men but women shall prophesie; ... not onely those that have University-learning but those who have it not; even servants and handmaids' (238). And Hester Biddle also declaims against the spiritual impoverishment and lust for worldly power of university scholars, sniffing around each other for their advantage: 'They that come forth of Oxford and Cambridge, they are such as Isaiah was sent to, to cry woe against, greedy dumb-dogs that never have enough, and love greeting in the market-places, and long prayers in the synagogues and the upper seats at feasts, and be called of men, masters' (165).

As well as centers of classical languages, the universities were training grounds for rhetorical skill, another area theoretically closed to women. Grace Mildmay (1617) excuses herself from using 'Eloquence, exact Method, or learning, which could not proceed from me who have not been trained up in universitie Learning' (31). Margaret Cavendish (1664) also asks: 'how should I write orations, who know no rules in rhetoric, nor never went to school, but only learned to read and write at home' (preface, *Sociable Letters*). Nevertheless, Jane Anger (1589) feels confident that whatever wisdom has been given to her by the grace of Mary will prove of more worth than the corrupted rhetorical skills acquired and misused by men. Her ignorance, after all, she ironically points out, saves her from sophistry:

> Give me leave like a scholar to prove our wisdome more excellent than theirs, though I never knew what sophistry meant. There is no wisdome but it comes by grace ... But grace was first given to a woman, because to our lady ... [T]herefore women are wiser than men ... They [men] run so into Rhetoric as oftentimes they overrun the bounds of their own wits and go they know not whither. (182)

Sarah Ginnor (1659), like Jane Sharp a midwife, also laying claim to a specific kind of women's learning, asserts their right to the display of public eloquence in their own defense: 'Why then should we suffer these Caterpillars to eat up our vine? Let me tell you, it is as lawful for us to be Judges & plead our own Causes in our own gowns as Lawyers to plead for others' (sig. A2).

Rachel Speght, citing exemplars of rhetorical skill in women, praises Cornelia for her eloquence: 'A Roman matron that Cornelia hight, / An eloquent and learned style did write' (5). Bathsua Makin did not need to journey so far back in history to find female examples of rhetorical expertise; her list includes Elizabeth Tudor and Makin's contemporary, Anna Maria Van Schurman: 'We may suppose Schurman and the rest that wrote so elegantly could also speak eloquently upon a just occasion' (12). These examples support Makin's argument for the teaching of logic and rhetoric to women, a goal she shares with Van Schurman, who justifies her advocacy of logic and rhetoric in women's education because they are 'arts which have nearest alliance to theology and the moral virtues' (quoted in Goreau, 165).

On either side of Van Schurman and Makin, two women proposed an institutional resolution for women's mix of suspicious, angry, indifferent, competitive and desirous reactions to learning. Although Martha Moulsworth, writing in 1632, clearly understood that the acquisition of Latin, not being 'mariadge mettall,' might work against her personal marital destiny, she still fantasized about a women's university outside the range of the male educational culture represented by Latin, Greek and rhetorical method. This women's university would overshadow the 'Two Universities we have of men,' and 'in witt, and tongs surpasse / All art of men thatt is, or ever was' (5). Mary Astell, more systematically, in the two volumes of her *Serious Proposal to the Ladies* (1694 and 1697), defending women's intellectual claims to a serious and rigorous education, developed a full-fledged proposal for a separate women's college, outlining its curriculum, its goals and its potential satisfactions, again outside the control of male dictates. Unlike Moulsworth, Astell seeks not to compete with male models of education, but to formulate an independent women's community, grounded in its own satisfactions and pleasures.

Women's textual construction of the 'inside' meaning of their contract with literacy was clearly neither unconscious nor naive about its terms and risks. Sixteenth- and seventeenth-century women's alibis for their learning dramatize the recognition, emphasized by Hélène Cixous, that women pay a 'certain price for the use of a discourse,' but that still preferring 'uneasiness, questioning' to the 'dry and taut' thread of male discourse, they may, nevertheless, 'accept the challenge of the discourse controlled by the phallus,' and affirm each other and their pleasure 'somewhere other than in silence, the place reserved for her in and through the Symbolic' (*Newly-Born Woman*, 92–93). The textual messages of early modern women, in other words, assert the operation of a cultural will to reinscribe the male pedagogical goal requiring exile or submission; these texts establish learning as a source of subjective pleasure for women.

Whatever 'outside' value was placed on women's learning was arguably founded in sixteenth-century liberal humanist idealism about education and its ethical influence. Yet most justifications for both men's and women's education were tied, not to the ideal, but to the weight of pragmatic usefulness. The professions of scholarly study, teaching, the holy ministry, law, medicine and politics, to which women had little or no access, supplied the most obvious practical reasons for men's education. Even as aristocratic courtiers, men had a certain function to perform that was enhanced by wit and learning: to be graceful and at ease in the social and politically charged interchanges at court. But what safe application might women find for their education? Elaine Beilin's view is that 'Tudor theorists were at best ambivalent and at worst prohibitive when considering how women might use their education' (*Redeeming*, 3), for only in exceptional cases were women engaged in the public life that could justify the practical value of a higher education. In those few cases, Castiglione's intellectually able, ideal courtly lady was the model: 'her agreeable and comely conversation suited to the time and place and station of the person with whom she speaks ... was to be the adornment of the social life of the Renaissance courts' (Stock, 37).

Because it might unravel the hierarchical threads of the social fabric, other less privileged women's education needed to be carefully directed to a designated domestic end. The wife who could read, write and possibly also keep accounts, and who became thereby a helpful associate for an up-and-coming, entrepreneurial husband, demonstrated an acceptable use for non-aristocratic women's education. In addition, such a wife might become a useful tutor for servants and children and, like her aristocratic counterpart, prove an entertaining companion to her husband and his friends. Although it seems always to have generated anxiety and resistance in some early modern pundits (for example, in 1614 Thomas Overbury's character of 'The Wife' unequivocally asserts that 'Books are part of a man's prerogative'), the increasing encroachment of women into this privilege was accepted when its application served dominant ideological interests, but was regarded as threatening if seen to subvert those interests. Never should it interfere with women's traditional activities; for Vives and Richard Mulcaster (1581), if the pen competes with the needle, the needle should prevail.

Support for women's education was often therefore vested in their ideologically necessary maternal role. In the seventeenth century, especially, women's education was increasingly valued in the Puritan household for its usefulness in teaching children and servants to read the Scriptures and lead a moral life. In 1620, *An Apology for Women: Or Women's Defense*, by the anonymous C.N., argues: 'Educing, education, and affection are the threefold cords that should tye each child to the love of its mother ... they ... suckle our mindes with the milke of good manners, training us up ... in religion and learning' (48–50). Even earlier, in the sixteenth century, the improved maternal instruction of children was a major justification for women's education. According to Spufford, the early teaching of reading to children was a task that was assumed to belong to the mother. Thomas More argues that 'children can receive a good education at home from their mothers, all except for cultivation and book learning'; for such advanced 'cultivation and learning,' boys would go to the university, where a girl could not follow (More, *Letters*, 95–100). Vives devotes a long chapter in his treatise to the wife's duty to educate her children:

> that they may have all one both for their mother, their nurse, and their teacher. And that they may love her also the more, and learn with better courage and more speed, by means of the love that their teacher hath toward them ... [I]t lieth more in the mother than men ween to make the conditions of their children. (123–124)

The fear of women's persuasive skills, lodged in Eve's inducement of Adam to join her in the fall to knowledge, appears to have been moderated by a confidence in maternal protectiveness, by a judgement that mothers will naturally refrain from teaching their children those things that might damage their chances for social success. Perhaps, as well, we see here an exercise of faith in top-down structures to control any potential upheaval in the social order.

Arguments both supporting and opposing women's education show that many women were at least able to read and also able to teach this skill to their children and to their servants. Suzanne Hull says that 'by 1640, reading by women ... was seen as a necessity' (131).[27] Fewer women could write than read, of course, and the less accessible skill seems to have acquired an aura that attached it to more professional instruction by women in the dame schools or elsewhere. It also was given a pragmatic justification: Martin Billingsley in 1618, advertising his own book on calligraphy, *The Pens Excellencie*, was able to assert that 'the art of writing is so excellent, and of such necessary use' (sig. B4) that it ought to be used by women as an aid to their recognizably limited memories. Its practical value, according to Billingsley, was such that 'no woman surviving her husband, and who hath an estate left to her, ought to be without the use thereof' (sig. B4v). *Pace* Cressy, who initially denied this possibility, women who could read and write seem to have had an important influence in expanding the literate public; the application of maternal caring included sharing with others in their care any instructive material at hand (Spufford, 'First Steps,' 435). Eventually, it proved that, in economically secure groups at least, 'an ill-educated wife or daughter is a sign of social inferiority' (Labalme, 11).

This socially approved, maternal justification for women's education of course inevitably made it possible, in the generation following Vives's and More's permission, for women such as Margaret Hoby, Dorothy Leigh and Elizabeth Joceline to adopt not only what was seen as safely private, but also what was feared as potentially disruptive, publicly instructive roles.[28] As I have argued in the previous chapter, maternity was a space of pleasure and agency for women, and the instructive role associated with maternity might also yield similar pleasure and power. Margaret Hoby writes in her diary on 30 August 1599, that 'she instructed som of my famelie' (67), but a week previously she had also instructed the 'poore and ignorant' (66) in her village.[29] Although her writing life was concentrated in a private genre with only herself for its presumed audience, she was able to express publicly, through teaching in the village, the very skills of reading and writing that made possible the diary's modest and secret pleasure.

Dorothy Leigh (1616) used the justification of maternal instruction to claim a role beyond the merely submissive. She asserts that she has gained authority from her husband to undertake the teaching of her sons, but since he is dead, his ghostly presence allows her to do what in any case she will (sigs A6–A8). She admits that she does not, 'according to the usual custom of women, exhort you by word or admonitions, rather than by writing, a thing so unusual among us, and especially in such time when there be so many godly books in the world that they mould in some men's studies, while their masters are marred because they will not meditate upon them' (14–18). She draws a pointed comparison between men's non-reading and a woman's writing, between men's intellectual passivity and her own activity, between male laziness and her energetic (maternal) virtue, between the misuse and good use of literate skills.

Elizabeth Joceline's *The Mothers Legacie to her Unborne Childe* (1624) uses her expected imminent death in childbirth and her maternal duty as excuses to deliver a set of instructions concerning the education of a daughter. In a prefatory letter to her husband, she circuitously exhorts him to pay particular attention to educating the child if it is a girl. She uses femininely submissive rhetoric to implant in her husband's thoughts the idea of a 'learned daughter': 'If thou desirest ... Yet I leave it to thy will' (sig. B6). Speaking directly to her unborn child, she urges it to 'reserve a time to sit downe to some good study' (48), affirming, in the implicitly risky language of pleasure, desire and temptation, not only the value of 'good study,' but its addictive appeal: 'And when thou hast fixt thy heart to this study, it will be so sweet, that the more thou learnest, the more thou wilt desire' (50). Although, according to Pamela Benson, Thomas More's letters advocating maternal instruction 'acknowledge and attempt to resolve the dilemma of an intellectual independent woman who must restrict her activities to the home' (158), no vocational justification for educating women, no matter how far-reaching, could supply a safe ideological account for women's embracing its innately pleasurable qualities. Justifying women's education in terms of its practical, domestic value for the instruction of servants and children opened the door to behavior and ambition more far-reaching than the dominant point of view permitted, but failed to construct an acceptable ideological domain for women's learning pleasure.

Turning the Outside In: The Pleasure of the Subject

As Elspeth Stuckey points out, 'Becoming literate signifies in large part the ability to conform or at least to appear conformist.' The 'outside' construction of that enacted conformity acknowledges only 'socially acceptable ... ranges of difference and deviance' and socially acceptable 'baselines of gratification' (19). Yet, even though established initially in socially acceptable terms, those 'baselines of gratification' point to the 'inside' pleasure entailed in an activity which women may eventually reconstruct as their own and in relation to which they learn to function as subjects. Mary Astell's description of the learning experience inside her imaginatively constructed female college vividly illustrates the possibility of its separatist and even sensuously gratifying subversive pleasure. Here, learning would be:

> A Joy whose perpetual Current always affords a fresh Delight, and yet every Drop of it is so entertaining, that we might live upon it to all Eternity ... Whilst our Souls are inebriated with its Pleasures, our very Bodies partake of its Sweetness; for it excites a grateful and easie Motion in the animal Spirits, and causes such an agreeable Movement of the Passions as comprehends all that Delight. (*Letters*, 29, quoted in Smith, 124–125)

While Bathsua Makin, in the seventeenth century, played down a public application of women's education and argued conventionally for its benefits to private piety and motherhood, she nevertheless went beyond any sixteenth-century humanist reformer's expectations for women by establishing her own school and insisting that 'the whole encyclopaedia of learning' should be open to any girl so inclined (24). Obviously, the full benefits of education were recognized as extending beyond its public or private application. A primary reason for women to study the usually prohibited physic, Makin says, is 'because this will exceedingly please themselves' (24). Although she somewhat disingenuously argues that housewifery requires a thorough grounding in languages and science, she urges women to discover in education a means to subjectivity, 'to set a right value upon themselves, according to the dignity of their creation, that they might, with an honest pride and magnanimity, scorn to be bowed down and made to stoop to such follies and vanities, trifles and nothings, so far below them and unproportionable to their noble souls' (41–42).

The same grounds of Makin's hope for the results of women's education had been a matter of concern for Edward Gosynhill in 1541, when he denounced a 'schoolhouse of women,' in which older women might teach the younger to 'Cherish yourself all that ye may' (141). Gathered together in gossips' meetings, Gosynhill feared, women would teach each other that which is detrimental to men: 'Thus learn the younger of the elders' guiding; / Day by day, keeping such schools, / The simple men they make as fools.' What is worse, this learning is accompanied by the subversive pleasure of 'good cheer.' While Makin encourages women to the intertwined pleasures of learning physic and setting 'a right value upon themselves,' Gosynhill's masculine perspective views the mixing of women's learning with 'good cheer' as dangerous. Even though the differences of construction in Gosynhill and Makin may be partially assigned to the changes in social attitude in the decades between 1541 and 1673, fears similar to Gosynhill's were still being expressed in 1697: women's learning communities, shockingly, may encourage women to think of themselves as subjects, 'to think there was something precious in you, meerly from the natural desire after what's forbidden, [so that you] should relapse from our [men's] Original Reason, and again learn to esteem and value that trifle Woman' (*The Challenge Sent by a Young Lady*, 54).[30]

The pleasures of learning and intellectual play, not obviously attached to any practical use, but potentially enhancing women's subjectivity, were apparent to education's advocates and practitioners, as well as its detractors. Kathryn King points out that for Anna Maria Van Schurman 'learning was divorced from both salon and seat of power, and was an end in itself' (179). Van Schurman sees women's leisure, so worrying for men as a crucible for women's mischief, as a space in which the pleasures of learning may be nurtured. She represents two of the most vehement hegemonic claims on women – chastity and domestic enclosure – as the very most favorable conditions for learning. If women are confined and sedentary, and/or un(hetero)sexual, what better way to spend their time than in quietly pleasurable, scholarly pursuits? Van Schurman points out that there will always be 'spare hours' from a woman's 'exercises of piety and household affairs' (3), that may be satisfyingly filled with study.

Their needles were obviously not always the preferred instruments of self-inscription for women in the seventeenth century. Some actively chose to find pleasure elsewhere, in their own mental or written inscriptions; some chose a pen instead of a needle, and some a combination of both. Anne Bradstreet disputes those who say 'a needle better fits' her hand than her pen; Lucy Hutchinson 'hated' her needle when it competed with Latin, and later, ambidextrously, learned to use needle and pen together. The authors of *The Women's Sharpe Revenge* reject the pricking of their needles as a substitute for a liberal education; the anonymous author of *Advice to the Women and Maidens of London* urges women to cease working with lace and needlecraft and learn instead to write and keep accounts. The speaker in the *Triumphs of Female Wit* asks indignantly whether 'the Excellency of a Female Soul could possibly be raised no higher than the management of a Needle or the ingenuity of a Pudding' (preface). Margaret Cavendish had no skill with her needle but was voraciously curious about intellectual disciplines; she chose to study and write poetry, to spin 'with the braine' (*Poems and Fancies*, dedicatory epistle). Catherine des Roches determined to retain the pleasures of both; neither Bathsua Makin nor Anna Maria Van Schurman accepted the necessity of choosing one to the exclusion of the other.

Some male commentators on women's education explicitly denounce pleasure as an end of women's learning, and language alluding less directly to that disquieting possibility also intrudes in many concerned discussions. In particular, the connection of pleasure with learning is seen as threatening women's patriarchally valued and monitored chastity. Stirred by the pleasure of their studies, which Erasmus acknowledges may incite a 'wilder enthusiasm than any other of the arts' (*De Institutione Christ. Matrimonis*, 663), and undisciplined by masculine Reason, women may intensify their already disturbing social challenge.

The whole range of intellectual pleasure available to women, decoded by the image of the curious and seductive Eve, is consistently linked in male texts with sexual temptation and corruption, which is why Vives forbids the texts of Ovid and other 'lewd' classical authors, as well as those of the romances of Tirant lo Blanc, Guy of Warwick and Bevis of Hampton which, he imagines, may incite this kind of response: 'What madness is it of folks to have pleasure in these books?' (Watson, 59). Such books, claims Vives, are analogous to the serpent who tempted Eve and may precipitate similar havoc: 'a woman should beware of all these books, likewise as of serpents and snakes. And if there be any woman that hath such delight in these books, that she will not leave them out of her hands: she should not only be kept from them, but also if she read good books with an ill will and loath thereto, her father and friends should provide that she be kept from all reading, and so by disuse forget learning' (61–62). For Richard Brathwaite, women, as inheritors of the 'lightness of their mother Eve,' make 'Pleasure their Vocation' (299), and this will only be enhanced by the wrong sort of reading. Daniel Tuvill reports the same fear, shadowed by women's role in Eden, in those who believe that 'the pen must be forbidden them [women] as the tree of good and evil' (Goreau, 35).

Vives's effort to dampen women's pleasure takes the form of recommending the reading of 'sad sentences' (Watson, 55) of 'wise and learned men' (62), perhaps of the kind that caused Christine de Pizan such unhappiness. His wish is that 'she that hath learned from inborn disposition or from books to consider this and such other things, and hath furnished her mind with holy counsels, shall never find to do any villainy' (49). Like Cleobula, the chastely learned woman should have 'clearly despised all pleasure of the body' (50). Women are, however, easily led astray from the 'goodly and pure pleasure' (54) of the mind which Vives hopes to foster in women's education; 'for how foul, how light, and transitory an image of pleasure she changeth: what a sort of ungraciousness she letteth in, what time she shutteth forth chastity: nor pondereth what bodily pleasure is, how vain and foolish a thing' (49). Although Vives intends that properly educated women 'shall leave all such light and trifling pleasures, wherein the fantasies of maids have delight' (52), the flaw in his plan for the control of their education is that once they can read, women, naturally 'disposed to pleasure and dalliance' (41), will surely where possible choose their own pleasurable reading matter. That this was frequently the case is made clear by Vives's peremptory recommendation that fathers and friends should prevent pleasure-seeking women from reading at all and thus make them 'forget learning.'

Thomas Salter states explicitly a fear of women's pleasure in recreational reading, which appears to be, from his point of view, always constructed pornographically. Women readers should be separated from 'lascivious books' about 'filthy love' and 'wicked adulteries and abominable fornications.' He goes on:

> [T]ouching recreation by learning, that cannot be granted her without great danger and offence to the beauty and brightness of her mind ... seeing also that in such studies as yieldeth recreation and pleasure, there is no less danger that they will learn to be subtle and shameless lovers, as cunning and skillfull writers of ditties, sonnets, epigrams and ballads. (sigs C1–C1v)

The significant merging in these passages of different kinds of sexual, reading and poetry-writing pleasures points up the contemporary male fear that all pleasure actively sought by women contains the seeds of sexual trouble. This 'trouble' is, perhaps, as much in the image of a woman pursuing pleasure for herself as in the sexual act itself.

Thomas More is beset by a similar worry, in reference to classical texts: '[M]any things that be written in the Latin and Greek tongue, compiled and made with great craft and eloquence, where the matter is haply sometime more sweet unto the ear than wholesome for the mind, it would of likelihood both inflame their stomachs a great deal the more unto that vice, that men say they be too much given unto of their own nature already' (Watson, 162–163). More, Hyrde and Mulcaster, like Vives, hope that the pleasures to be found in learning will combat women's essential 'instability and mutable nature,' their 'pleasure of a contentious mind' (More, in Watson, 163) and their 'peevish fancies' (Hyrde, in Watson, 167). While their natural 'towardnesse' (Mulcaster, 167) may make them apt pupils, 'their natural weakness ... as of a moonish influence' (176) may also render them undisciplined and unable to appreciate the purer 'fruit, profit and pleasure [that] cometh of learning' (Hyrde, in Watson, 168). *The Ladies Dictionary* in 1694 still lamented that 'the reading of many wanton things do heat by little and little ... after that these pamphlets and songs of wantonness, have made young maidens bold, it afterwards doth make them to practise what they read ... These are but cunning lessons, to learn young maids to sin more wittily' (Goreau, 58). Although male theorists of women's education recognize the intellectual pleasures of learning, they are wary of the possibility that this variety of pleasure, when experienced by women, may slide into the sensual.

For many nervous husbands, fathers and tutors, concern with women's chastity reaches the level of fetish. Women's ultimate and sufficient knowledge sometimes seems to be no more than knowledge of their chastity. They need to learn to perfect chastity, to be educated in its importance and to study how to protect it. According to Vives, 'these things ought to be seen unto, for as much as chastity in bringing up a woman requires the utmost diligence' (Watson, 55). Yet, disquietingly, only women can know whether they are chaste; this is not a sphere of knowledge that men may always control. Perhaps some of the concern associated with women's education is that, turning their attention to pleasure-producing learning endeavors, and ceasing to attend obsessively to their chastity, they may absent-mindedly or ignorantly mislay it; pursuing one pleasure, they may snare another. The study of her insecure chastity seems to be conceived as a full-time occupation for a woman, from which she will easily be distracted by the lure of any means of pleasure.

One believes, of course, that male agitation over women's suspected tendency to use reading as semi-pornographic stimulus derives from men's own such use.[31] As women reclaim their control over, and pleasure in, the experiences of learning, reading and writing, they hardly, if at all, construct the pleasure available from these pursuits in sexual terms. Pleasure and desire are inevitably multiplistic and complex, and always mediated through available cultural terms. Even so, women's own comments on their learning experiences reposition women as subjects of their own pleasure and choice. It is instructive to consider Elizabeth Walker's insistence on the factor of choice in the experience of pleasure, although this example occurs just within the range of our interest in early modern women (1690), and connects rather with issues of love than of learning. Having asked her husband to say why he loves her, she rejects his first claim to his conscience, explaining, with reference more to her own understanding of subjectivity than to his rhetoric of love, that she prefers to have him love her 'not as a duty but delight. For we are prone to reluctate against what is imposed, but to take pleasure in what we choose' (*Holy Life*, 27, quoted in Fraser, 50).

Although Judith Teague and Eugene Kintgen claim that early modern readers 'would not take up a book for amusement or simply to pass the time' (Teague, 367), vociferous warnings against this very habit among women, and women's own comments on their reading, suggest otherwise. Kintgen asserts that 'What is lacking in this whole process, from our point of view, is any conception of reading as an end in itself, as a pleasurable aesthetic experience valuable in its own right' (44); the term 'aesthetic' may be a problematizing factor in this claim, but the *dulce* of learning and reading did exist independently of their *utile* in early modern perceptions and practice, as is evident in the distinction Margaret Hoby draws in her diary between days when she did or did not read something 'recreational' (Hull, 84).

In the cultural effort to control the experiences of readerly and writerly pleasure in women, the dominant ideology supported a wished-for overriding of pleasure by profit, and also at the same time needed constantly to countermand the inevitable alternative. Kintgen quotes John Lyly as advising women to choose books that will 'last longest' and 'endure soundest' (9–10), but these comments are coupled with Lyly's understanding that women will choose books to please themselves, as they insist on choosing 'cloth that will weare whitest, not that will last longest, coulours that looke freshest, not that endure soundest.' In his dedication to *Euphues and his England* (1580), addressed to the 'Ladies and Gentlewomen of England,' Lyly hopes to benefit from this habit: 'I would you would read bookes that have more shewe of pleasure, then ground of profit, then should Euphues be as often in your hands, being but a toy, as Lawne on your heads.' Lyly acknowledges – and of course seeks to exploit for his own profit – women's ability to choose their reading pleasures. Yet he too sexualizes this choice – *Euphues* will share with 'little [pet] Dogges' the enviable position of alternating time in the hands, and lying in the laps 'ready to sport,' of his women readers (8–9).

The female counterparts to the male pedagogues who declaimed on women's education wrote in the seventeenth rather than the sixteenth century, but they sum up recognitions surely available from the beginning of women's increased literacy. Their discussions are unapologetically filled with paeans to the positively valued pleasures to be found in learning and reading. For Anna Maria Van Schurman, these pleasures are not (hetero)sexual; indeed they are most easily accessible to the woman who has independent control of her body, whose leisure and concentration are not interrupted by the duties of marriage; even in the very requirements of 'the Apostle,' who 'requireth women to be keepers at home,' there may be found the perfect conditions for a different kind of pleasure than that which St Paul sought to curtail in women:

> That which affecteth and replenisheth the Mind with honest and ingenious delight, is convenient for a Christian Woman: But, Learning doth so ... [N]othing is more agreeable to humane nature, then honest and ingenious delight ... Pleasure is by nature a Divine thing ... [T]here is no delight or pleasure (except that which is of Christians which is supernatural) either more worthy of an ingenuous soul, or greater then this, which ariseth from the study of Letters. (vii–xiv)

For Bathsua Makin, the illustrative text for women's enjoyment of learning outside the constructions of male commentators is, interestingly, Erasmus's dialogue between an abbot and a well-read woman, Magdalia. The abbot argues against women's learning, advising instead that they enjoy themselves in an indulgence of the senses. Magdalia, however, defends the greater pleasures of learning: 'What if I enjoy reading a good author more than you do hunting, drinking, or playing dice?' (*Erasmus on Women*, 175). For the abbot, there is only one kind of pleasure that women can be expected to enjoy. Magdalia, however, unravels the differences between her point of view and the abbot's, appropriating for women the pleasures of learning, scorned by the abbot, who says, 'I wouldn't want my monks to spend their time on books' (175).

For Erasmus, this dialogue offers a humorous comment on the corruption of the clergy which is so profound that even a woman knows better where to find more adequate pleasures. For Makin, the dialogue seriously resituates the emphasis on Magdalia's superior capacity for the enjoyment of intellectual pleasure: 'I remember a discourse in Erasmus, between an abbot and a learned woman ... [S]he found a great content in reading good authors at spare times' (23). The sensual, most often associated with women as an argument against their claim to the pleasures of learning, is reassigned here to men, who, it now appears, project their own sensual obsessions onto women. More pointedly, while advocating the building of schools for girls, Makin says, 'I expect to meet with many scoffs and taunts from inconsiderate and illiterate men, that prize their own lusts and pleasures more than your profit and content' (4). What Makin describes elsewhere as women's 'pleasure' in learning, becomes a quieter 'content,' when placed beside men's 'pleasures,' now associated with lust. The rhetorical tables have been well and truly turned.

We have already seen Makin's justification for women's learning physic in that it 'will exceedingly please themselves' (24). Her general defense of women's learning, echoing Van Schurman's, repetitively emphasizes its inherent and potential pleasures, unfairly withheld from women by men:

> Their quality ties them at home. If learning be their companion, delight and pleasure will be their attendants, for there is no pleasure greater nor more suitable to an ingenious mind than what is found in knowledge ... There is in all an innate desire of knowing, and the satisfying this is the greatest pleasure. Men are very cruel that give them leave to look at a distance, only to know that they do not know. To make any thus to tantalize is a great torment. (24)

Also, she says, if women were educated, 'the advantage would be very great: the women should have honor and pleasure, their relations profit, and the whole nation advantage' (27). In an elegy written for Lady Elizabeth Langham, who died in 1664, Makin again emphasizes the compensatory pleasure found by this woman in her studies: 'Her hours were all precisely kept, and spent / In her devotions; and her studies meant / To share some for her languages, which she / In Latin, French, Italian happily / Advanced in with pleasure' (*Kissing the Rod*, 226).

Any doubt that Van Schurman's claim to learning's pleasure was simply mimicked by Makin and that this emphasis in their two defenses is aberrational in women's writing, is easily dispelled.[32] And not just because Elizabeth Cary, with whom I opened this chapter, 'loved [reading] much' (*Life*, 186) and, when 'her whole employment was reading and writing' (264), was 'never more merry nor better content' (212). In both sixteenth- and seventeenth-century women's texts, where mention is made of their educational experiences, so also excitement about the pleasures of learning frequently recurs. Although there are few formal defenses of their right to learn, such as those developed by Van Schurman and Makin, among the passing comments by women on their reading and writing, an unusual number employ language that ranges from expressions of mild satisfaction to assertions of passionate pleasure. That this pleasure was often solitary or experienced in the company of other women supplied another cause for concern in women's patriarchal watchdogs and an added component of subjective differentiation for women themselves.

A well-known, poignant passage illustratively confirming a woman's intense solacing pleasure in solitary study is found in Roger Ascham's richly evocative account of his visit to the ill-starred Jane Grey. He writes: 'I found her in her chamber reading *Phaedon Platonis* in Greek, and that with as much delight as some gentlemen read a merry tale in Boccaccio.' When Ascham asks why she is not hunting in the park with her parents and gentlewomen, she replies with full didactic conviction, 'I wisse, al their sport in the park is but a shadow to that plesure that I find in Plato. Alas! Good folk, they never felt what true pleasure meant.' Compared to the misery of her objectified life away from her studies, 'so without mesure misordered,' and fraught with harsh parental discipline, 'my book hath been so much plesure and more, that in respect of it, al other pleasures in very deed be but trifles and troubles to me' (sigs Eiii–iv). In her discovery of pleasure in the study of Plato, this sad young woman also discovers a subjective authority that enables her to pity the athletically occupied parents who normally fail to pity her. Jane Grey's cleaving to her studies as a resource for subjective confidence is not unlike Elizabeth Cary's disobedient retreat from her mother's and mother-in-law's discipline to her books. Both these women found in the process of learning a precious space to realign their social inscription as obedient and subdued daughters.

Another royal woman, like Jane Grey caught in the toils of conspiratorial politics, found comfort in the pleasures of studying and interpreting not the classics but the Scriptures. Elizabeth Tudor, for the moment imprisoned, exerted some control over her situation by self-sufficiently cultivating the sweet food of her reading; in the blank space in the margin of her copy of Paul's Epistles, she wrote, 'I walk many times into the pleasant fields of the holy Scriptures where I pluck up the goodlisome herbs of sentences by pruning, eat them by reading, chew them by musing ... that so having tasted the sweetness I may the less perceive the bitterness of this miserable life' (Nichols, I.9–10). Anne Dowriche's preface to her translation of *The French History* (1589) also confirms the self-confident subjectivity revealed to women by means of the pleasures to be found in study and writing. To her brother she proclaims, '[I]f I were sure that you would take but half so much pleasure in reading it, as I have in collecting and disposing it, I should not need any further to commend it' (sig. A2 ii).

Women poets, especially, frequently reiterate the pleasures of writing, reading and learning. Dedicating her *Sweet Nosgay* (1573) to Charles Mainwaring, Isabella Whitney hopes that he will 'take pleasure' in her poetic offerings. In her own reading of the compositions of Hugh Plat, she tells us in her address from 'The Auctor to the Reader,' she herself has been enabled by Fortune to 'pleasures feele' (sig. 3A). The process of writing her poems she likens to the sensuously pleasurable gathering and distributing of a bunch of sweet-smelling and health-producing herbs. Those who read her poems will in them comfort and 'pleasure finde' (sig. 3Bii). The subjectively satisfying pleasures of writing and reading empower Whitney confidently to declare, 'for this I say the Flowers are good / which I on thee bestow' (sig. 4A).

Rachel Speght (1621) teases out still more definitively the tropes used by Whitney. Speght experiences '*Ignorance*' as 'griefe' (2). Afflicted by it, she says, 'I feele disease, yet know not what I ayle, / I finde a sore, but can no salve provide; / I hungry am, yet cannot seeke for foode' (2). Her cure is found in '*Knowledge*,' located in '*Eruditions* garden,' and supported by '*Desire*' (4). The presence of desire in justifying this poet's claim to knowledge marks a process of subjective construction at odds with the controlled inhibition of women's learning ordained by male commentators. 'Wherefore,' asks Speght, 'shall / A woman have her intellect in vaine, / Or not endeavor *Knowledge* to attaine' (71). The revealing appearance of 'choyce' in this process of knowledge acquisition, set in motion by desire, and ambiguously assigned to God or Mary, establishes women's subjectivity inside a framework of divine intent: 'The God of *Knowledge* nothing gave in vaine. / 'Twas *Maries* choyce our Savior did approve' (71). And, finally, the claim of knowledge is confirmed by its almost addictive 'pleasure'; Speght tells the reader that any sacrifice would be acknowledged as worthwhile, 'If thou didst know the pleasure of the place, / Where *Knowledge* growes' (72). Her own intent, reinforced by desire and the expectation of pleasure, is firm:

> When *Truth* had ended what shee meant to say,
> *Desire* did move me to obey her will,
> Whereto consenting I did soone proceede,
> Her counsell, and my purpose to fulfille;
> And by the help of *Industrie* my friend,
> I quickly did attaine my journeyes end.

Where, being come, *Instructions* pleasant ayre
Refresht my senses, which were almost dead,
And fragrant flowers of sage and fruitfull plants,
Did send sweete savours up into my heade;
And taste of science appetite did move,
To augment *Theorie* of things above.

There did the harmonie of those sweete birds,
(Which higher soare with Contemplations wings,
Then barely with a superficiall view,
Denote the value of created things.)
Yeeld such delight as made me to implore,
That I might reape this pleasure more and more. (72)

An Collins (1653) confesses to her reader that the 'inflaming' pleasures of poetry have for her also been well-nigh addictive: 'To be brief I became affected to poetry, insomuch as I proceeded to practise the same; and though the helps I had therein were small, yet the thing itself appeared unto me so amiable as that it inflamed my faculties to put forth themselves in a practice so pleasing' (sig. A1). She finds 'no small content' in 'Songs or counterfets of Poesies' (Preface to *Divine Songs*). The enviable pleasures of learning, available to men but not to women, are represented by Jane Barker (1688) as 'Luxurious Banquets of this dainty Fruit' (4). The language of luxury and desirous 'longing' emphasizes women's sense of the pleasures available in the fruit of knowledge, originally forbidden by God, but earned by women in Eden, now again unfairly refused them by men who themselves eat at its feast:

... Altho' our Eyes
Do serve our longing Souls to tantalize,
Whilst kinder fate for you do's constitute
Luxurious Banquets of this dainty Fruit.
Whose Tree most fresh and flourishing do's grow,
E'er since it was transplanted amongst you.
('Invitation to My Friends at Cambridge,' 3–4)

Bathsua Makin, too, agrees that 'women were the inventors of many of these [seven liberal] arts [including poetry], and the promoters of them, and since have studied them and attained to excellency in them' (21). Yet, in spite of their original and continuing ownership, their pleasure in learned poetic accomplishment is undermined by the male 'account' of women poets, as 'giddy-headed gossips, fit only to discourse of their hens, ducks, and geese,' who, if they should be 'suffered to meddle with arts and tongues ... by intolerable pride ... should run mad' (16). But Makin is able to point to the poetic achievements of Anne Bradstreet, Katherine Philips, Jane Grey, Queen Elizabeth, Mary Sidney and Lord Burghley's three daughters, to refute this 'outside' construction (19–20).

Margaret Cavendish, like Mary Astell some years later, responded to the same 'outside' disapproval by imaginatively constructing a private 'convent of pleasure' (1668) as a space in which women would regain control over their learning lives and retreat from an order in which men 'hold books as their crown, and the sword as their sceptre, by which they rule and govern' (*Poems and Fancies*, sig. A3). There they will nurture their subjective pleasures, merging the three crucial satisfactions of subjectivity; freedom, learning and gratification of the senses: 'my Cloister shall not be a Cloister of restraint, but a place for freedom, not to vex the Senses, but to please them' (7). Free to choose a conjunction of intellectual and sensuous pleasure, they do so, not as the seducers of male peace nervously warned against in male texts, but, independently, inside a separate community of women.

An extra spice added to the pleasures of study was the solitude that sometimes accompanied it. If the early modern period nurtured a social concern about any form of pleasure experienced by women outside masculine control, this anxiety intensified when the pleasure could only be suspiciously imagined because occurring in a physical space not available to the male gaze. The increasingly fashionable 'closet' in which early modern people often read and wrote[33] was a place of possible solitude which evoked worry about the dangers of an inner life not subject to cultural sanctions. Robert Horne's *Christian Governor*, for example, in 1614, warned that when in their private rooms, people should 'do nothing that shall be uncomely' or anything they 'should be ashamed should it be brought before the face of men' (sigs G8, H1).

Roger Chartier comments, 'personal communion with a read or written text liberated the individual from the old mediators, freed him or her from the control of the group, and made it possible to cultivate *an inner life*' ('The Practical Impact,' 116). If, as Chartier contends, 'reading contributed to the emergence of a sense of self, as the reader scrutinized his own thoughts and emotions in solitude and secrecy' (151), this process of private subjectivity, when engaged in by women, was often coded in early modern texts as a dangerous escape from patriarchal control.[34] An *Acte for thadvauncement of true Religion*, passed in 1542, held the private reading of the Bible as a special privilege permissible only to noblewomen and gentlewomen, presumably thought not to embody a serious threat to society because of their material investment in the *status quo*. Otherwise, 'no woomen nor artificers prentises journeymen serving men of the degrees of yeomen or undre, husbandmen not laborers' could read the English Bible 'privatelie or openlie.' Vives, trying to close both sources of trouble, says girls should never be alone, except for prayer, nor in a crowd, for the sake of their chastity (84–89). Their studying is to take place in an in-between space, permitting maximum supervision of the student by the instructor or her mother. Grace Mildmay's footsteps were constantly dogged by her appointed companion, 'And when I was not with her she would be sure to be with me at my heels to see where and with whom I was and what I did or spake' (quoted in Warnicke, 132).

Of course, privacy and solitude were also seen, conversely, as admirable states for women. According to Henry Smith's *Preparative for Marriage* (1591), the chaste woman, caring to please only one (presumably her husband), 'keeps her closet as though she were still at prayer' (79). Smith's contemporary Philip Stubbes (1591) lavishly praises his own wife because she was solitary:

> And so solitary was she given, that she very seldom or never, and then not neither except her husband were in company, go abroad with any, either to banquet or feast, to gossip or make merry as they term it: insomuch that she was noted by some (though most untruly) to do it in contempt or disdain of others. (*Christal*, sig. A2 ii)

In 1638, John Ley, preaching a sermon on the death of Jane Ratcliffe, both acknowledged her 'incredible desire and delight' in reading 'good Books,' and praised her for attempting to 'keep her skills in scripture reading and teaching [her children and servants] a secret' (Clarke, 416–417). And a century after Stubbes, *The Ladies Dictionary* (1694) was advising that the most desirable state for a woman was to be enclosed inside her husband's house. Women's writing, if at all approved, was preferably associated with manuscript circulation: Jeffrey Masten argues that in Mary Wroth's *Urania*, manuscripts passed between women are represented as a 'withdrawal into a privatized discursive space,' as opposed to the undesirable 'making public, the circulation, of a woman's story' ('Shall I,' 79).[35]

Yet Richard Brathwaite acknowledges the double-barreled and therefore even more uncontrollable significance of women's solitude: 'Privacy is the seat of Contemplation; though sometimes made the recluse of Tentation' (294). Similarly ambivalent in its implications, silence, accompaniment to solitude, is 'our sweetest Conference; where the retired becomes either the best or worst friend to himselfe' (294). Brathwaite warns that a woman welcoming privacy, congratulating herself that 'the walls encompasse mee, darkenesse o're-shadowes mee, the Curtaine of night secures mee,' is speaking 'the wordes of an Adulteresse' (297); he worries lest she will choose to read 'Sibariticke stories' (297) in the privacy of her closet. Here again, the expressed concern is that women's pleasurable solitude will compound their illicit urge to sexuality, in particular that their secret reading will intensify this obsessive need. Enacting submission to enclosure and privacy, women might move to independent solitude and then to secrecy, with unpredictable results.

Many women, Elizabeth and Lettice Cary among them, did indulge in the sometimes secret luxury of private reading; Lettice was 'oft-times at a book in her Closet when she was thought to be in bed' (quoted in Fraser, 30). Dorcas Bennet, in the preface to her *Good and Seasonable Counsel* (1670), says she studied 'while others slept.' The Copley sisters had their books in bed with them when, suspected of Catholic sympathies, they were interrogated at night. This incident seems to suggest that women's practice of secret night reading stimulated suspicion against them. The sisters cleverly left their copy of Virgil out as a red herring to turn off their interrogators, but concealed their more precious and more subversive Catholic texts in the bedclothes (Grundy, 136–137). Anne Clifford retreated to her closet for the comfort of books during periods of marital strife (January 1617), though she was not always alone there; at times during the winter of 1617, members of her household, Rivers, Moll Neville, Kate Duchin and her cousin Maria, read to her.

Women's writing, being especially dubious, often took place in an atmosphere of secrecy. As Sara Mendelson points out, the characteristic woman's genre of the diary is a mode of secret writing, especially when, as in the cases of Elizabeth Bury and Elizabeth Dunton, the diaries were written in a private shorthand (Mendelson, 'Stuart Women's Diaries,' 184). While shorthand was a method of writing and note-taking not confined to women, it provided yet another means for women to remove their writing from masculine surveillance.[36] Anne Clifford, Alice Thornton, Grace Mildmay and Margaret Hoby kept faithful and detailed diaries and journals. The daily writing of a private diary, in the same way that Chartier suggests of private reading, enhances introspection, self-evaluation and the possibility of writing the self as subject through concentrated attention on the diary's 'I.' That women felt the urge to protect the privacy of their writings from the censoring masculine eye is evident in the comments quoted by Sara Mendelson: Katherine Austen said her diary 'concerned none but my self & was a private exercise directed to my self'; Elizabeth Walker asked her husband not to read her diary as long as she lived ('Stuart Women's Diaries,' 184–185). This sense of the privacy of the written word undertaken by the female subject extended to other forms of writing: Brilliana Harley asks her son to destroy the letters she secretly sends him: 'Your father dous not knowe ... Nobody in the Howes knows I send to you' (16, quoted in Walker, 36).

Just as the pleasure of writing is especially celebrated by poets, so also solitude is a regular accompaniment and even stimulus to their poetic composition. Isabella Whitney is 'all sole alone' when her *Sweet Nosegay* of poetry begins to come into being. Left solitary by the exodus of Margaret Russell and Anne Clifford from Cookham, Aemilia Lanyer turns to the writing of her long poem. Katherine Philips, enacting social expectations, writes self-protectively and passionately, in the 1664 preface to her *Poems*, about the invasion of others into her precious imaginative space. For her, as for Whitney, it was solitude or 'want of company' that 'seduced [her] to write': 'I thought a rock and a mountain might have hidden me, and that it had been free for all to spend their solitude in what reveries they please ... but 'tis only I who am that unfortunate person that cannot so much as think in private, that must have my imaginations rifled and exposed.'

For Jane Barker, in 'An Invitation to my Friends at Cambridge' (1688), the solitude of a studious life compares to the pleasures of Paradise:

> 'Tis such a pleasing solitude as yet
> Romance ne're found, where happy Lovers met
> Yea such a kind of solitude it is,
> Not much unlike to that of Paradise. (3)

A 'Virgin Life' also permits a personal space for learning. The virgin's closet is a place of solitude in which she can enjoy her own society and books:

> Her Closet, where she do's much time bestow,
> Is both her Library and her Chappel too,
> Where she enjoys society alone,
> I'th' Great Three-One ... (13)

At those times when one seeks human as well as divine company, the virgin life offers the extra pleasurable dividend of the right to choose one's own friends:

> She drives her whole Lives business to these Ends,
> To serve her God, enjoy her Books and Friends. (13)

The denial to women of a public life and public acquisition and application of their learning drove them to secret and solitary reading and writing pleasures, transforming the socially required private woman into a worrisome image of illicit subversion, but for women, the discovery of the intrinsic pleasures of learning justified their enclosure and made their solitude precious.[37] Anna Maria Van Schurman (1659) deployed the social expectation of women's privacy to argue for their right to learning: 'The study of letters is convenient for them, for whom it is more decent to find themselves both business and recreation at home and in private than abroad among others' (quoted in Goreau, 167). Bathsua Makin (1673) also insists that private persons, most usually women, are best suited for learning.

Postscript: Dressing Pleasures

The association of women's learning with the pleasure that generated concern in its male overseers and desire in women themselves is confirmed by an apparently odd, but relatively frequent, analogy of women's taste for learning's pleasure, which adorned their minds, with their taste for the pleasures of fashionable dress, which adorned their bodies. A few comments on this intriguing connection will conclude this chapter. Like a web of interwoven threads, the network of ideas in the early modern English mind relating to women's reading and writing contained among others the following images, most of them readily visualized: women reading and writing; their intellectual and, from a suspicious point of view, sexual pleasure; the spaces of secrecy and solitude sometimes connected with these experiences; the innate frivolity that characterized and dictated women's reading and writing; and, finally, the external, sensuous expression of their frivolity in their fascination with luxurious and fashionable dress.

The spider at the center of the web, named or not, is of course Eve, who, gaining access to knowledge, subsequently needed to clothe herself for shame. In the sixteenth and seventeenth centuries, women, as daughters of Eve, are still seen as dangerously desiring learning and taking improper pleasure both in knowledge and in the dress that should be the covering of their shame, but instead has been manipulated into a further source of pleasure. We have already seen earlier in this chapter the humorous comments by Lyly about women's preference for books that will give them pleasure, analogized to their preference for the whitest linen and freshest colors over something more durable, and Thomas Elyot's concern about women misdirecting their 'wit,' which may help them learn, to the 'trymmynge them selfes with praty devyses' (*Defense*, 33). Philip Stubbes's *Anatomie of Abuses* links a lengthy diatribe on the vanity of women's preoccupation with dress to an attack on their potential abuse of educational privilege. Richard Mulcaster worries about the pleasure women take in amorous books, ballads, songs and sonnets, but almost in the same breath he worries about their bodily adornment: it is 'shameful and unseemly ... for any woman to learn from another how to adorn herself after the latest fashion, so to display her bodily beauty without respect for the comelier virtues of the mind' (23). Mulcaster thinks that women's education, properly directed presumably by a male instructor, should lead to virtue, but misdirected and falling into the hands of another woman it will surely focus on the frivolous and luxurious pleasures of fashion and adornment. Thomas Salter (1579) attacked schoolmistresses and those other teachers, mothers, for their love of expensive dress; he urged a 'practical education' as an antidote, perhaps fearing that an education enjoyed for its own intellectual pleasure might foster in women the ability to choose other sources of their own gratification, in clothes this time, rather than in 'filthy love' and 'abominable fornication' (sigs C1–C1v).

Edward Hake complains that daughters and wives of ordinary gentlemen and citizens spend as much on clothes in two years as would keep a (male) university student for four or five years (D2r); the suggested competition for family funds has some interesting undercurrents. Women's dress appears to be opposed to men's education in a way that suggests that their sensuous pleasure in dress may be regarded by Hake, and perhaps by women too, as compensation for the alternative intellectual pleasures of a university education which they are denied. For the male commentator, the connection between women's learning and clothing is drawn through notions of frivolity, excess, waste and the always underlying issue of women's self-claimed pleasure. If directed by male husbands or teachers, women's learning and clothes-wearing may be seen as passive and appropriately restricted, but if women themselves choose for pleasure what they read or wear, they may tap into their capacity for subjective agency. The notorious 'Counterfeit Lady' epitomized the cultural fear that women's education would lead to deception and social disruption through their self-assertion. K.F., the narrator of the lady's story (1673), tells us that she posed successfully as a woman of rank, though she was not one, thereby subverting social and class hierarchies. Here, too, connections among women's education, conscious self-representation, their pleasure and love of finery, are established:

> I can say little of her education, only those that knew her when young, relate that she was very much addicted to her pleasure, loved fine Clothes and gallantry, and endeavored to exceed her betters in the bravery of her habit, that she took much pleasure in reading,

> especially Love Books ... and from her frequent and often reading, she believing all she read to be true, was much in love with the actions of those great and renowned Heroes, and supposed herself to be no less than a *Heroine*. (9–10)

The royal road to social perdition is apparently paved with women's pleasure and the encouragement, by their reading and writing, to think of themselves as subjects, to suppose themselves to be '*Heroines*'!

The connection between the comforts of pretty dress (Thomas Elyot's 'praty devyses') and the comforts of reading and writing appears also in some women's texts, perhaps implanted there by male pressure concerning both spheres of women's possible choice. Anne Clifford's diary for January 1617 records that on the 8th, 'my lord and I had a falling out,' and on the 9th, 'I went up to see to things in the closet and began to have Mr. Sandys' book read to me about the government of the Turks, my lord sitting the most part of the day reading in his closet.' The wife finds comfort in books in her closet, while the husband, estranged, also reads in his. On the 28th, though, 'at this time I wore my plain green flannel gown that William Punn made me, and my yellow taffety waistcoat. Rivers used to read to me in Montaigne's plays, and Moll Neville in the *Faerie Queene*.' The pleasure connection exists in the same diary entry between a 'yellow taffety waistcoat' and the usually forbidden, for women, *Faerie Queene*.

Margaret Cavendish in 1656 also recorded her love for both reading and writing and 'fine dressing,' the one sometimes competing with the other:

> However little that wit I have it delights me to scribble it out and disperse it about ... addicted from my childhood [more] to ... write with the pen than to work with the needle ... passing my time with harmless fancies (their company being pleasing, their conversation innocent), in which I take such pleasure as I neglect my health ... But my serious study could not be much, by reason I took great delight in attiring, fine dressing and fashions, and especially such fashions as I did invent myself, not taking that pleasure in such fashions as was invented by others. (*Natures Pictures*, 383 and 388)[38]

In 1697, the female speaker in *The Challenge sent by a young Lady* unapologetically defends women's right to improve their appearance with dress: 'The Body must be adorn'd with such improvements as it is capable of.' The mind, she acknowledges, perhaps more deserves to be adorned, but 'the other ought not to be undone' (33). The competition between the two, evident to Cavendish, is not an issue in this defense.

Women's association with the pleasure of dress and the pleasure of reading and writing emanates from their power to choose both. Both may implement resistance to objectification in a move that reconstructs, through choice, imposed sober reading into reading and writing for pleasure, and imposed sober dress into sensuously pleasing fashion. The taste for the fashionable and delightful influenced women's choice of books and their choice of clothes, to the dismay of their male protectors. Frances Dolan points out that Thomas Tuke's 1616 denunciation of women's use of cosmetics 'positions women simultaneously as passive objects of male censure and lust and as agents who inhabit and transform their bodies in order to pursue pleasure. Though he presents women as texts, he also presents them as authors and readers' (230). On the same continuum, women's fashionable choices of clothes may be analogized to their choices as readers, and the pleasurable dressing of their bodies to their self-gratifying role as writers. Margaret Cavendish even claims that women's exercise of 'Fantasticall' *choice* in dress, and in the art of needlework, provides them with proper training as poets:

> Besides, *Poetry*, which is built upon *Fancy*, *Women* may claime as a *worke* belonging most properly to themselves: for I have observ'd that their *Braines* work usually in a *Fantasticall* motion, as in their *severall*, and *various dresses*, in their many and singular choices of *Cloaths*, and *Ribbons*, and the like, in their *curious shadowing*, and *mixing of Colours* in the *Wrought workes* and divers sorts of *Stitches* they imploy their *Needle*, and many *Curious* things they make, as *Flowers*, *Boxes*, *Baskets*, with *Beads*, *Shells*, *Silk*, *Straw*, or any thing else ... For *Fancy* goeth not so much by *Rule*, & *Method* as by *Choice*. (*Poems and Fancies*, sig. A3)

The economic climate in sixteenth- and seventeenth-century England made fashion a viable issue – as I will discuss in the following chapter – that connected to women's writing and reading, as well as to print culture. Books, read and written by women, and dress, chosen and worn by them, submit to both private choice and public display. Frivolity is the 'outside' meaning applied by the dominant view to both these spheres, but it is rerouted by women in its 'inside' meaning, as subjective choice and pleasure, both, of course, problematized by the terms of the dominant culture, but still effectively operable, even inside an oppressively gendered system.

For a woman to reach a position as a subject, she must reclaim pleasure in discourse, says Luce Irigaray, especially because 'there is, *for women*, no possible law for their pleasure. No more than there is any possible discourse ... And if women – according to him – can say nothing, can know nothing, of their own pleasure, it is because they cannot in any way order themselves within and through a language that would be on some basis their own' (*This Sex*, 95). It is gratifying to see, despite Irigaray's forebodings of its near impossibility, that early modern women discovered a discourse of pleasure linked to their access to the language of reading and writing. Early modern women's texts, which inscribe women's relationship to their learning, fully confirm Margaret Miles's and Frigga Haug's claim that

> [T]o understand people as socially constrained or repressed is seriously incomplete without a simultaneous hypothesis about the social production of motivation, desire, and pleasure ... The simultaneous and complementary processes of socialization ... and subjectification are also invested with learning and the development of competencies – in short, of pleasure 'arising from the activity of learning itself.' (Haug, 166; Miles, 188)

Notes

1 See the work by Peter Clark, Sandra Clark, Olwen Hufton, Margaret King, Ann Kussmaul and Margaret Spufford for discussions of the circumstances of working-class women and maidservants. Also see Fraser, 128–129 for a few instances of women of lower ranks who learned to read and write.

2 Tryon was a public advocate of vegetarianism, a practice, given the heavy meat content of most meals considered desirable in early modern England, that must have seemed more eccentric than it does now.

3 There is, also, in the details of Cary's experience, some evidence of class as a factor intertwined with gender, affecting women's relationship to learning, both in the fact that Cary's father, of a lower social class than his wife or Elizabeth's mother-in-law, unlike them, liked his daughter to learn, as well as in the ironic twist of Elizabeth's dependence on her likely unlettered servants for their assistance in her learning and education.

4 The contributions to this task of reconstruction have been too numerous to list exhaustively. However, see the works listed in my bibliography, of J.W. Adamson, H.S. Bennett, K. Charlton, Peter Clark, David Cressy, Dorothy Gardiner, Margaret George, Suzanne Hull, Ruth Kelso, Myra Reynolds, R.S. Schofield, Joan Simon, Margaret Spufford, Phyllis Stock, Retha Warnicke and Louis Wright.

5 Anne Laurence provides a quick overview of the quite widespread instances of women's learning and teaching (especially chapters 11 and 12). Walter Ong and others typically assume that the acquisition of literacy is always a mark of civilization. However, Levi-Strauss's warning that literacy makes for easier political indoctrination and subordination should be kept in mind.

6 Under Elizabeth, 80 per cent of men were illiterate by this measure and 95 per cent of women. At the beginning of the seventeenth century, 89 per cent of women and 85 per cent of male laborers could not sign their names. However, 'Female deponents from the City and suburbs improved from 78 per cent unable to sign in the 1670's to 64 per cent in the 1680's and 52 per cent in the 1690's' (*Literacy and the Social Order*, 147).

7 Jean Brink, while accepting that gentrified Martha Moulsworth's level of education, including instruction in Latin and rhetoric, 'cannot be generalized to the extent of claiming that most seventeenth-century women were literate and educated,' nevertheless makes the important point that 'Moulsworth's views on education challenge the revisionist studies that persistently debunk the view that humanism opened up educational opportunities for women' (183).

8 As Cressy himself has acknowledged, he has only been able to arrive at approximate estimates because they depend on counts of signatures appearing on extant legal documents – baptismal certificates, depositions of witnesses in ecclesiastical court cases, oaths of political and religious orthodoxy (for example the Protestation Oath of 1642), marriage licences, wills and so on – where women's signatures would not necessarily have been either expected or legally required.

Betty Travitsky says that 'it could be misleading to calculate the interests of Renaissance women on a quantitative basis. Indeed, one could argue that the secular manuscript writings by women argue for a high degree of interest and hard-won erudition on their part' (*Paradise*, 90). Elizabeth Hageman and Sara Jayne Steen also suggest that women's ownership, production and decoration of books offers another indication of their interest.

9 Suzanne Hull proposes that the increasing publication of books specifically targeted to a female readership 'is persuasive evidence that a substantial number of women knew how to read English by the end of the sixteenth century, and that their needs and interests were being recognized by both writers and booksellers' (1). Contributing to the profitable possibilities in books for women readers were the 'continuing growth of a middle class with some leisure for its women; increased opportunities for education, particularly reading instruction in English for both boys and girls; a new emphasis placed on women and their roles as the result of successive reigns by two educated queens; the rise of a professional class of writers dependent on book buyers as well as the chancy largesse of patrons; and the booksellers' need for new markets' (1). Jacqueline Pearson adds, 'This conflict between the need to limit women's reading in the interest of conservative ideologies of femininity and the need to expand it in the interests of the market and the growing professionalization of literature, might well have opened up a liberating space for individual women readers' ('Women Reading,' 91). Hull endorses Adamson's speculations about how girls learned to read, in small grammar schools and pettie schools, taught by local priests and sometimes by an usher (2–3). Adamson cites the ancient canonical duty of the parish clerk 'to keep school' (181), and suggests that chantry schools and pettie schools admitted girls (183). A manual, *The Englische Scholemaister* of Edward (or Edmund) Coote (1596), was directed to those men and women who 'eked out a livelihood by teaching children to read, and perhaps to spell' (187). This group of potential readers was apparently large enough to make the publication of such a manual worthwhile.

10 On the other hand, 'Girls of distinguished social position had their own traditional type of education, whether they found it in the homes of their parents or in the households of their social equals or in nunneries, either as wards of the abbess or as school-girls instructed by a nun or nuns ... [F]or girls the earliest English *Primers* were made; and these books were before the era of the printed book' (Adamson, 188). Girls were often educated with their brothers by private tutors or in small schools in villages, and Adamson thinks 'it may not have been uncommon for girls to be admitted to grammar schools' (193).

11 Margaret Spufford estimates that children who stayed in school until they were seven would probably be able to read and that writing was probably taught in the eighth year ('First Steps,' 412). Spufford also suggests that reading was more widespread because seven was also the age at which most boys were considered able to be put to profitable work (414). Margaret Ferguson says that, 'Despite the modern assumption that if one knows how to read one can teach oneself to write, the journey from reader to writer – with the latter term understood even in the most material or literal sense – seems to have been full of complex stages (and obstacles) for early modern women' ('Renaissance Concepts,' 149). Reading literacy was not only acquired separately from writing literacy, but each skill was taught by different methods and often by different teachers and in different schools, the acquisition of both these skills inflected in large part by gender (Teague, 'Judith Shakespeare' *passim*).

12 See Cressy, *Literacy and the Social Order*, ch. 3, for citations of contemporary comments that seem to suggest a perception of widespread literacy. For example, Thomas More in his 'Apology made by hym anno 1533 after that he had given over the office of Lord Chancellour of Englande,' says that 'farre more than fowre partes of all the whole divided into tenne could never reade englishe yet,' suggesting that up to 60 per cent could read. Adamson also points to the Act of Henry VIII, 34–35, c.1 (1543), which forbids reading of

the English Bible by women, artificers, prenticemen, journeymen and so on. The Act gives gentlewomen permission to read the Bible 'privately but not to others' (172). Cressy prefers his signature count as a means of measuring literacy, but Spufford and Bennett are both more persuaded than Cressy by the contemporary remarks. Margaret Ferguson suggests a further consideration, whose validity I recognize without being able to pursue it any further here, that, in the early modern period, there are inherent difficulties in 'defining literacy as the ability to read and write, and ... problems [in] ... measuring literacy when it is so construed' ('Renaissance Concepts of the Woman Writer,' 147).

13 R.S. Schofield ('Measuring') asks about the relation between signing and different levels of literacy. Does literacy in a period mark the ability to read a handbill, a newspaper, or the works of John Locke? Frances Dolan ('Reading') quotes Elizabeth Cellier's assertion in *Malice Defeated* (1680), that the chief witness against her required a letter in her 'own writing.' Dolan says that 'In the context of suspicion, accusation, and prosecution, one's "own Hand-writings" are taken as irrefutable evidence that they are the ... "last word"' (147). Cressy, on the other hand, warns that 'we must shed the notion that literacy was necessarily as important in the past as it appears to be in the present,' with which we associate 'ability, facility, capability, and perhaps even virtue' ('Literacy in Context,' 306). Yet he also points out that at least seventeenth-century Puritans as well as sixteenth-century humanists saw literacy as a means to 'religious, social, and political discipline' as well as a 'variety of secular benefits' ('Literacy in Context,' 307).

14 See Wendy Wall, 341–347, for a discussion of a contemporary recognition of this view. In *2 Henry VI*, Jack 'Cade's sense that printing is bound up with social tyranny and political repression is heard in critical accounts that associate publishing with the oppressive measures used to secure a hierarchical social order' (342). Also see Jacqueline Pearson's discussion of women's reading as figuring power ('Women Reading,' 87–88).

15 See Margaret Ferguson's discussion of this point in 'Renaissance Concepts of the Woman Writer,' and Frances Dolan's enlargement of it. Keith Thomas also considers the tensions attaching to the meaning of literacy in early modern England.

16 The popularity of the *Book of the City of Ladies*, at least in some educated women's circles, is evident in the commemorative tapestry made in 1513 for Marguerite of the Netherlands, copies of which were owned by Elizabeth and by the mother of Mary Queen of Scots. Elizabeth's hung in her wardrobe room.

17 Frances Teague says that 'the idea that there was a single cultural attitude toward learned women is simply inaccurate' (*Bathsua Makin*, 45).

18 For discussions of Vives's largely unrecognized ambivalence on women's education, see Janis Butler Holm, Valerie Wayne, Pamela Benson, 172ff and Margaret King, 163ff. Pamela Benson supplies a valuable analysis of the ambivalence of the central humanist texts of More, Hyrde, Vives and Elyot regarding the education of women: 'thought about women's intellectual and moral capacity and about their education at the beginning of the sixteenth century was diverse and in the process of developing' (181). Also see Kathi Vosevich's discussion of Vives's principles for the education of Princess Mary and the different views of Ascham concerning the education of Princess Elizabeth.

19 Amusingly enough, Bathsua Makin puts a reality check on Agrippa: 'Let not your Ladyships be offended that I do not (as some have wittily done) plead for female preeminence. To ask too much is the way to be denied all' (2).

20 As Juliet Fleming ('Dictionary English') also points out: 'The three dictionaries that followed it, John Bullokar's *An English Expositor* (1616), Henry Cockeram's *The English*

Dictionarie (1623), and Thomas Blount's *Glossographia* (1656), were also directed at least in part to women' (175).

21 Thomas Overbury is also anxious about the reading choices of those women who have access only to the vernacular. In his character of a chambermaid, he writes, 'She reades Greenes workes over and over, but is so carried away with the *Myrrour of Knighthood*, she is many times resolved to run out of her selfe, and become a Ladie Errant.'

22 Yet a number of women, including Grace Mildmay's teacher, Mistress Hamblyn, taught. Aemilia Lanyer set up a school in St Giles in the Fields in 1617 'to teach and educate the children of divers persons of worth and understandinge' (petition over rent for the property, Woods, *Lanyer*, 33). Bathsua Makin taught in the school of her father, Henry Reginald, later set up her own school and even developed a philosophy of education based on the theories of Comenius (Teague, 31). And of course many women, Anne Halkett for example, were taught by their mothers (Fraser, 134).

23 Yet Makin seems to capitulate in a half-hearted way to that same social suspicion: 'My intention is not to equalize Women to Men, much less to make them superior. They are the weaker Sex, yet capable of impressions of great things, something like to the best of Men' (29). Irony is not impossible here, however, in the likelihood that she is reserving only the 'best' of men as the appropriate comparative base for educated women.

24 Alice Thornton's perception of the 'best education the kingdom could afford,' which she says she and her mother received, does not include Latin, but the 'French language, writing and speaking the same, singing, dancing, playing on the lute and theorbo,' also working silks and making sweetmeats, 'religious instructions, examples, and admonitions, teachings, reproofs, and godly education' (entries for 1633 and 1634, see Graham, *Her Own Life*, 151). See Elaine Hobby's discussion of the place of Latin in women's education between 1649 and 1688 (*Virtue*, 190–203).

25 It has by now become clear that the view expressed by Bathsua Makin toward learned women in the sixteenth century, and endorsed by some early scholars of the period – including Myra Reynolds, who believed that the growth of women's learning in the sixteenth century gave way to a dearth in the seventeenth century – was mistaken. See George, 233.

26 For further development of these points, see chapters 4 and 6 of this volume.

27 Jacques du Bosc, in the chapter, 'Of Reading,' in *The Compleat Woman* (1639), says skill in reading 'affords a certain lustre to such as have it in an eminent degree, and lessens much their *imperfection* who have it not so great; it makes the one tolerable and the other admirable' (sig. G2).

28 See Valerie Wayne's discussion of women's maternal advice in 'Advice for Women from Mothers and Patriarchs.' See also Betty Travitsky, 'The New Mother,' and Kenneth Charlton's chapter on mothers as moral educators in *Women, Religion and Early Modern England*, 188–240.

29 Also: 'Mary Warwick was in the habit of catechizing her maids daily and reading to them books of devotion, in addition to her diurnal visits to the village girls' school. The educative abilities of a mistress of a household ... were of enormous importance ... Obviously, the Puritans, with their emphasis on Bible reading, had a particular incentive to increase the spiritual capacity of their dependents by teaching them to read' (Fraser, 50).

30 It is mildly amusing to compare the tenacious masculine fears of the consequences of women's mutual instruction to the profoundly different and benign goals outlined by Anne Whitehead in 1620 for women's meetings: 'We being met together, the Elder Women to

instruct the Younger to all wholesome things, Loving their Husbands and Children, to be Discret, Chaste, Sober, keeping at Home, that the Word of God we profess be not Blasphemed, &c. with many other matters pertinent to us' (6).

31 Samuel Pepys's *Diary*, in February 1668, records just such an experience in reading *L'Escholles des Filles*: 'it did hazer my prick para stand all the while, and una vez to decharger' (59).

32 It is interesting to note that when Mary Bewley died in 1658, the Reverend Dr Reynolds preached a sermon in which he listed a number of books a gentlewoman might profitably read. The list included 'Opera Anna Maria Aschurman' (George, 138). This 'profitable' item is surely Anna Maria Van Schurman's contribution.

33 Robert Darnton says that 'long after books acquired their modern form, reading continued to be an oral experience, performed in public. At an indeterminate point, perhaps in some monasteries in the seventh century and certainly in the universities of the thirteenth century, men began to read silently and alone' (160). Louise Schleiner (especially ch. 1) points to the continuation of reading groups among women in Tudor and Stuart England, and Margaret Ezell (*Writing*) discusses at length the frequently communal nature of women's reading and writing at the end of the seventeenth century.

34 Sasha Roberts concludes, as I do, that choices of reading, in privacy, signify the possibility of agency: privacy is a 'controlling act – the ability to choose your own companions, or to be alone – enabled by material conditions' (33). I also agree that 'the experience of privacy among early modern elite women was more diverse than Fumerton and Ferguson allow' (33).

35 See Jennifer Summit's discussion of Elizabeth Tudor's 'covert place of women's writing' (185–193).

36 Sir Ralph Verney objected to his god-daughter's learning shorthand; he complained that ' "the pride of taking Sermon-notes" had made "multitudes of women most unfortunate" ' (Gardiner, 296). Bathsua Makin also invented a form of shorthand she called 'radiography' (Mendelson, 'Stuart Women's Diaries,' 205 n. 19). See also Charlton, *Women, Religion and Education*, 154–167 for a discussion of women as audience and recorders of sermons.

37 The speaker in *The Challenge sent by a Young Lady to Sir Thomas – &c. OR The Female War* (1697) sums up the attractions of a nunnery. She sees it providing for a group of women the same rewards as many of those women I have quoted expected of the non-conventual solitary life: 'Privacy' and 'Quiet', 'Solitude', 'Peace', and 'Content', and 'Indisturbance, either from you [men] or from anything equally impertinent' (58). Women might there 'enjoy Friendship fit for Desire, above Scandal' (57). This comment suggests that the inhibition of women's pleasure, peace and solitude has a masculine source.

38 Elizabeth Cary resented the time given to dressing because it took away time for study: 'her women were fain to walk round the room after her (which was her custom) while she was seriously thinking on some other business, and pin on her things and braid her hair; and while she writ or read, curl her hair and dress her head' (*Life*, 194).

Chapter 4

Isabella Whitney. The Printed Subject: Print, Power and Abjection in *The Copy of a Letter* and *A Sweet Nosgay*

> [What] is implied [in the term 'poetry'] is that language, and thus sociability, are defined by boundaries admitting of upheaval, dissolution, and transformation ... '[P]oetic language' ... [is] an openness that is checked but that nonetheless occurs.
>
> – Julia Kristeva, *Desire in Language*, 25

A Foothold in the Printer's World

Pending further scholarly discoveries, Isabella Whitney's remains the first woman's name we are able to attach to a substantial body of published poetry in England.[1] For her contemporary readers, as well as for subsequent aspirants to poetry, she therefore publicly modeled the newly viable possibility of a woman's poetic subjectivity. As a woman writing verse, she disrupted the previously exclusive assignment of poetry to men. As a woman publishing serious poetry, even though it was certainly intended by her printer for the widest possible audience, she challenged what J.W. Saunders, Arthur Marotti and Wendy Wall have shown was a generalized cultural suspicion of print as inappropriate for all polite, preferment-seeking writers. As possibly the earliest forerunner in these newly combined roles, Whitney stands as a necessary aid to understanding the circumstances in early modern England that enabled women to achieve a poetic presence and to enter into print; her foundational relationship with early print culture throws into relief some of the wider cultural and attitudinal changes that needed to be in process for this emergence to occur.

In this study, which seeks to explain the ways in which some adventurous and resourceful women constructed for themselves a previously unrecognized poetic subjectivity, Isabella Whitney demands a primary place. Considered in relation to later women writers like Elizabeth Cary and Aemilia Lanyer, whose poetry also came into print, and who may have unconsciously benefited from Whitney's pioneering role, her tactics and self-representation deserve close scrutiny. That her poetry is whimsical, quirky, touching and clever supplies its own reward.

Isabella Whitney's publishing career is intriguing and revealing, not only for its novelty, but also because it does not, on the one hand, manifest the usual single-item published poem typical of many early modern women poets or, on the other hand, conform to an independent, individualist model of authorship. A string of works, spanning the years from 1567 to 1597, has been attributed to her with varying degrees of credibility, and her role as printed poet makes use of the particular kind of collaboration among printer, poet and a growing audience of readers-as-consumers that could only exist during the years when publication was possible, but individual authorial ownership protected by copyright laws was not.[2]

The first volume containing work certainly Whitney's appeared in 1567. Two of the four poems included in this volume are acknowledged on the title-page as 'By Is. W.' – *The Copy of a letter, lately written in meeter, by a yonge Gentilwoman: to her unconstant Lover* and *An Admonition to al yong Gentilwomen, and to all other Mayds in general to beware of mennes flattery.* The third and fourth poems in the volume use the personae of betrayed male lovers, the first of these by 'W.G.,' and the second (not acknowledged on the title-page and probably added as a filler) by 'R. Witc.' That the initialed attribution, 'Is. W.,' refers to Isabella Whitney can be established by cross-textual reference to her second volume of poetry. This later, certainly attributed work, *A sweet nosgay, or pleasant posye: contayning a hundred and ten phylosophicall flowers* (1573), was published by the same printer responsible for the first volume, Richard Jones (sometimes Jhones or Johnes). In this volume, the two opening dedicatory letters, to George Mainwaring and to the Reader respectively, are signed 'Is. W.,' and a following commendatory letter by 'T.B.' (Thomas Berrie) refers explicitly to Whitney by name and to this as her 'seconde worke.'

That neither she nor Berrie expected this to be Whitney's last foray into print is suggested by Berrie's assertion that:

> And when her busie care from head shall lurke,
> She practize will, and promise longer worke. (sig. Bi)

Isabella also, in her opening dedication to George Mainwaring, promises that she will write a 'more dayntier thing' to present to him in the future. The 'dayntier thing' or 'longer worke,' perhaps envisioned as the next in a sequence of increasingly lengthy and serious poetic endeavors, continuing the pattern begun in the movement from *The Copy of a letter* and *Admonition* to the *Nosgay*, did not, as far as we know, come into being. Yet, interestingly, this glimpse into Whitney's poetic ambition suggests that in 1573 neither she nor her poet friend and supporter, Berrie, regarded her as silenced by gendered literary or social ideology, a point whose implications will be considered a little later in this chapter. The sole surviving copy of the *Nosgay* lacks a title-page, so we do not know whether Whitney's full name proclaimed itself at the beginning of this more elevated poetic endeavor, but the disclosure by Berrie of her identity and her gender imply the expectation by the printer, at least, of a sympathetic audience for this 'philosophical' work and its attachments.

R.J. Fehrenbach speculates that Whitney's publishing career continued anonymously under the auspices of Richard Jones, the printer responsible for Whitney's earlier independent titles, in his miscellanies, *A Gorgeous Gallery of Gallant Inventions* (1578) and *A Handful of Pleasant Delights* (1584). If so, it is also likely that Whitney contributed to the lost predecessor of *A Handful of Pleasant Delights*, printed by Jones in 1566 and falling between Whitney's two definitely known publications (Rollins, *Handful*, x–xv). That almost all of the *Handful* seems to have derived from the material in this 1566 volume would suggest that the last date we can with real confidence attach to a poem by Whitney is 1578, the year of the publication of the *Gallery*. Yet an eleven-year publication career for this pioneer of women's printed poetry is worthy of respect and elucidation.

Admitted as a member of the Stationers' Company on 7 August 1564, Richard Jones continued printing until 1602. Tina Krontiris and Ann Rosalind Jones (*Currency*) have noted that Jones specialized in printing broadside ballads, but his printing range was wider than this. He was also responsible for well-known instructive titles like *The Schoolmaster* (1583) and *The English Courtier and the Country Gentleman* (1586) and, most revealing for our purposes, he was interested in producing books appropriate for women readers. For example, it was he who printed the first item likely contributed by a woman to the English *querelle des femmes*, Jane Anger's *Protection for Women* (1589), a list of suitable names for baby girls and several manuals on marriage, thus covering the range from 'feminist' protest to the ideologically normative point of view about women.[3]

Jones's publishing goal was clearly to whet contemporary appetites, and certainly his poetic collections appealed to current literary fashion; his miscellanies are full of the kinds of poetic epistolary complaints to and from lovers and their ladies that appear in Whitney's *Copy of a Letter* volume. Jones's miscellanies conformed to the two criteria typical of collections in this period: contemporaneity and novelty (Benedict, 6). Also characteristic of both of Whitney's volumes and Jones's later miscellanies is the lack of logical thematic or generic organization, and the addition of 'filler' pieces, such as the last letter from R. Witc, 'Against the Wilful Inconstancie of his deare foe E. T.' in Whitney's 1567 publication, and the poem most likely to be hers, at the end of the *Gorgeous Gallery*, 'The lamentacion of a Gentilwoman upon the death of her late deceased frend William Gruffith Gent.'

This loose arrangement in many of the early published poetry anthologies[4] – whose 'heterogeneous contents,' designed to 'attract multiple audiences,' was typical of the genre (Benedict, 11) – and the conscious addition of filler poems, betoken an attempt in early print culture to mimic the methods of pre-print, and print-boycotting, scribal communities at the level of the gentry and above, and of the manuscript collections of poetry produced in, and circulated amongst, courtly poetry circles (Marotti, 17–35; Love, 98). As Marotti points out, manuscript circulation allowed readers-turned-writers to emend and respond to the manuscripts that passed through their hands (chapter 1). That some of these readers, who altered others' manuscripts inserted their own poetic additions and gathered collections of manuscript poems, were women (48–61) is a detail worth remembering when considering Whitney's appearance in the world of Jones's printed poetic collections.[5] Printers like Jones were probably attempting a format that would re-create the amateur or occasional effects of courtly poetry practice, especially as the hope of patronage did not vanish with the advent of print (Miller, 94–136). But there was also the need to make available what was new and fashionable in order to profit from the purchasing power of the newly consumerist culture.

Isabella Whitney's role in this milieu, 'when the two systems [of manuscript transmission and print] ... not only competed but also influenced each other' (Marotti, 1), may be seen as that of a participating agent, undoubtedly seeking social and economic reward by cooperating in print's emulation of, and rivalry with, the social and literary status of manuscript poetry. This concurrently competitive and imitative status of print in relation to the coterie circulation of manuscript poetry favored by courtly and aristocratic poets has a gender-inflected component in Whitney's case, for her poetry also offers sometimes subtle, sometimes overt, appropriation of, and challenge to, established and specifically male social and literary practice.

Surprisingly because of her gender, Whitney seems to have had a more or less regular place among a group of writers tapped by Jones to supply poems for his publications. Perhaps in some cases these poets were paid, certainly in other cases not. For example, all of the ballads in the *Handful* volume had appeared elsewhere as broadsides, so apparently Jones simply collected them in a single volume and, without copyright laws firmly in place, felt no need to recompense their authors. This circumstance would also have applied to what Rollins calls the '(perhaps involuntary) contributors to the *Gorgeous Gallery*' (xxi). These included Thomas Churchyard, Jasper Heywood and Thomas Howell. Their poems Thomas Proctor, a friend of Anthony Munday and himself admitted to the Stationers' Company in 1584 (*Gallery*, xix–xxii), in manuscript tradition collected for Jones, altered to suit his taste and supplemented with his own compositions. On the other hand, Proctor may have been paid for his services – or at least promised some of the profit from sales, or offered payment in kind in the form of copies of the books themselves. And it is just possible that Jones commissioned Whitney, as well as W. G. and R. Witc, for the 1567 volume and Whitney as well for the *Nosgay*. Edwin Miller deduces that authors of pamphlets of six to ten signatures might be paid 40 shillings, but that many received less than this (154–158). Whitney, as a woman, would find her fee, if any, even further reduced.

It is also possible, though less likely, that some of the poets who produced original poems for the *Gorgeous Gallery* received some small payment, but Jones's typical casual practice in all cases, including Whitney's, may be the one he implemented regarding the author of *The English Courtier and the Country Gentleman*. 'Without his leave,' Jones says, he published this author's work, and, Jones further proclaims without apology, 'I crave small praise for my Printing of it, and hee (being used to loose his labour) desireth nothinge' (quoted in Miller, 146). Whether the author's ignorance and lack of interest in financial reward is constructed by the printer to enhance the image of an amateur writer or to stimulate reader interest, it is still unlikely that Jones paid him. As Miller ironically observes, 'Unquestionably publishers traded upon the chronic poverty of writers' (168), an exploitation to which Isabella Whitney, seeking in London for some personal security and alleviation of her financial troubles, was certainly vulnerable.

Jones's 'stable' of poets, paid or unpaid, included Thomas Proctor, who was responsible for organizing the poems in the *Gorgeous Gallery* and writing some of them; Clement Robinson and I. Tomson, represented most frequently in *A Handful of Pleasant Delights*; Thomas Berrie, who contributes a commendation of Whitney and one of the 'familier epistles' in the *Nosgay* volume; R. Witc. and C.B., unidentified contributors to Whitney's two volumes; and William Gruffith, whose death Whitney's probable poem in the *Gorgeous Gallery* memorializes and who may be the W.G. who is the author of the third poem in the *Copy of a letter* volume. 'Elizabethan printers,' says Hyder Rollins, 'frequently wrote and published their own poems and ballads' (*Gallery*, xix). Whether Jones himself is responsible for any of the anonymous poems in his anthologies we cannot know, but he certainly made use of a number of poets whose work he obviously hoped would be saleable and popular. Of many of these poets we know nothing at all. It is one of the small ironies of literary history that in this unusual case we have been able to identify the woman writer in the group, and we do have at least a little scattered information about her, even if much of what we know is extrapolated from information about her more famous and successful brother, Geffrey, and though her very presence as a member of a collaborative group of printer and poets seems ideologically anomalous.

Finally, Henry Green, the editor of Geffrey Whitney's *Choice of Emblems* (1586), says that a commendatory verse in Thomas Morley's *A Plaine and Easie Introduction to practicall Musicke* (1597) is by Isabella Whitney.[6] This attribution, however, seems unlikely. The poem is signed 'I.W.,' not the 'Is. W.' more often favored by Whitney; by 1597 Isabella had otherwise sunk out of sight,[7] and R. Alec Harman, editor of the 1952 edition of the work, more plausibly attributes the poem to John Wootton or Wotton.

Isabella Whitney has been regarded by many critics as a 'professional' writer,[8] but this designation has a particular range of meaning in the years of Whitney's publication, not necessarily implying earnings from writing, a continuous or even fully committed writing career, or primary claim to ownership of one's writerly production. In moving on to consider the ways in which Whitney imprints herself as a writing subject in her poetry, we need to keep in mind the writing, printing and publishing world to which she at least marginally belonged, and the collaborative relationships typical of early print culture and miscellany or anthology production, inside of which her verse came into print and was preserved.

The Copy of a letter and *An Admonition*: Print and Fashion

In 1567, a volume appeared on the London bookstalls, purporting to be *The Copy of a letter, lately written in meeter, by a yonge Gentilwoman: To her unconstant Lover. With an Admonition to al yong Gentilwomen, and to all other Mayds in general to beware of mennes flattery*. Though the letter was a fictional construct, the 'yonge Gentilwoman' in this case was not. The book's printer Richard Jones had registered with the Stationers' Company only three years before, and he was to prove himself not averse to experimentation in his effort to attract an audience willing to pay for the pleasures of reading, especially when, as in this case, the venture required only a small outlay on his part. He was one of a tribe of printers concerning whose appropriation of their works authors more firmly established than Whitney, either coyly or sincerely, protested.[9] Without the aid of demographic surveys and computer-generated analyses, Jones sought to divine popular reading taste and supply the means to please it. He was, in the world of popular literature, both a follower and an arbiter of fashion, seeking to respond to current trends, but also, perhaps inadvertently, shaping them – especially, in the latter role, by publishing a woman. Jones's economic sponsorship and organization of the volume in which Whitney's poems first appeared established the fashionably allusive ground on which Whitney was able to build still further proofs of being poetically in vogue.

The four poems in *The Copy of a letter* volume, probably arranged in their two pro-woman and two con-woman structure by Jones,[10] taken as a group, imitate the formal debate about women's worth which had acquired new fervor in England in the early 1540s with the publication of Thomas Elyot's *Defence of Women*, Edward Gosynhill's *Schoolhouse of Women* and *Mulierum Paean*, Robert Vaughan's (?) *A Dyalogue defensyve for women*, and a translation of Cornelius Agrippa's *A Treatise of the Nobilitie and excellencye of woman kynde*.[11] This debate generated so many works and continued so excitedly through the following years that Jones's expectation of an interested readership for the 1567 *Copy of a letter* was entirely reasonable. His later publication of Jane Anger's *Protection for Women* continued his support for this literary mode. Many circulating manuscript collections, whose format both of Whitney's published collections emulate, also contained 'misogynistic pieces ... counterbalanced by poems in praise of women,' as well as love poems that 'set amorous compliments and complaints against palinodes and renunciations of love' (Marotti, 57). As Paul Marquis points out, '*The Copy* also recalls the second part of the *Heroides*, in which the plaintive epistles by women are answered by their male lovers' (317).

The similarities between the structure and contents of the poems in *The Copy of a letter* and this fashion of literary debate between men and women were undoubtedly perceived by Jones and Whitney as likely to attract the reader whose taste had already been shaped in this direction. To catch readers with other interests, the collection also exploited the growing appeal of the personal letter as a genre; this focus of attention was fostered by handbooks on techniques for composing a letter, one by Erasmus, for example, recommending Ovid's *Heroides* as a model for letter writing.[12] That Whitney structured the poems in her first volume as letters, turning for many of the illustrative examples to the same model cited by Erasmus, of which a new translation by Turberville appeared in the same year as *The Copy of a letter*,[13] reveals a highly conscious effort to participate in contemporary fashion. In addition, Whitney's use of the *Heroides* forges a link to yet another 'hot' literary fashion. The two poems by Whitney in *The Copy of a letter* volume supply variants on the female complaint poem whose vast popularity was initiated in the 1563 edition of *The Mirror for Magistrates* by the inclusion at the end of the volume of a fictional poetic monologue by Jane Shore. As Wendy Wall points out, from the early 1560s on:

> Writing the complaint of the fallen woman became a literary craze ... ballads about such figures as Rosamond Clifford (mistress of Henry II) and Jane Shore (mistress of Edward IV) flooded the market ... [T]he choice of this form signaled a writer's affiliation with Ovid, whose *Heroides* offered the classic text of lamenting and forlorn heroines. (251–252).

As far as we yet know, until Whitney's version, the composers of these popular women's lamentations, as well as of poems in women's voices, by Surrey, Wyatt, Googe and others, appearing in collections like *Tottel's Miscellany*, were men.

But the desire to profit from an appeal to the fashionable requires careful maneuvering. One's audience may wish to feel included in the up-to-date, while not wanting at all to have its sensibilities shocked or made the subject of ridicule by the assault of the too avant-garde. Though Jones may have intended to avoid the inoffensively out-of-date as unlikely to help him turn a profit, seeking instead to satisfy the passion for 'newness' beginning to infect the early modern consumer,[14] he needed to proceed with caution. In Isabella Whitney he found a poet in tune with his goals, intensely alert to literary fashion, able to supply saleable popular verse exploiting current literary taste, and with some formal education and connections to the gentry level of society where he expected to find his primary audience. At least in this first volume, however, Jones was not so anxious to be on the cutting edge of fashion as to risk violating his readers' sensibilities by playing up the factor that was *really* new – the gender of the writer. Instead, he concealed her personal identity under her initials and equivocated the issue of her gender under the generic 'yonge Gentilwoman,' who might be understood by the reader to be just as fictional as the 'Jane Shore' of the *Mirror for Magistrates* lament. If Whitney's contributions to the volume induced some of her friends and gentry-level acquaintances to buy the book, so much the better. The casual purchaser, however, would have found no shocking indication on the title-page that the speaker in these poems differed in any respect from the 'virtual' voices of women ventriloquized by Gosynhill, Vaughan and the male writers of women's complaint.

But how did Whitney as a possible contributor to his enterprise come to Jones's attention at all? In 1567, Isabella was almost certainly living in London, attempting to support herself, quite likely in service in the household of the 'vertuous Ladye' she mentions in the *Nosgay*'s epistle to her brother Geffrey.[15] She may have come to Jones's notice because of her marginal association, through Geffrey, with university and London literary circles, for it is from the universities and the Inns of Court, says Marotti, that the majority of surviving manuscript poetry emanated: 'Although much poetic composition is associated with the court, many fewer poetry anthologies survive from this environment than from the universities and the Inns of Court' (37–38).[16]

In 1567 Geffrey Whitney was a student at Magdalen College, Cambridge, having already spent some time at Oxford, though from neither university did he earn a degree, and he was soon to be in London, probably studying for the profession of law which would enable him to qualify for the office of Under-Bailiff of Great Yarmouth in the early 1580s (Green, lviii–lxi). Geffrey himself was to become a poetic emblematist of greater renown, though of less originality, than his sister, but as yet, in the last years of the 1560s and the early years of the 1570s, it was she who was the published poet. Perhaps Geffrey, benefiting from the university scholarships available to sons of gentry and tradespeople, found himself in a circle of fellow undergraduates interested in writing poetry – as indeed, what young man, anxious to find a foothold in the courtly and/or commercial world of influence and power, was not? By introducing her to friends already writing for Jones, or to Jones himself, it is possible that Geffrey sought to help his clever and talented sister, with whom he very likely shared his early schooling in Cheshire, either at home in Coole Pilate or at a grammar school at Audlem about three miles away (Green, liii).[17]

Geffrey was in the early stages of a public career, eventually to hold public office, to travel to the Low Countries in the service of Robert Dudley, Earl of Leicester and, as the oldest son, to inherit most, if not all, of the family property.[18] Isabella seemed destined to a life more fitting for a gentlewoman, at first in service to a lady in London, and then in a suitable marriage. In the meantime, both she and Geffrey were short of funds and self-supporting. So Isabella might as well write poetry and, if the opportunity presented itself, earn a little income from it.

If Geffrey belonged to university poetry circles, as seems probable, given the subsequent compilation of his book of emblems, he would have been sensitive to the superior social cachet attaching to manuscript circulation of miscellanies, over print with its democratizing overtones: 'Whether or not they were from the ranks of the gentry, Oxford and Cambridge students who compiled miscellanies and anthologies thought of themselves as engaging in the leisure activities of educated gentlemen' (Marotti, 35). For Geffrey, with his socio-political ambitions, manuscript collection and circulation would have been the appropriate choice. For Isabella, exiled by her gender from the benefits of primogeniture inheritance, university education and political career, the possible social leveling and economic promise of print must not have seemed entirely undesirable. It is also possible, of course, that, independent of Geffrey's introduction, Isabella approached Jones to propose that he publish her verse, having learned of him in the London reading and writing circles to which, as Louise Schleiner suggests (4–18), she perhaps belonged.

Thus far, I have been engaged in weaving a speculative reconstruction of the material circumstances surrounding Isabella Whitney's pioneering entry into print, and I have attempted to mark off as clearly as possible, in the printer–poet collaboration, the areas of Jones's possible responsibility for that unusual event. If the story is as I have told it, it might seem that Isabella was strongly controlled in her poetic enterprise by her printer and perhaps by her brother, and that she performed as a kind of objectified writing machine at their behest. Although this would have made Isabella not much different – except for her gender – from the scores of male literary hacks who were writing for printers in London, and who typically were, like Whitney, educated, poor and ambitious members of the gentry, the anomalous fact of her gender impels a careful search for the moments in Whitney's poetry that disclose her presence as subject and reveal her authority over her text. Though Whitney was brought into print by the hovering presence of her printer, we may well ask in what way her text writes itself out of his control and allows the inscription of a woman's subjectivity.

The place to begin this search is with the volume's title-page, which finds it worth alerting the interested purchaser to the fact that the 'yonge Gentilwoman's' letter is 'written in meeter.' The idea of a 'Gentilwoman' connected with poetry must have resonated as more than a casual pointer, as possibly both celebration and warning, given the prevailing ambivalent feelings about women as poets and women in print. Yet, in the early 1560s, inveighing against women's writing and publication had not yet reached the raucous level of intensity it would achieve after the death of Elizabeth, in large part because the imagined threat represented by women's engagement with print was still as yet more potential than fulfilled. That Whitney was able to find a role as a published poet undoubtedly depended on the confluence in the 1560s of several moderately encouraging factors. It is true that Juan Luis Vives in 1529, and other like-minded pedagogues following him, had worried about women's access to poetry, but such concerns in the middle of the sixteenth century were modulated by the tentative humanist interest in women's education.[19] Perhaps also the public eloquence of the reigning female monarch, and her ventures into poetry, suppressed some of the stronger antagonisms to women's writing. The examples of women's poetry in manuscript collections may have encouraged both Whitney and Jones, and the established tradition of male-authored poetry with female personae must also have wedged open a potential space for the next, most obvious elaboration, of a woman-authored female persona.

More than all of these circumstances, however, at least before the inevitable backlash could gather strength, what Marotti calls the 'democratizing force of print culture' (34), together with the new public's taste for the fashionable, must have increased the publishing opportunities for Whitney and, subsequently, for other women poets. Barbara Benedict's comment about eighteenth-century collections applies equally to sixteenth-century printed miscellanies: 'Booksellers produced anthologies that mediated between the traditional manuscript culture of the court and the new public' (5). The new reading public in the sixteenth century as in the eighteenth included increasing numbers of women,[20] an equalizing cultural shift that surely altered conditions for women writers, who perhaps, in the opportunistic printer's race for profit and desire for novelty, were occasionally regarded as peculiarly able to attract this new, small but growing group of readers.[21]

Even in 1573, as we have noticed above, neither Whitney nor her friend Thomas Berrie considered her poetic career curtailed because of her gender, but expected it to go forward with a 'longer work' yet to come. Jones had been willing to print a second volume of hers, more personal and less conventional as to genre, and containing a much larger proportion of her poems than the earlier volume. The sales of the *Copy of a letter* must have been sufficient to warrant Jones's taking a second, more deeply committed chance on this woman poet. The genre of the printed literary collection or miscellany, as opposed to the manuscript version, also democratically offered poetry to a mixed audience of men and women of different classes and different levels of education, who might otherwise 'have been discouraged by the demanding and serious attention that poetry can require' (Benedict, 10), but who had in common the willingness to spend some of their newly acquired money on such a book.

With a potential audience of people very like herself in terms of class, education and perhaps gender, a poet like Whitney was well suited to produce the right combination of tone, topic and poetic convention and innovation that would whet the new consumer's desire to buy. Jones's 'Printer to the Reader,' which opens Whitney's first volume, within the space of twenty lines urges the reader twice, not to read, but to 'Buy this same Booke,' and the second instance continues, 'you (I know) wyll say you have / bestowed your mony well.' Even though Jones, diplomatically or with a realistic understanding of where most of that money would come from, addresses himself to 'Maister mine,' he helped Isabella address *herself* quite directly to potential women readers. While efforts were quickly made to exclude women from its opportunities and its imagined corrupting power, the initial and ultimate effect of print was democratizing, disrupting previously stable hierarchical systems of class and gender and producing commercially-driven, consumer-influenced conditions in which women could gain a foothold.

Print as commerce fitted comfortably into the changing London economic and social scene. Thomas Platter, a German coming to London in 1599, recorded his impressions that year, but what he observed of the influence of fashion and commerce had been developing during the previous decades. Christopher Breward comments on Platter's observations:

> Perhaps the overriding impression left by Platter's description is of a city in which men and women from competing and disparate social levels coexisted in a scenario of increased commercial and fashionable activity ... There is little of the preoccupation with strictly defined moral divisions of class, gender and wealth that typified records of the medieval city. If anything, Platter highlights a sense of social easiness within which the outward signs of status or duty had become muddled. (53)

Among the new readers-as-consumers in 'status-muddled' Renaissance London, print satisfied the urge to own what one read. But the willingness to buy was driven by another force with which the clever printer–poet collaboration of Jones and Whitney cooperated. On the title page of the *Letter*, Jones emphasizes the novelty of their endeavor. In fact, he says, Whitney's poems are 'newly joyned to a loveletter sent by a bacheler.' What does that phrase, 'newly joyned,' imply? Does the 'newness' describe the whole collection of poems contained in the volume, or is it the conjunction of Whitney's poems with the other two, by W.G. and R. Witc., that is new? In other words, does this phrase tell us that Whitney's poems have already appeared elsewhere, either in print or in manuscript, independent of this new 'joyning'? Or, as seems perhaps more likely, that it is W.G.'s and R. Witc's poems that have been recycled here in a new conjunction with Whitney's new poems? Although our interest as critics is inevitably drawn to the lost details of the circulation of Whitney's poems, Jones's attention, as a man interested in making money, is on 'newness,' the quality likely to attract a new readership.

In his address to the reader, Jones insists for a second time on the newness of these poems: 'this same will serve your turne / the which is also new.' Novelty seems to be inextricably associated with marketing, advertising and the competition for profit – all processes gaining momentum in sixteenth-century England and manifesting themselves in literary as in all other forms of production. The conflation of 'the new' with 'something to buy,' called by Roland Barthes *neomania*, had begun. Another of Jones's titles also demonstrates his desire to capture the reader with a taste for the conjunction of newness and fashion, in this case relating to issues of dress: *Quippes for upstart newfangled gentlewomen, Or a glasse to view the pride of vainglorious women. Containing. A pleasant invective against the fantastical forreigne toyes, daylie used in womens aparell*. That necessary reminder that this is a 'pleasant' diatribe, meant to amuse and not to anger, draws rather than alienates the very 'upstart newfangled gentlewomen,' whom Jones wished to target. The marketing of poetry collections in printed form, like Whitney's and Jones's later miscellanies, also depended on the printer's and poet's ability to keep abreast of the new. The opportunity to enter into print was open to Whitney if she could satisfy the public's taste for the new and fashionable, without, at the same time, affronting them. On Whitney's and Jones's skill in manipulating the recognizably contemporary with the surprisingly novel, a combination that defined the new consumer's sense of the fashionable, depended their success.

In a somewhat controversial but intriguing argument interestingly applicable to the print revolution, Gilles Lipovetsky has suggested that the rise of fashion as a motivating force between the fifteenth and eighteenth centuries in Europe functioned as 'a special agent of the democratic revolution' (31). Not confined merely to the 'domain of dress,' the logic of fashion 'with its fads and its rapid shifts in direction' (15), in short, with its commitment to newness, pervaded culture with democratic consequences:

> By continuously introducing novelties, by legitimizing the practice of taking contemporaries instead of predecessors as models, fashion ... provided a climate favorable to acts of boldness and transgression ... among the bourgeoisie. Fashion must be conceptualized as an instrument for the equality of conditions ... It undermined traditionalist behaviors and values in favor of the thirst for novelty. But fashion could be an agent of the democratic revolution only because it was accompanied by ... the economic ascension of the bourgeoisie ... [and] the growth of the modern state ... Together these factors succeeded in giving reality and legitimacy to the desire for social advancement on the part of the classes who desired to work. This is the crux of fashion's originality and also its ambiguity ... On the one hand, it blurred the established distinctions and made it possible to confront and confuse social strata. On the other hand, it reintroduced – although in a new way – the timeless logic of signs of power. (31)

Inside the new ideological folds marked out by print and fashion, it seems Whitney, one of those 'who desired to work' and a member of the English equivalent of the bourgeoisie desiring social advancement, found a place. Willing, as a woman poet, to commit 'acts of boldness and transgression' by allowing, perhaps even urging, her poetry into print, she advanced where women had previously not found a place. In a small but important way, she contributed to the democratizing processes of print and fashion which blurred established class and gendered distinctions. Yet adherence to fashion involves one in ambiguity, for, as Lipovetsky argues, while fashion confuses and blurs social strata, it also invokes systematic signals of competitive power. As I have already suggested, in a profit-making print enterprise needing also to participate in the fashionable, it was necessary to assuage and mimic public taste for the conventional as well as to surprise and satisfy the taste for the new. In this balancing act, Whitney was singularly learned. The self-contradictions of her position as a woman poet in the largely male-controlled fashions of early print culture, neither independently empowered nor entirely disempowered by her relationship to her printer and her audience, surface in the doubling language and ideology of her poetry, and mark the mode of her subjectivity.

The Copy of a letter and *An Admonition*: Double-Speak

Ann Rosalind Jones, among others, has remarked on the apparently 'incompatible goals' in *The Copy of a letter*; does the persona 'want to expose the villainy of her betrothed or win him back? Is she writing to prove her forgiveness or to set up a public vendetta against the man who has abandoned her' (*Currency*, 47)? Jones suggests that this mixed message signals Whitney's more immediate practical goal 'to win multiple literary admirers' (47). Elaine Beilin has also discussed Whitney's inconsistent and 'selective moralization' (*Redeeming*, 92) as a rhetorically useful way of emphasizing her own virtue and pointing to the retribution that follows men who betray women. Yet the 'double-speak' in Whitney's goals and instructional position permeates her poems, even more intensively, in the representation of a persona who is both abject and authoritative, in the use of illustrative mythic examples, male and female, who are both heroically brilliant and dismally flawed, and in the semantic choices which strangely contradict what they seem to intend.

Tina Krontiris endorses Jones's suggestion that Whitney is mired in language 'saturated with suspicion of *women*' (49): 'Without any precedents for her to follow, her ideas could only be expressed in terms generated by male writers ... Even worse, the linguistic structure and idiom were already gendered at the expense of the female sex and hence a handicap to a woman writer' (33). These insights valuably point to the problems faced by a woman poet compelled to use the language deeded her by patriarchal culture. I dispute, however, Krontiris's further point that, in Whitney's case, or perhaps in general, it is 'self-undermining ... for a woman to contest meanings with a language ... pointed against her' (33).

I see, rather, that all of Whitney's poetry, including *The Copy of a letter*, lures from the psychological recesses of language, the ambiguous meanings and doubled self-representations that call into question, and offer to undermine, the inflexible binary relationships and fabricated singularity of meaning that support hierarchy and oppression in subject–object, male–female relationships. The doubleness of early print culture – both imitative and innovative, backward-looking and forward-facing, and the ambiguities of the fashionable – committed to the experimental, the ephemeral and the new, and also to the instantiation of competitive status structures, inform the self-representation and language of Whitney's poetry. Both ideologies of print and fashion, at one and the same time imitating the current forms of acceptability and also competing with them by promoting the new, plant in the cultural unconscious an alternative notion of language and self-representation that enriches possibility and refutes the exclusiveness of binary choice, that blur the distinctions of gendered power which silence and immobilize women. Both encourage the opening of a poetic space where a woman's desire for language collides with, but is not subdued by, patriarchal patterns, where a woman may write from both sides of her mouth, as it were, from a sense of power and a place of abjection.

An element in Whitney's stance that has surprised students of early modern women's writing is her lack of overt self-assertiveness concerning her initiatory action in the field of women's published poetry. Why does she not say, 'I am a woman doing something highly unusual,' or solicit admiration for her pioneering temerity? Certainly, poets coming after her, including Aemilia Lanyer, Anne Bradstreet and Katherine Philips, proclaimed themselves forerunners in women's poetry. The lack of this acknowledgment by Whitney is especially interesting in relation to her otherwise intimate and solicitous engagement with her reader. Elaine Beilin talks of the 'public caution' (*Redeeming*, 89) with which Whitney approaches her role. Except in the *Wyll and Testament*, says Beilin, 'Whitney's interest seems to lie more in her [morally instructive] mission than in developing her poetic voice' (98). Perhaps another answer to this puzzle lies in the possibility that, unlike Katherine Philips, for example, Whitney did know of other women who poetically preceded her, whose works are now lost, or who, anonymously, had entered into print before her, and for this reason, apparent to her though not to us, did not announce her poetic priority.

Even if this explanation is wide of the mark, however, I am still not impressed by any unitary purpose in Whitney, for, in ways known or unknown to herself, her choice of language and example betrays both her pride in her role as poet, as well as the mischief, perhaps even malice, mixed inside her externally virtuous and long-suffering self-representation. After all, Richard Jones's 'Printer to the Reader,' which introduces Whitney's volume, asserts more strikingly than it must have intended that, self-contradictorily and impossibly in the terms of binary logic, at one and the same time and in one and the same package, 'this Treatise is, / both false and also true.' Though Jones admits that his 'wordes [may] be thought, / uncredible,' yet, he says, in 'this same Booke,' Is. W., 'the Auctor,' will produce from the magic receptacle of her poetic language the surprising paradox of 'a trifle that is trew' and 'Fables that be fained.'[22]

Whitney's assumed persona and her very relationship to her text, from the outset, obscure the clear separation of the true from the false and masculine from feminine. In *The Copy of a letter* she is following the precedent established by earlier male poets who had assumed the guise of a female persona bewailing her treatment at the hands of a man or, more aggressively, had attacked all men for their failings. These earlier examples required a literary transvestism in their poets, who took on a woman's nature, experience and voice, but were able to rely on the understanding unquestioned by their readers that the authoritative poet behind the female persona was male. In Whitney's case, something more complex and several degrees more interesting occurs.

Because the title-page reveals only the initials of the poet responsible for the first two poems, and although Is. W. is described as 'a yonge Gentilwoman,' there is no guarantee provided to the reader, already used to male-voiced female laments, that the gender of poet as well as persona is not a fiction. However, the first two poems in this volume we, at least, know, are in fact the work of a female poet who, unusually, assumes a female persona within a literary fashion that until now has required the compositional authority of a male poet. The 'authentic' gender of the female poet is obscured by the initials which leave open the possibility that the 'real' poet is a male who has assumed a female persona. Whitney is able to stage her poetry, speaking a woman's experience of male betrayal, disguising her female authorship with (*possibly*) a male's initials, in order, paradoxically, to give authority to the pronouncements of her female persona. Because the conventions of this popular genre are so firmly evoked, the conservative and complacent reader could comfort himself with the belief that what he was reading was what he had seen before – something akin to Jane Shore's narrative, for example, presented by the male poets of the *Mirror for Magistrates*. On the other hand, the more revolutionary and discontented reader might have felt pleased by the conviction that she was reading the work of a woman whose testimony, advice and suffering were trustworthy because experienced by a woman whom she sympathetically recognized. The poet thus becomes both male and female, a doubling appropriate to the printer's and the poet's expectation of 'multiple literary admirers' (Jones, *Currency*, 47).

If the poet's identity is what it seems to be and not, 'both false and also true,' the cross-hatching of the apparently clear dichotomies of true and false, male and female, is reinforced in the classical allusions in Whitney's two poems in this first volume. Paul Marquis has shown that in the *Letter*, the speaker's wish that her ex-lover may share the fortunes of Xerxes and Croesus actually conceals a prophetic curse, for both these rulers suffered various combinations of defeat, imprisonment, assassination and dishonorable death (319). But many other examples in *An Admonition* as well as *The Letter*, chosen by Whitney from Ovid, ostensibly to illustrate man's perfidy and woman's innocence and virtue, carry the same buried self-contradiction or threat.

An Admonition is less densely packed than the *Letter* with these ambiguously weighted Ovidian *exempla*, a difference in emphasis that is perhaps explained by its explicitly designated audience of love-sensitized 'Virgins that from Cupides tentes / do beare away the soyle.' Its examples too, however, blur the sharp distinction the poem seems at one level to imply between the deceitful, wavering lover and the abused, rejected mistress. Scilla, for example, violated her filial duty, contributing to her father's death for the sake of Minos, whom she loved and who, for her reward, rejected her. Yet she was in turn loved by Glaucus, whom she in turn rejected; women, too, can turn away from reliable virtue or an ardent lover. Though this example is offered as a warning to 'mayds' who do not take sufficient heed of their lovers' worth, its latent message is more complicated. Though her human happiness was curtailed by Circe's vengeful intervention on Glaucus's behalf, Scilla, changed into a monster, became more powerful, angry and destructive of seafaring men than an unsuspecting reliance on women's passivity and long-suffering would allow for. Scilla's end may not have been exactly as she would have desired, but it was not entirely without compensation for an angry woman.

Poor Oenone fits the stereotype of the innocent woman done wrong, for Paris succumbed to the irresistible promises of Aphrodite and left Oenone to pursue the more beautiful Helen, but Paris met his just retribution in Troy. Yet the example of Hero and Leander which concludes *An Admonition*'s instructive mythological instances holds little comfort for the male or female reader. Hero carefully 'tried' Leander before committing her heart to him and found him 'constant, true, and just.'[23] Even so, she too was left bereft, for Leander's very love for her caused his death by drowning as he swam the Hellespont to reach her. Even a faithful man's love, this example shows, is not proof against the vicissitudes of 'spitefull Fate,' for the faithful lover may die in pursuit of love and leave his mistress still abandoned.

Turning to the more numerous mythological examples in the *Letter*, we find ambiguity and obscured threat intensified. Although Sinon, the Greek left behind to persuade the Trojans, with a story fabricated by Achilles, to take the wooden horse inside the walls of Troy, seems a straightforward example of 'falshood,' the three following couples are not clear, dualized exemplars of conscious male deceit and innocent female abuse and misery. Dido, truly loving Aeneas, *was* abandoned by him, but, as Aeneas reminds her when he is called by the gods to leave Carthage, he had never married, or promised to marry, her. So, the 'untrueth' assigned to him by Whitney's persona is something of a manipulation of the original story. Dido is, however, undoubtedly a sympathetic figure. Sympathetic, too, is the sorrow of Ariadne, forsaken by Theseus on the island of Naxos, after she had helped him defeat the Minotaur. Yet there are two versions of this separation, one maintaining Theseus's goodwill; this version tells that Theseus put ashore because Ariadne was seasick, and his boat was blown away by a storm. Even the other version in which Theseus is culpable does not leave Ariadne desolate, for the god of ecstasy, Dionysus, discovers her and loves and comforts her. And Theseus, we remember, is one of the few figures in Greek mythology whose nobility, virtue and wisdom are seen as exemplary, for he is the great king who established Athens as the home of liberty, a democratic commonwealth where the citizens (not women of course) could vote.

Perhaps neither Whitney nor her readers knew the blurring intricacies of these stories in classical mythology, but they would certainly have known more of Medea than the *Letter* allows. This third example is the most problematic for its announced purpose in this poem. Jason certainly married Hipsypile, the daughter of the King of Corinth, and abandoned Medea, who had helped him win the Golden Fleece, pleading that he was afraid of her. Jason's position from a commonsense point of view was not unreasonable, for Medea, in all the stories concerning her, is a lowering figure of evil, power and revenge. She betrayed her father to help Jason win the fleece, killed her brother so that she and Jason might escape, induced Pelias' daughters to kill their father, horribly murdered Jason's bride with the gift of a poisoned shirt that melted the flesh off her bones, and finally murdered her own and Jason's sons in vengeance against Jason. Under no circumstances is it possible to see Medea as a weak and innocent 'simple soule,' as the poem's persona describes herself.

And yet, surely these stories invite increasingly menacing comparisons between the mythic women and Whitney's poetic persona and the mythic men and the persona's lover. Sinon lied to the Trojans and caused the destruction of Troy. Is the persona, unthreateningly, like the Trojans, betrayed and destroyed? Aeneas abandoned Dido. Is the persona, like Dido, destined to commit suicide – or at least implicitly threatening to do so? Theseus lied to Ariadne and abandoned her (in the less happy version), but Ariadne was saved by the god Dionysus. Is the persona telling her ex-lover that she will be comforted by another, better and more priapically endowed than he; that he is not, after all, the only or best fish in the sea? The analogy between the Jason–Medea story and the persona and her lover is reinforced by the parallels between the word choice in the persona's reminder that if her lover marries her, 'So shall the promises be kept, / that you so firmly made,' and the 'vowes' Jason 'dyd make so faithfully, / unto his loving Spowes.' Jason abandoned Medea, but she had her terrible revenge by murdering Jason's bride and his sons. Is the persona telling her lover that if he marries another, death and vengeance will follow?

This chilling implication from the woman who describes herself, surely with some self-masking disingenuousness, as the lover's 'refuse,' and 'a simple soule' content to be 'forsaken' by him, echoes unsettlingly though amusingly against her odd hope that, instead of the lover's having cause to regret his abandonment of the speaker and his choice of another, the other should die before he weds her: 'And it may chance although not yet / you wish you had me taken':

> But rather the [sic] you shold have cause
> to wish this through your wife:
> I wysh to her, ere you her have,
> no more but losse of lyfe. (sig. A4)

Finally, the speaker begs and/or threatens the lover:

> And unto me a Troylus be,
> if not you may compare:
> With any of these parsons that
> above expressed are. (sig. A4)

Troilus, we know, was killed by Achilles on the field of Troy.

The persona's ultimate power to carry out her revenge is, however, less a matter of blood than ink. For the stanza quoted above tells the lover that if he persists in betraying her, he will be memorialized in her verse as one of the liars and betrayers with whom she has compared him and whose traditionally noble reputations she has rewritten, whose 'Fame,' like his, she can turn to 'Shame.'[24] Her conviction of the power of writing is evident in her exhortation to her lover at the end of the poem that he should keep her letter, with its documentation of lies and perfidy, safely 'in store.' What she has written, she tells him, is worth saving and is not to be discarded. She intends to fill in her absence, by being with him in word, if not in flesh. Though language is insecure, full of promises that cannot be relied upon and vows not kept, and never saying fully what one may think one means, nevertheless, the poet, in this case a woman, has as much control and power over and through language as is available. Whitney and her persona are clearly able to manipulate poetic language to produce a message not quite straightforward and transparent, not quite truthful, but 'both false and also true.' They are, after all, only adhering to Elizabethan rhetorical theory and theories of poetry which 'praise enigmatic rhetoric as the metamorphosis of secrecy into pleasure – or what we might call the free play of language' (Bell, 82).

The language of single 'truth' is the language of self-evident identity, where it can be relied upon that A will always equal A and never equal something other. But language always contains more possibility than this, and that other potentially ominous dimension enters Whitney's texts. While her poems seem to endorse the binary divisions of false men and true women, these distinctions, on examination, fall apart. The divided vocabulary is there: truth, constancy and faithfulness applied to women, and lying, boasting, falsehood, beguiling, forsaking and stealing applied to men. But we see, in the way in which both mythic and contemporary Elizabethan male and female relations are exemplified, that women have the power to implement something very much other than virtue and silence and patience. The language of these two poems certainly writes women in a way that patriarchal language fears but does not encourage, as powerful, threatening and verbally expressive. At a level deeper than the surface assertions, the poems ally the speaker with this possibility, more than with male-approved, conduct-book qualities. The 'polite' level of the poetic argument connects men with deception and falsehood and women with virtue and truth, but these dichotomized grounds for the female speaker's attack on men, placing the woman on a moral pedestal, actually offer the more predictable and conservatively permissible reading. This is the reading Richard Jones must have expected his readers to tolerate because it ultimately works inside, and holds no threat to, the established binary order of male–female relations. But Whitney, writing even in the language of the patriarchally permissible, allows another, even more disruptive, dimension of language to seep through.

Patriarchal language, enacted in the broken promises and betrayals that the poem recalls, is undoubtedly replete with lies, indeed, as the *Admonition* expresses it, with over-determined 'fained lies' (which, if 'fained,' may, unreliably, not be lies at all), and with seductions aided by the deceitful 'teares of the Crocodile.' But more deeply entrenched as an essential foundation for patriarchal language is the binary division itself which separates true from false, and male from female. It is not this binary demarcation that 'a subreading' (Bath, 31) of Whitney's text finds, but something subtler and more dangerous – a revelation of the layered possibilities inherent in language that open up meaning to self-contradiction, so that the inextricable connection of truth and falsehood, fact and fiction, suggested by Jones in his 'Printer to the Reader,' is maintained. If no longer even dichotomously contested, masculine spaces, writing and speech become scenes of ongoing, gendered *agon* or struggle, continuously open to the deconstruction of their patriarchal logic and power. The 'Fame' and 'Shame' of the *Letter*, and the 'trust' and 'deceit,' 'trueth' and 'painted talk' of the *Admonition*, are not then seen as exclusive alternatives; the items in the apparently opposed pairs simply merge into the same coextensive epistemological combination.

Even the syntactic choices in these poems also lead to these layered and disquieting ends. For example, the second stanza of the *Letter* reads:

> You know I alwayes wisht you wel
>   So wyll I during lyfe:
> But sith you shal a Husband be
>   God send you a good wyfe. (sig. A2)

The force of the 'But,' which turns the stanza in the third line, syntactically undoes the well-wishing of the first two lines. If, the stanza seems to say, the lover becomes a husband and God sends him a good wife, the persona will *cease* to wish him well, or, even more threateningly, it seems possible that the status of a husband with a good wife becomes the material for a curse antipathetic to any good wishes whatsoever. Once the submerged threat in the Ovidian stories has been exposed, this buried ill-wishing, effectively functioning concurrently with the surface well-wishing, begins also to emerge elsewhere, as a semantic consequence of a 'gender unconscious' (Bell, 79) comes into play. In the fifth stanza, then, which reads: 'But yf that needes you marry must? / then farewell, hope is past,' just exactly whose hope for happiness is 'past,' the persona's or the lover's?

This recognition of an unconscious language which subverts the overt expression of a gendered dichotomy between submissive, truthful, silent women and authoritatively-speaking, lying men goes a long way to explaining the role of the mermaids whose apparently illogical appearance has puzzled critics of *An Admonition*. Instead of keeping consistent the denunciation of male liars and seducers, the speaker warns the 'yong Gentilwomen' to beware of 'flattering tongues' such as mermaids use to seduce mariners, seeming to switch her gendered stereotyping to the image of the dangerous, manipulative female impeding the important journeyings of the serious male. Yet, at the very least, we should notice that in the story of the sirens, as the usual roles of male seducer and innocent female are reversed, it is women who become the ones with powerful control over language and song – and poetry.

As a matter of fact, there may be an etymologically plausible explanation for Whitney's apparently woman-undermining choice of mermaids to exemplify 'fayre and painted talke,' that is, that the mermaid was not always understood in Elizabethan England to be exclusively female. For example Isabella's brother, Geffrey Whitney's *Choice of Emblemes*, published in 1586 but circulated earlier, includes an emblem for the sirens calling to Ulysses. The sirens in the accompanying woodcut are depicted as mer-persons, with human torsos and fish tails. Although the explanatory poem, which identifies sirens with mermaids, refers to their 'womans shape,' in the illustration only one is quite definitely female, and the other two seem to be masculine or androgynous, without breasts. Also, according to the *NED*, the first use of the masculine 'merman' did not appear until 1601.

Perhaps, then, the only 'mermaids' available to Whitney as examples of seductive talk or song were understood to represent an all-inclusive gender. But it may also be that, as well as warning the women to whom the poem is addressed against the power of language which may 'pretend no good' to them, the speaker is also reminding them of the power of language they have in their control, if only they choose to use it. After all, the woman speaking to them models an authoritative speech, already manifest in the *Letter*, where she has her 'mind ... exprest.' 'I speake,' she forthrightly declares in *An Admonition*; more strongly yet, she asserts that 'good counsell ... I wyll, here in few wordes expresse.' Because she is able to do so, for what good reason should her 'tongue ... be slacke'?

Similarly, just as the mermaids seem to embody a cross-gendered reading, the little fish at the end of the poem who learns from bitter experience, is a 'he,' even though he is analogous to the woman speaker who 'was deceived late, / by ones unfaithfull

4.1 Geffrey Whitney's emblem of sirens

teares.' As has already been evident in the *Letter*'s manipulation of genre conventions, the speaker-poet here also seems to seize control of both male and female roles. The readers learn that piscine paranoia – 'now he pries on every bait, / suspecting styll that pricke' – may be justified for both male and female, though if the 'pricke' has the bawdy significance suspected by Paul Marquis, the joke plays against both hetero- and homosexual possibilities, through the gender of the speaker and the fish, respectively. Either male or female may betray or be betrayed, and women as well as men have the power to use language both offensively and defensively. The conclusion of this poem offers no innocent happiness to men or women, lovers or mistresses. Wisdom after the fact, in an untrustworthy universe directed by 'spitefull Fate,' after loss of innocence, after the fall into the insecurity of language, teaches that all, men and women alike, should take care.

The two poems become, then, not so much the traditional female complaint against male betrayal they seem to represent, as a submerged female challenge to undermine the power of male language over women, and a demonstration of the untrustworthy vicissitudes of binary social and linguistic structures. In any case, we, like the lovers perhaps, have learned that a woman with a message like this buried in her heart or mind, known or unknown by her, is hardly good material for a conventional and comfortable wife. The speaker does not at all conform to Henry Smith's 1591 prescription for a wife: 'To her silence and patience she must add the *acceptable obedience* which makes a woman rule while she is ruled' (87). In spite of her enacted submissiveness, Whitney's persona's willingness, desire even, to rule, is not bound by the conditions suggested by Smith. She is not patient in her heart, not acceptably obedient, not willing to *be* ruled and, above all, of course, she is not silent. She openly acknowledges to her lover that she is not 'quiet':

> And if you cannot be content
>   To lead a single life?
> (Although the same right quiet be)
>   Then take me to your wife. (sig. A2)

It is the single life he might have chosen, she admits, that would be 'quiet.' Marriage with her would not be quiet because she would not be. As part of her equivocal farewell to him, she dubiously wishes her lover, along with the (desirable and undesirable) fates of Xerxes and Croesus, as little or 'as much rest and quietnesse / as man may have on Mould.'[25]

These poems, then, show a poet and her fictional persona adroitly deploying multivalent language, neither quiet nor caught as victims in the middle of love, literary or print systems that might well have silenced them. The speaker expects that not only the 'yonge Gentilwomen,' but the lover and, by extension, other male readers, will heed her; she assures the faithless lover that she can make or break his reputation and, furthermore, requires him to save her letter as a valuable reminder of her authority to speak. These two early poems force dichotomous patriarchal language to double back to a place where both its inflexible binary deficiencies and its multivalent potential can be revealed. The message the speaker *should* send, the message desired, even required, of her by patriarchal culture, is not at all the same message that she, wittingly or unwittingly, desires to express, and sends.

That this poem's authoritative 'double-speak' surprisingly emanates from a persona who describes herself as 'a simple soule,' content to be 'forsaken' as her lover's 'refuse,' is formally appropriate. Also relevant to this apparently self-contradictory ambivalence is Elaine Showalter's concept of 'double-voiced discourse,' in which women often write because they are always in dialogue with, and addressing, two audiences, one male and one female. Addressing Whitney's somewhat more complex *Nosgay*, however, where the same anomaly appears, of an apparently disempowered speaker seizing powerful control of language, it will be helpful to turn to other decoding systems. Especially, Julia Kristeva's theoretical model of women's writerly subjectivity which finds, in semiotic or poetic language, a way to speak from abjection, seems a helpful liaison with the speaker in this second volume of poems, who is 'sick,' 'harvestlesse,' 'servicelesse,' 'husbandless,' indebted, 'fearful,' isolated, 'least of Fortune's favored' and death-desiring, yet a conscious manipulator of poetic style and genre, of cultural appropriation, of sophisticated rhetorical methods, of affective relationships and of the idiosyncracies of ideology.

A Sweet Nosgay: Abjection and Poetic Power

The Power of the Poet

Whitney's *Sweet Nosgay* opens and closes with the speaker essentially isolated from those possibly 'spightful' inner circles of London marked by privileged class and financial security. In her 'Auctor to the Reader,' which opens the *Nosgay*, she represents herself as 'servicelesse,' 'harvestlesse,' suffering from 'sicknesse,' craving death 'by reason of [her] luckless life' and 'all sole alone.' In the 'Wyll and testament,' which closes the volume, she says she has been released from prison by a 'Friendes procurement,'[26] she complains that London has not given her room or board (sig. E3), that she is 'very weake in Purse' (E3), 'wery' (E8) and has not been helped by those who 'should have sought to mend [her] luck; / which ever was too bad' (E8); alone, she departs from London.

Such desired, but absent, connections as she invokes in the first and last parts of this three-part volume are, at the beginning, with her hoped-for patron George Mainwaring and with her literary source Hugh Plat and, at the end, with the city of London and the fictional heirs of her 'wyll.' Between these two framing spaces of physical and psychological isolation, she reaches out in a series of 'familier' epistles to friends and relatives. Most of these letters remain unanswered, but embedded in the thirteen letters of the sequence there are three affectionate and encouraging replies from friends.[27] It is not clear that the connections with her brothers and sisters are any more financially reciprocated than her appeals for acknowledgment from Mainwaring, Plat or the city that rejects her. She does not, for example, know the whereabouts of her two brothers, and two of her sisters are in service in London and probably not economically secure themselves.[28] Yet the genre of the personal or 'familier' letter and the conventionally assumed closeness of familial and friendly relationships warm the epistolary community set up by Whitney in the middle of this volume.

The affectional climate of these interchanges encourages the persona, 'Is. W.,' to write openly, not only of her material and psychological needs, but also of her role as writer. The letter addressed to her married sister, 'Misteris A.B.,' contains two revealing stanzas often commented on by Whitney's readers.

Good Sister so I you commend,
  to him that made us all:
I know you huswyfery intend,
  though I to writing fall:
Wherfore no lenger shal you stay,
From businesse, that profit may.

Had I a husband, or a house,
  and all that longes therto
My selfe could frame about to rouse,
  as other women doo:
But til some household cares mee tye,
My bookes and pen, I wyll apply. (sig. D2)

Elaine Beilin has perceptively pointed to the use in the second stanza of the 'ironically contrasting verbs, *tye* and *apply*, [which] replace a domestic "me" who is the object of control and restraint with a reading and writing "I" who performs the active intellectual work' ('Writing,' 249). The comparison between married domesticity and the intellectual, writing life does not, however, strongly favor one over the other, but acknowledges the claims of each. Both, it appears, are choices available, if not to all women, then at least to some. Nevertheless, what is interesting in the manner of their representation is the different accessibility assumed to each. The domestic life is one that the writer may still reasonably expect to enter: '*til*,' not '*if*', she says, 'some household cares mee tye.' But a woman who has a 'husband or a house' will have domestic responsibilities that require her to 'rouse' (that is, stir about or be busy), quite separately from 'bookes and Pen'; for her, the option of a writing life is closed.

Anne Baron, Isabella's married sister, did not, after all, leave a legacy of poetry as Isabella did. She has a continued poetic presence only as the recipient of a poetic epistle from Isabella, who, when she writes, has *not* married. 'Misteris A.B.' has disappeared into a domestic space in which it is her 'prety Boyes' whose learning and education matter. Their Aunt Isabella herself hopes for them that when grown they may be in 'learning ... so strong; / That they may march among the best, / Of them which learning have possest' (sig. D2); to them, to encourage and enhance their classical education, their Uncle Geffrey Whitney willed all his books: 'Item, I bequeath my Liberarie of Books whole without dimishinge [sic] to Gefferie his sonne yf yt shall please God to indue him with learninge in the lattin tonge or else to anie other of his sonnes which shall attaine unto the same' (Green, xciii).

The married life holds out the possible pleasures of companionship, security and children, which would moderate Is. W.'s loneliness and indebtedness, but the writer of these poetic epistles must know that once inside marriage, she will probably not continue to write. Her mixed feelings over this prospect are betrayed in her word choice; she would busy herself like other women, she says, 'Had I a husband or a house.' Does the use of 'or,' instead of 'and,' imply that one of the two acquisitions might be detached from the other, and still represent the material difference to her life that she wishes for? Perhaps the 'house' and what it represents in terms of security would suffice, and might be imagined as desirable even separately from a husband? For the writer of these poems, who is fully aware of the power of her 'books and Pen,' sacrificing them would surely be painful.

Some critics have found the *Nosgay* less vehement in its 'feminist' sympathies than the *Copy of a letter*: Tina Krontiris, for example, speaks of the volume's 'lower tone' (39). Yet the number of ways in which Whitney insists in this set of poems on the power of language and on her own access to, and desired control of, this power is quite remarkable. The same sophisticated deployment of the double power of language both to unsay what it seems to say, and to say more than it seems to intend, is evident in the later volume, as it was in the *Copy of a letter.* In the *Nosgay*, however, instead of being employed mischievously to remind the reader of the poet's skill and presence, the power of language and its writer are openly declared. In this volume, the poet is wiser and less playful, more consciously commenting on both the authority in her writerly grasp and the personal costs of exercising this power. The *Nosgay* volume is grander than the previous one, early signaling its seriousness by its opening dedication to a possible patron. It is 'philosophical,' its poems treating themes of friendship, mutual obligation, compassion, the vicissitudes of fortune, sickness and poverty and the lessons they may teach.[29] The role of the persona signals her divided, but active, claim to subjectivity. She is materially poor, socially marginal, conventionally apologetic for the inadequacy of her skill and physically sick, yet she is able to cure through her writing, authoritative in her recommendations, confidently petitionary, wisely instructive and poetically expert.

The very nature of the intimate poetic appeal to her reader that characterizes Whitney's poems in this volume asserts the power of poetry to fill in the physical absence of the writer with a ghostly and curative supplement of words. In the 'Farewell to the Reader,' the poet confidently urges that when she is 'distant farre' from the reader, the 'nosgay' should 'worne be for my sake.' The particular genre of the 'familier epistle' works from the premise that writing may function as a compensation for presence. Is. W. tells her sisters and her cousin that her letters and theirs serve as powerful substitutes for the sight of each other. To her sisters, she says, her letter to them will serve, 'tyll I your selves do see,' and from her cousin she requests, 'Let me you see, or have some scroll, / that shall of you be pend.'

Furthermore, it is no accident that the term she sometimes uses in this volume to refer to her writing is 're-sighte' or 'resyte' or 'recyte.' In the 'Auctor to the Reader,' this wonderfully flexible word describes her creative and ultimately authoritative rewriting of Plat's original 'floures of philosophie': she 're-sites' or resituates them, she 'recites' or reperforms them, she 're-sights' or provides them with a new visual aspect. In this poem, too, her reading and rewriting of Plat's aphorisms will 'fill [her] gasing eye.' She urges the reader to 'see' the virtues of her writing and 'view' the ways in which she has used the products of Plat's 'garden,' and she excoriates those who 'come with spite to toote' (that is, peer or pry) into Plat's 'garden' or her own 'nosgay.' To her brother, B.W., she also says she will 'wryt, or yet resyte' until she sees him again and may speak to him. In her 'Wyll and testament,' she 'recytes' her legacy of London's riches. The repeating allusions to and puns on sight, as a capacity that resonates correlatively with the persona's writing, itself able to re-sight, resite and recite, acquire for that writing the controlling and constructive power implicit in the dominating gaze. Sight was, in fact, the very sense in the European Renaissance which, originally in painting and architecture, and subsequently in writing, was 'systematically and symptomatically prioritized' over the other senses, fostering a maximum sense of mastery for the viewer. That sense of mastery derives from the detachment of position sight allows and requires, while also supporting judgments of class, fashion and affluence, manifest in visual presentation (Massey, 224; Evett; Cropper, *passim*).

The products of her writing are, additionally, represented by Is. W. as so desirable that they may produce feelings of envy or hurt if one person receives them and another does not; their power makes them potentially conflictive. Is. W. tells her sister, A[nne B[aron], that, having written to her brothers and other sisters, she needs to prove her goodwill and gratitude by writing also to Anne, lest Anne think less of her. And in her dedication to Mainwaring, she foresees envy of her 'Flowers' of poetry by others because she 'presented ... or gathered them, bef[ore] they had done one, or both.' Also, though one may be materially poor, poetic language contains a kind of abundance in which one may nevertheless be rich, and which may even be invested as a means of assuaging material impoverishment. As this publishing poet surely understood, the power of immaterial language contains the potential for material production and material recompense. This recognition must lie behind both her own willingness to give her poetry a material form by bringing it into print and her dedication of this volume to George Mainwaring, an affluent friend and neighbor to the Whitney family in Cheshire, and a potential patron. And, closely coupled with her poetic petition to her brother Geffrey to let her know his whereabouts, so that she may write to him personally rather than publicly, is an equally important request for his material help. To her brother Brooke she also intends to 'wryt.' Not knowing the whereabouts of these brothers, she is still able to communicate with them through the power of the published poetic epistle functioning as a kind of early 'personals' column, and ask them for financial help.

A poetic composition itself may also serve as a valued gift. The dedication to George Mainwaring offers the 'nosgay' of poems as a 'Present' which Is. W. gracefully compares to a gift of water carried by a peasant in his hands to the 'Persian Prince,' and whose sufficiency to 'recompence' Mainwaring's generosity she conventionally decries.[30] Isabella herself is able generously to 'give' advice to her sisters, supplying them, even when she 'shal further from [them] dwell,' she promises, with 'wealth.' Unlike other gift-giving, however, this gift of language is indefatigable and incapable of satiation: 'I cannot speake, or wryte to much, / because I love you well.' The gift of Is. W.'s writing is so powerful it may even act as a kind of talisman, the daily reading of which, rather like the reading of the Scriptures, may protect her sisters from harm:

> Your business being done,
>   and this my scroule perusd,
> The day wyll end, and that the night
>   by you be not abusde,
> I some thing nedes must write,
>   take paynes to read the same. (sig. D1)

Finally, most powerfully of all, the poet's pen can immortalize its subject. Writing to her friend, T.B., self-confidently Is. W. assures him 'that thy Fame, for ever florish shall, / If Is. her Pen, may promise ought at all.' The ultimate and permanent absence of death can be eased, if not erased, by the poet's power.

Yet such a powerful medium cannot always be harnessed or made to produce results that are desired or predictable; it may have intended or unintended harmful as well as curative effects. Even though, as a poet, Is. W. claims the highest degree of power over the vagaries of language, she warns her sisters that words abused by others and turned to lies have the unreliability of the wayward wind and may be harmful in their effects:

> Your busines soone dispatch,
>   and listen to no lyes:
> Nor credit every fayned tale,
>   that many wyll devise.
> For words they are but winde.
>   yet words may hurt you so. (sig. D1)

Master T.L., who has foolishly not paid attention to Is. W.'s warnings against those who would take advantage of him and 'wold fleece [him] much,' she scolds: 'But all my wordes they weare as wind / my labour yll was spent'; even her own words, though curative in intent, she irritatedly acknowledges, may be ignored. Yet she continues to insist on her instructive and poetic power: 'Nor hand, nor tong, shal so be charmd / to make me holde my peace. / Wherefore I warne you once againe.' She is insistently determined that he shall heed her, that the authority of her speech will ultimately persuade him. *Her* writing, if properly attended to, can act effectively as a protection against the harmful and corrupting effects of 'lyes,' 'fayned tales,' and 'trifles' of gossip. Although she tells the reader that she is no 'Sorceresse,' and deserves no 'ban or curse,' her self-defense reveals her awareness of her almost magical power to manipulate words for curative purposes.

The speaker in 'The Auctor to the Reader' is quite explicit about the medicinal powers of her poetry, especially for the kind of melancholy disorder she herself seems to suffer. She proves her integrity and seriousness by not claiming too much; her poems will not cure already entrenched mental illness – 'if thy mind infected be, / then these wyll not prevayle,' but they may 'keepe thee sound, / which if thou use them well: / (paynes of my lyfe) in healthy state / thy mind shall ever dwell.' She still, however, needs to warn her reader that 'thou my Nosegay not misuse.' A distillation of her poems 'wyll safely thee preserve,' she says in 'A Soveraigne Receypt,' but in 'A Farewell to the Reader,' she again issues a warning against their abuse:

> I must request you spoyle them not,
>   nor doo in peeces teare them:
> But if thy selfe doo lothe the sent
>   geve others leave to weare them.
> I shall no whit be discontent,
>   for nothyng is so pure:
> But one, or other will mislyke
>   therof we may be sure. (sig. C5)

Language, even at its best-intentioned, can be misused and misunderstood, to the poet's or the reader's detriment, for it can both fill in an absence and reinforce it, be received gladly and also inspire envy, can serve as an adequate gift and also fail to 'recompense,' be enjoyed or not, can cure and harm. Its doubleness is as clearly manifest to this speaker as it was to the persona of the *Letter*. How then can this powerful and insecure medium of poetry, not entirely under the control of even its most skillful user, be turned to good results, and how may its user endorse herself as a subject in its slippery morass?

To answer these questions it seems necessary to look closely at Whitney's relationship of literary indebtedness to Hugh Plat, the very place where she might be expected to exercise the least opportunity for subjective agency, and also at Is. W.'s comments about what she imagines that relationship to embody. The most obvious alteration imposed by Whitney on Plat's *sententiae* is her rendering of them into verse. As Ann Rosalind Jones argues, this change made the mottoes 'memorizable' and 'popular' (*Currency*, 42), and here again we may see Whitney's eye for the saleable and fashionable at work. But in setting a series of male-authored prose pieces to poetry, she is doing something in terms of literary ideology much more interesting and challenging; she might even be regarded as enacting her authority over Plat's material.

The writing enterprise considered most acceptable for women during the years of Whitney's literary activity was translation of admired and authoritative male work into vernacular tongues; one well-known evidence of this expectation appears in the preface to John Florio's translation of Montaigne, where he speaks of the 'feminine' activity of translation. Or, because serious and original poetry was considered a male preserve, the ideologically more predictable gendered turn would have been a woman's translation of male poetry into prose. Whitney's role in relation to Plat *is* as a kind of translator of his morally serious work, but the highly unusual switch from male prose to female poetry suggests that Whitney is challenging and out-writing Plat in an 'anything you can do I can do better' move.

That Whitney was not averse to male–female competition and even conflict is evident in her first volume of poetry and also here in the few poetic flowers in her nosegay where she negatively judges men. Though women's anger, she says in her sixty-fifth flower, can be appeased by men's tears, 'men will not be pacified, / if Wemen weepe a flood.' In her sixty-third quatrain, she points out the disjunction between the lover's 'desire' and what she 'should require.' And in the seventy-sixth, in the bawdy manner Paul Marquis has pointed out in her earlier volume of poems, she writes mockingly of men's loss of reason and 'dying' in love, playing on the Elizabethan *double entendre* for this image of orgasm. Here, however, 'life' is restored upon sexual entry into another's body:

Affection fond deceaves the wise
        and love makes men such noddyes
That to their selves they seeme as dead
        yet live in other boddies. (sig. C1)

In other ways, too, Whitney seems to be suggesting Plat's deficiencies and repairing them. Ann Jones points out that Whitney cut down Plat's unwieldy material: 'she organized maxims into thematic groups (fortune, friendship, love); she expanded Plat's terse sentences into metrical mottoes written in a memorizable iambic heptameter' (*Currency*, 42). Panofsky also tellingly comments that 'Whitney disliked the miscellaneous ordering of Plat's sentences. Something in his concept is not congenial to her tastes for organizing and grouping' (xii).

Whitney's dissatisfaction with Plat's randomly planted garden and sententious prose is also evident in the final lines of 'The Auctor to the Reader': 'yf thou to *Plat* his Plot / Repayre: take heede it is a Maze / to warne thee I forgot.' In this maze, Whitney seems to say, the reader may get lost, and perhaps would do better to 'repayre' to Whitney's better-organized and potentially more health-giving 'nosgay.' After all, mazes, we know, had a notorious erotic association in Elizabethan culture as places for illicit assignations. Whitney's 'Flowers' may be more openly and wholesomely indulged. Writing to Mainwaring, she has said that her 'Flowers' are 'of others growing, yet ... of my owne gathering and makeing up.' It seems likely that this gathering and making up is being represented under the conventional self-deprecation as the more serious and important activity, especially when Whitney goes on to compare her poeticizing with the role of health-giver. Plat may be the gardener, but she is the apothecary. The man may grow the garden, but the woman's use of the products of the garden is what is ultimately potent. The selecting and arranging of the correct flowers or herbs to promote health surely requires more skill than – or at least as much as – their growing. In a facetious way, Whitney tells the reader that she is appropriating the products of Plat's (male) garden and prose to make her own (female) medicine and poetry.

In the 'Auctor to the Reader,' the poet assumes with confidence the role of medical herbalist, typically assigned to women rather than men in this period. Contemporary garden books and household handbooks for women assume that the business of growing and composing the remedies for the health of the household belong to women; recipes for herbal treatments and medicines are interspersed among cooking recipes, household hints and guides for conduct and table manners in works for women readers by Gervase Markham, John Murrell and Hugh Plat himself. In fact, Plat's authorship of several such garden and household conduct books makes him a congenial source of manipulable literary and herbal material for young women like Whitney in service in London households.

At the conclusion of her 'Farewell to the Reader,' Whitney hopes that 'some may say, God speede her well / that dyd this Nosegay make,' but she also provocatively considers the possibility that Plat himself might

> Fume ... to see them borne aboute,
>   and wysh he did mee know.
> And say in rage were she a man,
>   that with my flowers doth brag,
> She well should pay the price, I wolde
>   not leave her worth a rag. (sig. C5)

Panofsky reads these lines as 'a bit of teasing' (vi), although Krontiris finds in them an 'excessive concern' about the possibility of being sued for 'literary stealing' (29). It is true that plagiarism and notions of intellectual ownership had begun to affect the climate of publication by 1573, when the *Nosgay* was published, with Donne, Drayton and Greene complaining about literary theft (Miller, 231–241), and the seeds of the Harvey–Nashe and Shakespeare–Greene controversies already planted. But Isabella's brother, Geffrey, for example, in 1586 was still able to publish without apology a whole volume of emblems which he 'borrowed' from others, only sixteen of the 248 being original. Perhaps this difference between Geffrey's silence and Isabella's acknowledgment of literary indebtedness suggests the differing standards for male and female authorship and literary borrowing which Krontiris perceives. Yet, although Whitney may be playing to the understanding among her audience of this likelihood, here, as also in the dedication to Mainwaring and in her 'Auctor to the Reader,' she must also be slyly drawing attention to herself as a skillful practitioner of the rhetorical methods of *imitatio* and *copia*, much admired by Elizabethan readers.

Erasmus, whose advocacy of Ovid's *Heroides* as a model for letter-writing we have already noted as a possible influence on Whitney's first volume, also urged students of rhetoric to demonstrate the arts of *imitatio* and *copia*: 'Erasmus' aim was to enable his students to develop an ability to turn the same thought into many forms, so that the commonplace becomes the primary matter (res) of the artist, and the efficacious expression of forms of common knowledge the definition of his artistry' (Trousdale, 49). This practice of 'imitative' collecting and 'copious' elaboration of commonplace ideas which circulated freely in writerly communities explains more aptly, I think, Whitney's comments on her use of Plat's text than any real fear of being found guilty of literary theft.

Erasmus also advocated the use of 'proverbs, sententiae, similes, and exempla,' which were 'widely used in teaching Latin composition and formed a body of materials with which generations of schoolboys became familiar in the process of learning how to write' (Bath, 31). That rhetoric was the subject excluded from girls' education as valueless to a person destined for a private life need not have deterred Whitney, who, as rural, gentry-level girls typically did, probably shared her brothers' education up to the level of university, and who was clearly better educated than she here pretends. Although she laments her 'mased muse' and 'brused brayne' in response to the reading she chooses 'to edifye' herself – 'Scriptures,' 'Histories' and 'Virgill, Ovid, Mantuan' – the very choices demonstrate considerable learning, and, in any case, her brother Geffrey, in the preface to his emblems, similarly pleads 'wante of learninge, and judgement.' Ably demonstrating her rhetorical skill, Isabella can afford freely to deprecate it.

Michael Bath reminds us of the close connections between the moral epigram or adage, such as Plat and Isabella write, and the emblem, which Geffrey Whitney favored. Emblems began as verse epigrams, and were used in 'memory systems by which writers were traditionally trained to systematise ideas in order to be able to recall or retrieve them for use' (34). Isabella's efforts at thematic systematization of Plat's collection conform to this same methodology. The distinction commented on by several recent Whitney readers, between Plat's 'learned' and Whitney's 'popular' style, may not have seemed so great to an Elizabethan reader if 'no essential discontinuity was generally recognized between the learned apothegm or adage and the popular proverb' (Bath, 43).

Furthermore, Plat's, Isabella's and Geffrey's collections all fall under the same genre classification in Renaissance rhetoric, described variously as 'flowers,' 'posies' (both these terms were used as titles for George Gascoigne's 1573 and 1575 publications), 'florilegium,' miscellany or anthology. Isabella's description of her culling activity in the 'Auctor to the Reader' clearly expects her reader to recognize the connections outlined by Walter Ong:

> The conceptual apparatus of 'flowers' and 'collecting' is tied in with the massive tradition of rhetorical invention (which includes poetic invention) ... 'Flowers' imply the busy rhetorical 'bee' who goes through the garden (or, at times, the forest) of invention to visit the 'places' (*loci*, *topoi*) from which the 'arguments' are to be extracted ... and constituted as bouquets of flowers. (Ong, 99, quoted in Bath, 44)

Isabella, as well as Geffrey, then, should also be seen as working ably in the same rhetorical or poetic tradition, even though the social level of their audiences and the material status of their publications are different. But Geffrey's emblem book was still in the future when Isabella's *Nosgay* came into print, and the markers of difference between the country gentleman who received her dedication and the nobleman who received Geffrey's, and the less and more elaborate and expensive material production of the two volumes were not yet evident.[31] Isabella's conventional literary modesty therefore is moderated by her real pride in her participation in yet another new, but still more prestigious, literary and rhetorical fashion than those drawn on in the *Copy of a letter* volume. 'Respect my labour,' she urges Mainwaring, and in the 'Auctor to the Reader,' she boasts that she is 'bolde' to come to 'Plat's plot' when as '[she] wyll: / Yea, and to chuse of all his Flowers, which may my fancy fill.' 'For this I say the Flowers are good, / which I on thee bestow,' she announces. From Plat's writing she culls her nosegay and, though just before she begins her selection, she gracefully decries her ability to 'sort the same aright,' she still triumphantly declares her success: 'And now I have a Nosegay got.' In her 'Farewell,' emphasizing to her reader that to produce the nosegay, 'some payne I tooke, / and travayled many houres,' she forcefully demands that her work not be 'spoyle[d].'

The Abject Power of the Poetic Subject

Just as her poetry is acknowledged by Whitney as multiply layered, both curative and harmful, heeded by its reader and ignored, solidly authoritative and unpredictable as the wind, her own writerly power and self-confidence are underwritten with another layer of what Julia Kristeva calls 'abjection.' In the *Copy of a letter*, even while forthrightly denouncing her lover's errors, the persona characterizes herself as 'forsaken' by her lover and 'content' as his 'refuse':

> But if I can not please your minde,
> For wants that rest in me:
> Wed whom you list, I am content
> Your refuse for to be. (sig. A4)

This self-representation, referring most obviously to the speaker's having been 'refused' by her lover, startlingly also evokes the idea of that which is literally thrown away, as the 'refuse' that is no longer useful to the male lover.

It is difficult to resist finding in this term a suggestive correlative with Julia Kristeva's theory of the 'remainder,' the originally maternal and semiotic otherness rejected by patriarchal monological systems of signification as threatening to themselves because it can never be fully domesticated or completely expelled: '[N]o signifier can uplift it [the maternal] without leaving a remainder, for the signifier is always meaning, communication, or structure, whereas a woman as mother would be, instead, a strange fold that changes culture into nature' ('Stabat,' 259). Persistent because internal, this multi-referential otherness inspires speech of the kind forced from 'anyone or anything identified with cultural remainders' (McDonald, 98); it is a site of cultural or linguistic transgression inside the socio-symbolic order, emanating from the pre-Symbolic maternal body, which is for Kristeva the only site of fissure in the patriarchal Symbolic. Its linguistic otherness finds expression in non-logical, indeterminate, non-analytic and, frequently and most naturally, poetic, language. Though women and their language, because of women's particular association with maternity, are most easily identified with the abject, and therefore most efficiently exiled from Symbolic power, it is a condition exclusive neither to mothers nor to women (Oliver, 7, 101–105, 111–113). In just such terms of abject poetic power, however, even as her poetic language and illustrations expose the anger and pain mixed with her acceptance of her fate (she is 'content'), the 'forsaken' speaker in *The Copy of a letter* may be seen as enacting her evasion of the control of masculine love, and of binary strictures advocating women's silence and muffling their non-binary eloquence and discontent. Kristeva's transgressive 'speaking subject' is imagined as one who accepts his or her abjection in the patriarchal, Symbolic order, but finds in it a place for the 'other' speech of the flexible, precarious subject.

The *Nosgay* volume, much more intensively than the earlier poetry, and in much greater detail, records the symptoms of abjection. In the 'Auctor to the Reader,' the speaker is 'subject unto sicknesse.' She is unemployed ('servicelesse') and diffusely – biologically, psychologically, creatively, or materially – unproductive ('harvestlesse'). 'Servicelesse,' she may be both unserved and unserving, 'harvestlesse,' she may be both unharvested and unharvesting, in both cases both potential receiver and giver, both potential object and subject. She suffers mental confusion and disorientation and a failure of creative inspiration ('mased muse' and 'brused brayne') in response to authoritative male intellectual documents; she is burdened by a 'luckless lyfe,' and craves death. In the dedication to Mainwaring, and the epistle to C.B., she is beset by the 'spightfull.' In the letters to her family members and in the 'Wyll and testament,' she is impoverished. In the epistle to her brother, G.W., she describes herself as the 'least of Fortunes favour[ed],' and in her epistle to her brother, B.W., as full of 'feare and deepe dispaire.' In the 'Wyll,' she has been imprisoned in Ludgate, probably for debt, and London has treated her pitilessly and rejected her.

In her most abjected lament, 'A Carefull Complaynt by the Unfortunate Auctor,' she identifies with the condition of another miserable woman, Dido, claiming that, following Dido, she has been chosen by fate to 'augment / misfortunes lucklesse line,' suffering still 'greater cause of griefe' than Dido because fortune has converted her 'health to heapes of payne,' and 'sweares [her] death.' She is 'gript with endles griefes: / Dispayre (alas) amid my hope, / and hope without reliefe'; 'heapes of deadly harmes,' she says, 'styll threaten my decay,' and she begs, 'O Death delay not long, / thy dewtie to declare.' Her letter to C.B., 'Bewaylynge Her Mishappes,' continues in the same vein, listing her 'dryrie daye in dole' and 'noysome nightes,' 'distresse,' 'perplexitie,' and 'endlesse miserie.' Her answer to G.W.'s attempt to comfort her pretends for the moment that, being 'wery of writyng,' she will cease to write until she has discharged herself of her griefs by vomiting them up, and will 'more quietnes ... trye.' Yet, inevitably, this powerful speaker does not abide by this resolution. She bursts out again into even more eloquent speech in the immediately following 'Wyll and testament.'

The intensity, extremity and repetitions of this persona's complaints appear to double the marginality intrinsic to her situation as a woman writer, at the same time as they also seem more to promote than to impede her writing. Her very condition, it seems, has driven her to write, to claim the right to write. Her loss of identity as a serving maid in a London household, and her ensuing misfortunes, are the very circumstances which have forced her inscription of herself as the subject who writes of these experiences. Seeking to explain Is. W.'s construction of her subjectivity, it is essential to take seriously her insistence on her emphatic embodiment – sick, vomiting, insomniac, mortal, death-desiring and death-fearing, in 'heapes of pain,' for Kristeva sees the metaphor of the anguished body, most clearly, but not only, evident in the pain and joy of childbirth, as the site within which the drama of the conflicted, marginal speaking subject is enacted, a drama of 'his/her mortality' which the subject accepts and in which he/she even finds joy (McDonald, 99). The conjunction and disjunction of pain and pleasure, sickness and health, sanity ('whole in body and in minde') and insanity ('brused brayne'), economic and social subjugation and authoritative writing, in Is. W.'s case, are precisely the manifestations of the split subjectivity that breaks through to speech beyond the patriarchal codes.

Wendy Wall has explained the way in which Whitney writes from deprivation: 'Troped as a recipe for personal preservation (a "soveraigne receypt"), her text comes to life through the account of her unfortunate personal circumstances' (298). Wall's argument focuses on the 'Wyll and testament,' which closes the *Nosgay* volume. Here Is. W. gives away in a poetic will, that is, in a substitute gift of writing, material objects she does not possess. The poetic 'Wyll and testament' itself becomes her deeded heritage; poetic and intellectual capital in her poem successfully compete in value with material property. Later in her book, however, Wall makes a summary statement about early modern women's writing in general, whose phrasing I want to apply specifically to Whitney: 'Women writers had to stay the threat of a double "fall," both sexual and social, when they chose to wander into the literary marketplace' (339). With this comment in mind, we need to return to the first of the two stanzas quoted at the beginning of this section, from the epistle addressed to Misteris A.B.

In this revealing stanza, Is. W. tells her sister: 'I know you huswyfery intend / Though I to writing fall.' The term 'fall,' as Wall implies, has a sexual connotation uniquely applicable to women, as in the phrase, 'a fallen woman.' In colloquial usage, the term is still used in the twenty-first century to denote not merely loss of virginity, but pregnancy. The *NED* records its first use in legal proceedings in this sense as occurring in 1722, but the sequence from the Edenic 'fall' from grace and innocence, to woman's sexual 'fall' from virtue, to her punished 'fall' into pregnancy and painful labor, is an ancient connection. Is. W. / Whitney's 'fall' to writing, then, renders her captured by, even made 'pregnant' by, writing.[32] This little phrase, with irresistible and uncanny resonance, states exactly the conditions proposed by Kristeva for women's writing – exiled from the patriarchal, embodied, poetic, abjected and metaphorically maternal. That Whitney and her persona are embedded in, and pressured by, a vast set of binary values and choices surely helps induce the mysterious sickness and misfortune that beset her. For a woman who wants to write and who also desires economic stability, the inextricable oppositions she faces are unresolvable: 'real' motherhood and 'huswifery' versus metaphoric, maternal 'fall' to writing; marriage and maternity versus spinsterhood and writing; domestication versus employment; material indebtedness, psychological dependence and accusations of plagiarism versus economic, personal and writerly autonomy.

Yet, even while negotiating these binary codes, the speaker still, like the speaker in *The letter* who is both 'refuse' and 'content,' claims pleasure for herself, the essential joy or 'jouissance' available to the abject speaker, and registered as a claim to subjectivity. While walking home, 'all sole alone,' she is guided by Fortune who, she says 'made mee *pleasures feele*.' The following lines, unusually in these poems, confirm her pleasure in richly sensuous terms:

> For she to Plat his Plot mee brought,
>   where fragrant Flowers abound:
> The smell whereof prevents ech harme,
>   if yet your selfe be sound.
> Amongst those Beds so bravely deckt,
>   with every goodly Flower:
> And Bankes and Borders finely framde,
>   I mee reposde one howre. (sig. A6)

That this possible pleasure is sensuous explains in part the speaker's earlier rejection of male authoritative and instructive writing, which, just as it always fails to speak adequately for the paradigm of maternal experience, also failed to speak to her 'feeling' body, her physical and emotional pain and illness and her hope for joy. The complex combination of pleasure and pain, seen by Kristeva as releasing women (or men) from binary logic and language through the real or imagined experience of maternity, or similar embodied experiences, also has other metaphoric counterparts in Is. W.'s narrative of her writing experience.

In the first case, she likens her volume's dedication to Mainwaring to the gift of water carried in his hands by a 'poore man' to the 'Persian prince.' Here again, as in

The Copy of a letter, we see Whitney disregarding binary gender boundaries; though she is female, the donor to whom she compares herself is male. The gift of water, the metaphor for her poetry, also escapes control; potentially both life-saving and, as a gift to a prince, superfluous, it is not bounded, seeping through the cupped fingers of the giver. The second weighted metaphor for Is. W.'s poetry occurs in 'The Auctor to the Reader.' While she herself is 'bolde' to come and pick from Plat's garden, and has from it 'frame[d]' a 'Posye,' she says that if others also wish to cut from the garden they must do so 'with order.' Though they 'may gather whilst they list':

> Then pittie were it to destroy,
> what he with payne did plant.
> The moderate heere may be suffisde,
> and he no whit shall want. (sig. A6)

At the poem's end, she is more insistent still that care be taken when cutting from Plat's plot:

> For though he make no spare of them,
> to such as have good skyll:
> To slip, to shere, or get in time,
> and not his braunches kyll:
> Yet barres he out, such greedy guts,
> as come with spite to toote:
> And without skill, both Earb and Flower
> pluck rashly by the roote. (sig. A8)

The action here being described is clearly more significant than simply clipping a few flowers, and in fact bears a close resemblance to the careful art of pruning to induce growth and increase the health and productivity of the plant. Whitney is, on the one hand, undoubtedly alluding to her quite drastic 'pruning' of Plat's numerous sentences, for the sake of improving their usefulness and health-giving properties, but a current emblematic allusion may also be active here. A motto reproduced and recognized as controversial in Elizabethan England was that inscribed on Mary Stuart's signet ring and used by her as a self-reference: *Virescit vulnere virtus*, or 'Virtue flourishes by wounding.' In an embroidered version, on a cushion made as a gift for the Duke of Norfolk, Mary joined the motto to a visual depiction of a hand holding a pruning knife and, as William Drummond described it to Ben Jonson, 'cutting down the vines as they use in the spring time' (Bath, 18; Freeman, 51).[33]

If the literary virtue of Plat's numerous prose aphorisms has been given new life by Whitney's skillful reducing, revising and poeticizing, so the poetic and moral speech and virtue of the persona herself may be seen as increased by the wounding or suffering she insistently describes herself as experiencing. In this metaphoric emanation, then, the speaker's sick, 'wounded' body again returns us to Kristeva's

4.2 Mary Stuart's *impresa* of a pruning hand

notion of women's poetic or semiotic creativity as psychoanalytically inflected by their abjectly suffering and yet joyously creative bodies.

Of course, without the mediation of Kristeva's psychoanalytic explanation for women's culturally marginalized desire for creative language not under the control of the patriarchy, Whitney's contemporary audience must also have understood in their own socio-symbolic context the warranty her speaker's misfortune, 'sicknesse,' and 'heapes of pain' issued for her poetic speech. The early modern period saw physical affliction as a condition intimately associating the sufferer with God, and offering a spiritual opportunity for patience and virtue. Andrew Borde's *Breviary of helthe* (1547), for example, advising the sick to think of Christ's death, Passion and pains, assigns ultimate power over physical well-being to God: 'Lordes, Ladies and Gentylmen, lerned and unlearned, of what estate or degre so ever you be of, thynke not that no man can be holpen by no maner of medicines, yf so be god do send the sicknes for he hath put a time to every man' (sig. B3). This awareness is manifest also in C.B.'s answer to Is. W.'s epistle, where C.B. offers advice that Is. W. too should remember that Christ himself was beset on earth by misfortune and that she should follow the example of his patience:

> Yf evel words and other wants,
> have brought thee to this woe:
> Remember how that Christ him selfe,
> on earth was even so. (sig. D7)

Adversity and sickness were also seen as chastisements by God for sin, and sometimes the sick person was seen as released from illness by a special dispensation from God. Lady Margaret Hoby's diary, for example, records in 1599 that she suffered a headache and a stomach-ache as God's 'Just punishment.' On 6 March 1602, after an illness, she rejoices, 'Praise God I had health of body'; when ill, God had allowed 'Satan to afflict my mind.' Is. W. speaks in her epistle to C.B. of her 'sinne,' admonishing herself to accept 'pacientlye / Correction in adversitie':

> Wherefore (my God) geve me that gyfte,
> as he did JOB untyll:
> That I may take with quietnesse,
> whatsoever is his wyll. (sig. D6)

Suffering also, however, more importantly for women otherwise urged to silence, earns for the sufferer the moral right to testify and instruct. C.B. encourages Is. W. to 'Impart thy woes, and geve to mee, / the greatest of the same.' The narrative of illness and misfortune, then as now, was encouraged to assuage the suffering and to establish an exemplary record of strength and endurance. Is. W. says she writes to C.B. to ease her 'perplexitie':

Therefore, in this perplexitie,
  To you deare frende I write:
You know my endlesse miserie. (sig. D6)

Early modern women, frequently ill because of their reproductive roles, were responsible also for the health care of others. Lucinda Beier, writing of women in the seventeenth century, says they 'had a special relationship with illness and healing by virtue of their sex. Their physiology made them particularly vulnerable to disease ... Their particular talents for nurturing and healing were seen as inherent in their female nature' (241). The 1655 edition of *Natura Exenterata: or: Nature Unbowelled*, ascribes, unusually, half of its medical recipes to women. Women thus found in these closely related capacities a means to justify their speech and writing. If ill, especially if afflicted in ways connected with the socially crucial maternal function, women might ask for attention, for protection, for remedy or for the right to tell their story. The diaries, journals and handbooks of many women like Margaret Hoby, Grace Mildmay, Alice Thornton, Elizabeth Freke, Anne Clifford, Elizabeth Grey, Mary Trye, Jane Sharp and Anne Halkett, take advantage, eloquently and in detail, of the hard-won right to record the intense association of women with sickness – their own and that of others.[34] Is. W. also gains authority for her poetic speech in part because human suffering opens up and legitimates a claim to speech, for the cry of suffering is difficult to deny. In fact, the narrative of illness may instantiate the presence of the sufferer, revealing her in her suffering as the speaking subject of her own felt experiences and legitimated story.

Finally, Is. W. may be seen as suffering from that most characteristic affliction of Renaissance creativity – the symptoms of melancholy.[35] The melancholic temperament uses writing to alleviate the 'hevinesse,' 'dolour,' solitariness, studiousness and 'losse of goodes' (66–69), which Thomas Elyot's *Castell of Helth* (1541) says characterize the condition, all of which symptoms Is. W. also experiences, along with other manifestations of the disease, such as insomnia, her 'dryrie daye[s] in dole,' and 'noysome nightes.' Robert Burton, writing the definitive commentary on melancholy half a century after Whitney, adds to the list of causes and symptoms still others amply documented in Is. W.'s case (xv–xvi): 'solitariness' (Is. W. is 'sole alone'); 'idleness' (she is 'servicelesse'); 'the force of the imagination' (her 'mased muse'); 'sorrow,' 'fear,' 'cares, miseries, &c.' (she suffers from 'feare and deepe dispaire'); 'Love of Learning' (clear in her reading and writing); 'poverty and want' (she is in debt); and 'scoffs, calumnies, and bitter jests' (the 'spightes' directed at her).

Some aspects of Burton's diagnostic system would undoubtedly have marked Is. W. as a prime candidate for the melancholic disease, for, in addition to her clear symptomatology, melancholy is most extreme, he argued, in women just like Is. W., who are not 'well placed, and married' (355), whose 'fire of lust' is not assuaged by marriage (357, cited in Schiesari, 14). Melancholy was also, according to John Weyer's 1563 text, *De praestigiis daemonum*, crueler in women because 'more

4.3 Albrecht Dürer, *Melencolia*

opposed to their temperament' (cited in Schiesari, 14), which was expected to be naturally cheerful and nurturing. An earlier woman medical observer, however, agreed with neither of these male opinions and would have supported Is. W.'s slow approach to marriage as appropriate to her psychology. Hildegarde of Bingen saw melancholy women as 'saner, stronger, and happier when without husbands than with them, because if they were with husbands they would become debilitated' (89, quoted in Schiesari, 152).

Despite his easy solution to women's melancholy, Robert Burton might have found in Whitney/ Is. W. a fellow writer and melancholic who, as with his own case, wrote to seek alleviation of 'perplexitie' and 'endlesse miserie,' but whose writing also feeds on and feeds the affliction. Yet his theories would not have encouraged Burton to expect this writerly communication with Whitney / Is. W., whose occupation as a serving maid, and presumably therefore of an insufficiently fine and sensitive temperament, he would have expected to exempt her from melancholy: 'For seldom shall you see an hired servant, a poor handmaid, though ancient, that is kept hard to work and bodily labour, a coarse country wench, troubled in this kind' (355). On the other hand, though from the country and poor, Is. W. is hardly 'ancient' or 'coarse,' and neither, apparently, is she engaged in 'bodily labour,' both because at the time of her melancholy she is unemployed, and also because she is, it seems, of a class of serving maids more akin to companion or housekeeper than to those primarily committed to physical work.[36]

Burton's recognition of a fellow writer would also have been inhibited by his opinion that while melancholy makes men creative and expressive, it makes women inarticulate or raving:

> [B]y fits it takes them now and then, except the malady be inveterate ... Many of them cannot tell how to express themselves in words, or how it holds them, what ails them, you cannot understand them, or well tell what to make of their sayings; so far gone sometimes, so stupefied and distracted, they think themselves bewitched, they are in despair & ready to weep. (354)

As she has done consistently in both volumes of her poetry, Whitney here too leaps over a gendered boundary, in this case the one set up by Burton between melancholic male creativity and melancholic female inarticulateness.[37] Burton's judgment of what more sympathetic readers have come to recognize as women's legitimate creative expression sadly echoes and foretells conventional male judgments of women's writing, both in the early modern period and in the centuries following. The 'you,' who 'cannot understand them or well tell what to make of their sayings,' is certainly the male reader with whom Burton shares a commitment to monological and binary language systems. Burton is surely not addressing twentieth-century readers, by whose positive construction of early modern writers he would surely be immensely surprised.

That Burton's description of melancholic women's expression also echoes the descriptions of women's reclaimed subjectivity, their language and their abject expression, found in the theories of Julia Kristeva and other feminist psychoanalytic readers, is an eerie and, to me, pleasing coincidence. These theorists have suggested that behaviors that Burton classified as stupefaction, bewitchment and distractedness are signs not of inarticulateness, but of women's escape from the control of patriarchal language. They have helped us to discover in Whitney and other women poets a subjective presence and an articulate, though not masculine, speech. Whitney, we have seen, writes in a doubling language, undermining binary relationships, and she enacts the conditions of abjection and melancholy to claim the right to poetic and printed subjectivity. Kristeva says that suffering allows an absence 'from other people's meaning.' We might equally well claim that Isabella Whitney's strategy of suffering allowed her to circumvent the language and meaning represented by readers like Robert Burton.

Notes

1 Unpublished verse by women exists in some earlier manuscript collections. See Marotti, 25–26, 38–40, 48–61.

2 For a fascinating related study of the collaborative relations that prevailed in this period among dramatists, see Jeffrey Masten's *Textual Intercourse*.

3 Jones's list of publications of interest to women includes: *The passionate morrice* (1593), Francis Meres's *Gods arithmeticke* (1597), Thomas Pritchard's *The schoole of honest and vertuous lyfe* (1579), *Quippes for upstart newfangled gentlewomen. Or a glasse to view the pride of vainglorious women. Containing A pleasant invective against the fantastical foreigne toyes, daylie to be used in womens apparell* (1595), Philip Stubbes's *A christal glasse for Christian women* (1591), and William Warren's *A pleasant new fancie of a fondlings device* (1581).

4 The etymology of the word 'miscellany', like the Latin *satura*, implies a jumbled, possibly disorderly 'collation of fruits gathered in one banquet to suit a variety of tastes' (Benedict, 9). See also Juliet Fleming's insertion of the concept of 'posies' into the practice of wall-writing ('Graffiti,' 325).

5 See also the testimony of Thomas Whythorne, a music master, in his autobiography, that one female student 'devised certain verses in English, writing them with her own hand; and did put them between the strings of [my] gittern' (quoted by Ilona Bell, 78, from *The Autobiography of Thomas Whythorne*, 21).

6 A Noise did rise like thunder in my hearing,
When in the East I saw darke clowdes appearing:
Where furies sat in Sable mantles couched,
Haughty disdaine with cruel envy matching,
Olde Momus and young Zoylus all watching,
How to disgrace what Morley hath avouched,
But loe the day star with his bright beames shining,
Sent forth his aide to musicks arte refining,
Which gave such light for him whose eyes long hovered,
To find a part where more lay undiscovered,

That all his workes with ayre so sweete perfumed,
Shall live with fame when foes shalbe consumed.

7 Unless R.J. Fehrenbach is correct in his guess that the 'Sister Eldershae' mentioned in Geffrey Whitney's will is the now married Isabella.

8 For example, Krontiris, Travitsky and Walker. For a useful discussion of print culture, see Elizabeth L. Eisenstein's *The Printing Revolution in Early Modern Europe*.

9 Nicholas Breton, for example, 'in *The Pilgrimage to Paradise*, accuses Jones of publishing his poetry "without my consent or knowledge"' (Miller, 148).

10 Paul Marquis has very effectively argued the claim of the volume to be read as a whole: 'the *Copy* was published as a literary assemblage and therefore should be read as such' (316); the 'four epistles together establish a resonance based on thematic images and opposing ideological concerns' (317).

11 Of course, these were not the first. Various debates about women and their nature go back at least to the Greeks; even in sixteenth-century England, one may see the 1521 translation of Christine de Pizan's *Book of the City of Ladies* as a predecessor to Elyot and Gosynhill. Works untranslated into English by Erasmus and Cornelius Agrippa also precede Elyot. For a discussion of Whitney's place in this debate, see Travitsky, 'The Lady Doth protest.'

12 For discussions of the Elizabethan interest in the personal letter, see Kim Walker (27ff, 152), Claudio Guillen, Peter Burke (23ff) and Molly Kirsten Whalen.

13 The Elizabethan interest in Ovid is further underlined by Arthur Golding's translation of the *Metamorphoses* appearing in 1565 (first four books) and 1567 (all fifteen books).

14 The appeal to the new is aptly exemplified in the preface to John Murrell's *A Daily Exercise for Ladies and Gentlewomen* (1617): 'As there is nothing new under Heaven ... so nothing old can please the Soule, or Sense. Yet on olde Grounds are new Descants daily, as full of rarietie, as varietie.' The passion for the new is evident in the regular assertion on title-pages of the newness of the material in the volumes they advertise. Hugh Plat's books, closer than Murrell's to Whitney, are particularly prone to this habit. See also Lorna Wetherill's and Ronald M. Berger's discussion of the increased consumption of 'new' goods in early modern England.

15 For more extensive biographical details about Isabella, see the entry in the *DNB* under Geffrey Whitney, R.J. Fehrenbach's essays, Richard Panofsky's introduction to the *Floures of Philosophie*, Henry Green's introduction to Geffrey Whitney's *Choice of Emblemes* and the reprint of Geffrey's will in the same volume.

16 Marotti also argues that prisons were another locus for poetic production (4–7). This point suggests an interesting connection with Whitney's 'Will and Testament,' in which she implies that she may have been imprisoned in Ludgate for debt.

17 See Amy Erickson's discussion of the tendency to educate brothers and sisters together, especially in non-urban settings (56–57).

18 Even Isabella's other brother, Brooke, was not well off in 1586. Geffrey's emblem addressed to Brooke speaks of Brooke's 'small store' of possessions (Green, 88).

19 For Whitney as a beneficiary of sixteenth-century humanist influence, see Elaine Beilin, 'Writing Public Poetry,' and Betty Travitsky, 'The Lady Doth Protest.'

20 As has been noted by David Cressy. Margaret Spufford and Suzanne Hull discuss the increased number of books designed for female readership between 1475 and 1640. Jacqueline Pearson ('Women Reading') discusses suggestively the social symbology of women's reading.

21 Margaret Tyler, for example. For a discussion of her prefatory material, see the first chapter of this book.

22 Consider, for comparison's sake, Philip Sidney's 1595 pronouncement that to fulfill his [sic] goal to 'teach and delight,' 'the poet, he nothing affirms, and therefore never lieth. For, as I take it, to lie is to affirm that to be true which is false ... The poet never maketh any circles about your imagination, to conjure you to believe for true what he writes' (123–124).

23 Paul Marquis has drawn out the elaborate bawdy puns embedded in the references to 'trying' and 'shrinking' in this poem.

24 See Ann Rosalind Jones's interesting reading of the way in which Whitney 'deconstructs ... classical heroes by applying a pro-woman rather than an epic criterion to their careers' (*Currency*, 44–50).

25 It should be noted that the very arrangement of the poems in this collection privileges the physical and psychological position of the woman's poems. The second 'bacheler' poem, by R. Witc., is not even mentioned on the title-page, but the two male poems follow and take second billing to the two poems by the 'gentilwoman' that open the collection and represent a woman's point of view. A provocative shift has occurred here from the 1563 edition of the *Mirror for Magistrates*, where the woman's lament trails the male voices, appearing at the end of the volume almost as an afterthought. The organization of material in collections like this cannot be taken to be innocent:

> Anthologies embody the principle of clustering together different but similar items. They thus presuppose that all their contents are alike enough to be compared, yet unalike enough to spur readerly evaluation. By beginning with a text that defines the genre and then arranging entries to emphasize contrast, these books stimulate readers to compare, judge, and thus rank the separate items. (Benedict, 4)

26 To my knowledge, it has not been noted, in this context, that in Old English law, a 'procurator' is an agent or attorney who represents a judicial court. Procuration is a legal fee allowed to scriveners or brokers for payment of loans. The poem's allusions indicate that the speaker has been placed in prison for failing to pay her debts.

27 The authorship of these letters raises interesting questions. In a few instances, word choice and repetition of phrases suggest that Whitney may have poeticized or invented some of the letters herself. Her experience turning Plat's prose into poetry may have stood her in good stead in the epistles as well. In two letters from Is. W., to her sisters and to C.B., words are described as 'wind.' More suggestively, in the epistle from G.W. to Is. W., the story of the mariner who survives the storm and tells his tale when he returns to 'friends and kyn' repeats the same story in Is. W.'s epistle to T.B., where the mariner delights 'oft among friends and Kin, / To tell what danger earst his lyfe was in.' The repetitions occur in *The Copy of a Letter* as well. The phrase 'pensive mone' appears in the letter from W.G., and in the letter by R. Witc. we are told that 'pensive men do mone.'

28 See Anne Laurence on conditions of service for young women in London, 129–137.

29 For an analysis of the appearance of these themes in the collection of 'Flowers,' see Ann Jones, *Currency*, 41–43, and Panofsky, vi, ix–xiv.

30 See Jane Donawerth's comments on Whitney's poetry as gift as an example of a contemporary convention (14–16).

I do not see Whitney's apologies for writing as any more than the conventional self-deprecation engaged in by most poets in the period, especially when they are entering into print. I am more inclined to agree with Panofsky's sense that the concluding lines of Whitney's 'Farewell to the Reader' are less serious in tone and do not demonstrate particular concern with issues of literary theft and ownership.

31 See also my discussion of the ideologies of writing and publication apparent in Isabella's and, by comparison, Geffrey's work (*Teaching*).

32 Of course, a much more famous example of this same metaphor appears in Philip Sidney's description of himself in Sonnet 1 of his sequence as 'great with child to speak.

33 Technically, Mary's version is what is known as an *impresa*, containing only two elements to the emblem's three: motto and picture; the emblem adds an explanatory verse. For a discussion of the differences between the *impresa* and the emblem, see Daly, 21ff.

Geffrey Whitney also included the motto in his emblems, but diplomatically accompanied it with a different, less politically volatile, explanation and illustration than the one associated with Mary Stuart, who in 1586, the year of Geffrey's publication, was accused of engineering a plot to murder Elizabeth:

The dockes (though troden) growe, as it is dailie seene:
So vertue, thoughe it longe bee hid, with wounding waxeth greene. (Green, 98)

34 For some interesting excerpts from these women's narratives of suffering and healing, see Otten, parts 5 and 6. Also, for a fascinating study of women and illness as portrayed in paintings of the early modern period, see Laurinda Dixon's *Perilous Chastity*.

35 Writing to T(homas) B(errie), Is. W. invokes the influence of Saturn, the planet of the melancholic, as responsible for spoiling 'Berryes joy,' and encourages him to wait out the influence of Saturn through the sadness of early spring, for eventually:

... when *Saturnus* hath declarde his might:
And *Winter* stints to turne the world to teene
Then pleasant *Ver* shall cloth the groud [sic] in greene
And lusty *May* shall labour to restore,
the things that *Winters* spit had spoyled before.

Although Is. W. begins the poems in this volume in harvest time, that is, in the autumn, her own melancholy symptoms have not abated with the change of seasons, but seem firmly established beyond seasonal influence, or, as Burton says, 'inveterate.'

36 Lena Corwen Orlin points out that 'many servants were of a status broadly speaking, with their employers' (21). 'Difference was more often experienced in terms of wealth and status than 'class' as we think of it today' (22). It is also relevant that, as part of the woman question controversy, two volumes were published in the same year as Whitney's first publication that relate specifically to the issue of appropriate behavior for serving maids. Edward Hake's now missing *A boke intituled a mery metynge of maydes in London* (1567) was answered by *A Letter sent by Maydens of London*, which purports to be a group composition addressed to their mistresses by London maidservants who answer Hake's accusation of their frivolity. Whitney's confession in her 1573 volume that she is a maidservant who has been dismissed, her allusions to her 'sinnes,' her self-defense and her respectful reference to her erstwhile mistress, as well as her use of the letter form in her 1567 volume, are all reminiscent of *A Letter sent by Maydens*. One wonders about Whitney's possible involvement in this volume, although R.J. Fehrenbach argues plausibly that the legal language and allusions indicate a male author.

37 For a thoughtful discussion of Luce Irigaray's contention that women are exiled from the discourse of male, creative melancholia, see Schiesari 63–69.

Chapter 5

Elizabeth Cary. The Nomadic Subject: Space and Mobility in the *Life* and *Mariam*

> You are moving. You never stay still. You never stay. You never 'are.' How can I say 'you,' when you are always other?
>
> – Luce Irigaray, *This Sex Which is not One*, 214

Opening the Texts

Two related issues of absorbing interest to scholars working to legitimate early modern women's writing have dominated many of the ground-breaking studies of Elizabeth Tanfield Cary. The first has been how to situate Cary as historical personage and biographical subject in the growth of what might be called 'feminist' thinking,[1] and the second, how to read the role of women in relation to male power in Cary's closet drama, *The Tragedy of Mariam, The Fair Queen of Jewry*. A typical approach to these interpretive questions has used the fascinating glimpses into Cary's life, supplied in the biography written by one of her daughters, to decipher her equally engrossing and, to some readers, frustrating play. So frequent has been the habit of reading *The Lady Falkland: Her Life*[2] as a key to *Mariam* that the practice has induced the misgivings expressed by Margaret Ferguson, Dympna Callaghan, Marta Straznicky, Stephanie Wright and Shari Zimmerman.

At the beginning of modern Cary criticism, Nancy Cotton Pearse claimed in 1977 that the 'sentiments expressed in the play are autobiographical' (605). Elaine Beilin ten years later observed that 'the coincidental parallels between the lives of Mariam and Elizabeth Cary are striking' (173). In 1992, also reading from the biography to the play, Tina Krontiris asserted that 'Cary's reluctance to support openly rebellious behavior in her life carries over into her literary work' (81). Donald Foster in 1993 saw no boundary between Cary's art and life: 'Cary was a product of continual interplay between her life and her art, as each was made to imitate the other in acts of self-conscious recreation' (145); and Barbara Lewalski, also in 1993, proposed that both of Cary's plays, *Mariam* and *The History of the Life, Reign, and Death of Edward II*, 'may be usefully contextualized with reference to the circumstances of her own life' (180).

To a large degree, Cary's current critical reputation has depended on the strategic juxtaposition by modern scholars of *Mariam* and the *Life* as texts able to reveal something important to each other as well as to the critic, and it must be admitted that a dramatic text more openly declaring its point of view than *Mariam* would less temptingly invite a second text to decode it. Many critics, questioning whether the play exemplifies a credible anti-patriarchal position, have found both the enigmatic role of the play's heroine and its general ideology difficult to pinpoint.[3] Resort to the biography has been an almost irresistible response to the play's inscrutability and apparent inconsistencies.

Beyond the question of how critically justifiable and productive such cross-reading has been, it is evident that turning to the biography as a means of unlocking the secrets of the play has certain theoretical consequences. The use of biographical material to ground the reading of literary and cultural texts may, especially from a post-structuralist point of view, be charged with at least three sins of critical naivety: 1) an Enlightenment bias which assumes a stable, unique and coherent autobiographical subject from which an authentic voice is presumed to speak; 2) unjustified faith in the transparency of a retrievable, truth-telling, life-revealing text; and 3) the privileging of lived experience (ostensibly captured in the biographical text) over recognizably problematized textual emanations.

Dympna Callaghan has warned against some of these errors.[4] From Callaghan's point of view, the emphasis, reinforced by attention to the biography, on Cary's reified female experience has deflected attention from the 'material conditions in which she wrote and in relation to which she herself was placed as other' (167). Margaret Ferguson also warily regards the biography as a 'crucial but problematic document' ('Running,' 39). Marta Straznicky worries that stressing the biographical 'confines both writer and text to the space of the domestic' (107), and Stephanie Wright emphatically insists that 'the anxious biographical validation of Cary's works is no longer necessary and is, in many ways, regressive and harmful' (64). Shari Zimmerman most pertinently reminds us that the 'biography, after all, is not a transparent record of a lived life, but an act of interpretation on the part of a daughter' (583).

In this chapter I do not intend to use either the biography or the play as a means of pursuing what Callaghan calls 'the elusive and perhaps inscrutable woman who lurks behind [these texts]' (165), but neither am I abandoning the pleasures of reading *Mariam* and the *Life* side by side. Even if the dramatic heroine fails to offer a neat fictional parallel to the dilemmas of the 'real' historical person, and even though the *Life*'s portrayal of Elizabeth may not supply a resolved and authentic portrait of the historical Cary, yet there are still other productive results to be gleaned from viewing the play and the biography in relation to each other.

Instead of the biography being used to represent some special truth which will explain the fiction of the play, one may read both play and biography as semi-fictional manipulations of semi-historical events, both texts influenced by the concerns of the cultural and historical circumstances which produced them. Although the play derives from Josephus's *Antiquities of the Jews* (published in Lodge's translation in 1602),[5] which draws on Biblical sources and features characters who lived at some point in recorded time, its literariness inevitably manipulates its use of historical event; an obvious example is the conflation of several historical and Biblical Herods into one complex character.[6] And also, as Isobel Grundy has emphasized, the biography is hagiographic and so rhetorically constructs what the Catholic daughter obviously considers the edifying circumstances of Catholic conversion. The second half of the work, in fact, once Elizabeth has safely entered the Roman church, seems to lose interest in her life, and turns its attention instead to the circumstances of her children's conversion.

It seems plausible, even, that much of the first half of the biography, though apparently written by one of Cary's daughters, was in some way influenced by the same consciousness that produced the play. The first half of the work contains many details which the daughter could not have known had they not been supplied directly or indirectly by the mother. The daughter could have had no direct experience of any of the circumstances of her mother's early life, her mother's innermost thoughts, or even some of the events that took place in private spaces. Someone must, for example, have told the biographer that her mother had learned the improbable language of 'Transylvanian' and forgotten it. Who told her that her father married her mother 'only for being an heir' (188)?[7] Elizabeth's fear of riding and dislike of hunting register vividly in the biography as if coming from the woman whose feelings these were. The passage which tells us that she collapsed into depression during her pregnancies, 'thinking her husband would then be most sensible of her trouble' (195), surely and poignantly describes thoughts that could have been known only to Elizabeth and might have been revealed by her.

Perhaps some family intermediary provided this information to the daughter, but it seems just as likely that Elizabeth imparted many of these details directly; the early part of the daughter's narrative is full of details the mother might well have wanted recorded. Given Elizabeth's passion for writing, it is even possible that the daughter worked from a now missing diary or journal. The *Life* does, in fact, mention the existence of a kind of daybook – 'a paper or two (several papers) which were found of hers, wherein she did make a disposition of the day for herself, designing to all her duties a due part' (216). The disappearance of these 'several papers' would be consistent with the evidence of an attempt by some reader, possibly the biographer's brother, to censor certain potentially embarrassing passages in the *Life*, as in the scoring through of the section which reads: 'She being continually after as long as she lived with him [her husband] either with child or giving suck' (194).

In the second half of the *Life*, the style changes from narrative to a more polemic mode. Longer, more haranguing sentences take the place of the shorter, more vividly detailed sentences of the first half. Arguments for reconciliation with the Roman church, together with angry complaints about William Chillingworth's efforts to impede this process for Cary's children, largely efface the titular subject of the biography. Compatibly with this emphasis, the second half of the biography attempts to exert some discipline over its unorthodox heroine's waywardness and 'forgetfulness' (215, 224, 270). Imposing narrative closure, the biographer writes with what sounds like satisfaction that in her last sickness Elizabeth 'was very quiet, pliable and easily ruled, which were not very natural to her' (274).

Wanting to explain a process of female subjectivity inscribed in the two Cary documents, one written about and the other by her, I find most suggestive those early sections of the *Life* containing material about the mother's unsettled pre-conversion experience, which the daughter could not have retrieved from her own memory, and which are not solidified into the Catholic celebration and rhetorical persuasion of the second half. The first half of the biography invokes the image of a restless, desirous woman induced to both frustration and risky invention by her inability to discover within conventional filial, marital or maternal structures a place in which to position herself and her discourse; this is the image which connects the biography and the play.

Play and life are similar verbal constructs. Both texts write the complex tale of a determined woman's engagement with language – speech, reading and writing – as the means to self-defined freedom and congenial space. The idioms that weave throughout the play, of mutable psychological and physical place, of desired freedom for body and mind and of the associated risk, resurface in the biography modified by a perception that constructs Elizabeth's turn to Rome as an adequate and appropriate resolution of her conflicts. Both play and life tell the story of an unquiet woman's mobile, 'errant' and thus non-coherent, multiply positioned subjectivity, and the complex means of enacting it. Her restlessness and mobility challenge the patriarchal order, which, insecure itself, requires that the 'safe' woman be physically static and mentally 'stable.'

My reading of *Mariam* does not look for logical coherence of character or point of view or resolution of contradiction, but takes pleasure in the inconsistencies of the heroine's modeling of a mobile and fluid subjectivity.[8] Although a unified and reconciled characterization of its heroine is not to be found in *Mariam*, the very fascination of the role is that it does *not* yield to the demands of rational consistency on which the logical Law of the Father relies, but connects more closely with the kind of female expression and pleasure imagined by Luce Irigaray:

> Woman never speaks the same way. What she emits is flowing, fluctuating. *Blurring*. Whence the resistances to that voice that overflows the [male] 'subject' ... What seems difficult or even impossible to imagine is that there could be some other mode of exchange(s) that might not obey the same logic. Yet that is the condition for the emergence of something of woman's language and woman's pleasure ... in some place other than that of woman's integration and recapture within the economy of purely masculine desire. (*This Sex*, 112)

The language of *Mariam* reaches toward this space outside the range of masculine logic and desire, blurred and blurring because unsatisfied with the oppositional structures that require a woman to be subject *or* object, obedient *or* rebellious, chaste *or* whore, silent *or* shrew. The dense contradictoriness of the play invites the feminist reader to discover a cannier means of entry than that permitted by expectations of logical unity or consistency.

Both *Mariam* and the *Life* imagine, inside patriarchal structures, semantic, syntactic and metaphoric approaches to what Rosi Braidotti, in agreement with Luce Irigaray, has labeled 'nomadic' female subjectivity. Nomadic consciousness, according to Braidotti, is recognized by its 'subversion of set conventions' (5) and its 'affirmation of fluid boundaries' (6). It belongs to the subject 'woman' when she is acknowledged as 'the site of multiple, complex, and potentially contradictory sets of experiences ... blurring boundaries without burning bridges' (4). This recognition of mobile subjectivity, able to move back and forth across categorizing boundaries, avoids the theoretical problems of essentializing each heroine into a solidified position, and also removes the critical burden of discovering logical consistency in the play's version of Mariam or the biography's depiction of Elizabeth Cary.

Both central characters are represented as struggling within the restricted spaces of socially imposed, confined and static ideals of womanly and religious behavior. Both intend wifely virtue and familial commitment, but both find themselves in states of inchoate and frustrated longing outside the range of the patriarchally permissible. Neither succeeds in reconciling patriarchally defined duty with her own desire, yet, as they both fail to exemplify the coherent and unified position admired and necessary within ordering hierarchical systems, they succeed in discovering an alternative space of freedom, perhaps in the only terms available to women in the early modern period (or elsewhere). For, according to Cixous, it is precisely when the 'permanence of identity is not fetishized' that the space 'where woman is wandering, roaming (a rogue wave), flying (thieving)' (*Newly Born*, 91) may intoxicatingly open up.

The texts in which these protagonists are represented, because written by women, and the characterizations of the protagonists themselves, self-contradictorily submissive and resistant to patriarchal control, disrupt the expectations of their culture; at the same time they evoke the unconfined, because as yet undefined, bodily, mental and discursive modes of feminine subjectivity. The concept of subjectivity that does not 'hold still,' that 'splits apart without regret' (Cixous, *Newly Born*, 90–91) seems indispensable to understanding the multiple positionalities of both the play's Mariam and the biography's Elizabeth.

Cultural Context and Women's Space

The instability and heterodoxy associated with the heroines of these two texts were disturbing in historically particular terms. Between 1517 and 1640 in London, there were 'at least 96 insurrections, riots and unlawful assemblies' (Manning, 187). In the period immediately preceding the composition of *Mariam*, between 1581 and 1602, there were 'no fewer than 35 outbreaks of disorder' (187). The question of national or individual alliance with Catholic or Protestant camps was equally volatile and disruptive; the varying religious loyalties of the Queens of England, from Mary and Elizabeth Tudor to Anne of Denmark and Henrietta Maria, gave the issue a visible feminine dimension. During the same period, vagrant women, displaced by the effects of increasing urbanization, became an icon for social disturbance.

Especially in a culture already mired in change, because her changeability may allow her the chance to elude designation and retribution, an indefinitely placed and mobile woman becomes as socially threatening to systems of power as a definitively rebellious one. But, says Hélène Cixous: 'This power to be errant is [woman's] strength; it is also what makes her vulnerable ... No matter how submissive and docile she may be in relation to the masculine order, she still remains the threatening possibility of savagery, the unknown quantity in the household whole' (*Newly Born*, 91). Inconsistency, variability and errancy, though fraught with the risk of punishment, may contain the opportunity to escape from patriarchal control and categorization.

Women's mobile elusiveness hardly ever wins patriarchal approval. Elizabeth Cary's husband, Lord Falkland, expressing his anger in language that is revealingly similar to Cixous's and Braidotti's, unwittingly testifies to the power and 'savagery' unleashed in his household by the 'unknown quantity' of his wife's errancy and escape from domestic duty after twenty-three years of marriage: she is, he says, 'replete with serpentine subtlety ... semblances ... and oblique ways' (*Life*, 1861, 152). She practises 'feminine wily pretences' (142) – self-protective maneuvers that a feminist reader might endorse, but which Falkland obviously found infuriating.

The affinities of *Mariam* and the *Life* can perhaps be ascribed to the fact that the same individual sensibility intervened in both as I have suggested above, but additionally to both texts' responsiveness to a shared cultural consciousness.[9] Both of these texts show what women's language was capable of inscribing over or under or within the dominant patriarchal language. As Luce Irigaray and Hélène Cixous have proposed, it is in spaces forced open by women's thieving or maverick use of patriarchal language and thinking that women may learn a language which will allow them access to the writerly experience enfolding their subjectivity.

In both *Mariam* and the *Life*, these spaces of women's subjectivity open up semantically and syntactically in places where the text often unsays what it seems to be saying. Thematically and metaphorically, also, both texts return again and again to ideas of bodily movement and freedom. Both texts rewrite the way in which women's spatial and subjective opportunities were confiningly represented in popular conduct books in early modern England. The language and imagery of physical and subjective movement appear with suggestive regularity throughout *Mariam* and the *Life*, reflecting a cultural preoccupation, but indicating as well a conscious or unconscious desire to circumvent the restrictions imposed on women's ability to move freely within physical and discursive spaces and to rewrite women's placement and displacement in both arenas.

Space, and position in space, are more than innocent locations; they are also codes constructed by people in culture and decoded by people within or outside that culture. Space is a '"morphic language," one of the means by which society is interpreted by its members' (Spain, 17). Where a man's or a woman's body may or may not safely go partly prescribes his or her gendered sense of discursive as well as physical capability. As Nancy Hartsock says, 'Women and men ... grow up with personalities affected by different boundary experiences, differently constructed and experienced inner and outer worlds' ('Feminist Standpoint,' 295). The ability to move by choice from place to place without major hindrance is at least one marker of subjective freedom and power, more readily available to men than to women. The ability to textualize one's own or another's placement is another such sign, a crucial indicator of sociocultural power.

An influential series of Italian and English conduct books, published in England during the sixteenth and seventeenth centuries, testify to this understanding. Francesco da Barbaro, Desiderius Erasmus, Agnolo Firenzuola, Henry Smith, Juan Luis Vives, Richard Brathwaite, William Gouge, Gervase Markham and William Whateley, among many others, all dictate women's confinement to the home and the control and restraint of their bodies as appropriate arenas of modesty and virtue. They praise the woman who keeps to her home, 'as though *home* were chastity's keeper ... Chastity careth to please but one, and therefore she keeps her closet, as though she were still at prayer' (Smith, 55).

Juan Luis Vives, in 1540, prescribed that 'A woman should be kept close, nor be known of many' (95). Richard Brathwaite refers to a common emblem which depicts a woman as a snail 'because shee still carries her house about her' (*Gentlewoman*, preface) and he reminds women: 'You are taught to enter your chambers and be still ... Still from the clamours and turbulent insults of the world; still from the mutinous motions and innovations of the flesh' (48). The tenacity of these ideals is evident as late as the 1671 commendation of Lucy Hutchinson for her attachment to patriarchal territory; she is described admiringly as a 'great lover of her father's house' (17). Elizabeth Cary's husband, in an angry letter complaining about his wife's defection, supported these repressive views: 'Surely her residency ought to be according to her husband's election, and not her own' (*Life*, 1861, 142).

Yet the intended containment of a woman inside her husband's or her father's home, the restriction of her body to enclosed or private rooms, was insufficient to calm fears of woman's capacity for disruptive escape, for even in an enclosed space, her mind may roam. 'Doe not say,' Brathwaite warns women, 'the walls encompasse mee, darkenesse o're-shadowes mee, the Curtaine of night secures mee; These be the wordes of an Adulteresse: Therefore doe nothing privately, which you would not doe publikely. There is no retire from the eyes of God' (*Gentlewoman*, 49). In the absence of surveillance of husband or father, the judging eye of God is invoked upon the enclosed woman.

Worrying about the opportunities for independent or rebellious behavior afforded the unobserved woman inside the very confined space judged by cultural norms as necessary for her control, Brathwaite further forbade women from furnishing their private chambers with 'wanton pictures, Aretine tables, Sibariticke stories' (*Gentlewoman*, 297). One wonders what Brathwaite envisioned as occurring in this private space – adulterous liaisons, masturbation, minds straying into some conceptual space of their own desire, stimulated by erotic pictures and sybaritic stories? Or perhaps even more appalling, that, like Elizabeth Cary when confined to her room by her mother-in-law, they might begin to write their own stories and wrest discursive control from repressive instructors like Brathwaite. Imagining just such a possibility of escaping the language that opposes male and female space, Luce Irigaray confronts the patriarch with the futility of his endeavor: 'Everywhere you shut me in. Always you assign a place to me ... You mark out boundaries, draw lines, surround, enclose ... What is your fear? That you might lose your property. What remains is an empty frame. You cling to it, dead' (*Elemental*, 24–25).

Not content with restricting a woman inside the walls of a home, however, Renaissance conduct books also insist that the woman's body itself be inhibited and controlled in its movement. Vives prescribes that, 'In going let the woman walk neither over-fast or over slowly. Now when she is in company of people, let her show great soberness, both in countenance and all the gesture of her body' (97). Francesco da Barbaro announces that 'the wandering of the eyes, a hasty gait, and excessive movement of the hands and other parts of the body ... are always joined to vanity and are signs of frivolity' (148). Again, Brathwaite writes, 'The habit or quality of the mind is best discerned by the carriage or composure of the body ... Light Habits suit not well with grave hearts, nor wandring eyes with setled minds' (*Boulster Lecture*, 239–240). The woman's soul and mind, according to the patriarch's wishful thinking, is visibly embodied in her 'Gate, Looke, Speech, Habit' (*Gentlewoman*, 315). As Sharon Fermor points out, 'movement was seen as an index of inner states, as well as of moral and social composure' (133). Her behavior should not be 'flinging, nor puffing, nor discontented, but savouring of all lowliness' (Whateley, 18).

Grace Mildmay's journal records her father's view of women's bodily movements:

> Alsoe my father could not abyde to see a woman light or unstable in her carriage, to hold her head one way, her hands another, and her feet a third way, her eyes tossing about in every places and her features disfigured by an evill countenance; but he lyked a woman well graced, with a constant and settled countenance, and a good behaviour throughout all her parts, which presenteth unto all men a good hope of stablished mynde and a virtuous disposition in her. (Weigall, 121–122)

The control sought by these judgments over the deployment and positioning of women's bodies in space is clearly a marker of both the subjective and social power of the arbiter and also of the effort to slot women into a controlled object position. 'The cardinal rule for women's behavior at all times was to avoid calling attention to themselves,' says Ruth Kelso; 'the girl must be trained to stand quietly, feet together, without meaningless movements of head, shoulders, hands, and feet ... [H]er face should be grave and her eyes habitually lowered' (50).

The language of gendered space appears, then, in contemporary conduct books, which intend to define the constraints within which women were expected to act and think of themselves. Efforts to inscribe confinement on women increased as women's mobility in sixteenth- and seventeenth-century England increased. As Doreen Massey observes, 'The limitation on mobility in space – the attempted consignment/confinement to particular places on the one hand, and the limitation on identity on the other – have been crucially related' (179). It is against early modern efforts to impose confinement and coherence on women's bodies and self-perceptions that the different language in *Mariam* and the *Life*, of women's bodily and imaginative mobility, signifying their nomadic subjectivity, should be read.

Given this goal, it is worth registering the comments of a foreign visitor to England on the mobility of local women. Not invested in the desire to control the potentially dangerous movements of Englishwomen, as the writers of the native texts are, this observer sees evidence of behavior other than that prescribed in the conduct books, remarking instead on what appears to him an unusual opportunity for movement available to the women of England:

> But although the women there [in England] are entirely in the power of their husbands except for their lives, yet they are not kept so strictly as they are in Spain or elsewhere. Nor are they shut up ... They go to market to buy what they like best to eat ... [T]hey sit before their doors, decked out in fine clothes, in order to see and be seen by passers-by. (Van Meteren, 72)

Elizabeth Cary's sense of the opportunities available to women for spatial and subjective mobility outside the control of patriarchal intent was perhaps affected by such scenes as those described above,[10] as well as by her own wide bookish journeying in Abraham Ortelius's *Le Miroir du Monde*, which she translated early in her life and which contains descriptions of China, India, Turkey and America. She also, of course, vicariously accompanied Josephus and Lodge in their literary excursions to Rome and Palestine.[11] In both her own *Mariam* and in her daughter's *Life*, we find a writerly breakaway from confining boundaries and unified positions, leading not to an equally fixed repositioning, but to flexible enactments of textual power and subjectivity in spaces where imaginative freedom is negotiated.

The *Life*: Writing the Mobile Body

To write is to claim a space inside repetitive social and textual codes whose very constraints and iterability, as Judith Butler observes, make variable subjective performances possible: 'repetition is what enables a subject' (95). Writing occurs in Western culture in contexts which make clear that the language of subjectivity and power is also the language of physical and spatial location. Cultural members expect to occupy a designated 'place' in the world. If successful, they claim a 'space' of their own. They 'situate' themselves. They 'settle' somewhere and are 'positioned' more or less advantageously in relation to sites of cultural privilege.

Nor is this manner of expression the idiom only of modern culture; it also communicated effectively in early modern England, as, for instance, in John Donne's *Canonization*. 'Go away and "get you a place,"' cries the infuriated persona to the friend who has intruded on him. The speaker or writer himself wants to be left undisturbed in the space where *he* is occupied in establishing, concurrently with his body and through the process of writing, his own erotic and poetic 'pretty roomes.' Though Donne's role as poet in turn-of-the-century London failed to gain for him the courtly role he sought, his poetic persona is still able to position himself with eloquent assurance. Far more confidently than his contemporary Elizabeth Cary and her dramatic heroine Mariam, both Donne and his poem's speaker command spaces for their writing and speaking roles. They function within long-standing male-defined poetic conventions in which they both have an acknowledged place.

Cary's efforts to negotiate a writing space for herself and a speaking space for her heroine were more complicated, for the established codes of writing were not designed to include her. The *Life* underlines the cultural antagonism to women's learning and writing, and bodily and mental freedom, by depicting a central character who, even in the space of her parents' or husband's home, was discouraged from pursuing her reading and writing desires. As a woman writing in early modern England, Cary defied the generally-held cultural views that connected women's imaginative writing and eloquence with their moral depravity. In spite of her participation in the literary and aristocratic Pembroke Circle,[12] Cary was not free of these constraints. Both her gender and her social position worked against her attempts to write.

Before fully understanding its implications, her new husband's esteem for Elizabeth is said to have risen after he discovered her writing skill. For a time, she took advantage of this increased regard to write poetry, not for his approval, but for her own secret pleasure: 'From this time she wrote many things for her private recreation, on several subjects, and occasions, all in verse' (189). However, her husband's benign acceptance of his wife's hobby did not extend to permission to publish; one of her compositions, probably *Mariam*,[13] was 'stolen out of that sister-in-law's (her friend's) chamber, and printed, but by her own procurement was called in' (189–190). This section of the biography testifies to the patriarch's control of language, for the woman, it is implied, writes with permission of the husband. The comment that tells us that Cary's writing ventures were stolen and published and then 'called in' by herself, speaks to the power of social control. The writer self-censors her work by withdrawing it from publication. But it is too late, for the disruption of publication has already occurred.

The biographical depiction of her mother by Elizabeth's daughter preserves Elizabeth's subject status as reader and writer from the effort to erase it by contemporary social standards of proper womanly behavior. The last pages of the biography summarize and justify Elizabeth's accomplishments in paragraphs that begin, successively: 'She had read' (268), 'She had writ' (269), 'She had conversed' (269), 'She spoke' (270), 'But yet she always seemed to have a most hearty good will to God and his service' (270). Although the narrator's primary attention is focused on Elizabeth's conversion story, the language of the narration draws the reader's attention to images of a devout woman's entry into the space of reading, writing and speaking.

An ever-present element in the narrative, Elizabeth's writing activity is strikingly represented as occurring in very specific, framed, spatial locations. Running alongside and resonating with these scenes of writing are other, equally arresting scenes of Elizabeth's bodily location, reminding us that where and how a woman's body moves in physical space may serve as a representation – a metaphor, or perhaps a metonym – for where her mind may move in conceptual space. This mental ranging encompasses her understanding of how she is valued by others and by herself, and whether and how she may inscribe this sense of self in writing.

As I speak now of 'Elizabeth Cary,' I am referring to the character who achieves a vivid textual presence in her daughter's narrative. This woman's body, appearing in various postures throughout the *Life*, is remarkably clear to us. It is short and inclined to be 'very fat' (248), so that as long as Elizabeth cares to project a commanding figure in the courtly world, to enhance her height and presence, she wears thick-soled chopines. These inhibit her ease of movement, requiring that she go about in a carriage. When she is freed of both her husband's economic support and concomitant expectations of her, she exchanges the chopines for more comfortable shoes and travels by foot whenever she goes 'abroad to court and other places about her business,' which, significantly, she now does 'very much' (224).

Her body has never been of the kind to stir male passion or female admiration. Even when young, she was 'nothing handsome' (188). Elizabeth does not willingly adorn her body, dressing elaborately as suits her station only at her husband's insistence. Left to her own devices, after she and he separate, she dresses in 'nothing graceful' (270), preferring the ease and economy of wearing either widow's black or what is 'cheapest and would last longest' (248). Except when fasting, she 'seemed not to have full power over herself in matter of diet' (216). She is not very agile and has trouble getting up and down, especially from a kneeling position (199), yet, once released from the marital and social obligations which prevent her from reading and writing, she is happy to sleep in a chair (246). She is loquacious (270), not silent as the conduct books urge. She has frequent colds and is ultimately fatally tubercular (264). Her body is not athletic; she hates to ride. What this body does love to do is read and write; it certainly compounds her sadness that she finds limited space and opportunity to do either as long as she lives with her husband.

Yet Elizabeth's body is submissive and serviceable to her husband's sexual and procreative needs. She is frequently pregnant or nursing, giving birth to eleven children 'alive,' nine of whom survive to adulthood (191). There are, in addition,

5.1 Elizabeth, Lady Falkland by Paul Van Somer

other pregnancies resulting in stillbirths or miscarriages. Her many pregnancies are probably not of *her* choosing, for maternity does not agree with her. She is frequently depressed, sleeping at will, 'when she had occasion to have sad thoughts waking' (196). Depression turns to nervous collapse at least twice while she is pregnant. She falls on both occasions into such 'deep melancholy' as to lose 'the perfect use of her reason' (195). The judgemental narrative voice implies that Elizabeth might have controlled her lapses into 'plain distractedness' (195): her apprehensions 'were always apt to go as far as she would let them' (195). A twentieth-century woman, though, may feel more sympathy at the thought of Elizabeth's sustaining more than eleven pregnancies during the space of seventeen years, as she did between her husband's return from Holland and her final leave-taking of his house in 1625.

Her body is not 'still,' as the conduct books prefer. It is restless, moving from place to place and position to position, seeking a space where the disjunctions between reading or writing subject and filial or procreative object relax. There is no such easily achieved or comfortable space for a woman who wants to write in early seventeenth-century England. Her 'self,' like her body, is unsettled, 'nomadic.' Her body *language* is necessarily mixed, even self-contradictory. The choices offered her by her culture are oppositional – obedience or rebellion – but both oversimplify her desires. So, not without risk, she resides in both spaces, moving back and forth across boundaries that prove more permeable than they are made to seem in the dominant discourse, turning conditions of confinement into spaces where a play of freedom opens up.

Submissively and painfully, all her life, she positioned herself on her knees in front of her seated mother 'frequently for more than an hour together' (199). Yet, 'so was she bent on reading,' that she chose to disobey her mother and 'frequently read all night,' secretly bribing the servants against her mother's commands to supply her with candles' (187–188). In this secret, confined and forbidden space Elizabeth reads alone in her room within the orbit of the candle's glow. She is encircled by the dark and confined by her mother's prohibition. The night-time space in which others sleep, and in which she has been ordered to do so too, is turned to a space of imaginative freedom in which the child can exercise her will. Yet the space is not quite safe. She risks her mother's displeasure and punishment. Her reading body contradicts her normal gestures of filial respect and obedience. At a cost, she nevertheless gains the control Roger Chartier says was made possible by reading, especially the silent private reading that began to be more often practised in early modern Europe: 'In retreat the individual is free, master of his time, and his leisure or study' (136). In this case, out of the norm, the freedom belongs to a 'her.'

In a parallel but more explicit example, Elizabeth's mother-in-law, attempting to discipline her, confines her to her room, 'which seeing she cared little for, but entertained herself with reading, the mother-in-law took away all her books, with command to have no more brought her; then she set herself to make verses' (189). Again, Elizabeth maneuvers inside a physically confined space to gain an alternative freedom. Locked up, then disallowed from reading, she is subjected to the conditions of an intended punishment. Yet, by the flexibility of her resistant behavior, by ingeniously raising the stakes from reading to writing, the young woman voids the punishment. Crucially, the opening up of a space which is meant to confine is achieved through writing. Into the very space of verse-writing, where early modern Englishwomen were forbidden to go, Cary nevertheless advanced. A woman writing creates a space within which ruptures of the conventional order may take place. 'Let her write!' (*Newly Born*, 88) says Hélène Cixous, 'a feminine text cannot not be more than subversive' (97).

In Elizabeth's relation to patriarch as well as matriarch, she also adopts a usefully mobile and ambiguous position; exploiting her fluency in patriarchal language to enact her submission, she is able at the same time to modify its suppressive intentions. As a child, though manifestly an obedient and loving daughter, she boldly instructs her lawyer father how better to examine an intimidated woman accused of witchcraft; she finds an opportunity literally to question the law of the father by demonstrating her superior ability to decode a woman's overly compliant speech, and gains the woman's release (187). As the little girl has the skill to make clear, female language 'almost always falls on the deaf, masculine ear, which can only hear language that speaks in the masculine' (Cixous, *Newly Born*, 92).

After her marriage, while being dressed and coiffed by servants to please her husband, Elizabeth 'seriously think[s] on some other business' and subversively reads and writes to please herself (194). Although 'most fearful of a horse' (194), and finding dressing a 'torture,' in the early years of her marriage, with wifely obedience she agrees to ride and to dress to please her husband; yet some years later she disobeys his wishes in the most extreme and embarrassing way,[14] by taking the vows of a Catholic, ironically enough, in a stable. On frequent occasions, performing ambiguously as both subject and object, she maintains her claim to her body, her conscience and her language. This is, of course, a hazardous enterprise. Still, complete and safe submission to parents and husband Elizabeth cannot achieve. Especially, wanting to be both scholar and wife, both writer and written, trying to bring the self-effacing marital and maternal roles approved by her culture into conformity with her own desires for writerly subjectivity, she finds herself still having to confront oppositional choices not entirely her own. The ambiguous subjectivity achieved in relation to mother and mother-in-law and in the dressing ritual cannot always be safely maintained, for fluid passage across behavioral borders is not part of a culturally condoned model for Renaissance women.

A series of comments in the biography emphasize her husband's 'very absolute' (194) power over Elizabeth's body and her conflicting efforts both to submit to his desires and to escape from his control. He requires her, although she is afraid, to ride, until during her fourth pregnancy, she falls from her horse, when he excuses her from riding again. 'As long as she lived with him' (194), Elizabeth was either pregnant or nursing; for Naomi Miller, Cary's maternity exerts 'an incipient counterforce ... to masculine supremacy in the household' ('Domestic,' 363). She does negotiate some degree of control over her body, but at a price. Difficult options are impressed on her body. Freedom from the need to ride, which she dislikes, is bought at the cost of successive pregnancies, which are, however, occasions of melancholy. During her second and fourth pregnancies she 'lost the perfect use of her reason, and was in much danger of her life' (195). During the fourth pregnancy she fasted for fourteen days. Her pregnancies, loss of reason, depression, fasting and excessive sleeping are all states which have a negative definition in the patriarchy, but another in the realm of the feminine. They are bodily states akin to mystical transport and hysteria which, according to Irigaray, hold some hope of women's escape from the control of patriarchal language and from embeddedness in the patriarchal order. Though they may allow freedom, however, they also entail risk. Being pregnant allows Elizabeth to escape from the masculine realm of hunting, but the pregnancies become incessant; her body is reappropriated by the masculine. The biography speaks of Elizabeth in pregnancy and lactating as of a valuable material commodity, a useful and profitable, though perhaps quirky, mechanism. Lord Falkland, we are told, 'was extraordinary careful of her when she was with child or gave suck, as being a most tenderly loving father' (195). As progenitor, the father is careful of the woman when she is a vessel for his procreation, but we are not told that he is tender of her 'for herself,' or that he is a 'tenderly loving husband.'

The description of Elizabeth's official conversion to Roman Catholicism, after she leaves her husband, reinforces the impression of her as an accomplished and practised escape artist. Restrained initially by her friend Lady Denby, who tells her, 'You shall lie in my chamber and shall not go forth' (205), Elizabeth seizes a brief moment of Lady Denby's absence and goes immediately to a Catholic priest to be reconciled to the Roman church: she 'let not this opportunity slip, but got her ways in the lady's absence' (205). Of course, this conversion, so pleasing to Cary's biographer and so ultimately ensuring of Cary's space to write, may seem another half-escape, like the movement from hunting to pregnancy – that is, a retreat from one form of patriarchal jurisdiction to another. While aiding escape from domestic tyranny, admission to Catholicism may represent the subject's liberation into a mystic's freedom, or the object's oppression beneath the weight of a patriarchal and hierarchical church, or, more complexly, as it seems in this case, may contain elements of both.

Elizabeth's removal of her body from her husband's jurisdiction allows her to escape from the 'melancholy' of reproduction and the 'torture' of adorning her body for the pleasure of the patriarch. Withdrawing to celibacy and nun-like clothing, after she left him, 'she never went out of plain black, frieze or coarse stuff, or cloth' (194). The biography now emphasizes two consequences for Elizabeth after, we are meaningfully told, her husband 'was angry with her' (194). On the one hand, she faces physical privation – 'confinement' (variations of this word are used to describe her circumstances eight times within a few pages), hunger, lack of furniture and clothing, cold and limited company (205–209). These conditions are regarded by her husband as punishment for her disobedience: 'If she complain of wants, I do believe it is true that she sustains them ... That she is not relieved in them by me is most true ... [because] she is, and lives that, there, and as I would not have her' (*Life*, 1861, 153). On the other hand, she now begins a period of intensive reading and writing:[15]

> She began her translation of Cardinal Peron's works, of which she translated the *Reply to the King's Answer*, in thirty days ... Sometime after she procured it to be printed ... dedicating it to her Majesty ... She likewise here begun the rest of his works which she finished long after but was never able to print it ... About this time she writ the lives of St. Mary Magdalene, St. Agnes Martyr, and St. Elizabeth of Portingall in verse, and both before and after many verses of our Blessed Lady. (*Life*, 213)

Her writing is accompanied by voracious reading: 'She now also spent her own time almost wholly in reading' (248). The phrase 'her own time' draws attention to Elizabeth's altered situation. Towards the end of her life, 'her whole employment was writing and reading' (264).

The language of the biography, in the end, is the simplified language of successfully achieved liberty, moving its heroine from confinement to deliverance: 'thus God delivering her' (205), in a 'little old house ... ready to fall on their heads,' hungry and cold, Elizabeth and her maidservant, Bessie Poulter, yet 'did affirm they were never more merry nor better content in their lives than they were then' (212). Elizabeth finally ends her life 'assisted by the prayers and visits of her Catholic and Benedictine friends ... without any agony quietly as a child' (275).

The *Life* supplies the ingredients for a conventionally happy ending to the 're-membered' Elizabeth's story; she is 'very merry,' she is able to write again, she has reclaimed her body from patriarchal use, she gains control over her children and their faith (significantly persuading all of her remaining daughters, after the eldest dies in childbirth, to a conventual, celibate life) and she dies in the arms of the Roman church. The biography's narrative purpose and Catholic polemic shepherd its heroine into studious quietness and ultimately to death, from ambiguity to resolution, into singularity and Catholic coherence. The oppositional alternatives necessary to patriarchal logic and the need for narrative closure ensure this result. Her inconsistent character (216, 270) is resolved at last by the biography's need to see Elizabeth's entrance into Catholicism as both narrative and spiritual resolution. The conclusion allows Elizabeth religious security and the power to write a lot and publish a little. She seems to have fulfilled her desires. But the textualized Elizabeth loses something in this narrative closure; perhaps, from a culturally conservative point of view, something too subtle to mourn. As her subjectivity stabilizes, what is taken from her is the adaptable and fluid feminine subjectivity of the earlier sections of the *Life*, of the kind that has 'the capacity to flow readily between different aspects of itself' (Flax, 93).

Mariam's Indeterminacy: 'Hanging in the Air'

The biography says that, after reading the definitive exposition of the Anglican *via media*, Hooker's *Ecclesiastical Polity*, Elizabeth remained unimpressed: 'It seemed to her, he left her hanging in the air, for having brought her so far ... she saw not

5.2 Elizabeth, Viscountess Falkland, effigy on Tanfield tomb

how, nor at what, she could stop, till she returned to the church from whence they were come' (190). The central character of the *Life*, though a capable negotiator of the terms of fluid subjectivity, is nevertheless destined for Catholic and narrative resolution. She is represented as desiring stability and singleness of meaning, as moving toward a place where she may settle, as wanting not to be left 'hanging in the air.'

In *Mariam*, the case is different. The biography's linear narrative drive toward simplification and closure is resisted by the play, which provides no equivalent to the centric force exerted by Catholicism in the *Life* and no simplified resolution of the heroine's conflicts. The whole play may be said to 'hang in the air,' to avoid a cathartic resolution of pity and fear, but more especially of the sense of disturbance it summons up. The play's atmosphere is looming and full of uncertainty and the characters dislocated and fearful. These are the usual conditions of tragedy, but, *un*usually, this play does not work from an established normative base.[16] The chorus, which would typically be expected to represent this position, assumes and desires stability, but it is also imperceptive and lacks persuasive force. It asserts with more sentiment than conviction, 'Oft we see that some in humble state, / Are cheerful, pleasant, happy, and content' (I.vi.505–5), yet no evidence of such content appears in this play. In fact, the pervasive quality of the central character's psychology is the discontent abhorred in women by the writers of English conduct books; women's behavior should not be 'discontented, but savouring of all lowliness,' says Whateley (18). What the chorus fears as future social disruption has already come to pass in the lives of the characters and the events of the play. Weller and Ferguson agree: 'their gnomic, conventional utterances seem somewhat off the mark' (35); Gwynne Kennedy also suggests that their 'conclusions do not fit the play's events' (123).

The action of the play takes place at a time when, as in early modern England, traditional grounds of political and moral security have been disturbed. Maccabean rule in Palestine has been usurped by representatives of Roman ascendancy. Herod has slaughtered the Hasmonean heirs and, by marrying Mariam to reinforce his power, has subverted her status as a Jewish princess. The undermining of the sources of Jewish stability is emphasized by Herod's ill-conceived offer to violate David's grave to supply Mariam with riches:[17] 'I'll rob the holy David's sepulchre / To give thee wealth' (IV.iii.105–106). Rome, too, is in a state of transition following the death of Julius Caesar. The setting, the characters, their circumstances and especially the foundations of power, are caught in a destabilizing process, moving from 'sand' to 'loathsome mud,' unable to come to rest in the 'settled state' wistfully advocated in the first act by the chorus (I.vi.496, 516).

The uncommitted nature of Senecan closet drama, hovering between conceptual and visual potential, is an appropriate packaging for the play's unsettled *angst* and its heroine's nomadic and inconsistent subjectivity. It is a form that seems, like its heroine, to edge away from clarity of resolution. Neither intended for performance nor entirely non-dramatic, closet drama exists somewhere in imaginative, literary space without claiming the possibility of theatrical enactment. To an early modern female author, characters and audience, it offers a moderate advantage. It escapes the traditionally cross-dressed male actors' appropriation of female roles, by sacrificing the immediate, if male-impersonated, presence of the female image and voice on the stage. But it retains the possibility of a forceful and, because mentally 'performed,' potentially more subversive place for a female character. In this sense, closet drama allows an evasion of the binary choices set up culturally for women's theatrical as well as social roles – either to be represented by men or to be publicly, and therefore shamefully, 'staged.'[18]

If narrative form, as Freud argued, is a source of formal consolation, assuaging anxiety and imposing order, the looser shape of poetic closet drama appears a better frame for the concerns of the unstable culture and restless heroine represented in *Mariam*. Although the five-act structure and its adherence to the unities of time, place and character create the expectation of the neatly rising and falling action of formulaic tragic complication, climax and resolution, there is in fact, as Nancy Gutierrez has argued, no sense of closure in this play (246). This lack is reinforced by the 'unfinished' feel of the final act, which has only a single scene, as against the six, four, three and eight of the preceding four acts. As the play ends, the fates of Pheroras and Graphina are left unknown, Alexandra and Doris are unaccounted for and Mariam herself, having physically disappeared in the fourth act, hovers in an interpretive space where she is both powerless victim and heroic agent,[19] both aspiring to virtue and a socially disruptive force, both dead and alive.

Although the Christian revelation waits in the wings, the Jacobean audience of this play would certainly have recognized the similarities between the anxious world of pre-Christian Palestine and the equally uncertain conditions of contemporary England; it might even appear that the Christian dispensation had not wrought any profound change in the material conditions of fallen human society. Mariam's fate could hardly offer consolation in an early modern world where political, sometimes capricious, beheadings were the order of the day. The last words of the play enforce the historical parallels:

> This day's events were certainly ordain'd,
> To be the warning to posterity:
> So many changes are therein contain'd,
> So admirably strange variety. (V.i.289–292)

The focus in this emphatic final moment of the play on changeability and variety as the important lines of continuity from the past to the present is interesting enough, but the odd half-commendation of 'variety' as 'admirably strange' is even more arresting when placed beside both the open fear expressed in sixteenth- and seventeenth-century conduct books of variety and change and the assertion by the chorus at the end of the first act that 'To wish variety is sign of grief' (I.vi.511). To 'admire' in the sixteenth century was double-valenced, meaning to 'wonder at,' but also carrying the meaning, closer to its twentieth-century sense, of 'to regard with pleased surprise'

(*New English Dictionary*). Apparently, anxiety is not total. Variety and change and the mobility they imply are to be warned against, but, as we have also seen in the preceding chapter on Whitney, to be wondered at with fascination.[20]

The fear of some, yet sense of opportunity for others, inspired by the prospect of individual and social change and mobility, were evident in Cary's rapidly changing society, and are clear as well in her play. The ideological indeterminacy partially revealed in the play's last lines, about whether conservatively to advocate socially commendable 'stillness' or more radically to explore the dangerous and freeing attractiveness of change, lies at the heart of the play's language and permeates its representation of Mariam herself. Without the control, as in the biography, of a directive narrative voice, this play's language flows in all directions, keeping in play multiple, contradictory possibilities.

The Senecan closet drama was a form which reflected, encouraged and frequently left unresolved the ideological arguments taking place throughout Jacobean society. It was therefore 'perceived as dangerous by Elizabethan and Jacobean censors' (Lewalski, *Writing Women*, 179), in part, one assumes, because it frustrated the punitive measures essential to social surveillance. Karen Raber sees the genre as 'highly duplicitous, using the pretense of deliberate containment to effect, not hinder, a woman's public voice' (325). In addition, the 'complexity and ambiguity' (Lewalski, 194) with which issues of tyranny and rebellion are treated by this genre, the 'prominence of women as heroines and villains, and a chorus which speaks from a limited rather than an authorized vantage point' (191), all make the closet drama a genre useful for submerged protest against women's oppression as well as for depicting a heroine who copes with oppression by moving within a fluid subjectivity which escapes easy categorization.[21]

In a Senecan drama like *Mariam*, narrative and dramatic activity are at a minimum (Gutierrez, 236), but narrative drive and/or dramatic tension are needed to promote a satisfying tragic resolution. The closet drama's (inconclusive in *Mariam*'s case) 'philosophical discussion and [especially] poetic mediation' (236) and its 'obsession with desire' (238) move it out of Freudian and into Lacanian territory where resolution, unity and fulfillment of desire are perceived as illusion: 'Seek these things if you wish,' says Lacan, 'and if you're prepared to settle for baubles and lies' (*Ecrits*); it is not in cause–effect logic and simplified unitary conclusions, but in multiplicity and continuing process that meaning and the subject reside: 'Even if I lose myself in the process, in that process, I am' ('Insistence,' 96). For those like Herod who have power and need coherence, stability and clarity as a condition of their authority, the recognition of their unattainability is frightening. But for others like Mariam, without power, this understanding may be liberating.

Mariam displaces issues of clear sovereignty of self and determinacy of meaning into a highly problematic dimension; because there is no reliance on false reconciliations or resolutions, certitude of meaning and selfhood are not enacted. Even if 'the primary issue [for plays written in imitation of Garnier's Senecan dramas] is that of self-definition' (Gutierrez, 236), Mariam does not achieve self-definition in the usual apparently absolute, binary terms, by pitting a superior integrated 'self' against an inferior other; in relation to masculine power this option is unavailable to her. The nature of her subjectivity blurs the boundaries between superior and inferior, subject and object, which Herod, representing patriarchal power, attempts to maintain. Although Mariam judges herself superior to other non-Hasmonean women in the play – Salome and Doris in particular – she remains an 'object' to Herod (IV.i.15), whose social and class alliances are closer to his sister and ex-wife than they are to Mariam, but whose masculinity and political power allow him to dominate Mariam.

Mariam's strategies of self-definition are equivocal and multiplistic rather than coherent and singular. She is, as Straznicky describes her, not a finished product but a 'work in progress' (125). Neither the central character nor the language of the play assumes the onus of resolution or catharsis. Mariam's subjective situation is contingent, partly on the inconsistencies of the language in which she and others attempt to define her, partly on masculine political power, partly on the incoherence of all subjectivity – the 'self's radical ex-centricity to itself' (Lacan, 'Insistence,' 101). Mariam's mobile, inconsistent, feminine subjectivity has been attuned by her experience living with masculine tyranny to an adept fluid positionality. Her death is the tragic consequence of the risks assumed by a woman whose nomadic subjectivity could remind the patriarch of the 'self's radical ex-centricity to itself,' in a society which must reject this understanding to protect its hierarchical systems of power. Herod's fate is to represent and implement that social refusal.

Refusing the Ex-Centric: Positing the False Ideal

The 'ex-centricity' of self to itself, which he involuntarily manifests, is nevertheless denied by Herod, who sees the retention of power as requiring the projection of impermeable strength and uncompromising position, even while he vacillates from adoration of Mariam to murderous rage against her. In some ways a model of spousal acquiescence, offering, contrary to all edicts of husbandly authority, to let Mariam be his 'commandress' and 'sovereign guide' (IV.iii.98), Herod still accepts, on the flimsiest testimony, that she is a 'painted devil' and a 'white enchantress' (IV.iv.75–76). In a single speech, he describes her as both 'unchaste' and 'heavenly true' (IV.vii.433, 452). Self-contradictorily he declares: 'Even for love of thee / I do profoundly hate thee' (IV.iv.200–201). An anxiety-inducing division of himself, that leads to compensatory intransigence and tyranny, he also unwillingly reveals: 'But Herod's wretched self hath Herod cross'd' (V.i.132); his emotional conflict, he says, 'pulls [him] piecemeal' (IV.iv.244).

These moments in which he briefly and painfully discloses his self-division are precipitated by Herod's fearful glimpse of a similar division in Mariam: 'a beauteous body hides a loathsome soul' (IV.iv.178); 'Hell itself lies hid / Beneath thy heavenly show' (IV.iv.203–204). Herod initially constructs his own dominant subjectivity in relation to a projected, false image of Mariam as stable, ideal and coherent. Not accepting the transience of her beauty or the variability of her feelings and sense of self, Herod wants too intensely to believe that Mariam's lovely exterior speaks an unchanging heart. If her body is beautiful, so must her chaste virtue also be: 'She is like Heaven, and must be heavenly true' (IV.vii.452). Focused on Mariam's physical appearance, Herod needs to be able to trust that it is a transparent wrapping of Mariam's 'self' and a reflective assurance of his own identity and power, for she is to him a 'precious mirror' (V.i.125). Herod concentrates obsessively on the details of Mariam's appearance, dwelling on the soft 'fleece' of her hair (IV.vii.413), her starry eyes (IV.iv.220), her 'looks' (IV.iv.254) and her 'heavenly show' (IV.iv.204), and he longs to feast his impatient eyes on her after his absence in Rome (IV.i.34). He exemplifies Irigaray's observation that 'More than the other senses, the eye objectifies and masters' ('Interviews,' 50). Herod demands of Mariam that she fulfill a clearly observable ideal of womanliness, a perfectly beautiful body containing a perfectly virtuous soul.

If Mariam is perfect, however, she must also be static, for what is already perfect cannot change. Herod therefore constructs Mariam not as a flawed, mobile, 'nomadic' subject, but as an immobilized 'object' which will his 'desires suffice' (IV.i.35). In this static, objectified form, whose whole recognized 'self' is what appears on the beautiful surface, Mariam can safely be accepted by Herod as his guide, for in such a role she offers no threat to him. 'Her looks alone,' he says, 'preserv'd my breath' (IV.iv.254). She is like the sonnet mistress to whom the poet is willing to swear undying loyal service because she is immobilized, objectified and sometimes, like Petrarch's Laura, dead. Praising her piece by piece, fragmenting her wholeness, the sonnet's speaker reduces the challenge embodied in the beautiful woman he longs to possess. The sonnet rhyme schemes in the poetry of the fourth act, which echo in and out of Herod's musings on Mariam, are peculiarly and poetically apt. Excessively implementing the sonnet's example, Herod's beheading of Mariam grimly and literally fragments the body he desires.[22]

As Herod begins to fear that Mariam's pure appearance conceals a false, hidden heart – 'Oh, thine eye / Is pure as Heaven, but impure thy mind' (IV.iv.190–191) – his world becomes unstable. He himself is fragmented, split, pulled, as he says, into pieces (IV.iv.244). The conviction expressed by Francesco da Barbaro's *De Re Uxoria* that men 'can penetrate ... into the most guarded thoughts' of wives by carefully observing their 'faces, countenances, and gestures' (148) is the false basis of Herod's security also: 'Methinks I should discern her if she feign'd' (IV.vii.495). Having fixed his love on Mariam's beauty and relying on her stability, he miserably accepts Salome's assertion that he has been deceived by Mariam's cosmetic speech and looks: 'She speaks a beauteous language, but within / Her heart is false as powder' (IV.vii.429–430).[23]

When, as he thinks, he can no longer penetrate Mariam's guarded thoughts, Herod must have her killed, so that his reality will not turn 'topsy-turved' (I.vi.424). After her death, Herod reconstructs his earlier idealization in different terms; now he asserts that 'Her heav'nly beauty 'twas that made me think / That it with chastity could never dwell' (V.i.243–244). Mariam once condemned to death, the reparation of the ideal image begins: her skin will repel the axe, rivers refuse to drown her and fire refuse to consume her, says Herod (IV.vii.362–380). Finally dead, Mariam can be definitively revisioned as perfect, with hands that 'did the whiteness of the snow impair' (V.i.151). She is now a 'pure unspotted ghost' (V.i.115), once again 'matchless.'

In early seventeenth-century England as well as in pre-Christian Palestine, 'good' women had an idealized iconic status. This idealization is evident in the popular pamphlet *Hic Mulier*, printed in 1620. Inveighing against some women's increasingly 'impudent' and 'monstrous' behavior, the writer praises the alternative impossible ideal in language very similar to Herod's wishful but mistaken depictions of Mariam:

> You good women, you that are in the fullness of perfection, you that are the crowns of nature's work, the complements of men's excellences, and the Seminaries of propagation; you that maintain the world, support mankind, and give life to society; you that, armed with the infinite power of Virtue, are Castles impregnable, Rivers unsailable, Seas immovable, infinite treasures, and invincible armies; that are helpers most trusty, Sentinels most careful, signs deceitless, plain ways fail-less, true guides dangerless, Balms that instantly cure, and honors that never perish. (265–266)

Good women, just as in Herod's desiring idealization of Mariam, are perfect, 'impregnable,' 'immovable'; they are 'signs deceitless' and 'true guides.' Fixed in the home, chaste, silent and obedient, they both represent and ensure a stable society. They act as necessary lodestars for male travelers and adventurers like Herod, Henry Cary and Renaissance English explorers. Without their stabilizing and centering force, however, the men who take their bearings from them are made ex-centric – to the women to whom they turn, but also to themselves.

Crucially, as objectified images, these iconic representations of women serve as projections of male belief in their own coherent subjectivity. For Herod, Mariam's suspected infidelity, her uncontrolled speech and her refusal to share his bed, representing violations of the ideals of chastity, silence and obedience, threaten the social order as well as his own sense of unitary identity. It is not accidental that his sense of having 'cross'd' himself and being pulled apart 'piecemeal' precipitates Herod's need to remove Mariam from his sight in an attempt to annihilate what her un-ideal actions and physical person have come to represent. Mariam's beheading, Herod hopes, will permit a necessary adjustment of the proper hierarchies of power; it will allow him to reimagine his self whole and dominant, instead of pulled to pieces and 'train'd / To endless bondage' (IV.vii.493–494). Mariam is sacrificed to assuage Herod's anxiety. In killing her body, he believes, he can also erase Mariam's challenging and frightening claim to freedom and subjectivity.

Just as woman's immobilized identity and objectified status undergird social stability and male subjectivity, so her mobility and instability are seen as indicators of social disruption. Despite Herod's hopeful construction of her, Mariam does not represent the ideal of a good wife. Though she may be chaste, she is neither silent nor obedient. Even her vaunted chastity, including Herod in its refusal, is not what a husband might wish. Her manipulation of language and her claim to ownership of her body represent her rejection of the terms of static, objectified idealization. In violating the social requirement that a good wife be still and unchanging, she lays claim, not to the integrated, autonomous identity designed for himself by the male subject, but to the nomadic subjectivity more useful for the woman who needs to find a place for herself in bodily and linguistic spaces outside the range of masculine appropriation. This is the kind of subjectivity, as Jane Flax observes, which may be viewed as in process rather than 'judged by a normative standard of unitary structure' (93). Mariam does not embody an ideal; her own behavior, her speech, indeed the other characters' construction of her, are not consistent or unitary. All of the play's representations of her are multiplistic and self-contradictory.

If at some level this play wants to represent an ideal, obedient wife tried by marital tyranny beyond the limits of her conscience, it fails. But the Griselda-like woman who would remain obedient and submissive, chaste and silent in response to Herod's jealous, murderous, ambitious manipulations cannot be credibly represented, perhaps especially not by a woman writer. In fact, just as perfect womanhood lies beyond the possibility of physical enactment, so the project of depicting an ideal of submissive wifely behavior lies beyond the range of literary representation. To manifest an ideal is more than self-referential, self-contradictory, non-transparent language has the capacity to do. Verbalized, the ideal disappears.[24]

In Renaissance sonnets, for example, with which this play seems to argue, the frustrated effort to depict an ideal woman is typically either displaced by the poet's self-display or bypassed by the fragmented image at the heart of the *blazon*. In fact, the male poet's trope of self-abasement in relation to the image of an ideally virtuous and beautiful woman might *require* that the lover, self-stylized as adoring object, give way to the expert poet as subject. But a woman writing about an idealized female character might find that *her* text's refusal to produce this ideal image does not encourage an exactly parallel maneuver.

Cary offers a skillful writerly display, exploiting the power of the poetic medium in her carefully paced poetic drama and her clever mixture of blank and rhymed verse and sonnet structures, while the use of a dramatic form supports the heroine's potential for subjectivity. The play form enables the representation of Mariam as a fully motivated character who is not objectified by her creator's claim to writerly subjectivity, for a play is able to unfold without the writer having to say 'I' in relation to her character's 'you.' The subtlety of the closet drama and its un-public form also accord with subtle strategies of relationship between writer and heroine; rather than triumphing over her female protagonist while drawing attention to herself, Cary can become a complicit partisan, watching from the wings, but off-stage both from her heroine and from the public stage of the playhouse. Both heroine and writer adopt subject-positions, not divided from, but related to, each other; both Mariam and Cary are women striving toward linguistic subjectivity, neither dislodging the other.

Several readers, responding to the crisis of identity that appears to be occurring in the play, have struggled with the issue of Mariam's subjectivity. Dympna Callaghan says that, except perhaps for the 'insipid Graphina,' there is 'no female subject position available in the play that is both viable and virtuous' (177). Maureen Quilligan observes that Mariam's virtue does not guarantee her 'sufficient power to claim any freedom for herself to define what her role will be' ('Staging,' 224). While these critics seem dubious about Mariam's claim to subjectivity, Catherine Belsey on the other hand sees her as an autonomous, integrated subject, speaking from a definite position (171–172). My own view rests somewhere between these. Mariam does, I believe, quite certainly enact a subject position, but I see it as mobile and variable, not coherent and definite. Like Margaret Ferguson, I see her unsettling the binary choices imposed on women. She refuses objectification and dies for it. She risks and loses her security for the sake of a brief freedom. Because she is embodied and vocal, the ideal image projected onto her by Herod is dismantled and flawed. The woman in the center of the imagined stage of this play is fallible and un-ideal. But loss of her ideal status does not therefore rob her of subjectivity. On the contrary, the static ideal object is replaced by a fully embodied, mobile and flawed subject. Her mobility and her insistent embodiment, preventing her ideality, ensure her subjectivity.

Walking on the Ridge

Speaking of the ideal wife who internalizes her own control for the benefit of her husband, and perceiving Mariam's failure to live up to this standard, the chorus at the end of Act III declaims: ''Tis not so glorious for her to be free, / As by her proper self restrain'd to be' (III.iii.219–220). The language of this judgement didactically rewrites Mariam's own endorsement at the beginning of the play of 'freedom ... unrestrain'd' (I.i.72). The ensuing question of the chorus metaphorically reveals Mariam's motivations and desires, but fails to sympathize with them: 'When she hath spacious ground to walk upon,' they ask perplexedly, 'Why on the ridge should she desire to go?' (III.iii.221–222).

What the chorus fails to understand is the restless lack of contentment which makes Mariam want to 'range' beyond the safe and 'spacious ground' fenced in by patriarchal control, beyond the space that encloses the woman to ensure the patriarch's security. The 'ridge,' on the other hand, offering an alternative prospect for women's subjective power and freedom, is a place of wide views and adventure. Unenclosed, it is not an easy place to walk, requiring adept balancing skills on its insecure footing. Choosing to 'go' on the ridge, Mariam must expertly balance her body and language, negotiating the circumstances of their confinement and mobility, juggling conditions of freedom and risk, power and danger. Salome, plotting against Mariam later in the play, plans to 'make some swear that she desires to climb' (III.ii.91). Although Salome is not interested in the truth or falsity of this accusation, but only in its usefulness to her purpose, and although the climbing she has in mind is materially acquisitive, she speaks more truth about Mariam than she knows. It is not 'estate' that Mariam wants to climb to, however; she aspires to skill in her balancing act on the 'ridge,' from which open up vistas of freedom and the conditions of subjectivity.

Even to the point of death, Mariam enacts a nomadic subjectivity that climbs ridges, does not hold still and is self-contradictory, characterized by Hélène Cixous as 'boundless, diffuse, abundant' (*Newly Born*, 91). The feminine subjectivity that is represented through the action and speech of this dramatic heroine remains uncongealed, fluid. Not stable, not consistent, not predictable, it inspires fear and retribution, for it drives 'reason, the principle of unity, mad' (Cixous, *Newly Born*, 91) and 'jams sociality' (96). Unlike Anne Donne (who, in any case, also died young), immutably planted in the object position that kept her husband's 'circle just' and helped him 'end where [he] begun,' Mariam, more radically, may be said to exemplify the challenging sensibility expressed by Luce Irigaray: 'The time is past when I stayed still to enable you [the patriarch] to keep moving' (*Marine Lover*, 18). Mariam is not a fixed objectified other; she achieves her role as subject by keeping ex-centrically on the move. Unlike Elizabeth in the *Life*, Mariam never enters a space of unity and resolution where subjectivity 'solidifies into rigid structures' (Flax, 93); she dangerously stays in a liminal, (un)balanced space where she is 'simultaneously victimized and responsible; [where] neither negates the other' (108). Mariam is not only simultaneously victimized and responsible; she is also 'dissembling' and transparent, free and 'restrain'd'; arrogant and humble, chaste and adulterous, sensual and celibate, vocal and sparing of words, persistently mobile and briefly 'unmov'd,' pulsingly beautiful and dead.

The language of the play, densely allusive, poetic and metaphoric, is frequently repetitive and frequently self-conflicting, avoiding the control of logical statement and opening a space in which the heroine can move beyond the restrictions of consistency. Especially as it refers to Mariam, the self-contradictory language, read from a point of view that does not anxiously supply the missing bridges to logic and consistency, reinforces the understanding that meaning cannot be contained by logic, that language always contains spaces which evoke something beyond cultural prescription and that women on the margins of cultural power may profitably, although with considerable risk, explore those spaces; 'when women want to escape from exploitation ... they disrupt the entire order of dominant values, economic, social, moral, and sexual' (Irigaray, *This Sex*, 165). This is the process that may be discovered in *Mariam*.

Many critics, for example Belsey and Ferguson, have commented on the crucial importance of Mariam's first speech as an introduction to the heroine and as establishing Mariam's claim to language as an essential means to her subjectivity. The complex poetic language of this speech also, however, introduces the idioms of physical and psychological mobility and freedom that constantly recur throughout the play; it reveals a desirous woman seeking a place for her 'self,' her feelings and her discourse; and it early makes clear that Mariam is not the ideal, stable and consistent wife Herod needs her to be. In this speech, Mariam reveals herself as a subject – restless, verbal, mobile and multiply positioned.

In the first line she tells us that she has a public voice which has been allowed, both by herself and her husband, to 'run on.' The image of physical movement associated with her language is quite typical in this play. The connections between linguistic power and bodily restlessness seen in the *Life* are here too. The static, the 'still,' are the conditions of the ideal, but also of the silent. Mariam is neither. In this first soliloquy, she speaks eloquently of 'ranging' (26), of 'flight' (19, 69), of 'change' (24), of 'liberty' (25) and, crucially, of 'freedom' (16, 72), a dangerous and seductive concept introduced here for the first of the nineteen times it is invoked throughout the play.[25] Mariam's emotions are also in turmoil, veering back and forth between lamentation and relief, love and scorn. To her love for Herod, 'which once on him was firmly set' (20), has been added a wish that the 'news [of his death] may firmly hold' (52).

Her body as well as her language is expressive, multiply positioned and passionate. She weeps 'rivers' of tears (33) and drops 'some falling tear' for her husband (53) as she recalls 'the tender love that he to Mariam bare; / And mine to him' (32–33). She reminds herself, with some complacency, that Herod has been her 'truest lover' (66), feeling for her 'the deepest love that ever yet was seen' (56). Neither has *her* love for her husband always been the unpassionate love of a merely dutiful wife:

> Why, now methinks the love I bare him then,
> When virgin freedom left me unrestrain'd,
> Doth to my heart begin to creep again,
> My passion now is far from being feign'd. (71–74)

This ambiguous passage evokes an extraordinarily interesting set of possible readings.

In the first place, the 'virgin freedom' which left Mariam 'unrestrain'd' resonates suggestively with Luce Irigaray's contention that 'A virgin is one as yet unmarked' by and for the desiring patriarchy, 'not yet imprinted by their sex, their language' (*This Sex*, 211), a reading encouraged by the association of Mariam's 'unbridled speech' (III.iii.183) with her subjectivity. In the second place, it is possible that the love Mariam recalls may be the intense, romantic, but unconsummated love felt by an as yet unmarried girl for her devoted and passionate suitor. Yet again, the lack of restraint remembered by Mariam as the condition of her earliest, freely-given love may also, especially in contrast to her later decision to refuse her body to Herod's desire, imply an abandonment that is sexual. That is, before the fixed obligation of wifely submission, the new lover freely, of her own agency, *chose* to lose herself in unrestrained love; Mariam elsewhere in the play also equates love and sex: 'I will not to his love be reconcil'd, / With solemn vows I have forsworn his bed' (III.iii.133–134). These readings do not, as we might expect in this play and of this heroine, logically connect with each other. All allude, however, to the interdependent linguistic and bodily spaces of feminine subjectivity and pleasure which may be found at the margins of patriarchally constructed and controlled female behavior.

The idea in this passage, of love freely given because 'unrestrain'd,' plays against Mariam's earlier assertion that it was Herod himself who, by 'barring [her] from liberty' (25) and by preventing her from 'ranging, taught [her] first to range' (26). Herod, in a different situation, later tells us that neither he nor any other 'creature,' possessing Mariam, could ever 'wish to range' (IV.iv.484). It is the balance of power that ensures the difference, of course. As wielder of domestic and political power, Herod is able to proclaim that he has sold his freedom for delight in Mariam (IV.iv.226) and that he never from Mariam 'would be mov'd a cause of change to find' (IV.iii.152). But, oppressed by that same power, Mariam specifies it as the very stimulus to the nomadic subjectivity of a woman who is the 'site of multiple, complex, and potentially contradictory sets of experiences' (Braidotti, 4).

Mariam's 'ranging' is not simply a contrary or rebellious response to oppression, though it is that too. More significantly, it provides a means of establishing herself as capable of agency. Herod has not only sought to confine Mariam's body, but also to produce a static, objectified, obedient mind – a goal endorsed both by the chorus, which anxiously fears that 'in a wife it is no worse to find, / A common body than a common mind' (III.iii.243–244), and by Richard Brathwaite's contemporary conduct book for Renaissance gentlewomen: 'You are taught to enter your Chambers and bee still ... Still from the clamours and turbulent insults of the world; still from the mutinous motions and innovations of the flesh' (*Gentlewoman*, 296). Mariam's response to these inhibiting expectations has been to 'range' from one position to another, without concern for logical consistency. Mariam works within a 'mode of exchange(s) that might not obey the same logic' as the male (Irigaray, *This Sex*, 112). By keeping constantly on the move, she claims some freedom, some power, and also, for a while, avoids categorization and punishment. She achieves a brief moment of escape before the retribution of the anxious tyrant captures her.

Mariam occupies many positions at once, some ordained for her by masculine need, some negotiated by herself as a means of undermining the power of a tyrannical husband and finding a subjective space for herself. The line in Mariam's first speech, 'My passion now is far from being feign'd' (74), opens up one of the many linguistic and situational contradictions that accompany her throughout the play. If *now* Mariam's passion is not feigned, this line may well suggest that there *have* been times during her marriage when it has been. She has, after all, until now continued to share Herod's bed, even after he has murdered Hircanus and Aristobolus, and Alexandra chides Mariam for not being sufficiently hostile to Herod: 'What weeps't thou for thy brother's [murd'rer's] sake?' (I.ii.81). Yet elsewhere Mariam insists that she cannot now, and never has, dissembled her looks and feelings and that her language has always been transparent to her purpose: 'I scorn my look should ever man beguile, / Or other speech than meaning to afford' (III.iii.165–166); 'My lord, I suit my garment to my mind, / And there no cheerful colors can I find' (IV.iii.91–92); 'I cannot frame disguise, nor ever taught / My face a look dissenting from my thought'

(IV.ii.145–146). The references to 'speech,' 'mind' and 'thought' on the one hand, and 'garment,' 'look' and 'face' on the other, underscore the inextricability of language, mind and body in the mobile process of Mariam's subjectivity.

The contradictions buried in the language of dissembling are also there in other descriptions of variable bodily and psychological positionings that metonymically bespeak a shifting sense of self.[26] In a moment of self-conflicted disgust with Herod, Mariam proclaims, 'Yet had I rather much a milkmaid be, / Than be the monarch of Judea's queen' (I.i.57–58), but this assertion of humility connects doubtfully with other moments in the play. Her mother, Alexandra, in the next scene, conjures up the ambitious image of Mariam sharing a throne even more powerful than Herod's: 'Then Mariam in a Roman's chariot set, / In place of Cleopatra might have shown' (I.ii.195). Constabarus, from a different point of view, connects the idea of men's dislocated class and gender with women's increasing grasp of power (I.vi.421–430). But it is Mariam's reductive relocation of herself as a milkmaid that epitomizes the very conjunction of disrupted class and unstable woman feared by Constabarus.

In any case, humility does not sit well with Mariam when it comes to its implementation. When Alexandra slyly suggests that Doris might replace Mariam in Herod's affections, Mariam rises to the bait with an outraged expression of self-congratulatory scorn: 'Doris! Alas, her time of love was past, / Those coals were rak'd in embers long ago / [Of] Mariam's love' (I.ii.131–133). Although she hastens to add, 'Nor did I glory in her overthrow' (134), she goes on to boast in a decidedly un-humble way that Herod cared 'not a whit' for Doris's son because he 'was not mine' (135–136). Similarly, in her immediately following confrontation with Salome, Mariam invidiously compares Salome's 'baser birth' (I.iii.233) to her own, addressing her as a 'mongrel' (236), and telling her, 'You scarce have ever my superiors seen': / For Mariam's servants were as good as you' (224–225).[27]

Speaking later in the play of Salome, Herod and her mother-in-law, Mariam again boasts, 'I could overthrow them all ere long' (III.iii.163). Yet, at the same time, she partially contradicts this urge by scorning, she says, 'To be commandress of the triple earth' (175), if the price exacted is an 'impure' spirit (178). Mariam may be willing rhetorically to consider herself a humble milkmaid, but the language of others as well as her own does not support the seriousness of this claim, especially when Mariam comes face to face with Doris or Salome, to whom she shows little compassion or humility, although she has more in common with both than any of the three is willing to admit.[28] Mariam's verbal embrace of the role of milkmaid rests problematically against all other language which does not evince humility; the chorus, in fact, indicts her and other culpable women, perhaps like Cary herself, on exactly the grounds of employing un-humble, assertive public language: 'Then she usurps upon another's right, / That seeks to be by public language grac'd' (III.iii.239–240).

Mariam's explanations of her downfall are equally complex, referring confidently on the one hand to the sufficiently protective powers of her innocence and beauty, but on the other, speculating that perhaps humility was always a necessary and too lately recognized ingredient. At first, she reassures herself that her innocence of adultery, alone, is a unique defense: 'Oh, what a shelter is mine innocence' (III.iii.171); 'Mine innocence is hope enough for me' (III.iii.180). Yet in the next act she says that she has also thought her *beauty* alone a protection: 'Ay, I it was that thought my beauty such, / As it alone could countermand my death' (IV.viii.527–528). Mariam, like Herod, has overvalued her beauty, as she has also overvalued her innocence. Dismayed that her beauty has failed her, she speaks plaintively here of her 'cheek of roses' (530) and 'an eye whose shine doth most excel' (531).

Belatedly, now, she sees the humility which she has lacked as the essential catalyst for the persuasive working of her innocence and beauty on Herod:

> Had I but with humility been grac'd,
> As well as fair I might have prov'd me wise.
> But I did think because he knew me chaste,
> One virtue for a woman might suffice. (IV.viii.559–562).

Even now, however, her language is not humble: 'Who sees for truth that Mariam is untrue? / If fair she be, she is as chaste as fair' (580). She congratulates herself on her innocence: ''tis my joy / That I was ever innocent, though sour' (567–568).

This phrasing seems weirdly to applaud the sourness with the innocence. It recalls William Whateley's adjuration that women's behavior should not be 'flinging, nor puffing, nor discontented, but savouring of all lowliness' (18), that is, not sour but humble – a conventional lesson Mariam has resisted and even now seems undisposed to learn. Acknowledging this 'sour' dimension in herself, even so, Mariam boasts, Herod has been unwaveringly faithful to her. He has even resisted Cleopatra's blandishments for love of Mariam (IV.viii.537–552), and would never have ordered her death had she herself not 'conspir'd' against herself (533); without that, 'No plot, no adversary from without / Could Herod's love from Mariam have retir'd, / Or from his heart have thrust my semblance out' (534–536). Mariam at one and the same time recognizes humility's usefulness, and is also still boastful of the power of her 'semblance.' 'Semblance,' we should note, is a word that conveys the meanings of both appearance and pretense – harking back, still indeterminately, to the issue of Mariam's *dis*sembling.

Although Constabarus, a comparatively sympathetic male figure in this play, admires Mariam and ostensibly wants to exempt her from the generalized denunciations he makes against the whole 'wavering crew' of women (III.iii.311), his specific complaints are directed to the 'pride' (324) of which Mariam is clearly guilty. It is difficult to find in his absolutist indictments a space in which to position Mariam as an exception to his totalizing rule. 'But none of you are inly beautified' (323), he says. 'Your best,' that is, in Constabarus's view, exemplified by Mariam, 'are foolish, froward, wanton, vain' (333). It appears that Constabarus, though wanting to play the role of advocate for Mariam, nevertheless convicts her of the very defects of character that are implicated in her fall. Here, too, as in Mariam's own comments about herself, the language of the play turns upon itself to insist once again on Mariam's un-ideal, mixed construction. The response of the chorus to Mariam's error is just as complex: 'Sway'd' by 'sullen passion,' they say, she has 'fixed her thoughts all injury above' and thus has been guilty of the strangely mixed sin of 'virtuous pride' (IV.viii.663).

The play's language is equally self-conflicted and indeterminate concerning the central question of Mariam's 'innocence.'[29] Again in her first speech, Mariam declares that, though she has been sorely tried by Herod, she has never been able 'To learn to love another than my lord' (28); this she regards as sufficient proof that she is innocent of the unchastity of which Herod, all the same, universally and unequivocally accuses her: 'never wert thou chaste' (IV.iv.204). Antipater, Doris's son, equally absolutely asserts, 'foul adultery blotteth Mariam's brow' (II.iii.278). Although Mariam insists that she has not chosen adultery for herself, she cannot escape the construction or the accusation. Neither is Antipater's charge the trumped-up version later engineered against Mariam by Salome. Antipater means quite literally and sincerely that Mariam is a guilty party to adultery.

Doris subsequently repeats and explains this conviction, accusing Mariam of living for nine years in adultery with Herod, whom she regards as still her husband. Mariam, no less than Doris or Salome, suffers the consequence of social and legal gendered double standards, as they surface here in the Mosaic divorce laws. Salome wants to eliminate the inequity in these laws, making divorce available to women as well as men, so that she may initiate her own divorce from Constabarus. Doris also rejects the double standard, but with a different purpose, insisting that neither party should be recognized as able to divorce a blameless spouse. On this ground she accuses Mariam of adultery; in Doris's eyes, Mariam is living with a still-married man.

Mariam, unlike the other two women, has trusted in the validity of the divorce laws' double standard and has believed herself to be chastely married to Herod. When Doris suggests that Mariam is not Herod's true wife but an adulteress, Mariam asks in either dismissive scorn or guilty and embarrassed surprise (both are possible), 'Was that adult'ry?' (IV.viii.587). Recognizing that, even while believing herself 'guiltless' (608), she has injured Doris and possibly committed adultery, with a momentary humility she now kneels, begging Doris to protect her children: 'Oh, Doris, now to thee my knees I bend / That heart that never bow'd to thee doth bow' (604–605). Her compunction, however, is short-lived. Her last words to Doris are cruel: 'I hope the world shall see, / This curse of thine shall be return'd to thee' (625–626).

The shifting ground of women's sexual guilt or innocence is, in any case, as much a matter of social perspective as it is a matter of individual bodily placement. Women's adultery and promiscuity are broadly, not narrowly defined, and in these terms, Mariam is undoubtedly guilty. Richard Brathwaite's *English Gentlewoman* makes this clear; the woman who congratulates herself on her privacy, who says, 'the walls encompasse mee, darkenesse o're shadowes mee, the Curtaine of night secures mee,' speaks 'the wordes of an Adulteresse' (297). Mariam's complaint that Herod prevents her 'ranging,' together with her lament upon his return from Rome, 'And must I to my prison turn again?' (III.iii.151), indict her, especially when placed beside what a point of view unsympathetic to Mariam might construe as Herod's generous and tolerant offer to give her 'more space':

> Or if thou think Judea's narrow bound
> Too strict a limit for thy great command:
> Thou shalt be empress of Arabia crown'd. (IV.iii.101–104)

Yet Herod himself, underwriting the popular conjunction of women's language and bodies, also accepts Mariam's promiscuity on terms not measured by her physical chastity at all, but by her eloquence: 'Her mouth will ope to every stranger's ear' (IV.vii.434).

These instances raise the question of whether Mariam has the power to define the terms of her own chastity. The answer seems to be, as is often the case in this play, at one moment and in one place, yes; at and in another, no. Mariam's sexuality is a social construction as much as a personal behavior; within both of these arenas she has to comport herself. Her body is part of a social exchange system, in which her personal conviction and assertion of chastity, while from her perspective sufficient, are still not enough to make her chaste in the eyes of others, or, in the end, to save her from death. For, it appears, adultery is more than an issue of the material body, and guilt more than an issue of chastity. Mariam is both chaste and not, both guilty of adultery and not. Though this mixed construction of chastity leads to Mariam's death, Herod's inability to contain absolutely either her body or her speech in a simplified, objectified form, and her own capacity to negotiate inside and outside her social construction, the very conditions of her short freedom, demonstrate the limitations of social constructions. For, though the chorus anxiously hopes for women's entire compliance and willing self-disposal – 'When to their husbands they themselves do bind / Do they not wholly give themselves away?' (III.iii.233–234) – the hope is vain.

Though Herod has the power to put Mariam to death, he does not have the power to contain her threat. Both because of her refusal even to defend herself against his suspicion with her usual eloquence, as well as because of the unsure social construction of her virtue, she embodies the worst of patriarchal anxiety. If, as the proverb says, it is a wise man who knows his own father, it is also an omniscient man who knows his own wife's fidelity. Cultural equivocation and inconsistency, resulting partly from women's refused compliance, and partly from excessively worried effort to enforce it, produce contradictory consequences. If Mariam does not have the cultural power to own her own body entirely and to testify reliably to her own chastity, how can Herod ever know that she is virtuous? But Mariam's ability to move in and out of the patriarch's containment, to assuage and whet his anxiety, to be both one thing and another, establishes the terms of her mobile body and discursive subjectivity.

For Mariam's body, like Elizabeth's in the *Life*, is both vividly present and variably positioned, able to move readily among different aspects of itself. It, too, is busy crossing borders of inadequate definition, heavily weighted with self-conflicted meanings, speaking a mixed language which allegorically evokes her escape from patriarchal jurisdiction. Mariam's body metaphorically both walks in 'spacious ground' and climbs on the 'ridge.' It has a different momentum than Herod's own wide-ranging travel in far-flung places, but just as much inspires nervousness and speculation, for it moves to the rhythm of restlessness and discontent. As the chorus for once truly says, 'her wishes drive her to she knows not what' (I.vi.526); her goals lie beyond the reach of definition because they are not sanctioned in patriarchal language. Mariam's body and mind are nomadic, her mind resiliently and widely so, her body 'ranging' within its own frame and the narrow spaces of the palace, restlessly in motion. Her body is mobile and expressive; it weeps passionate tears and is insistently vocal. It is maternal and sensual, sexual and celibate. It is arrogant and prideful, yet, in distress, kneels to Doris.

Mariam's body is passionately desired by Herod, but it is also at least potentially an object of desire by others. Sohemus says of her that her 'eyes' grave majesty keeps all in awe, / And cuts the wings of every loose desire: / ... Yet though we dare not love, we may admire' (III.iii.209–212). As well as desired, she is desiring; she has loved Herod immoderately. Yet, believing Herod to be dead, she swears future celibacy: 'With purest body will I press my tomb' (I.ii.201); her body will not be moderately 'pure,' but superlatively 'purest.' After Herod's return, she continues in her excessive enactment of the chastity the patriarch has desired of her, even under indictment for adultery, interrupting the masculine desire that seeks to control and design women's bodies and language. 'Even if it exacts its price from the woman herself,' as it certainly does in Mariam's case, a woman's continued refusal of heterosexual pleasure is a 'position resistant to the patriarchal requirements of heterosexuality' (Grosz, *Sexual Subversions*, 133). Believing in their effectiveness, Mariam still chooses not to use her sexual wiles to survive; she tries something else more extreme and farther outside the range of the acceptable – refusal of sex with her tyrant.[30]

This tactic constitutes a particularly frustrating challenge, for, unlike Elizabeth Cary as she appears in her daughter's biography, Mariam possesses the stunning beauty that defines her as an object of desire. She is 'sweet-fac'd' (I.vi.487); her eyes are stars (IV.iv.220; IV.vii.441, 450); her hair is like a golden fleece (IV.vii.413); 'her forehead like the sky' (IV.vii.451). Everyone in the play speaks of her beauty. Herod is obsessed by it; even Salome reluctantly acknowledges it (IV.vii.405); Alexandra constructs ambitions of power on it (I.ii.180–198); Doris envies it (II.iii.223); Sohemus admires it (III.iii.205–214). Mariam, somewhat smug about its power, trusts its influence on Herod overmuch: 'I know I could enchain him with a smile: And lead him captive with a gentle word' (III.iii.163); but choosing not to smile on Herod, she has, nevertheless, mistakenly 'deem'd my face must needs preserve my breath' (IV.viii.526). Women's beauty is an almost universal literary figure of fragility, decay and change, yet only once does the play, through Salome, issue the reminder that 'Beauty is a blast' (III.i.20). Mariam's beauty is ostensibly the one aspect of her that is left undisputed and apparently stable in the language of the play. But it too is finally changed by the grimace of death.

One of the irrefutable lessons to be drawn from Mariam's fate is that even if a woman makes an effort to conform to social demands, she may still not survive. Nothing is sufficient in an insatiably demanding culture that permits tyranny in a husband and demands total submission in a wife. Early in the play, Mariam becomes aware of the voracious literalness with which Herod has held that in marriage, they have become one body, hers assimilated to his. If Herod's body dies in Rome, Sohemus has told Mariam, hers is also to be put to death. Even Mariam's response to this foretaste of her husband's later and final order for her execution is not unmixed; tangled in a sense of Herod's devotion to her, half-forgivingly Mariam says, 'It was for nought but love he wish'd his end / Might to my death but the vaunt-courier prove' (I.i.60). Though appalled by it, Mariam also seems taken with the romance of this controlling desire.

Finally, Mariam's 'body is divided from her head' (V.i.90). Refusing one kind of objectification through idealization, she has another forced upon her in death. Yet even her beheading, which seems so definitive, is not.[31] 'Therefore, shall she never more be free' (IV.iv.258), Herod absolutely decrees, but the apparent finality of Mariam's death is problematized by Herod's subsequent regret, by the after-the-fact general testimony to Mariam's fidelity and by the typological Christianizing of Mariam as a 'phoenix' (V.i.24), as a 'dying swan' (V.i.65), as someone whose death induces her betrayer, Judas-like, to hang himself and as a martyr who 'three days hence, if wishes could revive,' would once more come 'alive' (V.i.77–78). The language of the play seems to assure us that not even her beheading will impose stillness on Mariam.

Even in her typological emanation, however, Mariam remains elusive and mobile, for here too the message of the play is utterly mixed. Is she dead absolutely or, like the Christ figure of whom she is a 'type,' to be in some way resurrected? Of course, Mariam's undoubted role as a type of Christ does not make her equivalent to Christ.[32] The point of typological precursors is that they are flawed because without benefit of the grace derived from the advent of the unique Christian dispensation. They are un-ideal and err inevitably, though they manifest a foretaste of virtuous heroism. Even this awareness, though, must be further tempered by the context which has also oddly allowed Herod to cross the line between death and life. For, even more definitively than the language of the play speaks of Mariam's death, it tells us that Herod has been impossibly 'reviv'd,' as his brother Pheroras says, 'from certain death' (III.ii.41). What are we to make of this? Is Herod's metaphoric 'resurrection' physical and Mariam's spiritual? Perhaps Mariam's typological claim is real and Herod's spurious? The answers to these questions remain unclear, but the fact that the play raises them at all certainly confuses Mariam's claim to Christ-like resurrection or purified typology. Still, Mariam and what she represents cannot easily be disposed of. Her 'space' is not so easily filled in, for it is fluid and ambiguous, neither enclosable nor able adequately to be classified and policed.

Though her execution ends Mariam's marriage and her mortal life, the audience is allowed to imagine that she has escaped to 'live' somewhere else. The image of the headless woman, sharply evoked in the blunt report that Mariam's 'body is divided from her head,' encourages this response, for the headless woman appears frequently in early modern iconographic depictions which testify to its ambiguous power (Borin, 214–218). All body, all sexuality, no longer directed by even the minimal rationality contained in a woman's mind, the headless woman is an object of fear, a figure of chaos. But, paradoxically, it may also be an image of ultimate, restrained female virtue exactly because it is separated from the misdirection and deception contained in women's minds.

In equally strange and paradoxical ways, although her beheading testifies to Herod's life-and-death power over her, it also undermines Herod's control. Attempting to assert absolute ownership of his wife's body and curtail her rebellion, Herod actually looses Mariam from his dominance, and she sends him an oblique message to tell him so: 'Tell thou my lord thou saw'st me loose my breath' (V.i.73). Herod, using a reference to Mariam's language to stand metonymically for the bodily object of his controlling but futile desire, replies, 'Oh, that I could that sentence now control' (74). In at least a metaphoric sense, Mariam's death also signals Herod's. 'Live without her? ... I'm sure I cannot' (IV.vii.380–382), he tells Salome.

Mariam's body is now divided from her husband, her 'head,' the social representative of her rationality, the control of her bodily dangerousness, her speech ('sentence') and her irrationality. William Gouge, among other influential contemporary commentators, explains 'How a Husband is his Wife's Head': 'The place of an husband ... is expressed under the metaphor of an *head* ... A wife must submit herself to an husband because he is her head ... As an head is more eminent and excellent than the body, and placed above it, so is an husband to his wife' (*Domesticall Duties*, treatise I, section 114). Though headless, Mariam has escaped from spousal dominance and thus is potentially heedless, unreasonable and disruptive. Yet, for a passing moment, on the way to her execution, Mariam is untypically 'unmov'd': 'She came unmov'd, with pleasant grace / As if to triumph her arrival were: / In stately habit and with cheerful face' (V.i.55–57). But the memory of Mariam and her posthumous image continues to move nomadically even across the border of death. As she leaves 'real' space, she takes over imaginative and mental space as a public figure and as a representative of a set of soon-to-be Christian values that will take their place in public discourse. Disembodied now, she undermines in a very powerful way the effort to reduce women to a contaminated physical body under their husband's headship.

Mariam's subjective space is not only sketched out by her body's elusive nomadism, but also by her flowing speech; both are eloquent.[33] Her public voice 'run[s] on' (I.i.1); 'she seeks to be by public language grac'd' (III.iii.240). Yet, although her speech violates restrictive edicts of the virtuous woman's silence, her 'world-amazing wit' is admired by Herod and her 'beauteous language' admitted by Salome, who acknowledges its power in her complaint that 'Herod's ear ... doth so firmly to his Mariam bend' (III.ii.87–88).

Mariam's speech, like her body, is described in images of movement, of multiple positionings. Like an unbroken horse, it is unpredictable and potentially dangerous:

'Unbridled speech is Mariam's worst disgrace' (III.iii.183), says Sohemus, using a metaphor which appears often in contemporary conduct books like William Whateley's, suggesting the social need to tame women's natural tendency to run out of control:[34]

> It is a laudable, commendable, a note of a virtuous woman, a dutiful wife, when she submits herself with quietness, cheerfully, even as a well-broken horse turns at the least turning, stands at the least check of the rider's bridle, readily going and standing as he wishes that sits upon his back. (36–43)

Mariam's speech represents her resistance to her oppressive construction and is also a mode of subjective inscription – a way of choosing her own way of going rather than 'readily going and standing as he wishes that sits upon [her] back.' Language, especially speech, is itself a shifting process and so serves as an appropriate vehicle for Mariam's subjectivity-as-process (Flax, 93).[35]

Mariam's speech, too public, too challenging and too vagrant, is, with her body, the means by which she lays claim to errant subjectivity, but also the cause of her downfall. Even her socially unamenable volubility unpredictably fails to come into play at the moment when it might have been most useful. Accused by Herod of attempting to poison him and of adultery with Sohemus, Mariam says briefly and unsurely, 'Did I? Some hateful practice this will prove, / Yet can it be no worse than Heavens permit' (IV.iv.161–162). In the face of Herod's accusations, she is not vehement in her denial and argues nothing to clear herself. Offering no evidence of her innocence other than her own very brief assertion, even at this crucial moment she withdraws from the binary structures of accusation and defense, leaving open and ambiguous her verbal and sexual innocence. Indeed, this non-binaried fluidity of women's position, so emphatic in the play, is the very source of both opportunity and trouble, for Mariam and early modern culture.

In the interests of consistency and making logical sense of this astonishingly variable text, a reader might be tempted to adjust its self-contradictions, sorting them separately into the 'true' and the 'false,' or categorizing them as the comments of reliable and unreliable speakers. But this is to accept the priority of oppositional binary constructions, which categorize women as oppressed, and to deny the slippery self-contradictions at the heart of language itself, those very possibilities that nurture women's language and subjectivity. It is also to bypass the self-contradictions induced by the anxieties of insecure power, evident both in Cary's recreation of Palestine shortly before the birth of Christ and in early seventeenth-century England.

The contradictions tell us about cultural stress, and also about women's efforts to negotiate a space for themselves in discourse between Herod's absoluteness – 'And therefore shall she nevermore be free' (IV.iv.258), and Mariam's desire – 'Oft have I wish'd that I from him were free' (I.i.16). Of course, the pursuit of freedom always involves risk. Yet though the risk may be extreme, freedom as concept and goal remains. The tyrant may kill the woman who asserts her claim to freedom, but the very killing keeps alive the notion of freedom; the extremity of the punishment validates the importance of the effort.

As Michel Foucault suggests, 'at the heart of power relations and as a permanent condition of their existence there is an insubordination and a certain essential obstinacy on the part of the principles of freedom [so that] there is no relationship of power without the means of escape or possible flight' (*Michel Foucault*, 225). This might be taken as a commentary on Mariam's situation. The obstinacy of her claim to freedom is induced by the principles of tyrannical power. The danger of asserting her desire for escape is evident in her end, but the space of freedom has been carved out even in its inevitably limited, problematized and only partially knowable way. This freedom marks itself against the tyranny which asserts its own coherence, knowability and universality. All of these claims, though false, inhibit the feminine, which nevertheless still locates itself in the world of the unknowable, the world of equivocation.

The problem represented by Mariam, as perceived from the male perspective, is how to situate a woman so she will be 'safe.' The problem perceived from a female perspective is how to situate herself so as not to be victimized by the over-anxious male, how to find a subjective space. Spaces of feminine meaning must be found in the reputedly logical and binary language of the patriarch because this is the only social representing system available. But feminine texts can be written in the ceaseless seismic displacements of language where the plates of logic do not in fact meet.

Mariam prevents the reader from entering the security of language which relies on consistency and binary logic. This is what has caused many readers' discomfort with the play, yet it is the very strategy that saves the play for a feminist reader. To dismantle the oppositional terms of culture, says Luce Irigaray, we need a miracle, an angel (*Ethics*, 15–19). For Mariam, miracles are unavailable and she dies. Nevertheless, she has engaged in the search for a space where she is not entirely restricted by choices between either/or on the one hand, or both/and on the other. In the effort to avoid this binary structure, she becomes a nomad, moving across borders and boundaries, balancing on a ridge. She engages in a dodging maneuver that allows her to acquire a brief, vagrant power over her body and language. Though the chorus warns against hearing 'a tale with ears prejudicate' (II.iv.401), this is exactly how this play invites us to listen to Mariam's tale and to hear the nuances of its text. The conflicted and slippery language of the play itself requires that we 'confound the meaning, change the words' (407), for *Mariam*'s disruption of the binary constructions that are essential to logical language is the rupture that opens the space for feminine meaning and subjectivity.[36]

Notes

1 For discussion of the ways this term can be applied in the English Renaissance see the opening of the following chapter on Aemilia Lanyer.

2 Questions of authorship relating to this document are discussed by Weller and Ferguson in the introduction to their edition of the play (1–2, and especially 51 n. 3).

3 Margaret Ferguson speaks for a number of Cary critics when she says that the play has seemed confusingly 'both feminist and non-feminist ... [T]he play's ideological statement is so mixed, so contradictory' ('Running,' 38); in a later essay, 'The Spectre of Resistance,' Ferguson also considers the play's mixed message regarding women's response to male authority. Tina Krontiris asks whether or not Cary endorses Mariam's rebellious behavior and responds: 'The answer is not straightforward. Cary's own attitude is ambivalent but also revealing of the tension between internalized cultural restrictions and individual desire' (84). Catherine Belsey comments that 'the play as a whole seems to oscillate between endorsement and disapproval of Mariam's defiance' (174).

4 Callaghan objects that focusing on the biography as a means of access to the play has led readers into an awkward anachronism, for the marriage traumas that critics have seen in both Cary's life and play had not made themselves known to Cary at the time the play was written. I think this point needs some qualification. The dating of the play is still somewhat doubtful, though it was probably written after Cary's marriage in 1602 and before the birth of her first child in 1609 – most likely after Sir Henry Cary left for Holland in 1604. The play was known to Sir John Davies in 1612 and parallels between the two plays suggest that it was possibly known by Shakespeare when he wrote *Othello* in 1607. During the first year of their marriage, Elizabeth's husband lived at court and at his parents' home, while Elizabeth stayed with her own parents. She seems to have known quite clearly that Cary had married her only for her money (*Life*, 188). In 1604, Henry went to Holland to fight for the Protestant cause against Spain – the same year in which Elizabeth was possibly already considering Catholic conversion (Mahl and Koon). If she was entertaining sympathies for Catholicism during the years that her husband took up arms against Spanish Catholicism, this and the other circumstances of her marriage during the years in which she could have written the play, suggest an early lack of marital harmony not out of line with the sense of marital tyranny and discord projected in *Mariam*. Also see Meredith Skura's suggestion that 'rather than *repeating* the story of her difficult marriage, the play quite remarkably *foretells* the story; what it does reproduce is Cary's early relation to her parents' (28). Skura hooks 'the maternal subtext' of *Mariam* to Cary's experience as a mother and with mother figures.

5 Lodge's translation would not have been essential to the polyglot Elizabeth's comprehension, but its publication would have alerted her to its potential usefulness for her own writing.

6 For a discussion of the sources for this combined character, see Weller and Ferguson, 20–22.

7 Most of the references to the *Life* are to the Weller and Ferguson edition. Occasionally, I quote from the letters in the Appendix to the 1861 edition; in those cases, I parenthetically specify that edition by its date.

8 Karen Raber has argued that the vacillations and self-splitting of Mariam's 'self' reflect the political realities of the 'mutually constitutive positive power of absolutism and patriarchy' and that 'the gendered subject is the progeny of a sociopolitical matrix' (331).

9 The thirty or forty years between the composition of the play (1602–1609) and the biography (1643–1650) did not substantially alter the cultural attitudes toward women's available space and freedom, though women themselves slowly began to adjust their thinking about their own potential. See Joy Wiltenburg for an interesting analysis of the representation of disorderly women in the street literature of early modern England and Germany. The biography also represents the culturally conservative position of a writer attempting to idealize the past.

Betty Travitsky judiciously refers to both documents, not to pursue Cary in one or the other, but to see how both reflect similar prevailing social and cultural attitudes to women; Travitsky sees 'chilling evidence of the pervasiveness of the patriarchal attitudes that underlay and determined women's place in Renaissance English society.' The play was 'written when her own efforts to subordinate herself wholly to her husband were presumably at their height and ... provides a mirror for the somber facts of women's subordination in marriage in seventeenth-century England' ('Feme Covert,' 192). Also see Shari Zimmerman's subtle discussion of the 'broad cultural questions' addressed in both texts (583 and *passim*).

10 Female vagrancy, also, may have represented to an aristocratic female observer a both distasteful and partly seductive example of women's freedom. But aristocratic women moved about England with some freedom too. In the second half of the seventeenth century, Lady Brilliana Harley, Alice Thornton, Katherine Evans and Sarah Chevers, Celia Fiennes, and numerous others, journeyed around and sometimes outside of England for various purposes. Contemporary with Cary, in London, middle-class women like Aemilia Lanyer passed through the city independently and often, as witness her visits to Simon Forman; and Isabella Whitney roamed the streets of the city she apostrophized in her poetry.

11 This sense of spatial possibility would perhaps have been enhanced by the newly acute cultural attention to the depiction of space in art and architecture. David Evett says that 'From the late 1570s onward ... openings begin to appear, both literal and metaphorical' (194) in paintings and buildings. Evett also cites Wylie Sypher's 'attention to the perforated space of Renaissance art' (159) and, speaking of the influence of these new perceptions on the dramatic scene and masque he comments on the 'striking ... development of the playwrights' spatial imaginations' (270).

12 Louise Schleiner has an interesting discussion of the activities of this circle (ch. 3).

13 This conclusion is Schleiner's as well as mine. See Schleiner, 184–185. Cary's complicity in the publication of her play seems likely, given that there is 'nothing surreptitious about the play's entry in the Stationer's Register' (Krontiris, 159).

14 The embarrassment of having a wife clearly out of his control was compounded for Falkland by his position in Catholic Ireland as Lord Deputy, representing Protestant England.

15 See Louise Schleiner's discussion of this escape into writing, 184ff.

16 Laurie Shannon argues that '*Mariam* unambiguously underwrites one particular moral value: constancy' (137). I find it hard to see that the play actually does this, although that may have been its intent. Nothing in this play seems 'unambiguous' to me.

17 According to Josephus, Herod did in fact rob David's sepulchre for his own advantage, not merely promise to do so for Mariam's sake. Cary's version makes Herod a little more sympathetic.

18 Maureen Quilligan says that 'The very choice of closet drama would, at the very least, seem to underscore the fact that the public theaters barred women' ('Staging,' 225).

19 Elaine Beilin says that the final act simplifies the conflict at the heart of the play by making Mariam a kind of Christian precursor. However, even if this appears to be the intention of the play, this is a place where the text overflows its intended meaning. The typological dimension is certainly there, but it does not erase the self-contradictoriness of the play's language or the problematic circumstances of Mariam's life, personality and death.

20 Another admiring contemporary comment on variety is voiced in Shakespeare's *Antony and Cleopatra*: 'Age cannot wither her, nor custom stale / Her infinite variety' (II.ii.245–246). The historical links between Mariam's family and Cleopatra and between Herod and Antony make this association more pleasing. Alexandra did in fact write to Cleopatra to ask for help when Herod murdered her son, probably assuming the Egyptian Queen's influence over Antony, to whom, as *Mariam* opens, Herod has been called to account for his actions. See Weller and Ferguson, pp. 41ff and pp. 63ff, and the play's 'Argument.'

21 Nancy Gutierrez argues that Cary's use of Senecan drama was not 'self-effacing' (238) and marginal, as it has sometimes been assumed, but an assured entry into an elitist, aristocratic genre. Cary undoubtedly took into account the likely response of her coterie audience, carefully skirting their possible disapproval. If Cary had wished for unequivocal approval from her local audience, she might have produced a straightforward translation exercise of the 'wise and sad men' recommended by Vives, or perhaps a treatise on wifely obedience. Or, if she wished to practise the Senecan drama popular in the Wilton circle and among her friends, she could have depicted a heroine more clearly embodying the virtues admired in her culture, or placed in the play an authoritative voice endorsing dominant cultural values. That she did none of these things suggests that she wanted to say and do something she expected to be culturally dubious, and also wanted not to incur cultural disapproval. Closet drama shares with all drama the distancing, even concealment, of an authorial point of view. Drama rarely offers the equivalent of the authorial intrusion and direction possible in fictional and biographical narrative, or the personal revelation available in some poetic forms. The form of the closet drama interferes with easy judgements concerning the blame or esteem attributable to the characters and, by extension, to the writer.

22 See Nancy Gutierrez's very interesting analysis of the way Mariam's use of the sonnet recasts the power configuration of this kind of poem (240).

23 Weller and Ferguson see this as a reference to gunpowder (130), but, following the lengthy descriptions by Herod of Mariam's physical attributes, it seems more likely that the falsehood of which Herod accuses her is associated with the deceptions of cosmetics.

24 See Elizabeth Cropper's brilliant discussion of the ways in which the representation of ideal beauty equally eludes the Renaissance painter and his compensatory maneuvers.

25 I.16; I.72; I.257; I.310; I.337; I 419; I.487; I.517; II.108 (twice); III.146; III.217; III.219; III.245; IV.226; IV.258; IV.298; IV.438; IV.570. The words 'liberty' and 'liberties' also appear regularly.

26 Shari Zimmerman has brilliantly teased out the implications of the issue of dissembling in Cary and Milton's *Doctrine and Discipline of Divorce*.

27 For the racial overtones of Mariam's response to Salome, see Dympna Callaghan's fine essay.

28 Again it is the echoing language of the play, not its apparent intent, that enforces these connections, but they are quite definitely there. Salome's husband describes her as a 'painted sepulchre' (II.iv.325); Mariam's husband, not dissimilarly, calls her a 'white

enchantress' and a 'painted devil' (IV.iv.175–176). Both Salome and Mariam declare themselves as wanting to be quit of their husbands. Both decide to remove themselves or their husbands from their beds: 'But now I will divorce him from my bed' (I.iv.317), says Salome; Mariam's version is: 'With solemn vows I have forsworn his bed' (II.iii.133). Like Mariam, Salome recalls her earlier love for her husband and its conflict with her present frame of mind (I.i.*passim* for Mariam and I.iv.274–292 for Salome). Both speak desirously of freedom (I.i.16 and I.iii.310). Both are trapped by the double standard of Mosaic divorce laws, Mariam in the adultery perceived by Antipater and Doris, Salome in a marriage she no longer desires. Both are accused of 'wavering' thoughts, Mariam by the chorus at the end of Act I and by Herod in IV.vii.510, and Salome by Constabarus in I.vi.474. Both have their defenders of their purity: Herod, after Mariam's death, speaks of 'The King of Jewry's fair and spotless wife' (V.i.198), and Silleus accuses Constabarus of slandering Salome's 'unspotted name' (II.iv.297). Both have their freedom curtailed by Herod's return. Salome tells Silleus, 'My brother's sudden coming now / Will give my foot no room to walk at large' (III.ii.117). Mariam greets the same news with, 'And must I to my prison turn again' (III.iii.151). Both are voluble. Both complain of their situations. Both are lumped together in the chorus' denunciations. And, finally, in a mistake that underlines all of these similarities, Herod confuses Salome and Mariam: 'I will requite / Thee, gentle Mariam – Salom, I mean' (IV.ii.83–84).

Mariam's connections with Doris are emphasized by Alexandra, who says that if Herod could replace Doris with Mariam, he could equally dislodge Mariam and return to Doris (I.ii.127–130). Mariam's petitionary posture to Doris at the end of the play: 'Oh, Doris, now to thee my knees I bend, / That heart that never bow'd to thee doth bow' (IV.viii.604–605), recapitulates Doris's earlier prayer: 'And with dejected knees, aspiring hands / Have pray'd the highest power to enact / The fall of her that on my trophy stands' (III.iii.248–250). Connections among the women in the play, through their maternity, are explicated by Naomi Miller ('Domestic Politics').

29 Obviously I differ here from Gwynne Kennedy's point that Mariam's 'chastity and sexual obedience are never suspect' (119).

30 See my discussion in chapter 2 of the ways in which chastity may establish a resistance to patriarchal goals. If Cary was examining the attractions of Catholicism at the time she was writing *Mariam*, as the biography seems to suggest, Mariam's choice of chastity might represent a comment on the disappearance of women's conventual chastity from Protestant England. In a Catholic culture, convent life might have tempted an intellectual woman like the young Elizabeth Tanfield. For a discussion of the way in which Mariam deploys her sexuality as a form of resistance inside a context which implies the threat of rape, see Catty, 156–170.

31 Margaret Ferguson sees the beheading as 'an over-determined allusion – to Christ's harbinger, John the Baptist, beheaded by Salome; to a recent queen of Scotland, Mary, whose son ruled England when Cary wrote her play and who was in the eyes of many English Catholics a victim of Protestant tyranny; and also, perhaps, to Anne Boleyn, killed by a royal husband who had broken with the Catholic church to divorce his first wife and who was explicitly linked to the tyrant Herod by some of his disapproving subjects' ('Running,' 55). Stephanie Wright points out that Herod's sister Salome is not the same Salome as his step-daughter who claimed the head of John the Baptist.

32 Subsequent discussions of this typological aspect in *Mariam* are dependent on Elaine Beilin's initial analysis.

33 Margaret Ferguson's essay, 'Running On ...', has supplied the definitive analysis of the function of women's speech in this play as a means to represent women's subjectivity.

34 A popular dramatic depiction of the process of 'training' a woman, analogous to the training of an animal, to behave in socially conformist ways, appears in Shakespeare's *Taming of the Shrew*.

35 All of the inconsistencies and ambiguities of Mariam's placement are framed by language that intensively evokes the restlessness of constant motion and displacement. Words like 'loose,' 'control,' 'free,' 'tamed,' 'restrained,' 'overthrow,' 'bent,' 'rear,' 'bind,' 'usurps,' 'fall,' 'thrust,' 'cast off,' 'subvert,' 'dejected,' 'aspiring,' 'raised,' 'winged,' 'wavering,' 'lift,' and 'uprear' fill the play.

In addition, the play emphasizes the uncertainty of displacement. Herod has displaced David's heirs, Hircanus and Aristobolus; Mariam has displaced Doris, but Doris stands ready to re-displace Mariam; Mariam's children have displaced Antipater, although eventually, according to Josephus, Antipater displaces Mariam's children whom Herod strangles; Sillcus displaces Constabarus; Constabarus has displaced Josephus; and so forth.

36 The motto, 'Be and Seem,' which the *Life* tells us Elizabeth Cary had inscribed on her daughter's wedding ring, has helped to construct the reading of *Mariam*. Several critics have seen it as expressing 'a high ideal of personal integrity' (Lewalski, 184). Ferguson paraphrases it as: 'never be satisfied that you really are as virtuous as you may seem to yourself – but always be what you seem' ('Running,' 50). As an addendum to this chapter, I wish to offer my own reading. The motto is, I think, peculiarly resonant and ambiguous. It is a statement, like many in *Mariam*, that is apparently clear, but makes available more meanings than it seems to intend. If one resists a binary reading which sees being and seeming as potentially and undesirably oppositional states, the injunction may be read to say, 'Be anything you want to be and at the same time seem anything you want to seem.' All possibilities of what one may be and seem are left open because the verbs have no restricting objects or predicates which define what one must be or seem. The words of the motto do not say, 'Be only what you seem to be,' or 'Do not be anything you do not seem to be.' Elizabeth Cary's own life seems to have had hidden recesses of secrecy and reserve, and Mariam's soliloquies tell us that she is not all that she seems to be. What can be enacted and made evident, in any case, is only the 'Seem.' The 'Be' is in the private, enclosed space of the woman's thoughts and conscience. The early modern conduct book expectation is that, ideally, one will conform to the other, but this perfect match also requires an unavailable ideal marital and social context in which the patriarchal imposition of a woman's seeming will conform to the woman's own conscientious being. Also see Zimmerman, 555–560, which, in large part, agrees with my reading of the motto's equivocal message.

Chapter 6

Aemilia Lanyer. The Feminist Subject: Idealization and Subversive Metaphor in *Salve Deus Rex Judaeorum*

> First, adequate representation of women must be self-representation ... Secondly, the work of self-representation must occur in public, in the institutions and arenas in which the discourse that both reflects and shapes society takes place ... The third requirement for adequate representation of women is the construction of a collective voice.
>
> – Margaret Miles, *Carnal Knowing*, 170–171

From the moment of its publication until the present day, Aemilia Lanyer's *Salve Deus Rex Judaeorum* has aroused audience response at both extremes of the possible range for early modern women writers. Following its first appearance in 1611, the text attracted neither wide reader interest nor aristocratic patronage.[1] If, however, her poetic venture failed to gain for Lanyer the preferment of patrons or the acclaim of a book-buying public, it was not because it was inattentive to one or the other hoped-for audience. That the volume's method is mediated by the discourse of patronage is evident, but Lanyer's work, like Whitney's second collection, made overtures as well to a second, rather different reader. Whitney and Lanyer (and their publishers) evidently hoped to make both the traditional system of patronage and the newer book-buying market work to their advantage: Lanyer's multiple dedications make a forceful claim for aristocratic patronage, but the fact of its publication and the volume's structure, including the dedicatory poems, invoke a different set of allusions to other increasingly influential contemporary literary practices. Emulating aristocratic and courtly manuscript circulation, the 'posie'-gatherings in early modern print 'anthologies' (from the Greek, meaning a collection of flowers), as I have discussed with reference to Whitney's collections, typically mixed prose and a variety of poetic forms, as does Lanyer's publication. What might seem to a twentieth-century reader a group of mismatched items randomly jumbled together (dedications, the central poem in praise of Christ and including a defense of Eve, vehement prose pieces and

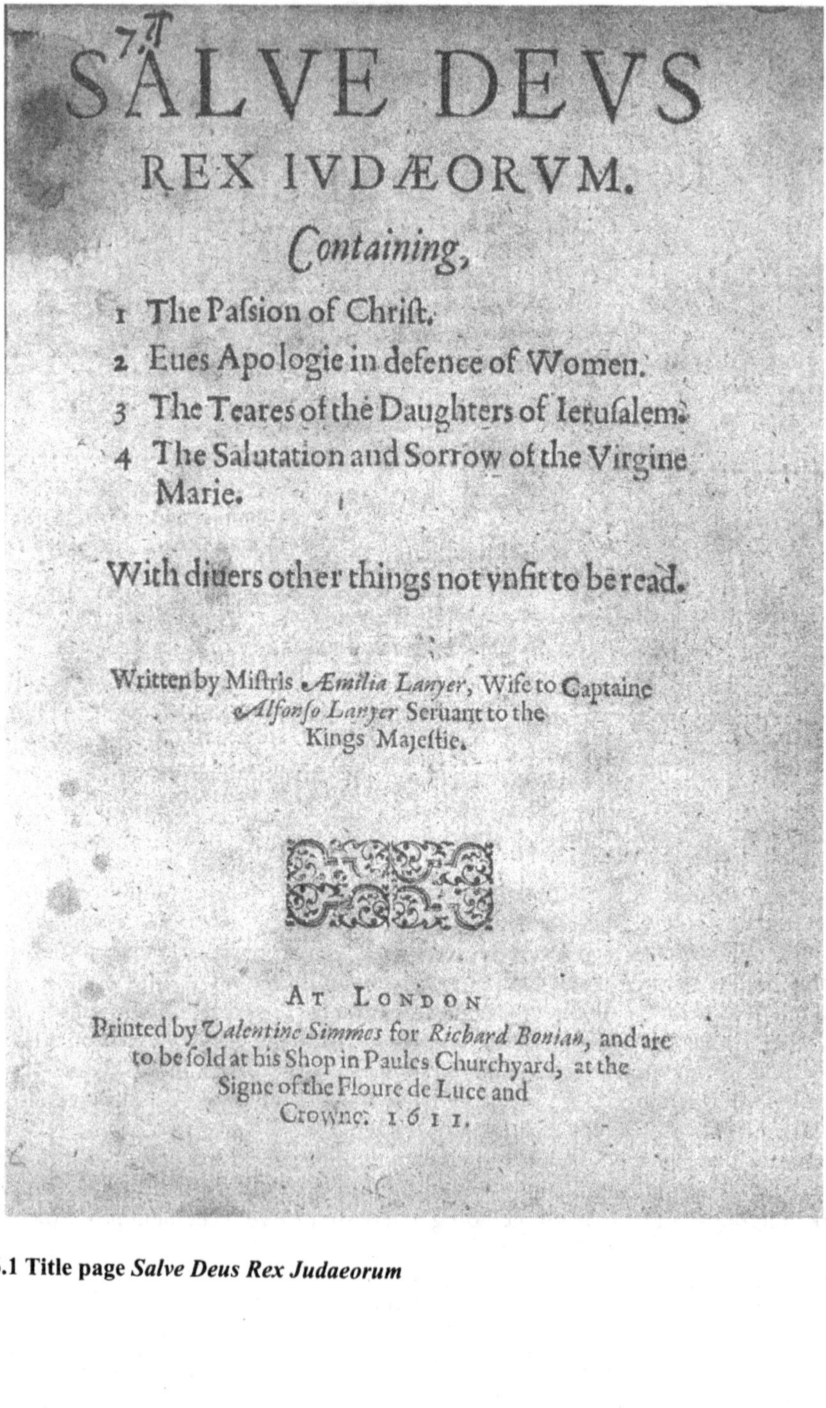

SALVE DEVS
REX IVDÆORVM.

Containing,

1 The Pasſion of Chriſt.
2 Eues Apologie in defence of Women.
3 The Teares of the Daughters of Ieruſalem.
4 The Salutation and Sorrow of the Virgine Marie.

With diuers other things not vnfit to be read.

Written by Miſtris *Æmilia Lanyer*, Wife to Captaine *Alfonſo Lanyer* Seruant to the Kings Majeſtie.

AT LONDON
Printed by *Valentine Simmes* for *Richard Bonian*, and are to be ſold at his Shop in Paules Churchyard, at the Signe of the Floure de Luce and Crowne. 1611.

6.1 Title page *Salve Deus Rex Judaeorum*

a country-house poem) would not have jarred the expectations of the early modern reader already accustomed to the methods of the miscellany.

Unlike Whitney, Lanyer had at least presumed access to a group of aristocratic dedicatees whom she attempts to persuade into benevolent membership in a fantasized women's community by poetically invoking the attractive and idealized discourses of maternity, religion and women's nurturing love for each other. The construction of her volume, with its independently detachable dedications, could emulate the flexibility of manuscript circulation: with one or more dedications discarded, individual copies might be customized for different potential patrons or tailored as presentation copies.[2] In the volume's second issue an effort was apparently made to excise the more controversial dedications to suit a less radical readership than the first edition supposed, and Barbara Lewalski ('Of God,' 284) and Mary Ellen Lamb ('Patronage,' 39–43) have argued that separate presentation copies were tailored for individual dedicatees, including Prince Henry and Thomas Jones, Archbishop of Dublin.[3]

At the same time, the volume, as a published, not manuscript entity, can be seen as the kind of 'collection' favored by early booksellers and book-buyers. In that case, the intimate, slightly gossipy glimpses into the spiritual lives of aristocratic women might attract readers of a different taste and station. The appeal to social equality and inclusive, woman-focused values would perhaps lure the same reader. No matter how intimidating or problematic the necessary qualification of Virtue, how satisfying for the socially aspiring reader to read, 'What difference was there when the world began, / Was it not Virtue that distinguisht all?' (42). The anti-misogynist 'To the Virtuous Reader' would also resonate familiarly for the reader of popular pamphlets in the ongoing 'woman question' debate. In spite of these hopeful adjustments and forays, however, the whole work, before the end of the seventeenth century, had subsided into the special oblivion once reserved for most early modern women writers.

Nevertheless, although it seems in its own time not to have succeeded in achieving either patronage or wider audience appeal, in the last fifteen to twenty years this poetic work has acquired perhaps the most interested readership available to any example of early modern women's writing. As the scholarship relating to early modern Englishwomen has matured, and even as we have come to realize that Lanyer's most radically provocative arguments in defense of women are not unique, this work still resonates with profound sympathy for the modern feminist reader.[4] Its current success is measured in different terms from the economic and social rewards for the poet to which the poem sometimes delicately, and often more insistently, alludes. The *Salve Deus* is arguably now the most frequently taught and anthologized example of early modern women's poetry,[5] having initially been partially represented in teaching texts, but now more frequently printed in full; it has also benefited as the topic of many highly sophisticated critical readings.[6] When anthologized in the twentieth century, the most frequently excerpted pieces have been 'Eve's Apologie in Defence of Women' and the self-contained country-house poem 'To Cookham.' Both these pieces stir modern political interests: the first exculpates Eve, the scapegoated mother of all evil, from the guilt of the Fall, and the second challenges the discounting of original female literary achievement, exemplified in the usual designation of Jonson's 'To Penshurst' as the 'first' country-house poem. Modern reader enthusiasm has been stimulated by the poem's political courage in defense of women as well as by its poetic skill.

Some time ago, in the early stages of Lanyer studies, I advocated the term 'feminist' as an appropriate designation for Lanyer's poem,[7] persuaded then to this anachronistic category by the poem's unusually assertive representation of a woman's writerly subjectivity, acted out inside an ideally and desirously represented women's collective culture. Those arguments still largely hold, I believe, especially when Lanyer's self-declarative subject position is read beside the equally skillful but less openly provocative approaches to subjectivity in the poetry of Whitney and Cary. Janel Mueller has described this same forceful stance in Lanyer's feminism, which, she says, like Christine de Pizan's, 'explicitly confront[s] misogyny and the injustices of male domination and prerogative,' as well as working to 'counter these with alternative, woman-centered constructions' (212). Supporting the presence of a direct feminist position in early modern women's writing, Ilona Bell has concluded that 'modern feminism, with its commitment to consciousness-raising among women and political action and social change on behalf of all women, has much stronger roots in the sixteenth century than most modern scholars have hitherto recognized' ('In Defense,' 192). The claims made by Lanyer's poem on behalf of women as a disadvantaged class link it to twentieth-century feminist sympathies.

Although, even in spite of recent political depredations, 'feminist' remains a useful ideological designation for Lanyer's mode of subjective representation, the term clearly needs particularization of its range of likely meaning in reference to this early seventeenth-century work. Feminisms, we know, are multiple, not ideologically unified, and variable not only during the twentieth century, but also throughout history, as well as within past historical moments. A modern feminist reader cannot therefore focus, in early modern women's texts, only on the reflected origins of our own political values.[8] This temptation is especially strong, perhaps even more now than ten or fifteen years ago, given the chords of fellow-feeling struck for the twenty-first-century feminist in Lanyer's depiction of her nostalgically shadowed, ideal women's community, and her half-acknowledged awareness of, and sorrow for, its deviations from ideality. Taking into account these reservations, however, the *Salve* does represent a subjectivity compatible with what even an ironically-beset, postmodern reader might aptly describe as 'feminist,' even though the term itself had no currency in Lanyer's time.

Lanyer's publication must have added its own fuel to the heated debate about the 'woman question' at the beginning of the seventeenth century,[9] especially because of the poem's serious moral intent and its suggested female separatism; in spite of an element of ironic self-reference, there is little in this volume of the slightly flippant effort to amuse that we find in texts by Gosynhill and Swetnam, or even in Whitney's first collection. Recognizing the terms in which the feminist element operates in

Lanyer's work confirms the slowly strengthening ideological current that ran counter to the dominant position concerning women in early modern England; even determinative, dominant ideologies, we are reassured, do not in the 'real' world determine everything. But, most pertinent to the concerns of this book, understanding what might be called a feminist point of view in Lanyer's poem will shed some light on the complex processes by which women in unfavorable and un-ideal social, educational and economic circumstances have been able to 'celebrate' each other as 'effective reader[s] and agent[s]' (Hutson, 154–155), and to represent themselves as multiply positioned, writing subjects.

Drawing on the insights of Joan Kinnaird, Hilda Smith and Moira Ferguson, Ruth Perry in 1986 proposed two major characterizing features of early modern feminism that remain helpful: it includes, she argued, a 'recognition of oppression and a conviction of women's intellectual and moral worth,' and a sense of 'what we now name "sisterhood" ' (18). This latter element, however, Perry believed, occurred only infrequently in the early modern period. Constance Jordan, using Karen Offen's distinction between 'individualist' and 'relational' feminism, believes that 'as a rule, Renaissance feminism is individualist' (8), that is, concerned with the 'autonomy of the female subject,' rather than linked to 'an appreciation of what women are and do in contrast to what men are and do' (7). Apparently, the search for an appropriate feminism in early modern culture is as elusive as is the early modern female subject. As I have proposed in this book, however, I doubt that the notion of a coherent, autonomous subject, female or male, had weighty currency in early modern England at all. Lanyer's text, certainly, seems to situate any claim it might make to a feminist subject position firmly inside a feminism that, however flawed in either its historical or poetic 'reality,' is still imagined as ideally and widely communal and relational. This subject position itself is relational and therefore multiply positioned, being both self- and other-reflective, addressed to both aristocratic and non-aristocratic readers.

Karen Offen has argued that relational feminism recognizes women as a *group* with rights distinct from men's, and that its proponents judge 'women's collective situation in the culture as unjust' and attribute its injustice to 'social and political institutions established by men' (141). Although Perry and Jordan consider this quality uncommon in the Renaissance, Hilda Smith discerns it in a seventeenth-century feminist awareness of women as a sociological group whose position was affected by another group, 'namely men, with the means and desire to establish social and political controls over women's lives' (8). Lanyer's *Salve Deus Rex Judaeorum*, in the first decade of the seventeenth century, also implements such a recognition in its depiction, within a poetic frame, of a female community imagined as mutually supportive, as also in its inscription of a self-proclaiming female poetic subject. 'The [feminist] individual's quest,' Bonnie Zimmerman believes, 'ends in the location of a supportive community of women' (120), where the individual feels herself at home. The oppositional stance of oppressed women in relation to oppressing men provides the ideological foundation for Lanyer's construction of a women's community. The community the poem envisages as an ideal unit, like many modern feminist communities, is vulnerable, in both poetic and historical emanations, to the strains of the varying class, wealth and success of its members. Yet the inscription of its wished-for possibility as a space of ideal emotional and social solidarity carries in its wake the implied challenge of wider political protest. Lanyer's poem may appeal to modern readers discouraged by late twentieth-century political erosion because it gives life to the idea of a mutually enhancing connection between a particular female narrative subject and the socio-political women's community in which such a subject discovers a way to inscribe herself. Lanyer's poet or persona writes for herself the necessary approving space within which she may, at least in a semi-fictional, semi-autobiographical mode, confidently construct herself as subject.

Almost all commentators on Lanyer's poem have noted the disproportionate amount of space devoted to women in a poem whose title-page suggests that it will focus on Biblical scenes and praise of Christ as Saviour. Betty Travitsky first argued that, despite its title, the central 'subject of the poem is the commendable qualities of women' (*Paradise*, 97). Barbara Lewalski claims that Lanyer's multiple dedications to women were 'intended to call [her] to the attention of past patronesses, and perhaps to attract new ones' ('Of God and Good Women,' 206; *Writing Women*, 219–220),[10] and Elaine Beilin has suggested that Lanyer should be 'understood as a millenarian advocating the establishment on earth of God's will through the particular agency of women' (181).[11] Lorna Hutson wryly denies the possibility that Lanyer 'wrote a narrative of Christ and absent-mindedly kept apostrophizing the Countess of Cumberland because she could not keep her mind off the richest woman in England' (160), although certainly the Countess's wealth was not absent as a factor in either the poet's extravagant praise of her, or in the poet's wishful positioning of herself as persona in textual proximity to her.

Luce Irigaray points out that the importance of a women's community for feminist understanding, whether desirously represented or physically evident, is to establish a space in which women may practice the tactical rewriting of their own desire:

> For women to undertake tactical strikes, to keep themselves apart from men long enough to learn to defend their desire, especially through speech, to discover the love of other women while sheltered from men's imperious choices ... to forge for themselves a social status that compels recognition ... these are certainly indispensable stages in the escape from their proletarization on the exchange market. (*This Sex*, 33)

Lanyer's poem offers exactly this variety of tactical strike. Irigaray's fantasy of women's space is just this, as she emphasizes: a 'morphological,' not 'essentialist' or 'real' possibility, designed to begin the project of releasing women's minds and love of each other from the constraints of patriarchal construction. So, too, with Lanyer's poetic construction of community and subject. Her wished-for goals as poetic persona and, one assumes, also as historical person are ideally comprehensive, involving both the claims of aristocratic patronage as well as the claims of mutually caring support from all other 'vertuous Ladies in generall.'

What, as historical personage, Aemilia Lanyer may have hoped for socially or financially, interestingly and subtly complicates, but does not undo, the powerfully moving rhetorical appeal to claims of love and comfort, as well as economic support, desired by the poem's persona from a community detached from the masculine, and responsive to women's intellectual, spiritual, material and erotic longings. Patronage controlled by women has the potential to enhance women's material security as much as women's religious community may nurture spiritual well-being. These different kinds of strategic goals may quite comfortably exist together on a continuum of women's nurturance of each other. Lanyer's feminist subjectivity, I assume, is not unconscious, accidental, or naive but manifest in a carefully crafted and calculated text which appeals to other women to save the poet and each other from the effects of male oppression. The appeal is economic as well as emotional, erotic as well as spiritual, directed to an aristocratic as well as a non-aristocratic audience, and assertively self-representative. All of these apparently disparate qualities are brought into play under the rubric of the female virtue that qualifies women for membership in this community.

In a few recent instances, arguments about this poem have fallen prey to the same trap as Cary's biography has presented for her play, *Mariam*. In both cases, the temptation to use the details of the life to gloss the poetry, and vice versa, to merge the poetic and historical subjects instead of reading the two in parallel, has sometimes seemed to simplify and reduce the complexly braided accomplishments of both poetry and life, even to produce an idea of this poet as disappointingly caught in naive socio-political and religious confusions. Rather, I think, what we are looking at in the *Salve* is a poem that calculatedly employed a fairly aggressive strategy of self-rescue, which may, because of the daring of its idealized stretch, have miscalculated the potential for its method's success. The autobiographical circumstance will, of course, intrude in the poem as a not fully conscious element that undermines and/or increases the plenitude of the text and splits the depiction of the subject position, but a non-coherent subjectivity is just what I have been arguing throughout this book is quite usual in early modern women's poetry and not, for that reason, any less functional or skillful. Although Lanyer's petition for patronage was apparently unsuccessful, the attractiveness of a supportive women's community is not any the less powerful. As Lanyer's poem illustrates, residing in the same hopeful subjective space may be both desire and disillusion. Because multiplistic and inadequately satisfied, women's desire is not therefore abrogated, but demands even more forcefully to be expressed.

Jonathan Goldberg (*Desiring*, 16–41) has persuasively used evidence concerning the contemporary 'scandalous' reputation of some of the members of Lanyer's community to argue that its construction responds to masculinist methodologies and same-sex eroticism in a way that detaches it from conventional feminine virtue or goodness as its cohesive claim. Yet claims to virtue, especially of the kind that would discount hierarchical class difference as a feature of a poetically constructed women's community, need not be invalidated because the historical actors involved were unable or unwilling to rise either to an ideal level of patriarchally envisioned virtue, or even to the level of ideal financial and emotional generosity proposed by the poet. Goldberg suggests that the Countess of Bedford and Anne Clifford were known to be erotically associated with other women, a possibility that, as I have suggested in my second chapter, was not especially unusual in early modern England. But if, knowing this, Lanyer flirtatiously but obliquely played in her poem on the possibility of her own role as erotic favorite, both of powerful aristocratic women and of Mother Nature, this only underlines Irigaray's view that women's communities, to be most favorable to women, *should*, at least imaginatively, 'discover the love of other women while sheltered from men's imperious choices' (33); the woman-friendly virtue discovered in these circumstances will simply be different from that of the conventional, early modern, patriarchally constructed, publicly exhorted 'good woman.'

Invocation of the ideal is a courageous or foolhardy tactic that may stir a responsive commitment, but it is subject to, and textured by, the pressures and disappointments of the existential process. The negotiation of Virtue in this poem as a claim for recognition and reward, like the women's relationships on which the claim is based, is complicated by the tensions between the promises of the feminist ideal and the necessity of the historically 'real' in the poem's and poet's goals. For example, the first dedication, to Queen Anne, does not place feminine Virtue inside the simplified binary opposition between female Christian rectitude and oppressive male error that Lanyer strategically exploits and subverts elsewhere. The supplicant speaker here characterizes herself in the most diminished terms, using epithets of abjection not unlike those seen in Whitney's *Nosgay*. The 'I' is 'unfortunate' and 'mean,' and her poem is 'defective,' 'rude' and 'unpollisht' (3–5). She is a victim of 'Affliction,' and lives closed up in 'Sorrowes Cell' (8). Even so, the speaker, safely inside the poem's protective boundaries, represents her Virtue as unquestioned. It comes in 'meane attire,' and will therefore, as for the 'vertuous Ladies in generall' to whom she will soon explicitly appeal in a following dedication, earn her a heavenly reward (6). Her virtue, like the virtue of others less materially fortunate than Queen Anne, allies her and them with Christ, who also lived in poverty and sorrow (5). In Christ's heaven the poet is confident that she will be blessed with the perhaps orthodoxly incongruous material and worldly rewards of 'lands' and 'honour' (6). Also reminiscent of Whitney's 'mased muse' and 'brused brayne,' this speaker suffers from a 'troubled mind' and a 'weake distempred braine and feeble spirits' (9), and needs to find a way to inspirit her 'sad dejected muse' (9).

Where, then, does Queen Anne fit in this construction? She, too, is 'grac'd' by Virtue's 'rare gifts,' but Anne's gifts, which the poet would share, are material and of this world. *Un*like the incarnate Christ, and *un*like the poet, she is possessed of earthly 'splendour' (4) and 'powre' (9) and 'Fame' (10). Whatever Virtue she possesses is clearly of a different order from that to be discovered in poverty, humility and the self-effacing Christian virtues. Even more problematically, Anne's 'powre' to 'raise my sad dejected Muse' (9), perhaps by material reward, is paralleled with Mother Nature's power to 'grace my barren Muse' (10). The Queen's materially blessed virtue is somehow linked to the vaguely incestuous, though nurturing, ability of

Mother Nature to make fertile her poet-daughter's 'barren Muse,' not, after all, a conventionally virtuous relationship, even perhaps more akin to the Sapphic, tribadic lust derided by Ben Jonson in 'female Poetesses,' but surely not for that reason any the less productive, supportive and inspiring. Why, after all, we are induced to ask, should a poetic and playful representation of ideal Virtue in women's relationships with each other not display the whole panoply of spiritual, emotional, material, erotic and poetic manifestations?

In a literary and social climate not conducive to women's poetic invention and success, Aemilia Lanyer negotiated the social proscriptions against women's poetry and the social suspicions of women's connections with each other, by textually creating an ideally inclusive women's world, congenial not to patriarchal but to her own and other women's interests, within which her poetic persona could 'defend [women's] desire' and challenge 'a culture which oppresses [women], uses them, makes of them a medium of exchange, with very little profit to them' (Irigaray, *This Sex*, 32).[12] Margaret Cavendish and Mary Astell devised similar fantasies of separate, sensuously and intellectually gratifying women's communities later in the century, but Lanyer's poem, before either of these (though after Christine de Pizan's construction of *her* city of virtuous ladies), sketches for herself, her patrons and other women readers 'in generall' the appealing and inspiring possibility of the caring and protection of women by women when and if independent of the controls of patriarchy.

Lanyer's poem does not discount at all the differences articulated on gender and class that work against the interests of women as a group, even, on occasion, infecting the best potential of the group itself. It argues, nevertheless, for the value of women's history and their intellectual and writerly abilities, and for the desirability of a female community that includes 'all vertuous Ladies.' A woman writer's appeal for patronage from other women is, in the early seventeenth century, an apt exemplification of this idea. That the response of Lanyer's designated patrons was less than she hoped adds poignancy to a feminist reading of Lanyer's poem, while also sharpening its feminist promise and reinforcing a view of female poetic subjectivity in this period as a necessarily variable position, imbedded in a courageous struggle and continuing process. The poem can pretend to make the represented ideal real, but it cannot do so; it cannot erase the barriers of social station that separate women from each other. Even so, Lanyer bravely undertakes her project of subjectivity in a textually represented ideal women's community, an imaginative space in which is articulated the desire for the illusory merge of representation and reality, that very space of unsatisfied desire where the split subject will emerge.

Lanyer's feminism does not overtly supply an agenda for structural political change. This reserve may not, however, so much mark a limited feminist sensibility as reflect what Deborah Shuger argues was a 'shared conceptual model' in early modern England that the adoption of a moral position did not require an accompanying 'form of self-assertion' directed toward revolutionary action (*Habits*, 98–99). Rather, a moral claim often found its most radical expression in textual forms and rhetorical advocacy to a change of heart, in Lanyer's poem as radically as in the culturally privileged male-authored sermons from which Shuger extrapolates her evidence. Yet, in writing into existence an ideally virtuous community of women whose primary nurturing relationships occur in their relationships with each other *outside* their relationships with mortal men, Lanyer's poem does after all explore an agenda for political change; in this case the represented ideal has a persuasive purpose and political role to play.[13] The poem also sponsors the possibility of change by invoking the sanction of Christ to destabilize male–female, subject–object relations; it rewrites this apparently patriarchal figure as a femininely nurturing, maternally abjected, erotically desirable object of women's gaze.

A Community of Virtue

If one of the hallmarks of 'relational' feminism is an 'appreciation of what women are and do in contrast to what men are and do' (Jordan, 7), Lanyer's poem tactically invokes this opposition to unite and defend women. The binary structure itself usefully and strategically reinforces the connections of the relational and contestatory 'us' against 'them' and, valuably for the purposes of the poem's critique, helps mask the breaks in the ideally represented 'us.' The notable deficiencies of failed male, as compared to idealized female, culture are evident in men's response to women, as well as, most importantly, to the Saviour, whom the poem counts as one of the 'us.' Men dishonored Christ (48–49) as they continue to dishonor women:[14]

> ... [W]hy are poore Women blam'd,
> Or by more faultie Men so much defam'd? (6)

Those men who betrayed Christ were 'bred in Adam's mud' (67), not in Eve's hard-won and generously shared knowledge, and the false male friends of Christ compare unfavorably to the faithful women who are his true friends. Even the disciples, being men, acted without courage, as all men do 'when dangers overtake them' (78).[15] The poem insists that man, not woman, was culpable for the Fall (84–85); furthermore, men boast of the knowledge they were only able to acquire through Eve, now rejecting and berating her for her role in this acquisition, while at the same time prohibiting her daughters from access to the knowledge she earned (86), laying 'the fault on Patience backe, / That we (poore women) must endure it all' (85). Eve's sexuality has been wedded to her curiosity and both subjected to masculine control and used to justify misogynist attack.

As they betrayed Christ's virtue, so men also seek to betray women's virtue (59). Refuting the traditional argument which blames women's beauty for men's downfall (Maclean, 16–17), Lanyer's poem chastises men for the fall of beautiful women. While men, contemplating women's beauty, formulate for themselves the limited, non-reciprocal goal of sexually possessing women's bodies, women, contemplating Christ, their true lover, are inspired by his beauty to a reciprocated desire for spiritual union with him (104–105). The erotic is not erased from, but emphasized in, the poem's description of Christ, and in the depiction of women's longing for virtue through him. As the portrayal of virtue in the dedication to Queen Anne embraces both the material and the spiritual, so the erotic element marries woman's soul to her body, for the presence of the sensually erotic intensifies the desire which transports and elevates the desiring woman above the mundane, rather than, like men's erotic desire, reducing the object of desire to used goods. The impossibility of making physically 'real' this textual transaction of women's desire with the body of Christ adds increased weight to the value of what is represented – the ineffable, the feminine, the communal and, most scandalously, the erotic, all operating outside men's history, law and logic.

Lanyer's text emphasizes lines of binary gender difference in order provocatively to expose their negative consequences for women: '*you* [men]', the poet says, 'in malice Gods deare Sonne betray' (86), while 'we (poore women) must endure ... all' the blame for Adam's original sin (85). This accusation that men have been dominant in a dichotomized and hierarchical system that has oppressed women, and have also betrayed Christ, the Eucharistic sacrifice and champion of female virtue, grants Lanyer the power, supported by her community of women, daringly to rewrite both Christology and women's experience in terms that challenge dominant male discourse. The poem retains binary hierarchical stereotypes as an inevitable fact of human history, but takes their failures seriously, pointing out from the 'other' side of the gendered opposition their negative significance for men and women; these stereotypes have intensified men's propensity for tyranny and vice, and diminished women's potential for virtuous influence.

Because masculine systems of control have required women to compensate for Eve's 'sin' by being 'good,' Lanyer's persona accepts that imposed requirement but challengingly extends it. Privileging the perspective of a woman self-proclaimed as virtuous, she emphatically enacts the idealized moral and epistemological consequences of this necessity of virtue, even ordaining herself with a priestly and instructive role. Her socially required 'goodness' becomes a condition of spiritually virtuous and poetic authority. From the perspective of a virtuous female observer, less virtuous male roles in human history indict men more resoundingly than male writers of history have allowed. The poem manipulates binary and gendered stereotypes to refute the Biblical justification for women's sexual subordination. If male-established binary structures have made men strong and women weak, from a virtuously empowered woman's point of view that strength carries with it an extra responsibility. Abnegated, that responsibility bears for Adam, as representative man, a greater burden of fault:

> But surely *Adam* can not be excusde,
> Her [Eve's] fault though great, yet hee was most too blame;
> What Weaknesse offerd, Strength might have refusde,
> Being Lord of all, the greater was his shame. (85)

The gender economy that conventionally identifies women in relation to men instead of in relation to other women also, we know, impacted the historical personages featured in the poem. Despite their difference in social position, neither Lanyer nor the poem's principal dedicatee, the Countess of Cumberland, escaped experiences of sexual oppression at the hands of socially powerful men. By the time Lanyer wrote her poem, she had been dismissed as the mistress of Elizabeth's Lord Chamberlain, Lord Hunsdon, and married to Alphonso Lanyer, a court musician, because of her pregnancy by Hunsdon.[16] Although it may have been acceptable for Aemilia Bassano to appear at court as the mistress of Elizabeth's Lord Chamberlain, as an unmarried mother of his illegitimate child, she needed to be otherwise disposed of.

In terms supplied by Irigaray, it may be said that Lanyer was protected by a phallic and paternal Law under whose auspices she was seduced and impregnated; but the protection of the Law failed when she became a mother and was no longer an object of sexual desire, for the paternal Law does not protect the mother unless she is also tied to the father by the Law of marriage (*Speculum*, 37–50). Lanyer, who, like the women in her poem (59–61), was possibly seduced because of her beauty, forfeited her position at court by becoming pregnant, so that her body was passed from one man to another.[17] After her husband's death, his brothers gained control of property that should have passed to Aemilia. Lanyer's biography exemplifies the prevailing 'reality' for women of her period, which her poetic representation resists, that their bodily and economic welfare typically depended on male identification and male control.[18]

The Countess of Cumberland's aristocratic rank did not protect her from similar sexual and economic objectification.[19] She was cast off by her husband, George Clifford, Earl of Cumberland, who, frequently absent from his wife and home, impoverished both his own and his wife's estates, and was also enamored of another woman. Despite a deathbed reconciliation with his wife and despite the existence of an ancient legal agreement that made possible inheritance through the female line, Clifford left his northern estates to his brother, who also inherited the title (Lewalski, *Writing Women*, ch. 5); the last section of Lanyer's volume records Margaret Russell Clifford's forced exodus from her temporary home at Cookham.

Other examples of aristocratic women disadvantaged by the Law of Patriarchy include Arbella Stuart who, because of the threat she represented to James's claim to the throne, had been forbidden to marry without the King's permission; Lucy, Countess of Bedford, who in the early seventeenth century had fallen into a precarious financial position which threatened her status as a patron and at court; and Mary Sidney, Countess of Pembroke, who, in the aftermath of her widowhood and almost certainly as its result, had been threatened with loss of authority over the Pembroke estates in Cardiff by lawsuits brought against her by William Mathew (Hannay, 177–184). The binary structures of male–female sexuality and their inevitable hierarchization of advantaged male and disadvantaged female have obviously not worked for these women's economic or emotional benefit. If women are economically and sexually at the mercy of men, and men are unreliable, where then but to each other should women turn for support? The similarities in Lanyer's and Margaret Russell's experiences perhaps stimulated Lanyer to make poetic overtures of intimacy to the Countess, proposing a connection between the two women stronger than their connections with men and apparently also stronger than the Countess was willing to accept. The background of known financial and sexual scandal and misfortune associated with these women might, furthermore, have evoked the empathy (and/or titillated the interest of), Lanyer's less socially privileged, but perhaps equally harassed, readers.

Lanyer's protest, in a published poem, against the fruitlessness of women's identifying themselves only as dependent wives and mothers through the attachment of their sexuality to male requirements of sponsorship and rank, is remarkable in early modern Englishwomen's writing. Though Isabella Whitney and Elizabeth Cary critique the dependency of women's security on the fluctuations of male interest, they do not openly refute the necessity of this connection. As a corrective to the insufficiency and hostility of the male-dominated social, sexual, political and religious systems, Lanyer, however, turns to women as a source of spiritual and economic protection and poetic inspiration. Positioning herself in a poetically represented community of women, she encourages them and herself in a process of mutually enhancing self-discovery.[20] She also writes for Margaret Russell an alternative to her husband's abandonment and infidelity: the feminized, de-masculinized and faithfully loving Christ will be her 'spouse.'

Though the conditions and extent of their oppression differ, the 'reality' of their shared experience of oppression at the hands of men sympathetically connects women with each other. The *Salve* represents women, Lanyer among them, as treated unjustly by the social structures which refuse them political entitlement and honor (42–43) and the legal and economic means to redress their wrongs. The poem can offer no 'real' or structural solutions in this world, but does rhetorically appeal to the Christian representation of Paradise, promising Margaret and Anne Clifford that all will be well for them when male-designed worldly class and status differences have been erased (42), and a true nobility of Virtue, to which deserving women will have the superior claim, is established.[21] Yet, the poem's toleration of complexity and ambiguity surrounding the issues of the material and the spiritual, evident in the first dedication, to Queen Anne, and embedded inevitably in both its patronage frame and the ultimate incompatibility of ideal and real, intrudes some unsettling questions here. What might the promise of Paradisial equality imply for Lanyer's aristocratic dedicatees? Their social position and wealth were surely valued by them, as confirmed by Anne Clifford's prolonged effort to regain her estates. How much comfort might Queen Anne, or the Countesses of Cumberland, Bedford and Dorset, find in the assurance that 'Greatnesse is no sure frame to build upon, / No worldly treasure can assure that place; / God makes both even, the Cottage with the Throne' (42).

The speaker, who has declared herself virtuous, might by a countess be regarded as presumptuous in her claim that 'Titles of honour which the world bestowes, / To none but the virtuous doth belong' (42). Her efforts at persuasive influence over her dedicatees might also be disturbed by the speaker's disconcertingly fluid passage back and forth between roles of humble supplicant, covered with inadequacy, and contentious complainant, denouncing men, wealth and position, and claiming virtue equivalent to any, presuming on real or wished connections with the highest-ranked ladies in England. This is, after all, her aristocratic dedicatees would know, and perhaps disapprove of, a woman who has been the mistress of one of their men and the mother of his illegitimate child. Nevertheless, the poem embodies a hope that women might respond as a group linked by their gender, rather than separated by their social and economic differences.

So, while they wait for Paradise, Lanyer self-defensively or wisely, depending on her reader's point of view, exhorts women not to 'speak unadvisedly against the rest of their sexe' and 'not to regard any imputations that they [men] undeservedly lay upon us' (49).[22] Instead, rising above possible fissures within their ranks, women would do well, she advises, to concentrate upon the bonds that have drawn them together for mutual support. Avoiding the difficulties and potential conflicts of the present, she invokes as models and connections the virtuous women of the past: Deborah, Judith, Hester, Pilate's wife and Joachim's wife (49 and 114ff). Sheba, a little out of the norm, merits special mention as an image of female strength because, refusing to be restricted by 'niceness and respect of womankind,' she traveled 'forth of her native Land' in pursuit of her own 'Desire' (119). Sheba's example points nostalgically to a time when a queen's desire at least could be acted upon without reference to ideological formulations of the 'niceness' of womankind. She was a queen, it appears, more independent than the reigning Queen Anne, and able to enact a personal and adventurous independence from women's 'niceness' that Lanyer herself perhaps envies.

The poem also expresses sympathy for women who have been caught in the trap of male desire. Cleopatra she speaks of as 'Poor blinded Queene' (60), led by Antony to 'worke *Octaviaes* wrongs' (60); Cleopatra and Octavia were positioned in an unnecessary hostile relationship with each other because of Antony's betrayal of his wife.[23] Here is an example of the ways in which women, who forget 'they are women themselves,' may get caught up in male desire, and, following male models, 'by all their powers of ill speaking ... eclipse the brightnes of [other women's] deserved fame' (48). Perhaps some personally defensive indignation is buried in this warning against women's evil-speaking against each other. In any case, Lanyer's poem positions itself on a moral high ground, offering the poet's commendations of women as a more legitimate and productive model of appropriate female solidarity.

An exemplary model of a mythological woman breaking through male oppression to self-assertion is found in Philomel, introduced into the landscape of Cookham. Philomel was raped by Tereus and made mute to silence her testimony against him; Lanyer does not emphasize the implications of this figure, but its reference to her own probable sense of injury and to Margaret Clifford's situation is there to be drawn out by the alert reader.[24] In addition, of course, Philomel's ingenious telling of the story of her assault in a tapestry-text she weaves for her sister Procne has application to

Lanyer's poetic tale, also decipherable by her 'sisters,' and invoking justice for them. Both the mythological and early modern instances offer examples of women emerging from male-imposed bonds of silence into forceful expressions of their communal subjectivity and desires, speaking to and comprehending each other by means of a fluent language of women's making. Among those to whom Lanyer addressed her dedications are also other examples of politically muffled women: Lady Arbella, dangerous to the Stuarts' claim to the throne and incarcerated in the Tower after her marriage to William Seymour; and Susan Bertie and her mother Catherine Willoughby who, because she 'liv'd unsubjected' (19), was forced to flee from England as a Marian exile.

The supportive relationships possible between mothers and daughters as they connect through 'the first music of the first voice of love,' which Hélène Cixous sees as the source of woman's speech and writing (*Newly Born Woman*, 93), are also invoked not only in the mother–daughter connections of Susan Bertie with her mother and of Anne with Margaret Clifford, but also in Lanyer's dedications to Queen Anne and her daughter Princess Elizabeth, and her commendation of her work to the daughters of Katherine Knyvet (38).[25] According to feminist psychoanalytic theory, the original dyadic relationship between mothers and daughters is damagingly interrupted by the entry of the authoritarian father as representative of male Law and language. This third, dominating male element is apparent in Lanyer's world, but it remains off-stage, drafting undesirable conditions for women's lives. Aemilia replaces male scholarship and art with Mother Nature as her personally inspiring muse, and Eve is invoked as the mother of women's learning. Within her definitively female context, Lanyer reminds sons that they only exist at all because of the mothers who bore and nourished them (48–49), and she especially commends Mary, the mother of Christ (94), whose exemplary Son, himself a victim of the Law, befriended women rather than disparaging them, assuming a nurturing, maternal role himself.[26] Before the imposition of male language and authority breaks apart the connections with the maternal, feminist rewriters of psychoanalytic theory have argued, a language is available between mothers and their daughters in which, if recovered, women's subjectivity may be entrenched.[27] Lanyer's appeal to Mother Nature to grace her barren muse yearns toward the possibility of this women's language and subjectivity.

A further line of connection among women especially pertinent in this poem is drawn through the attributes of knowledge deeded to women by their first mother, Eve. Eve's actions are defended as less heinous than Adam's, perhaps even praiseworthy, because, beguiled by the serpent, she sinned 'for knowledge sake' (86). Lanyer unashamedly allies herself with Eve by also petitioning the serpent to be her guide to wisdom (14), and she takes issue with the contemporary and traditional male suspicion of women's learning as dangerous because it may lead women to re-enact Eve's tempting man to sin. She declares her own bias in favor of women's virtuous learning against men's corrupt knowledge by describing the evil men who killed Christ as 'unlearned' (75).

Women's good use of the knowledge inherited through Eve is evident in those women who surround Lanyer; as a whole they constitute a larger group of learned women within which women who write form an essential sub-group.[28] Mary Sidney is praised as a poet, to be esteemed for the 'many Books she writes' (30) and also because she is superior, in Lanyer's flattering appraisal, to her brother Philip, 'for virtue, wisedome, learning, dignity' (28). Susan Bertie possesses gifts 'that grace the mind' (18). Lucy, Countess of Bedford, is a literary woman and a well-known patron of other writers. And Anne Clifford wrote an extensive biographical diary.[29] In addition, because it is published, the poem addresses itself to a potential group of women who can read and who might therefore choose to own Lanyer's book. There is considerable legitimacy, then, to Lanyer's claim that she has chosen to honor in her poem women who might grace the Muse (16). This Muse for Lanyer is either Margaret Russell or Cynthia (51). The invocation and seduction of a female muse by male poets has a history almost as old as writing itself, but Venus, goddess of heterosexual passion, Lanyer expects to 'frown' on her endeavors (13). Cynthia, on the other hand, has a special significance for a female writer; she is a Muse specifically woman-identified, associated with the moon, which governs women's cycles, and outside the range of male desire because virginal or 'barren' (10), but possibly therefore seducible by this woman poet. Lanyer's own poetic activity is unassailably legitimized, she says, by her having been charged to write by the 'Eternal' and 'celestiall powres' (36, 65, 113), Christian as well as classical. After all, her ultimate sanction is Christ, whom she petitions to 'illuminate my Spirit' and 'guide my hand and Quill' (65). Lanyer further insists that divinely inspired women who write have an irrefutable claim to virtue (34, 35, 36). Virtue for women, it seems, in spite of the contrary views of some male pundits, is here unapologetically informed by knowledge and education.

Ultimately, then, Virtue is the necessary qualification for membership in this women's community. The third dedication, coming after the dedications to the two highest women in the land, Queen Anne and Princess Elizabeth, and before the dedications to the Lady Arbella and the following Countesses, is addressed 'To all vertuous ladies in generall.' Although, as Leeds Barroll has shown, strict hierarchical order is not observed by Lanyer in the arrangement of her dedications to the Countesses, the place of this third dedication places the 'vertuous ladies in generall,' though not quite at the level of Queen Anne and Princess Elizabeth, still at a higher rank than the Countesses. Virtue herself is nominated as a queen: 'Let this faire Queene not unattended bee, / When in my Glasse she daines her selfe to see' (12). All women, of whatever rank, need to wait upon Virtue, who will lead them like virgins or priestesses to their Bridegroom, Christ.

Yet, this third dedication, to the devotees of virtue, is not so far removed from the dedication to Queen Anne that the attachment of Anne's 'Naturall, Morall, and Divine' (6) virtue to worldly 'powre,' 'splendour' and 'honour' can have been already forgotten. Here, too, the poem returns twice in ten lines to the 'hope' and 'bait' of 'worldly pleasures,' which should be resisted, of course, but whose attractions are evident enough to lead the reader to speculate about how women's virtue might be reconciled with worldly pleasure, and what role poetry might play in this reconciliation. Perhaps some worldly wealth might legitimately and fortunately come the way of the poet who can exemplify virtue in herself by praising the virtues of the deserving powerful. Yet who are these 'vertuous ladies in generall,' for must not that 'generall' category include more than the powerful?

Lanyer seems to have turned here, as well as in the more combative dedication 'To the Vertuous Reader,' to her second general audience of book purchasers, rather than to aristocratic patrons. In the dedication 'To the Vertuous Reader,' she declares that she has 'written this small volume, or little booke, for the generall use of all virtuous Ladies and Gentlewomen of this kingdome,' as well as for 'some particular persons of our owne sexe ... that I dare undertake Fame dares not to call any better' (48). Yet, in spite of the fame of the aristocratic ladies, 'the vertuous Ladies in generall' in the third dedication are congregated as a kind of priesthood, described in the most enthusiastic and sensuously attractive terms. Dressed in the colors of love and Virtue, 'purple scarlet white,' carrying 'Lillies' that outshine Solomon's glory, they come to a temple decked not in gold, but in daphne and laurel, where hope drowns wealth, and hyssop marks the door of the chosen, to ward off the riotous 'Sinne' which would make 'Virtue poore' (12–13). This procession is swollen by the Muses, devotees of Pallas, 'whose Virtues with the purest minds agree' (13). This Virtue, like Christian-humanist *virtus* combining learning and morality, appears to contain Old Testament, New Testament and classical qualities. The Hebraic patriarchs – Aaron, Solomon and Moses; the classical female deities – Daphne, Minerva, Cynthia, Pallas and the Muses, Phoebus, the classical forerunner of Christ; and Christ himself are the patterns of virtue that earn for the ladies who embody them a place as saints in 'the eie of heaven,' or 'sweet *Elizium*, by the Well of Life' (15).

Swept away by the ideal representation of the leveling Virtue that equalizes 'all vertuous Ladies in generall,' however, Lanyer in the end needs to be recalled to the facts of material and historical circumstance that, in 1611, had not yet replaced aristocratic with economic power. She represents herself as being called by name, 'Lest unawares I in an error fall' (15). This error, it seems, is to 'place' the 'generall' vertuous Ladies with 'the rest, / Whom Fame commends to be the very best' (15), that is, to forget that her pragmatically proper dedicatees are those who might offer her some immediate material benefit through their patronage. Her efforts at wide feminist inclusion are finally restrained by the necessities of favor and ambition. Yet the subject who seeks the rewards of patronage, fame as a poet and prestige as a social personage is monitored by the subject who still desires to promote an ideal feminist community within which to define herself. Speaking from the isolation of the petitioner for patronage, Lanyer still murmurs the desire to belong to a broadly supportive feminist community. Her role as poet must therefore find a way to be both self-sanctified and sanctified by the community.

The Poet-Priest

Lanyer's persona makes frequent comment on her role as poet, praying for 'Power and Strength to Write' (64) and, in a gesture that affiliates her with other early modern women writers, choosing 'plainest Words' (64), rather than decorative ones, for her task. Unlike men, she says, who are directed by scholarship and Art, she prefers to embark on a different project than is exemplified in male poetry. Jane Sharp, speaking to women later in the century about the different art of midwifery, similarly proclaims that 'It is not hard words that perform the work, as if none understood the Art that cannot understand Greek.' Sharp embraces 'our mother tongue' for her writing task.[30] Although Lanyer's alliance with the Maternal as her poetic source is only indirectly an alliance with the English language, she overtly acknowledges as her inspiration, Nature, another maternal figure, 'Mother of perfection,' who speaks to her 'Soule' (10). To a modern reader, she seems to abide by one of the conditions proposed by Josephine Donovan for a women's poetics because, marking a distinction between a detached, artificial male style of writing and an affiliative, affective female stye (Donovan, 104–105), she chooses the feminine mode. Lanyer also employs a 'feminine' structure for her poem that, to use Donovan's terminology, is modeled on the pattern of a web, more nuclear than linear (105; and Beilin, 207). Jacqueline Pearson significantly points out that 'in an Irigarayan sense ... the narrative functions as a series of enfoldings' ('Women Writers,' 47).

Although Lanyer, the patronage-seeker, employs the humility *topos*, referring to herself as lowly and inadequate to her poetic task, this conventional stance is complicated by ironic self-reflection and contradicted by an assertive confidence in her poetic role. Perhaps even more than exemplifying the poet's desire for patronage, the poem enacts the poet's ambition as poet. Comparing herself to Icarus attempting more than she should (63), at the same time she reassures herself with the story of the widow's mite (64) – a story about a member of the one category of women allotted in early modern England a degree of independence outside the range of male desire (Travitsky, *Paradise*, 70). The widow's mite, we remember, is ultimately recompensed with multiple blessings; it was, like her own poem, as Lanyer perhaps protests too much, 'more worth than golden mynes' (64). It is hardly possible to believe the poetic persona's assertion that she cares nothing for 'Fames lowd Trumpet' (64). Lanyer appears fully conscious of her temerity and originality in undertaking the poetic project of constructing a community of women and inscribing herself as poet within that community. Her understanding of the novelty of her task is apparent in her petition to her readers to:

> Vouchsafe to view that which is seldom seene,
> A womans writing of divinest things. (3)[31]

Lanyer was not, however, simply 'writing of divinest things' – though in 1611 that would have been novel enough; she audaciously rewrote and reconstructed them.

Lanyer's poem illustrates Margaret Miles's demand that 'adequate representation of women' should invoke a 'collective voice' (171) and supports Josephine Donovan's claim that a communal awareness of women's shared oppression may be a foundation for the development of a women's poetics (101). Lanyer's text offers a specific recognition of oppressive ideological determinations imposed on women as a group, as well as proposing their subversion, in particular with reference to the influential Pauline doctrine, both biographically and literarily antipathetic to a poet like Lanyer, that female silence was a necessary condition of female chastity (Hull, 155, 173, 206, 220; Hobby, 3, 6, 10). Perhaps having already lost her chastity in a public way as a courtier's mistress, Lanyer felt she had gained the right to the role of public poet. Lanyer's open assertion of herself as a woman poet is necessarily bound to her depiction of herself as framed by the imagined women's community she creates in her poem; in turn she uses her poem to frame her praise of women (41). This ideal female community, then, does not exist for its own sake, or only to provide a psychologically supportive base for its members, or even to praise the hoped-for patrons who make up its membership. Lanyer explicitly writes this community into existence in order to justify her writing herself as poet and persona into existence. The textual creation of a female community by a woman writer is not unique in the period; after all, Christine de Pizan's *Book of the City of Ladies* had been translated and published in England in 1521. But Lanyer's use of her broadly referenced women's community as a frame in which to embed the scene of poetic writing, which oscillates between the 'real' language of material patronage and the 'ideal' language of feminist community, is indeed rare.

The *Salve Deus* employs an acceptably conventional topic to protect a level of subversive discourse which pursues the rare possibility for a woman poet of collective and individual self-inscription. Religion is 'one of the few sites where women have some respite from the circuits of sexual, political, and social exchange' (Grosz, *Sexual Subversions*, 124). This 'safe,' and also potentially subversive, context for Lanyer's poem could be expected to collect the widest possible range of female readers, and perhaps a little mollify predictable male outrage. Within the discourse of Christianity, women have traditionally been allowed a limited autonomy to define themselves as subjects of their own experience. In the early church, women performed missionary and priestly functions (Pagels), in the Middle Ages they established Beguine, Carmelite and Cistercian communities sanctioned and unsanctioned by the church hierarchy (Bynum, *Jesus as Mother*), and in the Protestant sects of the early modern period women were often assigned primary responsibility for the spiritual welfare of their families, with recurrent comments throughout the seventeenth century by male as well as female writers acknowledging that women equaled men as spiritually enlightened and developed human beings.[32]

On all these precedents Lanyer's project depends. Still, no matter how apparently attached to accepted convention, women's texts always take place within 'a dominant male discourse, through acts of "revision, appropriation, and subversion" ' (Showalter, *Speaking*, 5). Women writers in the early modern period, attempting to escape from gender-based constraints on roles and behavior, inevitably turned to oblique codings and representations. Lanyer's 'cover' as she marks out a subversively separatist feminine discourse is the accepted stance of women as devotees of the Christian faith and maintainers of spiritual discourse. By exploiting this access to religious discourse, the *Salve* fulfills Margaret Miles's requirement for adequate representation of women that it 'occur in public, in the institutions and arenas in which the discourse that both reflects and shapes society takes place' (170). So, although the title of Lanyer's poem suggests a project of Christian praise which would have been regarded as a possibly appropriate task for an early modern woman intent on writing poetry, the work itself deviates considerably from the conventional norms for women's sacred poetry. Lanyer's Christian poem divides itself from its apparent purpose to become instead a celebration of women. Necessarily, the means employed by Lanyer to link her writing project to the construction of a female community are subtly coded.

As a foundation for her poetic endeavor, Lanyer establishes and sanctifies a self-supportive, female priestly community to whose care she commits the iconographic image of a Christ who is lover-like, seductively attractive and feminine, and whose own priestly function offers a congenial model to Lanyer and the other women in her poetic community. Lanyer invites 'all vertuous Ladies in generall' to assume a priestly role, following the example of Aaron – the first true priest and typological forerunner of Christ – and of virtuous women:

> Anoynt your haire with *Aarons* pretious oyle,
> And bring your palmes of vict'ry in your hands,
> ...
> Sweet odours, mirrhe, gum, aloes, frankincense,
> Present that King who di'd for your offence. (14)

Women, including Lanyer officiating as poet-priest, share with Christ the nurturing privileges of the priestly function, in some profound way facilitating his spiritual role as he does theirs.

Although the poem's assertive defence of women and its complaints about women's oppression are oppositionally positioned against mortal men, in the enhancing relationship of women to the divine but incarnate Christ, the gender difference is blurred and this opposition erased. In Lanyer's rendering, Christ is presented as just one, albeit a central, member of a community of loving women. In terms of sheer line numbers, the section on Christ's Passion occupies only about 500 of the poem's 3,000 lines. And although the description of Christ's Passion occupies the central position, women heavily and crucially frame the poem, giving it shape and justifying the terms on which the feminized representation of Christ is developed. In fact, the female body physically enfolds this male/female Christ. In a telling image, Christ is lodged as an icon in the heart of the Countess of Cumberland:

Therefore (good Madame) in your heart I leave
His perfect picture, where it still shall stand,
Deepely engraved in that holy shrine,
Environed with Love and Thoughts divine. (108)

In addition, he is harbored in Margaret Russell's breast (58); his 'constant soule doth lodge between her brests' (108). He is also seated in Lucy Bedford's breast (32), folded in the arms of Anne Clifford's soul (46) and lodged in the closet of her heart (47).

The erotic implications of these images are not accidental, for Christ is Bridegroom to all the virtuous women of Lanyer's poem (12, 20, 41, 54, 107), as well as to the Biblical vestal virgins.[33] All 'vertuous Ladies' are invited to come to Lanyer's poem as to a wedding with Christ, their Bridegroom, who awaits them in the sanctified space of the poem: 'Put on your wedding garments every one, / The Bridegroome stayes to entertaine you all' (12). Indeed, Susan Bertie is advised to 'take this faire Bridegroome in your soules pure bed' (20). He is represented emphatically as a faithful lover (35, 48, 80, 93, 111–112), depicted in the images of courtly love, but truer than any other man since the world began (38):

No Dove, no Swan, nor Iv'rie could compare
...
No rose, nor no vermilion halfe so faire
As was that pretious blood that interlac'd
His body, which bright Angels did attend. (39)

His cheeks are scarlet and his 'eyes so bright / As purest Doves that in the rivers are, / Washed with milke'; his lips 'like scarlet threeds' are sweeter than 'hony dropping dew' (107). Christ is an icon on which women focus their desiring gaze (101, 105); in him is 'all that Ladies can desire' (40). He embodies the space in which women may lose and find themselves in the 'libidinal multiplicity found in the presence of the divine' (Chewning, 118). Lanyer textually builds an ideal space in which the hopefully apprehended woman's communal body can join with the sensually apprehended body of Christ.

The women in this poem are not represented as objects looked upon by an all-knowing, all-seeing, judging God. Rather, the Christ figure becomes the *blazoned* object of the female gaze (5, 101, 105):

This with the eye of Faith thou maist behold,
...
And here both Griefe and Joy thou maist unfold,
To view thy Love in this most heavy plight. (101)
... this rich Jewell, which from God was sent,
To call all those that would in time repent
... I present deare lady to your view. (105)

Christ is depicted in the position that is usually inscribed, especially in Renaissance love poetry, as female and he is, at the same time, endowed with feminine characteristics, so that the gender relationships between Christ and his female followers are sexually complex. Lanyer's Christ is an androgynous figure, at once both male lover-Bridegroom and feminine in character and beauty. This depiction leans in part on the contemporary notion that in a fully civilized society 'virtues represented as feminine – temperance, patience, charity – are perceived in men as much as in women' (Jordan, 14). Lanyer is also, however, continuing the tradition – originated by patristic authors like Jerome (Clark, 83ff) and Anselm (Bynum, *Jesus as Mother*, 113ff), and still appearing in Renaissance homiletic – as, for example in Lancelot Andrewes's image of God's love overflowing like 'the breasts that are full' (*Works*, I:100) – that sees God as feminine. Lanyer, like other women writers in the early modern period,[34] exploited this likeness to claim that Christ belonged in some particular way to women; he is portrayed in Lanyer's text as at once both the embodiment and the reflection of female virtue.

Lanyer draws the connection between Christ and women by emphasizing Christ's virtues of humility, love, meekness, nurturance, giving, chastity and suffering (56, 73, 74, 76, 77). Like women, he feeds, washes and heals. He is the God of widows and orphans (53, 62), and comforts the meek and the humble (81). He belongs especially to those who seem 'Weaker ... in Sexe, or Sence' (63), so that he belongs particularly to women, culturally defined in precisely this way. They are not just his worshippers and attendants but his essential supporters. Not only is Christ like women; they are like him. They dress like Christ in humility (12) and like him shed blood (39) and suffer wounds (32).[35] In her dedications, Lanyer compares Princess Elizabeth to the dead Queen Elizabeth, both of whom she describes as phoenixes, as also is Lady Arbella. Later in her poem, this epithet is also applied to Sheba (123) and Margaret Russell (132). These five women are directly identified with the traditional association of the image of the phoenix with Christ who arose from death as the phoenix arises from the ashes of its own funeral pyre.[36] Women, then, not men, best exemplify qualities that are typical of Christ.

Thus Lanyer's feminization of the Christic icon appropriates it for women, making it the object of female contemplation. Because Christ is presented as being like women and supported by women, in contemplating him women are in effect gazing at an extension of themselves and thereby learning to love themselves, an important goal of this community. Altering the traditional relationship and dislodging the traditional gender opposition between women and a male God makes it possible for women to conceive of themselves as subjects of their own religious experience and for Lanyer to assume an authoritative position as poetic subject. Attaching women to Christ and emphasizing those Christian virtues culturally defined as feminine is not, however, a capitulation to a weakened position. It is, on the contrary, a startlingly radical attempt to rewrite the nature of power. The members of this poetically conjured women's community – the aristocratic patrons, and the non-aristocratic poet and 'vertuous Ladies in generall' – can achieve subjectivity together, further helped to this posture because Christ also implicitly embodies the possibility of leadership and revolution, thus exemplifying subversive spiritual and political implications for women:

> Sweet Lambe of God, his deare beloved Sonne,
> By this great purchase, what to thee remaines?
> Of Heaven and Earth thou hast a Kingdom wonne,
> Thy Glory beeing equal with thy Gaines. (69)

Christ's glory in heaven, which virtuous women may aspire to share, is described in the language of measurable material achievement and security with which the poem's awareness is more than a little concerned: by a 'great purchase,' Christ has 'wonne' a 'Kingdom,' his 'Glory' now equal to his 'Gaines.' Even though, on this earth, women may manifest their alliance with Christ by being meek, humble, chaste, nurturing of others and submissive, they may, at the same time, become arbiters of their own fates, directors of the fates of others, teachers, poets and models of power and virtue, and also expect, in the end, a spiritual reward whose satisfaction is marked, metaphorically at least, as equivalent to that derived from material 'Gaines.'

Encouraged by this hope, the poet casts off humility, and in the middle of her contemplation of Christ's Passion, militantly exhorts men to:

> ... let us have our Libertie again,
> And challendge to your selves no Sov'raigntie;
> You came not in the world without our paine,
> Make that a barre against your crueltie
> Your fault being greater, why should you disdaine
> Our beeing your equals, free from tyranny? (87)

In this way of rendering Christ's role in women's lives and in their writing, Lanyer alludes to the opening up of spaces of power for women like herself and the Countess of Cumberland whose earthly power, position and entitlement, though desired and deserved, are insecure.[37] The poem's feminine representation of Christ in both humility and power also shows both men and women a divinely exemplified lesson in circumventing oppressive gender and class oppositions, a lesson, the poem's ideal representation hopes, women are best able to learn. This lesson also values the particular quality of feminine subjectivity, the 'capacity to flow readily between different aspects of itself' (Flax, 93), evident in the fluidity of the iconic model of Christ as both male and female and both humble and powerful, and in the flexible positioning of the poem's speaker as both humble supplicant for material patronage from aristocratic dedicatees and insistent advocate for the inclusion, at least of all those women who read her poem, in a virtuous community.

Feasts and Mirrors

The *Salve*'s challenge to male oppression, issued most forthrightly in the dedication 'To the Vertuous Reader' and in the central stanzas of 'Eve's Apologie,' appears to establish a conventionally simple and familiar binary structure. Occurring less obviously throughout the poem, however, are two interwoven metaphoric webs that sustain a more surreptitious questioning of the negative valencing of women in binary constructions of gender. Both of these metaphoric systems seem, at first sight, simply traditional, but they are also amenable to feminist analysis of women's subjectivity. Both images are deeply embedded in the sacramental and didactic codes of medieval and Renaissance Christianity and draw on standard medieval iconography, yet their conventional associations are reoriented to support the poem's subversive message. Lanyer feminizes these metaphors of feast and mirror to make them congenial to her women's priestly community, so that, possibly disarming to an unsubtle male reader, however suspicious of female writing, they carry potentially incendiary tidings to an alert female reader.

Both images signal moments of exchange, the moments Luce Irigaray sees as crucial in a sexual economy (*This Sex*, 170–197), where 'what is exchanged is less important than the meaning or information the object of exchange signifies' (Grosz, 147). In both cases, however, Lanyer's framing of the exchange, with a woman as both giver and receiver, rewrites the conventional signification of these exchanges as reductive of women when they take place between man and woman or between man and man with woman as the object of the exchange. For, instead of remaining as both conditions and objects of the exchange, women in Lanyer's poem are positioned as subjects or active agents of the exchange relation, so that they may 'escape from their proletarization on the exchange market' (Irigaray, *This Sex*, 30). The images of feast and mirror work effectively together in association with women's socially determined position as passive consumers and spectators. Lanyer's manipulation of these tropes, however, rescues women from their culturally condoned passive role and urges them to active agency and the pleasures associated with sustenance and self-reflection.

That Lanyer calls on the rhetoric of metaphor to express what is repressed in dominant culture is particularly important. For both these metaphors spill over their conventional boundaries in ways that comport a challenge to the ideology that represses women. In psychoanalytic theory, the metaphor is a figure of condensation and concealment, compressing terms on the basis of overt similarities, while other more threatening similarities remain disguised. Metaphor relies on a relation of similarity between two terms, one of which represents while covering over or silencing the other. This procedure allows the 'unconscious to be expressed or deciphered,' thus 'gaining a compromise pleasure' (Grosz, 23). Appearing in women's writing, the metaphor would seem especially exemplary of the ways in which women's language might pleasurably, perhaps unconsciously, circumvent the interdictions of gender ideology.

Julia Kristeva claims metaphor and metonymy for the feminine realm outside the range of the masculine Symbolic realm. She argues that the Western patriarchal system has wanted to suppress this oblique, allusive mode of expression, seeking rather to be unified, rational and disembodied in its language. The metaphoric language of poetry Kristeva associates with the feminine because, she says, it carries the unconscious relation between the subject and the excessive and disturbing maternal body. In these terms, then, a metaphor can package, as Lanyer's feast and mirror do, in one and the same mechanism, an anxiety-assuaging acknowledgment to the dominant discourse which fails to represent women's interest and a subversive encouragement to, and enactment of, a critical transgressive discourse. Thus the woman writer's compromise pleasure is achieved by maneuvering metaphorically through and around the repressions of women's language in the received male discourse. Metaphor can open up a space in which a woman's own unrestrained linguistic pleasure can unfold. Luce Irigaray suggests mystical hysteria as a potential space in which a woman exaggeratedly mimes and parodies the male representation of her sexuality, so as to rescue something of her own desire. Also, the term 'metaphor' in the Greek means a carrying across, a bridge; Lanyer's use of metaphor, like her construction of feminist community, while aware of the inevitable division, yearns to bridge the space between the represented ideal and the real. The use of metaphor may be a rhetorical device by which, in this case, a woman writer may both enact complicity with and escape from restrictive masculine language and thus rescue something of her desire to speak.

As Lanyer performs her hieratic rites of female incantation and poetry behind the screen of her acceptably feminine use of Christian praise, the talismanic figure of the feast assumes a central role. The poem itself is represented as a figure of Christ (7) – a feast and Paschal Lamb as he is (7 and 11). Lanyer, the poet-priest, officiates at the feast of her poem, which she offers to women, proposing to feed them on mutually mirrored images of themselves and of Christ, from which they may gain sustenance:

> ... she must entertaine you to this Feast,
> ...
> For here I have prepar'd my Paschal Lambe,
> The figure of that living Sacrifice;
> Who, dying, all th'infernall powres oercame,
> That we with him t'Eternitie might rise:
> This pretious Passeover feed upon, O Queene,
> Let your faire Virtues in my Glasse be seene. (7)

As poet-priest, Lanyer celebrates the sacrament of her poem, nurturing women with a feast of female self-esteem, proclaiming her love for them and showing them how to love one another, at the same time also urging her female readers to participate with her in her priestly function (14). A connection may be implied here with medieval communities of religious women, whose conventual arrangements were lost in early modern England, but in which women had previously exercised some spiritual autonomy and power while sustaining emotionally and sometimes erotically nurturing relationships with Christ and each other (Bynum, Arenal and Schlau).[38] In fact, women religious in these communities in the twelfth and thirteenth centuries exercised sufficient clerical authority, including the benediction of their own nuns, the hearing of confessions and preaching, to provoke a disapproving response in 1210 from Pope Innocent III (Bynum, *Jesus as Mother*, 1–20).

Perhaps without direct allusion to this particular precedent, Lanyer still models her own persona as provider of the food of her poem – 'this holy feast' (18) or Eucharistic offering which will nourish her readers by initiating them into a feminine community enriched by its inclusion of and attachment to Christ – on Christ's role as feeder of his flock, as officiator at the Last Supper and as the Eucharist itself (124–127), 'sweet foode of life that doth revive the dead, / And from the living takes away all cares' (127). Lanyer's poem exploits an association of the image of a spiritual feast with feminine nurturance to connect the persona's role as poet-priest with the didactic and saving role of Christ. In the medieval tradition that emphasized the nurturing qualities of the Saviour, Christ as Eucharist, feeding the soul with his body and blood, was sometimes compared to a nursing mother (Bynum, 'And Woman His Humanity,' 263). Images of food, drink, brimming fountains and flowing streams of blood were used by thirteenth-century women religious to express their yearning for direct connection with Christ and for the power to handle Christ in the celebration of the Eucharist (Bynum, *Jesus as Mother*, 8; *Holy Feast*, especially chs 5 and 9).[39] The connections between eating and erotic desire as sources of pleasure, especially with reference to women, in the early modern period and in this poem, hover at the boundaries between conscious and unconscious expression: a handbook of the period advises that a girl should 'so eate as that shee may alwayes be an hungred ... lest shee see such meats as she might desire' (Battus, sig. T3r–v). Juan Luis Vives's instruction book for the education of young women is more forthright: 'unto the time they be married, much fasting shall be good, which doth not feeble the body, but bridle it and press it down, and quench the heat of youth' (64).[40]

To further validate her own role as provider of spiritual poetic food, and to substantiate this role as appropriate for a woman, Lanyer deploys another disruptive tactic. She revises the traditional representation of Eve as the progenitor of evil, justifying Eve's actions through the same metaphor of feeding that she uses to justify her own. An implicit acknowledgment of the unjust recriminations heaped upon all women who violate patriarchal constructions creeps into this argument; Eve has been vilified for disobeying the divine prohibition against knowledge, and women like Lanyer have been guilty of the same crimes of disobedience and immodesty for not heeding the contemporary social disapproval of women's writing and publication. Eve, says Lanyer, ate a significant food and then, for love, shared it with Adam and their descendants. Adam, however, did not deserve the sharing of the fruit, for he became the prototype of all men who ever thereafter denounced women for this act of generosity and sustenance (104). An alliance is suggested here between Eve and her daughter Aemilia: each presides over the respective feasts of the fruit of the tree of knowledge and the *Salve Deus*, and both are represented as female Christ figures, like him betrayed by men. A contrast is established between these women, resting under Christ's protection, and Adam and the men who refused Christ as the Eucharist, betraying him as he sought to nourish them.[41]

As Victoria Kirkham has pointed out, the Biblical precedent of God's urging Ezekiel to open his mouth and swallow the book of divine prophecy (II.8–10; III.1–3) is reiterated in Dante, Boccaccio and Augustine, so that in the Middle Ages knowledge is frequently represented as something to be consumed ('The Book and the Idea of the Book').[42] In the New Testament, before preaching the Apocalypse, St John the Evangelist eats the book of Prophecy. An example of this metaphor closer to Lanyer is to be found in the inscription written by Elizabeth, when imprisoned in Woodstock, in a blank space in a copy of a translation of St Paul's Epistles: 'I walk many times into the pleasant fields of the holy Scriptures where I pluck up the goodlisome herbs of sentences by pruning, eat them by reading, chew them by musing ... That so having tasted the sweetness, I may the less perceive the bitterness of this miserable life' (Nichols I.9–10). Lanyer incorporates into her poem this same image of spiritual knowledge as a food to be chewed and digested, but appropriates the right to prepare and eat it for women or for the maternal Saviour she presents metaphorically in ways echoed by Hélène Cixous: 'I adored God my mother' (*La Venue à l'écriture*, 26), 'a young man, elegant and maternal' (24); 'To write would be to nourish my own mother. To give to her [him?], in my turn, my milk?' (20). 'I was brought up on the milk of words ... I allowed myself to be nourished only with the voice, with words' (27, my translation).[43] In Lanyer's description, the maternal Christ is the source of the 'hony dropping due of holy love, / Sweet milke, wherewith we weaklings are restored' (125).

Lanyer's conflation of a maternal, nurturing God, woman's writing, and the nourishing, delicious food of knowledge invokes the 'sweet taste' of Christ's sufferings which tunes up her 'untun'd voyce' so that she can 'sing / Of sad Affliction' and 'praise pale Sorrow' (8), producing a book which she likens to 'heavenly food' (38) that 'delights the taste' (30) and will in turn be eaten:

> I doe invite [you] unto this wholesome feast,
> ...
> Though your faire eyes farre better Bookes have seene;
>   Yet being the first fruits of a womans wit,
>   Vouchsafe you favour in accepting it. (11)

Lanyer's persona, then, chooses to share the same food of knowledge which is especially women's, acquired for them by their mother Eve, with other women who may feast upon it with more gratitude and pleasure and make better use of it than did Adam. To these women Lanyer offers knowledge of themselves and instruction in how they may value themselves and exploit fully not only the food of Eden but also the food of Christian love. In traditional patristic readings, the corrupt feast of knowledge in Eden is purified by the feast of the Eucharistic sacrifice. Lanyer makes

6.2 An angel helps St John the Evangelist to eat the Book of Revelation

them both of a kind; both are beneficial efforts to share knowledge. Like the poet herself, Eve becomes a nurturer as Christ is, and not, as she is usually represented, antagonistic to him. She and he are both members of the same women's spiritual community bonded together in and with this Eucharistic poem, the writing of which becomes a sacramental offering. Luce Irigaray also recognizes the same potential for validating feminine connections across generations of women in the Eucharistic moment: 'If a woman were to celebrate the Eucharist with her mother, giving her a share of the fruits of the earth blessed by them both, she might be freed from all hatred or ingratitude toward her maternal genealogy, and be hallowed in her identity as a woman' (*Sexes and Genealogies*, 21).

Lanyer's act of writing produces a feast – a gastronomic and hallowing exchange between writer and reader. But the interchange set up at the scene of writing, between writer and reader, also invokes another process of *reflective* exchange. At the very beginning of her poem, Lanyer describes Queen Anne reading the text:

> Reade it faire Queene, though it defective be,
> Your Excellence can grace both It and Mee. (3)

The virtue of the royal woman reader makes both text and poet excellent, for a backward and forward flow is set in motion between reader and writer through the reflective medium of the poem. The implied image of a mirror becomes explicit several lines later:

> Looke in this Mirrour of a worthy Mind,
> Where some of your faire Virtues will appeare;
> Though all is impossible to find,
> Unlesse my Glasse were chrystall, or more cleare:
> Which is dim steele, yet full of spotless truth,
> And for one looke from your faire eyes it su'th. (5)

Glossed from Paul's letter to the Corinthians (I Corinthians 13:12), these lines appear to say that the poem is a reflection of a worthy mind (whether Lanyer's own, or Anne's, or Margaret Russell's remains strategically open), but, even so, it can reveal only *some* of the queen's virtues because the reflecting glass is steel, not crystal. The ideal world so longed for is always flawed. Though the poem's language aspires ideally to 'spotless truth,' it is only possible as yet for the poet and the reader to 'see through a glass, darkly.' Neither they nor any other mortal being can yet see 'face to face,' or know themselves or each other as they will ultimately be known by God. It is the world of the poetically represented that the mirror reflects.

The image of the mirror appears on a number of occasions in close proximity with the image of the feast (7, 18, 31, 41). A medieval tradition which continued into early modern England also associates the mirror with the Eucharist. As Herbert Grabes describes this tradition, 'just as the fragments of a broken mirror each furnish a complete image of an object, Christ is wholly present in each fragment of broken bread (the Host)' (107). This analogy appears in Aquinas, Lydgate and Wycliff, among others (Grabes, 107). The image of the broken and fragmented body of Christ presented as a mirroring object for the desiring gaze of the women in this poem (108–109) certainly reinforces this analogical means of connecting the metaphors of feast and mirror. It similarly participates in the contemporary sense of mirrors as 'platonically angled, tilted upwards in order to reflect paradigms' (Shuger, 'The "I" of the Beholder,' 26). But the mirrored image of fragmentation in addition points to the play of possibility, to a process of deconstruction and woman-referenced reconstruction, not as sources of restriction, but of social change.

As the image of the mirror continues to appear in Lanyer's poem, then, it attaches to itself resonances that associate it with the issue of women's self-construction and self-referentiality suggested in Lanyer's use of the feast. Deborah Shuger has pointed to instances in Vives, Milton and Andrewes that would seem to support the possibility of a 'habit of thought' in the Renaissance that 'love of one's own image is not evil but the ground of all love' (*Habits of Thought*, 236–239); elsewhere Shuger speculates that Renaissance persons, gazing into mirrors, saw a whole panoply of:

> saints, skulls, friends, offspring, spouses, magistrates, Christ. The mirror reflects these figures because they are images of oneself; one encounters one's own likeness only in the image of the other. Renaissance texts and emblems consistently describe mirroring in these terms, which suggests that early modern selfhood was not experienced reflexively but, as it were, relationally. ('The "I" of the Beholder,' 37)

As I have argued in earlier chapters of this book, the subject/self in early modern women's writing is often fragmented, though fully functional. The relational aspect of 'early modern selfhood' deduced by Shuger fits compatibly inside the relational feminism of Lanyer's poetic community where women's subjectivity is promoted in imaginative and desirous relationships with other women and a feminized Christ. Lanyer's mirrors are crowded with the image of Christ, the idealized images of the women she praises, the image of an ideally and widely inclusive women's community and her own self-image. They contain alternative images of desire or aspiration, reflecting imagined possibility as much as external reflection, bridging for an imaginative moment the space between ideal representation and the circumstantially 'real.'

In another early modern woman's text, in an appearance presaging Lanyer's own role, Lady Reason, in Christine de Pizan's *Book of the City of Ladies*, holds before Christine a mirror of which she says, 'I would thus have you know truly that no one can look in this mirror, no matter what kind of creature, without achieving clear self-knowledge' (9).[44] It is this hopeful use of the mirror image, rather than its negative construction as contributing to women's vanity, that Lanyer's poem also develops. The women in the *Salve* are invited to feed on their own images of virtue, for Lanyer's poem is a reflection of female virtue defined as beneficial and pleasurable for women

6.3 Jan David, *Speculum exemplare*, from *Duodecim Specula*

themselves – embodying learning, pleasurable connections with other women and spiritual enlightenment – rather than according to male prescriptions of chastity, silence, enclosure and obedience. The poet holds the mirror which provides a reflection of women undistorted by the male interpretation of the female. Instead of being presented as objects of the male gaze, these women receive from another woman a special commendatory glass in which to view themselves, each other and Christ. Lanyer refers to the poem as '*my* Glasse' and '*my* mirrour' (5, 7, 12, 31, my italics); in it she conjures up 'glittring' images of exemplary virtuous women (7) who may serve as models for each other and for other female readers of the poem.[45]

Like the figure of the feast, the mirror has a medieval history, a Renaissance cultural significance and a current feminist psychoanalytic analysis. The medieval dimension of the mirror image supplies a variety of interpretations. Classical in origin, the mirror remained a frequently employed metaphor in the Latin Middle Ages; its connotations were negative as well as positive, sometimes distorting, deceptive and narcissistic, sometimes representative of either the spotless Virgin Mother or the truth of God, the wisdom which is 'speculum sine macula' (I Corinthians 13:12) (see Curtis, *passim*). In courtly love, the mirror was frequently seen either as the mirror of Narcissus (Bernard de Ventadour's 'Can vei la lauzeta mover') or as showing the true image of the lady to her lover (Jean Froissart's 'Espinette Amoureuse,' Guillaume de Machaut's 'Remede de Fortune'). In the *Roman de la Rose*, God's mind is called the 'everlasting mirror' in which are reflected all things and all events (17451–17498). Similar examples appear in Alanus de Insulis and Bernard Sylvester (Gunn, *passim*). Iconographically, the mirror as a reflection of the divine is depicted, for example, in the *Sapientiae Christi*, where Christ is shown holding a mirror reflecting his image (Pierpont Morgan ms. 132, fol. 130). The mirror also featured heavily in works that can be associated with the *querelle des femmes*, such as the *Miroir aux Dames* by Alain Chartier or the *Miroir de Mariage* by Deschamps.

The popularity of the mirror in the Middle Ages did not diminish in the Renaissance. In fact, Herbert Grabes suggests, it occurs so frequently in titles and texts of the Renaissance that it might well be regarded as a 'fashion' (3), a point not likely to be lost on Lanyer, who, like Whitney, was seeking to negotiate the shoals of both patronage and fashion for her own benefit. The mirror's complexity of reference also continued into the early modern period; it was 'clearly suited to a particularly noteworthy variety of symbolic, analogizing and metaphorical applications: ... it met all the prerequisites for a use of metaphor that can be regarded as characteristic of a specific period in the history of literature' (3). Its frequent appearance and its slipperiness of application resonate with the insecurity of the Renaissance sensibility as it attempted to come to terms with drastic social change, including economic and population shifts, religious conflict, a rising populist voice and the precariousness of gender roles.

In particular, the mirror's referentiality to both the foundations of Christian belief and the seductions of human love may reveal a concern in the period for the ways in which both these spheres of discourse, while evincing the power of the patriarchy, also open up spaces of potential power for women. It appears frequently in titles of conduct books intended for women's beneficial instruction as well as in warnings against women's vanity and self-love.[46] In fact, the popular *Mirrhor of Modestie* by Thomas Salter published in 1579 might well be a text negatively reflected in Lanyer's contrary glass, for Salter inveighs against women's learning to the same degree that Lanyer vehemently defends it. And Robert Greene's *Penelope's Web ... a christall myrror of feminine perfection ...* (1587), which echoes the contemporary view that a virtuous woman should be as a mirror reflecting her husband's image (Jordan, 61),[47] might equally well have provoked Lanyer's response that women can learn a better and more useful lesson from each other's reflections than from less flattering male images. Perhaps the traditional emblem of the Virgin as a 'spotless mirror' provided a more congenially instructive icon even to English Protestant women than the lessons taught by male writers of contemporary conduct books.

In the early seventeenth century in England, then, Lanyer had a rich and complex tradition to draw on in her use of the mirror image. Her poem could hardly erase from her readers' minds the contemporary reference of mirrors to female vanity. It contends against this negative association, however, following its own advice to women not to speak against each other. Preferring to emphasize women's best potential, it draws instead on the representation of the mirror as it appears in the *Speculum Mundi* of Vincent de Beauvais, in Gower's *Confessio Amantis* and in the Elizabethan *Mirror for Magistrates*. The *Salve* positively reflects in its woman poet's reconstructive poetic power the originally constructive power of the Creator of the world. As Edward Peter Nolan has expressed it, the image of the mirror in the Middle Ages and Renaissance gathered about itself a range of connotations that allowed it to signify the liminal area 'between reader and text, subject and object, knower and known, creature and Creator' (2), an epistemological border territory within which Lanyer skillfully maneuvers.

The historian Georges Gusdorf has suggested that the 'technology of the mirror, perfected and marketed by Venice in the early sixteenth century,' made whole pictures of themselves available to people who had previously been used to the distorting effects of blown glass mirrors, so that, says Roger Smith, commenting on Gusdorf's insight, 'there was an enrichment of the sense of self' (53). These new 'whole' images are also evocative of Lacan's sense of the mirror stage in human psychological development as providing an illusory moment of coherence and autonomy which becomes the object of perpetually unsatisfied desire, inside of which the split subject constructs itself. Lanyer's poem maintains the 'reality' of a fragmented relational subjectivity addressed to the ultimately un-mergeable audiences of aristocratic patron and less privileged virtuous women, while also representing the ideal of material and spiritual unity among women toward which the poem urges women to aspire.

As Deborah Shuger also emphasizes, the interior mirror signified by Renaissance mirrors 'reveals what one *should* look like' ('The "I" of the Beholder,' 34), rather, or as well as, the flawed reality. The mirrored image displays both the self and the other that one would be. This multiplistic potential of the mirror's imaging allows it to reflect the persona's own mind, the mind of her virtuous ladies and Christ, 'the beauty of the World, Heavens chiefest Glory,' himself another mirror – 'of Martyrs, Crowns of holy Saints' (79). Lanyer exploits the mirror as metaphor, then, to reinforce ideal alliances of women with women and women with a feminized Christ. The mirror, like Lanyer's poem, shows women to themselves in a yearned-for and pleasing light. Attached to the image of Christ, the *Salve* does not refer to that image as an inflexible, invariable Presence. Rather, the image of Christ is loosened from patriarchal definitions and made flexibly responsive to women's needs. Because both infinite and spiritual, Lanyer's image of Christ is not an image of an immobilized center, but of the joyful affirmation of possibility. This Word, like Foucault's 'language to infinity,' engages 'in a play of mirrors that has no limits' (54).

A modern feminist reader will have been sensitized by feminist psychoanalytic theory to a further range of implications implied by the connection of Lanyer's mirror-poem as a vehicle of women's self-discovery, to religious experience as a sphere of women's power. This association invokes Irigaray's and Cixous's valorization rather than derogation of narcissism as beneficial for women in a prolonged mirror stage in the female construction of the self.[48] This narcissistic phase for women is a phase of connection between mother and daughter (there are many mothers and daughters in Lanyer's poem), a reinforcement of the self and a continuance of the feminine semiotic stage which Julia Kristeva sees as dense with metaphor and metonymy and operating outside the masculine Symbolic realm, in a process of resistance to the Law of the Father. Contrary to the tendency in Western philosophy to represent woman only as the self-reflection of the male subject, as its own solipsistic image (*Speculum*, 181), Irigaray proposes the use of a mirror that is concave instead of flat; upside down, it 'leads [the female soul] to that abyssal source [of pleasure] that she could never have found otherwise' (194).[49]

In language that is remarkably apt as a gloss on Lanyer's project, Irigaray speaks of the effort of woman to find her 'self' beyond the power of male construction. Outside the range of the system of exchange in which woman is valued as a commodity, women may be able to rescue their prodigality, their 'expansion and dissipation of self,' their 'mother-matter' from mastery (*Speculum*, 195). Here, in the 'abyss,' women find themselves in reflections of each other: a woman sees either herself or another woman as a 'living mirror ... (to) your resemblance as you are mine' (197). Through this process also, the feminized divine, the God who 'goes beyond all representation' (197), is able to find and validate the self-discovered woman:

> And if 'God,' who has thus re-proved the fact of her non-value, still loves her, this means that she exists all the same, beyond what anyone may think of her. It means that love conquers everything that has already been said. And that one man, at least, has understood her so well that he died in the most awful suffering. The most female of men, the Son. And she never ceases to look upon his nakedness ... at the wounds from the nails that pierce his body as he hangs there ... And she is overwhelmed with love of him/herself. (*Speculum*, 199–200)

Of course, Lanyer's vision of woman's movement toward self-discovery and connection with the divine is more controlled and attached to material necessity than Irigaray's celebration of the '*mysterique*,' the 'me-hysteric' of the escaped, abandoned, ecstatic woman. Neither does Lanyer dismantle the construction of divinity to the same radical extent as Irigaray. Yet feminist connections exist between Lanyer and Irigaray in the form of a shared insight into the male constructions that have inhibited women's access to subjectivity and language, in a common understanding of the need for women to undertake their project of self-definition in spaces constructed by and for women, in idealized (for Lanyer) and morphological (for Irigaray) representations of women's communities, in a similar feminized redefinition of the divine as a strategic maneuver toward this project and in the use of mirror metaphors to elucidate the way to self-definition through 'dazzling, multi-faceted' and infinitely potential self-reflection. Both writers seek other means of self-construction than those mirrors which reflect their images through 'phallomorphic disguises, masquerades, and demands' (*Speculum*, 143). And because, according to the fundamental post-structural insight that texts always say more than they are able to control, in particular at metaphoric moments falling outside intended boundaries, it might equally be said of Lanyer's seventeenth-century feminist text, as of Irigaray's twentieth-century one, that it too points to the attraction of 'a specular surface which sustains discourse' by the 'dazzle of multi-faceted speleology' (143) in which a new form of subjectivization might be represented, owned not by man, but by woman.

Aemilia Lanyer's *Salve Deus Rex Judaeorum* more strenuously insists on women's mutual self-valuation and more unequivocally professes a woman poet's writerly subjectivity than is at all usual in this period, but the poem's very existence establishes pleasingly for the modern feminist reader that these possibilities, though perhaps rare, were nevertheless available to early modern women. Speaking to each other across the centuries, the poetic texts of Aemilia Lanyer and Luce Irigaray mirror each other's visions as they both, in their separate historical contexts, yearn toward a space where a woman, allied with other women, and supported by her union with 'the most female' God, might speak, as a subject, from her sense of her own experience, however fragmented and decentered it and she might be.

Luce Irigaray:

> ... the horizon line [that defines the (male) subject] is already drawn, and drawn, in fact, by the 'subject' who defines himself at the same time, in a circularity that knows no end except the return, over and over again, upon itself/himself. The problem is to break down the walls around the (male) one who speaks, sees, thinks, and thereby now confers being upon himself, in a prison of self-sufficiency and a clarity made of the shadows of denial. The task [for the female soul] is to go back through the house of confinement and the darkness of the night ... The only possibility is to push onward into the night until it finally becomes a transverberating beam of light, a luminous shadow. Onward into a *touch* that opens the 'soul' again to contact with divine force, to the impact of searing light. She is cut to the quick with this shimmering underground fabric that she had always been herself, though she did not know it. And she will never know it herself *clearly* as she takes fire, in a sweet confusion

> whose source cannot at first be apprehended ... But a 'God' already draws near in these/her fainting states. What does it matter that all judge her mad if the 'prince of the world' has noticed her and if henceforward he will be her companion in solitude. (*Speculum*, 192–199)

Aemilia Lanyer:

> ... we [women] are not to regard any imputations, that they [men] undeservedly lay upon us, no otherwise than to make use of them to our owne benefits, as spurres to vertue, making us flie all occasions that may colour their unjust speeches to passe currant ... As also in respect it pleased our Lord and Saviour Jesus Christ, without the assistance of man, beeing free from originall and all other sinnes, from the time of his conception, till the houre of his death, to be begotten of a woman, borne of a woman, nourished of a woman, obedient to a woman; and that he healed women, pardoned women, comforted women: yea, even when he was in his greatest agonie and bloodie sweat, going to be crucified, and also in the last houre of his death, tooke care to dispose of a woman: after his resurrection, appeared first to a woman, sent a woman to declare his most glorious resurrection to the rest of his Disciples. (49–50)

Although Lanyer lacked the term to describe her politics, she forced the grounds of protest available in early seventeenth-century English culture to their most radical possible feminist claims. Expecting, in spite of her sex, the just rewards of a poet, she sought both patronage and book sales. Appealing for both material security and emotional gratification, she urged herself and other women to embark on a process of self-construction beyond the power of imprisoning male construction and male desire. Exploiting the binary oppositions of male oppression and female subjection, she also blurred the boundaries between the two. Unable to close the gap in masculine Symbolic language between the represented ideal and the real, she exploited the feminine possibilities of metaphor to allude to an alternative language of women's mutually enhancing pleasure. Appropriating the most powerful and sacred Christian ideological icon as authorization, she poetically invoked a supportive female community under whose auspices she established for herself the role of writing subject.

Notes

1 The work was registered on 2 October 1610 by Richard Bonyon (Bonion) and published by Simmes and Bonion in 1611. There was apparently a second issue with different dedications, some of the more controversial having been removed. Barbara Lewalski suggests that the British Library copy could have been a unique copy prepared for a particular patron ('Of God and Good Women,' 284). Mary Ellen Lamb also proposes the possibility of multiple different presentation copies. Also see Germaine Greer's comments (45), Susanne Woods's textual introduction to her edition of the poems, which I will cite in this chapter (xlvii–li) and Lewalski, *Writing Women* (218–219 and 321–322).

2 The presentation copies for Prince Henry and Thomas Jones, Archbishop of Dublin, politicly dropped some of the dedications (Woods, *The Poems*, xlvii–li). Also see Leeds

Barroll's detailed and thoughtful discussion of the dedications, and some of the errors of judgement evident in the poem's insufficiently rank-conscious arrangement of the dedications: 'As a female poet with a non-aristocratic social and educational background, Aemilia Lanyer was seriously handicapped in the Court game, yet one could argue that these are the very factors that made her presumed relationship with Kent, Cumberland, Hunsdon, and perhaps other nobles, so remarkable' (42). Also see Susanne Woods's subtle reading of the relationship between poet and patron.

3 The dedications omitted in the second issue were those addressed to: Arbella Stuart (taken into custody and sent to the Tower in March 1611 because her marriage in July 1610 to William Seymour strengthened her claim to the throne); the Countesses of Kent and Pembroke (both vehemently Protestant at a time when Protestant–Catholic factionalism in the Stuart court might have made it unclear which faction it was wisest to support); and the Countess of Suffolk (who, with her husband, Lord Thomas Howard, Lord Treasurer and Lord Chamberlain of the Royal Household, was arrested in 1618 for embezzlement and selling information to the Spanish, but who even earlier may have been the subject of the kind of rumor to cause the publisher or author of her praise some concern). The last dedication absent from the British Library copy is the one 'To the Vertuous Reader'; it is characterized by A.L. Rowse as 'a piece of rampant feminism, like nothing else in the age' (20). Tina Krontiris suggests that some of the dedicatees might have chosen to have their own dedications withdrawn rather than being associated with such 'feminist ideas' (120).

4 Gary Waller's comment about all historical textual criticism seems especially applicable to Lanyer's poem: '[L]ater readers who approach texts from the past with their own questions and concerns are often in a position to articulate what neither [the writer] not her writing were able to put into words' (252).

5 For example, it appears in *The Norton Anthology of English Literature*, *The Norton Anthology of Literature by Women*, *Kissing the Rod: An Anthology of 17th-Century Women's Verse*, and Marion-Wynne Davies's recent edition of *Women Poets of the Renaissance*. It also appears in Brown University's Full-Text Data Base Project of Women's Writing from 1339 to 1830. Lanyer now even has her own website.

6 For example, see Beilin, Bowen, Goldberg, Greer, the volume edited by Grossman, Herz, Hutson, Krontiris, Lamb, Lewalski, Travitsky, Wall and Woods (especially her recent valuable positioning of Lanyer in the broader literary context of the period). This list cannot, because of the critical enthusiasm inspired by Lanyer, include many other valuable contributions I am sorry not to be able to add. Thanks to A.L. Rowse's belief that Lanyer was Shakespeare's mysterious 'dark lady,' the entire text has been accessible in a modern edition for a comparatively long time, and is now available in Susanne Woods's excellent scholarly edition.

7 See '"Let Us Have Our Libertie Againe": Amelia Lanier's 17th-Century Feminist Voice.'

8 Barbara Bowen's fine essay on the 'otherness' promoted in Lanyer's text by her Jewish origins exemplifies attention to this caution. A twentieth-century reader exists in and reads from a context that necessarily embraces political alliances scarcely recognized by even the most radical Renaissance sensibility. Something like this retrospectivity is at work in Krontiris's reading of the poem. Although Krontiris calls Lanyer a feminist 'in a historically specific sense' (118), she emphasizes what she sees as inconsistencies in 'the feminist voice of the text' (118). In fact, these variations of position are integral to the kind of pro-woman stance that in the early seventeenth century was epistemologically possible.

Janel Mueller reminds us that 'our best wisdom, our most sophisticated and influential theories, are no *sine qua non* for a feminist poetics' (101).

9 For discussions of this phenomenon, see especially Henderson and McManus, Woodbridge and Hull.

10 Lanyer's multiple dedications to powerful women had an impressive precedent in Spenser's seventeen dedications of *The Faerie Queene* to members of the court, including the Queen and other aristocratic ladies. Spenser also has a dedication with a title reminiscent of one of Lanyer's: to 'all the gracious and beautiful Ladies in the Court.' He also preceded her in his praise of the Countess of Cumberland to whom he dedicated his *Four Hymns*. See Oates; see also Lewalski, 'Seizing Discourses.'

11 In a medieval precedent for this reading, Priscilla, a follower of Montanus, had a vision in which Christ appeared to her as a female to announce the descent of the heavenly Jerusalem. See Clark, 87.

12 As I use the term 'Lanyer' throughout this chapter, to refer to the speaker of the poem, I am not at the same time intending to describe the historical personage's views. What Aemilia Lanyer may or may not have believed or intended I cannot, though I wish I could, know. Where I refer to the early modern woman who lived in London and wrote this poem, I will try to make that clear.

13 For a crucially important analysis of the movement from idealization to political action, see Kaja Silverman's brilliant *Threshold of the Visible World*, especially chapter 3.

14 References to the *Salve* are to page numbers in Susanne Woods' edition.

15 This is not a 'universal' use of the masculine, for this section of the poem strongly establishes an oppositional stance by women against the men who were responsible for Christ's death.

16 Lanyer was twenty-three when she bore Hunsdon's child. She was married to Alphonso Lanyer on 18 October 1592. Lanyer possibly became Hunsdon's mistress around the time of her mother's death in 1587, when she was about seventeen. Her father had died in 1576. (See Woods, *Poems*, xvii–xviii, and *Lanyer*, 16).

17 Simon Forman says she 'was very brave in youth' and he himself 'finds her attractive' (Woods, *Poems*, xx–xxi).

18 Lanyer's fortunes declined still further. After the death of her husband, the stipend awarded to Alphonso Lanyer by King James in 1604 was taken over by his brothers, ironically named Innocent and Clement. Lanyer was apparently still seeking redress against them in 1635. See Woods, *Poems*, xv–xxx. Like the Countess of Cumberland and her daughter, Lanyer found herself seeking redress through the courts for appropriation of her rightful property. Without the hoped-for patronage of her female dedicatees either, Lanyer opened a school in her impecunious widowhood and helped support her grandson.

19 For an account of Margaret Russell's role as dedicatee for Spenser's *Fowre Hymns*, see Quitslund and Woods, *Lanyer*, 54–61.

20 I agree with Fisher and Halley that the concept of the self needs to be 'approached sceptically by those seeking the historical self of women.' Whether many women in the early modern period participated in what Fisher and Halley call a 'deep-seated belief in an essential self,' located in and variously called the 'soul or the heart or the mind' (2), is, I think, doubtful. The sense of self for women seems always to have been problematized in a way that twentieth-century psychoanalytic theory has discussed. It is in this highly-qualified sense that I use the term 'self' in discussing Lanyer. It should be noted also that this idea of the self in the early seventeenth century was probably for both genders

less secure than, though still dependent on, the concept of the self as formulated by the patristics, Anselm, Abelard and Bernard, in response to the increased emphasis on the affective level of religious experience in the twelfth and thirteenth centuries. See Robertson, 112. Also see chapter 1 of this book for a fuller discussion of this issue. For an interesting connection between the increased use and availability of mirrors and a changing sense of self in the Renaissance, see Grabes, 118ff. Also, however, see Shuger's argument against Grabes's view ('The "I" of the Beholder'). For a discussion of an equally interesting conflation between text and self, see Regan. For a view of the self as double and divided, see Shuger on Luther's *Zwei-Regimente Lehre* and on Perkins (*Habits*, 94–95).

21 Although George Clifford's will contravened a documented earlier legal agreement that specifically denied the need to entail the Cumberland estates through the male line, Anne Clifford's efforts to regain control of the estates she should have legally inherited were prolonged and frustrating. She was unable to find any support for the enforcement of her rights, even needing to resist pressure from the King to give up her claim on her family estates. Eventually, she regained her estates by outliving all male claimants. For further information about the Cliffords, see Holmes, Williamson and *Lives of Lady Anne Clifford*.

22 For a consideration of Lanyer's social class as a factor in the poem, see Ann Baynes Coiro's essay, comparing Lanyer's situation with Ben Jonson's. Also see Kim Walker 118 and Mary Ellen Lamb.

23 Jacqueline Pearson ('Women Writers') points to the connection between Lanyer's reference to Cleopatra, and the Countess of Pembroke's translation of Garner's *Antonie* and the Countess's commissioning of Daniel's *Cleopatra*.

24 It is worth noting Stephanie Jed's association of the image of the rape of Lucrece and the development of Renaissance humanist learning, especially in light of Lanyer's defense of women's learning. Also note Ann Rosalind Jones's interesting argument that at least in the case of two Italian women poets, the image of Philomel represented not just the silencing of women, but the possibility of their eloquent *riposte* ('New Songs').

25 Naomi Miller ('Mother Tongues') explores in more detail the significance of motherhood in the *Salve* as a potentially cooperative rather than a potentially competitive bond.

26 Luce Irigaray reminds priests of their ultimate indebtedness to women for their existence in a similar manner: 'And yet, when the minister of that one and only God, that God-Father, pronounces the words of the Eucharist: 'this is my body, this is my blood,' according to the rite that celebrates the sharing of food and that has been ours for centuries, perhaps we might remind him that he would not be there if our body and our blood had not given him life, love, spirit' (*Sexes and Genealogies*, 21).

27 I am obviously referring here to the extensive and complex re-writing of Freud by the post-Lacanian French psychoanalytic theorists, including most influentially Julia Kristeva, Luce Irigaray and Hélène Cixous.

28 Louise Schleiner sees Lanyer's community of learned women as both an exemplar and a reflection of Renaissance women's reading groups in which one or more women, often ladies-in-waiting, read to a group of women, many of whom, while listening, engaged in varieties of needlework.

29 See Lewalski's discussion of Anne Clifford and her diary (*Writing Women*, ch. 5, 125–151).

30 See also other instances of women's alliance with the vernacular in chapter 3 of this volume.

31 Elaine Beilin reads these lines as a 'confession of her inability as a writer' (185). Although I agree that this is the effect of these lines at the level of topos, I think they are more rhetorically packed than this.

32 See Hobby (17) and Maclean (20, 24), who cites Cornelius a Lapide and Agrippa. Other writers who emphasize women's superior spiritual gifts are Foxe (*Actes and Monuments*) and William Heale.

33 In a letter to St Eustochum, St Jerome speaks of the female martyrs and ascetics as 'brides of Christ' (Epistle 22). See Clark, 84. It is intriguing to speculate whether Lanyer could have known of these precedents or similar medieval precedents for the erotic imagery used by women writers to describe Christ. See Bynum, 'And Woman His Humanity,' 271.

34 For example, Margaret Fell Fox and Jane Lead, as well as other Quaker women. Julian of Norwich, in her fourteenth-century *Showings*, had also emphasized 'God's motherly bearing, feeding and tending' (vol. 2, 594ff). I find some of these maternal qualities in Lanyer's depiction of Christ, but Janel Mueller argues that 'Lanyer ... does not feminize her Christ in a medieval fashion as maternal. He has, rather, the cultivated graces and virtuous bearing associated with marriageable women of rank in the Renaissance' (235 n. 7). I was fascinated to hear recently a Philadelphia radio program featuring the gospel choir from the Church of Jesus Christ as Wife and Mother.

35 Luce Irigaray draws a connection between Christ's wounds and a woman's vagina, an association that allows women a particular kind of spiritual expressiveness (*Speculum*, 200).

36 The phoenix image was also, of course, regularly exploited in the iconography of the Tudor court.

37 Another seventeenth-century work, *Eliza's Babes*, also suggests that 'through withdrawal from the world in obedience solely to God ... women can attain a measure of self-definition and self-control' (Hobby, 59).

38 Wendy Wall suggests that the erotic quality in Lanyer's descriptions of Christ 'implicitly critiques Petrarchan strategies' (327) and enables the crucifixion to become 'the site for contestations between the sexes, an agonistic moment in history that makes women's virtue visible' (320).

39 See also Simone Roisin.

40 Diane Purkiss has pointed out the use by seventeenth-century women prophets such as Sarah Wight and Anna Trapnel of images of feeding: 'women prophets constantly deployed tropes of hunger, food, feeding and satiation in order to describe their privileged relation to God' (146).

41 Before Lanyer, participants in the pamphlet war defending women against misogynist attack had also regularly defended Eve, and after Lanyer, An Collins, Jane Barker and Bathsua Makin insist that women originally were the means of acquiring knowledge and learning and have since unjustly been excluded from sharing in its fruits by men.

42 A most notable example of this connection is the twelfth-century French historian, Chancellor of the school of Notre Dame, known as Peter the Eater, so-called because of his voracious appetite for reading. See also Regan, 59ff.

43 'J'ai adoré Dieu ma mère' (26) – 'un jeune homme élégant et maternel' (24). 'Ecrire serait nourrir ma propre mère. Lui donner à mon tour mon lait?' (20). 'J'ai été élevée au lait de mots. Je ne me suis laissée nourrir qu'à la voix, aux mots' (27).

44 The French actually says 'le fond de son âme.' It is arguable that knowledge of the depths of one's soul is the fifteenth-century version of self-knowledge.

45 Implications of a witch's crystal ball also seem to dance in and out of these references to the poet's 'glass.'

46 For example, among such books printed before 1611 was the romance *The Mirrour of Princely Deeds and Knighthood*, translated by Margaret Tyler, and featuring prominently a valiant and beautiful heroine. The preface claims that the work is dedicated to 'Ladies or Gentlewomen' (4). Instructive 'mirror' texts for women were written by Thomas Salter, Robert Greene, William Averell, James Yates, Anthony Munday, Philip Stubbes, possibly Stephen Gosson and Peter Colse.

47 See Tilney's injunction that a husband should be a wife's 'dayly looking glasse ... whereto she must alwayes frame hir owne countenance' (E iiiiv).

48 See also Scharfman's argument that narcissism is a healthy means for women to achieve autonomy.

49 The concave mirror and the burning glass are also associated as mystical and visionary symbols in the Renaissance, for instance by Spenser in *The Faerie Queene*, VI, Proem 6: 5–7; 7:19, and Henry More in *Psychathanasia or the Immortality of the Soul*, book 2, canto 2, st. 8.

Chapter 7

Epilogue

So finally I make an end, no longer can I tary. – (Isabella Whitney)

When I am dead ... [my] name in this may live. – (Aemilia Lanyer)

This day ... / In after times, the school of wisdom call. – (Elizabeth Cary)

The epigraph to my conclusion, a pastiche of quotations from the three poets highlighted in this study, captures in admittedly too-brief fashion the conflicting realizations and aspirations of women poets in early modern England. They wrote sometimes as a personal luxury, sometimes hoping for material reward, but always knowing they were not expected to 'tarry' in the world of poetic composition. Their gender demanded of them other more insistent occupations: maternity and wifeliness and domestic work; for some, their social station required that practical efforts more reliable than poetry be directed toward economic survival or enhancement. Yet, despite the humility tropes that conventionally decorated their writing, they aspired to win approving recognition for the poetry which absorbed their skills and energy, perhaps to be manifest immediately in material form, perhaps in the long term in acclaim and even fame. Abandoning our own humility for the moment, scholars of early modern women may claim to have finally established a 'school of wisdom' that has rescued these poets from the obscurity into which they had fallen and has offered them the commendation that is their due. I have endeavored in this study both to learn and teach in this school by exploring the psychoanalytic processes of subjective inscription in the poetry of women writing in early modern England.

When a woman in early modern England took up her pen to write verse, a degree of conscious understanding of herself in relation to her task was certainly at work. She could not fail to know that she was doing something daring, something unexpected, something not wrapped in the blanket of social approval. Her awareness of herself as a writing subject would have been inflected by one or more possible positions. Perhaps in rare cases a confident self-assuredness fostered by her station or wealth or accomplishments might have informed her sensibility, allowing her to dismiss inevitable complaints against her violation of socially approved norms. Perhaps she approached her poetic role rebelliously, discounting the right of patriarchs to restrict her range of skill. Perhaps she was indifferent to outside influence, perhaps even anxious or fearful of retribution. But in almost no case could she have had available a sense of her task as comfortably justified by relaxed cultural acceptance. Although she intended not to heed its behests, early modern culture provided her with clear expectations of her modesty and silence. Whitney embarks on a task proclaimed as 'new'; Cary determines to resist family pressures to read and write for her 'recreation'; Lanyer knows she is doing something 'seldome seene' in women. Engaged in a project one knows is 'new' and 'seldome seene,' which is not muffled by ideological constructions that allow it to be taken for granted, one is forced at least to the level of consciousness that induces some unavoidable questions: Do I want to do this or not? What will people think? What will be the consequences? Choice, and probably the pursuit of pleasure, both factors of subjectivity, are brought into active play.

Yet, no more than ideology is subjectivity unitary or monolithic. It is deeply and ineluctably divided, perhaps particularly so for an early modern woman poet. All of the terms of subjectivity stretch into areas of complicated and largely unconscious pressures and possibilities that divide, disturb and enrich both subjectivity itself and the unreliable language in which it must inscribe itself and by which it must be inscribed. For women, one of the 'languages' in which they are profoundly embedded and where they may access elements of their subjectivity is the construction of their physical embodiment. This understanding, explored in the second chapter of this book, is confirmed in the poetry of Whitney's 'abjection,' in the metaphors of physical mobility that depict Cary's 'errant' subjectivity, and in Lanyer's erotic and Eucharistic merging of her virtuous community's body with the feminized body of Christ.

More usually recognized social systems to which women needed access even to begin to engage with the possibility of subjective inscription are the ideologically coded systems of literacy and education, discussed above in chapter 3. Poetic language is deeply dependent on these systems, providing for women rich worlds of obliquity and metaphor that indirectly access their subjectivity's unconscious and the unconscious feminine recesses of language itself. Whitney's first poetic collection relies on, but at the same time radically undermines, binaried systems of gendered opposition between false men and faithful women. The language of Cary's play divides itself from its apparent intention of praising a chastely virtuous woman, laying bare the divisions in a representative woman's virtue and its alliances with (Herod's and Salome's) error. The language of Lanyer's long poem splits between patronage and book sales, between ideal feminist inclusion and advocacy and the desire for aristocratic support.

It goes without saying that the subjectivity of all women who wrote poetry in early modern England was not cut from the same cloth; the ways in which their subjectivity split were not predictable or duplicable. In this, their subjectivity does not adhere to the logical and empirical requirements of self-identity, reliability and replication, but moves into the spaces of a fluid language outside the masculine Symbolic. Though many early modern women probably shared similar responses to external pressures on their awareness, this sharing did not produce repetitive, assembly-line versions of subjectivity; the variations imply genuine subjectivity. It is not too much to claim that writing, including the writing of poetry by early modern women, nurtures a level of conscious subjectivity. But beyond the control of its user, the allusive and metaphoric language of poetry has a life of its own that taps into the unconscious and will appear to the graphic and phonemic light of day in unexpected forms, trailing unconscious, unintended, social, cultural and personally inflected possibilities that lie waiting in the fissures and sliding spaces of all language: 'In poetic language, [subjective] identity is infused with alterity without completely breaking down' (Oliver, 12). The validity of these claims is tested and supported in the poetic language of Whitney, Cary and Lanyer.

The lived circumstances of the three women whose poetry I have brought forward to display the divided and effective subjectivity I believe characterized women's poetry in this period all exemplify major, likely traumatic, shifts in social position, geographic location, economic circumstance, and occupation. Isabella Whitney grew up in what one imagines as a relatively happy set of family circumstances in a pleasant country house in attractive rural surroundings. Her family belonged to the ranks of minor gentry and had connections to wealthier neighbors. Her relationships with her two brothers and three sisters were close enough to make them addressees of Isabella's later, warmly concerned verse. She was apparently enough esteemed by her parents that she was well enough educated to know, if not love, classical writers. Evidently upon her parents' death and her eldest brother's inheritance of the family possessions, she left her home and, like many other rural gentry, went to London. Here she became a serving-maid. Perhaps this situation was also somewhat enjoyable. She writes that she regretted having offended her mistress and being separated from her, although these responses might have been induced by the anxiety that attended her worryingly reduced circumstances. Her first volume of poetry may have been published in an effort to improve her prospects. Some of her second publication post-dated her presumed imprisonment for debt, and almost certainly embodied a hope of recognition or reward. Severely impecunious, she was forced to leave London, probably as a condition of her release from debtor's prison, and disappeared from view. Her date of death and length of life are unknown.

Elizabeth Cary, unlike Whitney an only child, but also gentry by birth, was raised in much more materially comfortable circumstances than Whitney, perhaps also in a moderately happy situation; although her mother was very severe, her father appears to have been proud of her accomplishments and more indulgent. Her parents' wealth provided her with an aristocratic husband who married her 'for being an heir.' As a wife with the pressures of aristocratic behavior exerted on her, she was divided from her favorite activities of reading and writing. In thirteen years, she became the mother of eleven children. She moved with her husband from England to Ireland, and during the course of her married life more riskily moved from the socially acceptable Protestant English church to forbidden Catholicism. Consequent on her religious transgression, leaving her husband in Ireland she returned to London, where she was forced to replace luxury with poverty, but gladly returned to a studious life of reading and writing. Her writing is not associated with appeals for patronage designed to achieve financial or social favor. Publication of her early poetic play *Mariam* was perhaps an accident, but may have been an act of literary ambition or pride. Her later publications do not seem responsive to the slowly emerging recognition, which Whitney and Lanyer understood, that writing might be made financially lucrative. She died at the age of fifty-four and, memorialized with a marble effigy, was buried in her parents' vault.

Aemilia Lanyer, one of two daughters of an Italian immigrant family, was middling-sort and socially marginal, but was raised in courtly circles close enough to the centers of power that she felt herself favored by the Queen. She was influenced by her family's musical culture and well educated in aristocratic households. As a court dependent, she occupied a somewhat precarious position and, in spite of what she may have hoped, continued to do so after one of the most important nobles in the land chose her publicly for his mistress. Having become pregnant, she was moved from her courtly position into marriage with a member of the Queen's Music. In a reduced financial situation, but aspiring to return to a better one, she turned to writing as an activity that nostalgically asserted her connection with the aristocratic circles from which she was now exiled, and she used those links to seek financial help. Unsuccessful in recapturing her courtly connection, she raised a son, buried a daughter, became a grandmother, was widowed and dispossessed of her husband's income from a hay and grain patent, and opened a school in a wealthy London suburb. She seems to have left London from time to time for visits of varying length to the country estates of her wealthy patrons. Having prevailed in a series of awkward life circumstances, she lived to a good age for her time, dying at the age of seventy-six and able to leave a small inheritance to her grandson.

None of these women lived a life of unvarying peace and plenty. Their social and economic situations altered drastically, in part precipitated by and in part reflecting the upheavals in English culture at large. All moved about, whether between city and country or between England and Ireland. Their levels of independence varied during their lives. In Lanyer's and Cary's cases, we know, their maternal bodies significantly changed their situations, wresting Lanyer from a valued courtly life and Cary from her loved studies. About Whitney we know only that at least for a time poetry seemed a sufficient sublimation for a maternal life. All of the changes in their lives before they came into print undoubtedly loaded material into their unconscious, ready to be tapped by the layered conscious and unconscious levels of their poetry. Those changes that continued to beset Cary and Lanyer beyond the composition of *Mariam* and *Salve Deus Rex Judaeorum* may have enriched other unconscious aspects of their religious, writing and teaching lives. Again, about Whitney, we have no knowledge.

All three of these poets were immersed in a patriarchal world which required a certain capitulation to specifically gendered requirements. Whitney was immediately impacted by her brother's inheritance of her father's estate, Cary by her father's wealth and her husband's social position, Lanyer by her illegitimate maternity, her marriage and her husband's death. The languages of inheritance, law and marriage embroiled them in changes they did not choose and partly wrote their fates. Yet it seems possible to surmise, from the sample of these three women, that something changed in English culture and the world of literary publication between 1567 (Whitney's *Copy of a letter*) and 1611 (Lanyer's *Salve Deus*) that facilitiated access to a quality of subjective inscription that made a space for women's poetic power. It is also arguable, as I have argued here, that these women wrote their way out of the stifling dominance of the masculine Symbolic, discovering in poetry a flexible, divided and errant subjectivity that found ways to access the rich otherness of the linguistic unconscious, facilitating 'otherwise unlikely encounters and unsuspected sources of interaction of experience and knowledge' (Braidotti, 6). As a woman writing at the turn of the twentieth to the twenty-first century, I can only register immense gratification that, for other women writing at the turn of the sixteenth to the seventeenth century, this should have been so.

Works Cited

Acte for thadvauncement of true Religion and for thabolisshment of the contrarie, 1542–3. Statutes of the Realm, 34 and 35. Act of Henry VIII, c.1.

Adamson, J.W. 'The Extent of Literacy in England in the Fifteenth and Sixteenth Centuries: Notes and Conjectures.' *The Library* 4th ser. 10:2 (September, 1929): 163–193.

Adelman, Janet. 'Born of Woman: Fantasies of Maternal Power in *Macbeth*.' In *Cannibals, Witches, and Divorce: Estranging the Renaissance*. Ed. Marjorie Garber. Baltimore: Johns Hopkins University Press, 1987. 90–121.

Agrippa, Henricus Cornelius. *Of the Nobilitie and Excellencie of Womankynde*. Trans. David Clapham. London, 1542.

Alcoff, Linda. 'Cultural Feminism versus Post-Structuralism: The Identity Crisis in Feminist Theory.' *Signs* 13 (1988): 405–436.

Allestree, Richard. *The Ladies Calling*. Oxford, 1673.

Althusser, Louis. 'Ideology and Ideological State Apparatuses.' In *Essays on Ideology*. Ed. Louis Althusser. London: Verso, 1984. 1–60.

Amussen, Susan. 'The Gendering of Popular Culture in Early Modern England.' In *Popular Culture in England c. 1500–1850*. Ed. Tim Harris. New York: St Martin's Press, 1995. 48–68.

———. *An Ordered Society: Gender and Class in Early Modern England*. Oxford: Blackwell, 1988.

An Account of the Tryal, Condemnation, and Execution of Mary Goodenough at the Assizes Held in Oxon. in February 1692. London, 1692.

Andrewes, Lancelot. *The Works of Lancelot Andrewes*. 11 vols. Oxford: Library of Anglo-Catholic Theology, 1854.

Anger, Jane. *Her Protection for Women*. London, 1589. In *Half Humankind*. Ed. Henderson and McManus.

Arenal, Electa and Stacey Schlau. *Untold Sisters*. Albuquerque: University of New Mexico Press, 1989.

Ascham, Roger. *The Scholemaster*. London, 1571.

Askew, Anne. *The Examinations of Anne Askew*. Ed. Elaine Beilin. Oxford: Oxford University Press, 1996.

Astell, Mary. *A Serious Proposal to the Ladies ...* London, 1694.

Aughterson, Kate (ed.). *Renaissance Woman: A Sourcebook*. London: Routledge, 1995.

The Autobiography of Thomas Whythorne. Ed. James M. Osborn. London: Oxford University Press, 1962.

Averell, William. *A dyall for dainty darlings, rockt in the cradle of securitie. A glasse for all disobedient sonnes to looke in. A myrrour for vertuous maydes*. London, 1584.

Bakhtin, Mikhail. *Rabelais and His World*. Trans. Helene Iswolsky. Cambridge, MA: MIT Press, 1968.

Barash, Carol. *English Women's Poetry 1649–1741*. Oxford: Clarendon, 1996.

Barker, Arthur. 'An Apology for the Study of Renaissance Poetry.' In *Literary Views*. Ed. Carroll Camden. Chicago: University of Chicago Press, 1964. 15–43.

Barker, Francis. *The Tremulous Private Body*. London: Methuen, 1984.

Barker, Jane. *Poetical Recreations*. London, 1688.

Barroll, Leeds. 'Looking for Patrons.' In *Aemilia Lanyer: Gender, Genre, and the Canon*. Ed. Marshall Grossman. Lexington: University of Kentucky Press, 1998. 29–48.

Barthes, Roland. *The Fashion System*. Berkeley: University of California Press, 1983.

Bates, Catherine. *The Rhetoric of Courtship in Elizabethan Language and Literature*. Cambridge: Cambridge University Press, 1992.

Bath, Michael. *Speaking Pictures*. London: Longman, 1994.

Battus, Bartholomeus. *The Christian Mans Closet*. London, 1581.

Bauman, T. *Let Your Words Be Few: Symbolism of Speaking and Silence Among 17th-Century Quakers*. Cambridge: Cambridge University Press, 1983.

Beier, Lucinda. *Sufferers and Healers: The Experience of Illness in Seventeenth-Century England*. London and New York: Routledge, 1987.

Beilin, Elaine. *Redeeming Eve: Women Writers of the English Renaissance*. Princeton: Princeton University Press, 1987.

———. 'Writing Public Poetry: Humanism and the Woman Writer.' *MLQ* 51 (1990): 249–271.

Bell, Ilona. 'In Defense of their Lawful Liberty: *A Letter Sent by the Maydens of London*.' In *Women, Writing, and the Reproduction of Culture*. Ed. Mary E. Burke et al. Syracuse: Syracuse University Press, 2000. 177–192.

———. 'Women in the Lyric Dialogue of Courtship: Whitney's *Admonition to al young Gentilwomen* and Donne's "The Legacie".' In *Representing Women in Renaissance England*. Ed. Claude J. Summers and Ted-Larry Pebworth. Columbia: University of Missouri Press, 1997. 76–92.

Belsey, Catherine. 'Constructing the Subject: Deconstructing the Text.' In *Feminist Criticism and Social Change*. Ed. Judith Newton and Deborah Rosenfelt. New York: Methuen, 1985. 45–64.

Benedict, Barbara M. *Making the Modern Reader: Cultural Mediation in Early Modern Literary Anthologies*. Princeton: Princeton University Press, 1996.

Benhabib, Seyla. 'Feminism and the Question of Postmodernism.' Paper delivered for the Greater Philadelphia Philosophy Consortium, Haverford College, September, 1990.

Bennett, Dorcas. *Good and Seasonable Counsel*. London, 1670.

Bennett, H.S. *English Books and Readers 1475–1557*. Cambridge: Cambridge University Press, 1952.

———. *English Books and Readers 1558–1603*. Cambridge: Cambridge University Press, 1965.

———. *English Books and Readers 1603–1640*. Cambridge: Cambridge University Press, 1970.

Benson, Pamela Joseph. *The Invention of the Renaissance Woman: The Challenge of Female Independence in the Literature and Thought of Italy and England*. University Park, PA: Pennsylvania State University Press, 1992.

Berger, Ronald M. *The Most Necessary Luxuries: The Mercers' Company of Coventry, 1550–1680*. University Park, PA: Pennsylvania State University Press, 1993.

Billingsley, Martin. *The Pens Excellencie or The Secretaries Delighte*. London, 1618.

Blodgett, Harriet. *Centuries of Female Days: Englishwomen's Private Diaries*. New Brunswick: Rutgers University Press, 1988.

Borde, Andrew. *The breviary of helthe for all maner of sycknesses and diseases*. London, 1547.

Borin, Francoise. 'Judging by Images.' In *A History of Women in the West: Renaissance and Enlightenment Paradoxes*. Ed. Natalie Zemon Davis and Arlette Farge. Series eds. Georges Duby and Michelle Perrot. Cambridge, MA: Belknap Press of Harvard University Press, 1993. 187–254.

Bowen, Barbara. 'Aemilia Lanyer and the Invention of White Womanhood.' In *Maids and Mistresses, Cousins and Queens*. Ed. Susan Frye and Karen Robertson. New York: Oxford University Press, 1999. 274–303.

Bradstreet, Anne. 'The Author to Her Book.' In *The Complete Works of Anne Bradstreet*. Ed. Joseph R. McElrath Jr. and Allan P. Robb. Boston: Twayne, 1981.

Braidotti, Rosi. *Nomadic Subjects*. New York: Columbia University Press, 1994.

Brant, Clare and Diane Purkiss (eds). *Women, Texts, and Histories 1575–1760*. London: Routledge, 1992.

Brathwait[e], Richard. *A Boulster Lecture*. London, 1631.

———. *The English Gentleman and the English Gentlewoman*. London, 1641.

———. *The English Gentlewoman*. London, 1631.

Bray, Alan. 'Homosexuality and the Signs of Male Friendship in Elizabethan England.' In *Queering the Renaissance*. Ed. Jonathan Goldberg. Durham, NC: Duke University Press, 1994. 40–61.

———. *Homosexuality in Renaissance England*. London: Gay Men's Press, 1982.

Breward, Christopher. *The Culture of Fashion: A New History of Fashionable Dress*. Manchester: Manchester University Press, 1994.

A Brief Description of the Notorious Life of J. Lamb. Testimony of Mabel Swinnerton before the King's Bench. London, 1628.

Brink, Jean R. 'Educating Women and the Lower Orders.' In *'The Muses Female Are': Martha Moulsworth and Other Women Writers of the English Renaissance*.

Ed. Robert C. Evans and Anne. C. Little. West Cornwall, CT: Locust Hill Press, 1995. 181–188.

Broadview Anthology of Seventeenth-Century Verse and Prose. Ed. Alan Rudrum, Joseph Black and Holly Faith Nelson. Toronto: Broadview Press, 2000.

Brown, David. *The New Invention Instituted Calligraphia*. St Andrews, 1622.

Bruni, Leonardo. *Humanistische-Philosophische Schriften mit einer Chronologie seiner Werke und Briefe*. Ed. Hans Baron. Leipzig: B.G. Teubner, 1928.

Burke, Peter. 'The Self from Petrarch to Descartes.' In *Rewriting the Self: Histories from the Renaissance to the Present*. Ed. Roy Porter. London and New York: Routledge, 1997. 17–28.

Burton, Robert. *The Anatomy of Melancholy*. Ed. Floyd Dell and Paul Jordan-Smith. New York: Tudor Publishing, 1955.

Butler, Judith. *Bodies that Matter*. New York: Routledge, 1993.

Bynum, Caroline. ' "And Woman His Humanity" Female Imagery in the Religious Writings of the Later Middle Ages.' In *Gender and Religion*. Ed. Caroline Walker Bynum, Stevan Harrell and Paula Richman. Boston: Beacon, 1986. 257–288.

———. *Jesus as Mother*. Berkeley: University of California Press, 1982.

C.N. *An Apologie for Women: Or Womens Defence*. London, 1620.

Cahn, Susan. *Industry of Devotion*. New York: Columbia University Press, 1987.

Callaghan, Dympna. 'Re-reading Elizabeth Cary's *The Tragedie of Mariam, Faire Queene of Jewry*.' In *Women, Race, and Writing in the Early Modern Period*. Ed. Margo Hendricks and Patricia Parker. London and New York: Routledge, 1994. 163–177.

Carey, Mary. *The Little Horns Doom and Downfall*. London, 1651.

Carroll, Kenneth. 'Early Quakers and "Going Naked as a Sign."' *Quaker History* 67 (1978): 69–87.

Cary, Elizabeth. *The Life*. In *The Tragedy of Mariam, The Fair Queen of Jewry with The Lady Falkland: Her Life by One of her Daughters*. Ed. Barry Weller and Margaret Ferguson. Berkeley: University of California Press, 1994. 183–275.

———. *The Reply of the Most Illustrious Cardinall of Perron to the Answeare of the Most Excellent King of Great Britain*. Douai, 1630.

———. *The Tragedy of Mariam, Faire Queen of Jewry with The Lady Falkland: Her Life by One of her Daughters*. Ed. Barry Weller and Margaret Ferguson. Berkeley: University of California Press, 1994.

Castiglione, Baldassare. *Il libro del cortegiano*. Trans. Sir Thomas Hoby, *The Courtyer*. London, 1528.

Catty, Jocelyn. *Writing Rape, Writing Women in Early Modern England: 'Unbridled Speech.'* London: Macmillan; New York: St Martin's, 1999.

Cavendish, Margaret. 'The Convent of Pleasure.' In *Playes Never Before Printed*. London, 1668.

———. *The Life of the thrice noble, high and puissant prince William Cavendishe, Duke, Marquess and Earl of Newcastle* ... London, 1667.

——. *The Philosophical and Physical Opinions*. London, 1655.

——. *Natures Pictures*. London, 1656. Includes 'True Relation of my birth, breeding, and Life.'

——. *Poems and Fancies*. London, 1653.

——. *Sociable Letters*. London, 1664.

Cellier, Elizabeth. *Malice Defeated*. London, 1680.

——. *To Dr. — an answer.* London, 1688.

The Challenge Sent by a Young Lady to Sir Thomas &c. Or The Female War. London, 1697.

Chamberlain, John. *The Letters of John Chamberlain*. Ed. Norman Egbert McClure. Philadelphia: American Philosophical Society, 1939.

Charlton, Kenneth. *Education in Renaissance England*. Toronto: University of Toronto Press, 1965.

——. *Women, Religion and Education in Early Modern England*. London and New York, 1999.

Chartier, Roger. 'The Practical Impact of Writing.' In *A History of Private Life*. Ed. Roger Chartier. Trans. Arthur Goldhammer. Vol. 3. Cambridge: Harvard University Press, 1989. 111–159.

Chawaf, Chantal. 'La chair linguistique.' Trans. Yvonne Rochette-Ozzello. In *New French Feminisms*. Ed. Elaine Marks and Isabelle de Courtivron. Amherst: University of Massachusetts Press, 1980. 177–178.

Cixous, Hélène. 'The Laugh of the Medusa.' Trans. Keith Cohen and Paula Cohen. In *The Signs Reader*. Eds Elizabeth Abel and Emily K. Abel. Chicago: University of Chicago Press, 1983. 279–297.

——. *The Newly-Born Woman*. Trans. Betsy Wing. Minneapolis: University of Minnesota Press, 1986.

——. *La Venue à l'écriture*. Paris: U.G. d'Editions, 1977.

Clark, Alice. *Working Life of Women in the Seventeenth Century*. London: Routledge, 1919 and 1982.

Clark, Elizabeth. 'Devil's Gateway and the Bride of Christ: Women in the early Christian World.' In *Women and the New Academy*. Ed. Jean F. O'Barr. Madison: University of Wisconsin Press, 1989. 81–102.

Clark, Peter. *Country Towns in Pre-Industrial England*. New York: St Martin's Press, 1982.

——. 'The Ownership of Books in England 1560–1640: The Example of Some Kentish Townsfolk.' In *Schooling and Society: Studies in the History of Education*. Ed. Laurence Stone. Baltimore: Johns Hopkins University Press, 1976. 95–111.

Clark, Sandra. *The Elizabethan Pamphleteers: Popular Moralistic Pamphlets 1580–1640*. Rutherford, NJ: Fairleigh Dickinson University Press, 1983.

Clark, Stuart. 'Inversion, Misrule, and the Meaning of Witchcraft.' *Past and Present* 80 (1980): 98–127.

Clarke, Samuel. *The Second Part: Containing the Lives of Gustavus Ericson, King of Sweden ... as also divers other Christians ...* London, 1661.

Clifford, Anne. *The Diary of the Lady Anne Clifford (1590–1676)*. Ed. Vita Sackville West. London: Heinemann, 1923.

Clinton, Elizabeth. *The Countesse of Lincolnes Nurserie*. London, 1622.

Coiro, Ann Baynes. 'Writing in Service: Sexual Politics and Class Position in the Poetry of Aemilia Lanyer and Ben Jonson.' *Criticism* 35 (Summer, 1993): 357–376.

Collins, An. *Divine Songs and Meditacions*. London, 1653.

Colse, Peter. *Penelopes complaint: or, a mirrour for wanton minions*. London, 1596.

Craveri, Benedetta. 'Women in Retreat.' Review of *A History of Women in the West*. Ed. Arlette Farge and Natalie Zemon Davis. *New York Review of Books*. 19 December 1991: 67–71.

Crawford, Patricia. 'Attitudes to Menstruation in 17th-Century England.' *Past and Present* (1981): 47–73.

———. 'The Construction and Experience of Maternity in 17th-Century England.' In *Women as Mothers in Pre-Industrial England*. Ed. Valerie Fildes. London: Routledge, 1990. 3–38.

———. 'Printed Advertisements for Women Medical Practitioners in London, 1670–1710.' *Bulletin of the Society of the Social History of Medicine* 35 (1984): 66–90.

———. 'Women's Published Writings 1600–1700.' In *Women in English Society 1500–1800*. Ed. Mary Prior. London: Methuen, 1985. 211–282.

Cressy, David. *Literacy and the Social Order: Reading and Writing in Tudor and Stuart England*. Cambridge: Cambridge University Press, 1980.

———. 'Literacy in Context: Meaning and Measurement in Early Modern England.' In *Consumption and the World of Goods*. Ed. John Brewer and Roy Porter. London: Routledge, 1993. 305–319.

———. 'Literacy in Seventeenth-Century England: More Evidence.' *Journal of Interdisciplinary History* 8 (1977): 141–150.

Crooke, Helkiah. *A Description of the Body of Man*. London, 1615.

Cropper, Elizabeth. 'The Beauty of Woman: Problems in the Rhetoric of Renaissance Portraiture.' In *Rewriting the Renaissance: The Discourses of Sexual Difference in Early Modern Europe*. Ed. Margaret Ferguson, Maureen Quilligan and Nancy Vickers. Chicago: University of Chicago Press, 1986. 175–190.

Culpeper, Nicholas. *Arts Masterpiece*. London, 1660.

———. *Directory for Midwives*. London, 1651.

Curtius, Ernst Robert. *European Literature and the Latin Middle Ages*. New York: Harper, 1953.

Da Barbaro, Francesco. *De Re Uxoria. The Civilization of the Renaissance*. Ed. K.R. Bartlett. Lexington, MA: D.C. Heath, 1992.

Daly, Peter M. *Literature in the Light of the Emblem*. Toronto: University of Toronto Press, 1979.

Daniel, Samuel. *A Defence of Rime entituled Observations in the art of English Poesie, 1603*. Ed. G.B. Harrison. New York: Barnes and Noble, 1966.

Darnton, Robert. 'History of Reading.' In *New Perspectives on Historical Writing*. Ed. Peter Burke. University. Park, PA: Pennsylvania State University Press, 1992. 140–167.

Davis, Natalie Zemon. *Society and Culture in Early Modern France*. Stanford: Stanford University Press, 1975.

Davy, Sarah. *Heaven Realiz'd*. London, 1670.

De Pizan, Christine. *The Book of the City of Ladies*. Trans. Earl Jeffrey Richards. New York: Persea Books, 1982.

Derrida, Jacques. *Of Grammatology*. Trans. Gayatri Chakravorty Spivak. Baltimore: Johns Hopkins University Press, 1976.

——. *Writing and Difference*. Trans. Alan Bass. Chicago: University of Chicago Press, 1978.

Dixon, Laurinda. *Perilous Chastity: Women and Illness in Pre-Enlightenment Art and Medicine*. Ithaca: Cornell University Press, 1995.

Dolan, Frances. 'Reading, Writing, and Other Crimes.' In *Feminist Readings of Early Modern Culture: Emerging Subjects*. Ed. Valerie Traub, M. Lindsay Kaplan and Dympna Callaghan. Cambridge: Cambridge University Press, 1996. 142–167.

——. 'Taking the Pencil Out of God's Hand: Art, Nature, and the Face-Painting Debate in Early Modern England.' *PMLA* 108 (March 1993): 224–239.

Dollimore, Jonathan. *Sexual Dissidence*. Oxford: Clarendon Press, 1991.

Donawerth, Jane. 'Women's Poetry and the Tudor-Stuart System of Gift Exchange.' In *Women, Writing, and the Reproduction of Culture in Tudor and Stuart Britain*. Ed. Mary E. Burke et al. Syracuse: Syracuse University Press, 2000. 3–18.

Donovan, Josephine (ed.). *The Poems of Lady Mary Wroth*. Baton Rouge: Louisiana University Press, 1983.

——. 'Toward a Women's Poetics.' In *Feminist Issues in Literary Scholarship*. Ed. Shari Benstock. Bloomington: Indiana University Press, 1987. 98–109.

Dowriche, Anne. *The French Historie*. London, 1589.

Du Bosc, Jacques. *The Compleat Woman*. London, 1639.

Duncon, John. *A Letter Containing Many Remarkable Passages in the Most Holy Life Of the Late Lady, Letice, Vi-Countess Falkland, Written to the Lady Morison at Gt. Tew in Oxfordshire*. 2nd edn. London, 1649.

Eccles, Audrey. *Obstetrics and Gynaecology in Tudor and Stuart England*. Kent, Ohio: Kent State University Press, 1982.

Eisenstein, Elizabeth. *The Printing Revolution in Early Modern Europe*. Cambridge: Cambridge University Press, 1983.

Eliza's Babes: or the Virgin-Offering. London, 1652.

Elliott, Valerie. 'Single Women in the London Marriage Market: Age, Status, and Mobility 1598–1619.' In *Marriage and Society: Studies in the Social History of Marriage*. Ed. R.B. Outhwaite. New York: St Martin's Press, 1981. 81–100.

Elyot, Thomas. *Castell of Helth*. London, 1541.

——. *Defence of Good Women*. Facsimile. University Microfilms, University of Michigan. Oxford, Ohio: Anchor Press, 1940.

Erasmus, Desiderius. *A Devout Treatise Upon the Paternoster*. Trans. Margaret Roper. Preface Richard Hyrde. London, 1526.

———. *Erasmus on Women*. Ed. Erika Rummel. Toronto: University of Toronto Press, 1996.

———. *A Lytell Booke of Good Maners for Chyldren*. London, 1532.

Erickson, Amy Louise. *Women and Property in Early Modern England*. London: Routledge, 1993.

Evans, Katharine and Sarah Chevers. *This is a Short Relation of Some of the Cruel Sufferings (for the Truths Sake) of Katharine Evans and Sarah Chevers*. London, 1662.

Evett, David. *Literature and the Visual Arts in Tudor England*. Athens: University of Georgia Press, 1990.

Ezell, Margaret. 'The Myth of Judith Shakespeare: Creating the Canon of Women's Literature.' *NLH* 21 (1990): 579–592.

———. *Writing Women's Literary History*. Baltimore: Johns Hopkins University Press, 1993.

Fallopio, Gabriele. *Observationes Anatomicae*. In *Opera Omnia*. Frankfurt, 1600.

Fehrenbach, R.J. 'Isabella Whitney and the Popular Miscellanies of Richard Jones.' *Cahiers* 19 (April, 1981): 85–87.

———. 'Isabella Whitney, Sir Hugh Plat, Geoffrey Whitney, and "Sister Eldershae".' *ELN* 21 (September 1983): 7–11.

———. '*A Letter sent by Maydens of London* (1567).' *ELR* 14 (1984): 285–304.

Fell, Margaret. *Womens speaking justified*. London, 1666.

Ferguson, Margaret. 'A Room Not Their Own: Renaissance Women as Readers and Writers.' In *The Comparative Perspective on Literature: Approaches to Theory and Practice*. Ed. Clayton Koelb and Susan Noakes. Ithaca: Cornell University Press, 1988. 93–116.

———. 'Renaissance Concepts of the "Woman Writer".' In *Women and Literature In Britain 1500–1700*. Ed. Helen Wilcox. London: Cambridge University Press, 1996. 143–168.

———. 'Running on with Almost Public Voice: The Case of "E. C." ' In *Tradition and the Talents of Women*. Ed. Florence Howe. Urbana: University of Illinois Press, 1991. 37–67.

———. 'The Spectre of Resistance: *The Tragedy of Mariam* (1613).' In *Staging the Renaissance: Reinterpretation of Elizabethan and Jacobean Drama*. Ed. David Scott Kastan and Peter Stallybras. New York and London: Routledge, 1991. 235–250.

Ferguson, Moira. *First Feminists*. Bloomington: Indiana University Press, 1985.

Fermor, Sharon. 'Movement and Gender in Sixteenth-Century Italian Painting.' In *The Body Imaged*. Ed. Kathleen Adler and Marcia Pointon. Cambridge: Cambridge University Press, 1993. 129–145.

Ferry, Anne. *The 'Inward Language': Sonnets of Wyatt, Sidney, Shakespeare, Donne*. Chicago: University of Chicago Press, 1983.

Fiennes, Celia. *The Journeys of Celia Fiennes*. Ed. Christopher Morris. London: Cresset Press, 1949.

Fildes, Valerie. *Breasts, Bottles, and Babies: A History of Infant Feeding*. Edinburgh: Edinburgh University Press, 1985.

Firenzuola, Agnolo. 'Dialogo delle Bellezze delle Donne.' In *Prose di M. Agnolo Firenzuola Fierentino*. Florence, 1548.

Fisher, Sheila and Janet Halley. 'The Lady Vanishes: The Problem of Women's Absence in Late Medieval and Renaissance Texts.' In *Seeking the Woman in Late Medieval and Renaissance Writings*. Ed. Sheila Fisher and Janet Halley. Knoxville: University of Tennessee Press, 1989. 1–17.

Flax, Jane. *Disputed Subjects: Essays in Psychoanalysis, Politics, and Philosophy*. London and New York: Routledge, 1993.

Fleming, Juliet. 'Dictionary English and the Female Tongue.' In *Privileging Gender in Early Modern England*. Ed. Jean R. Brink. Kirksville, MO: Northeast Missouri State University Press, 1993. 175–204.

———. 'Graffiti, Grammatology, and the Age of Shakespeare.' In *Renaissance Culture and the Everyday*. Ed. Patricia Fumerton and Simon Hunt. Philadelphia: University of Pennsylvania Press, 1999. 315–351.

———. 'The Ladies' Man and the Age of Elizabeth.' In *Sexuality and Gender in Early Modern Europe*. Ed. James Grantham Turner. Cambridge: Cambridge University Press, 1993. 158–181.

Florio, John. *The Essayes, or Morall, Politike and Militarie Discourses of Lo: Michaell de Montaigne*. London, 1603.

The Floures of Philosophie (1572) by Hugh Plat and A Sweet Nosgay (1573) and The Copy of a letter (1567) by Isabella Whitney. Ed. Richard Panofsky. Delmar, NY: Scholars' Facsimiles and Reprints, 1982.

Fontaine, Nicolas. *The Womans Doctour*. London, 1652.

Foster, Donald. 'Resurrecting the Author: Elizabeth Tanfield Cary.' In *Privileging Gender in Early Modern England*. Ed. Jean R. Brink. Kirkville, MO: Northern Missouri State University Press, 1993. 141–173.

Foucault, Michel. 'The Discourse of Language.' In *The Archeology of Knowledge*. New York: Harper and Row, 1976. 215–237.

———. 'Language to Infinity.' In *Language, Counter-Memory, Practice*. Trans. Donald F. Bouchard and Sherry Simon. Ed. Donald F. Bouchard. Ithaca, NY: Cornell University Press, 1977. 53–67.

———. *Michel Foucault: Beyond Structuralism and Hermeneutics*. Ed. Herbert L. Dreyfus and Paul Rabinow. Chicago: University of Chicago Press, 1983.

———. *The Use of Pleasure: Vol. 2 The History of Sexuality*. Trans. Robert Hurley. New York: Pantheon, 1985.

———. 'What is an Author?' In *Language, Counter-Memory, Practice*. Trans. Donald F. Bouchard and Sherry Simon. Ed. Donald F. Bouchard. Ithaca, NY: Cornell University Press, 1977. 141–160.

Forster, Mary et al. *These Several papers was Sent to the Parliament*. London, 1659.

Foxe, John. *Actes and monuments of matters most special and memorable*. London, 1641.

Fraser, Antonia. *The Weaker Vessel*. New York: Knopf, 1984.

Freke, Elizabeth. *Mrs Elizabeth Freke, Her Diary: 1671 to 1714*. Ed. Mary Carbery. Cork: Guy, 1913.

Freud, Sigmund. *Civilization and its Discontents*. New York: Norton, 1961.

Friedman, Alice T. 'Inside/Out: Women, Domesticity, and the Pleasure of the City.' In *Material London*. Ed. Lena Corwen Orlin. University of Pennsylvania Press, 2000. 232–250.

Frye, Marilyn. *The Politics of Reality*. Trumansburg, NY: Crossing Press, 1983.

Fumerton, Patricia. *Cultural Aesthetics: Renaissance Literature and the Practice of Social Ornament*. Chicago: University of Chicago Press, 1991.

Gardiner, Dorothy. *English Girlhood at School: A Study of Women's Education Through Twelve Centuries*. Oxford: Oxford University Press, 1929.

Gargill, Anne. *A Brief Discovery of That Which is Called the Popish Religion*. London, 1656.

Gatens, Moira. 'Towards a Feminist Philosophy of the Body.' In *Crossing Boundaries: Feminisms and the Critique of Knowledges*. Ed. Barbara Caine, E.A. Grosz and Marie de Lepervanche. Sydney: Allen and Unwin, 1988. 59–70.

Gee, James Paul. 'The Legacies of Literacy: From Plato to Freire through Harvey Graff.' *Harvard Educational Review* 58 (1988): 195–211.

Gent, Lucy and Nigel Llewellyn (eds). *Renaissance Bodies: The Human Figure in English Culture c. 1540–1660*. London: Reaktion Books, 1990.

The Gentlewomans Companion. London, 1675.

George, Margaret. *Women in the First Capitalist Society: Experiences in Seventeenth-Century England*. Urbana: University of Illinois Press, 1988.

Giddens, Anthony. *Central Problems in Social Theory: Action, Structure, and Contradiction in Social Analysis*. Berkeley: University of California Press, 1979.

Gilbert, Sandra and Susan Gubar (eds). *The Norton Anthology of Literature by Women*. New York: Norton, 1985.

Gillis, John. *For Better, For Worse*. Oxford: Oxford University Press, 1985.

Ginnor, Sarah. *The Womans Almanack: or, Prognostication for ever ... With several Predictions very useful for the Female Sex*. London, 1659.

Giroux, Henry. 'Literacy, Pedagogy, and the Politics of Difference.' *College Literature* 19 (1992): 1–11.

Goldberg, Jonathan. *Desiring Women Writing*. Stanford: Stanford University Press, 1997.

———. *Writing Matter: From the Hands of the English Renaissance*. Stanford: Stanford University Press, 1990.

Goreau, Angeline. *The Whole Duty of a Woman: Female Writers in Seventeenth-Century England*. New York: Doubleday, 1984.

A Gorgeous Gallery of Gallant Inventions (1578). Ed. Hyder Rollins. Cambridge: Harvard University Press, 1926.

Gosson, Stephen (?). *A glasse, to viewe the pride of vainglorious women*. London, 1595.

Gosynhill, Edward. 'The Schoolhouse of Women.' In *Half Humankind*. Ed. Henderson and McManus.

Gouge, William. *Domesticall Duties*. London, 1622.

Grabes, Herbert. *The Mutable Glass*. Cambridge: Cambridge University Press, 1982.

Graff, Harvey. *The Legacies of Literacy: Continuities and Contradictions in Western Culture and Society*. Bloomington: Indiana University Press, 1987.

Grafton, Anthony and Lisa Jardine. *From Humanism to the Humanities: Education and the Liberal Arts in Fifteenth and Sixteenth-Century Europe*. Harvard: Harvard University Press, 1986.

Graham, Elspeth. 'Women's Writing and the Self.' In *Women and Literature in Britain 1500–1700*. Ed. Helen Wilcox. Cambridge: Cambridge University Press, 1996. 209–233.

——, Hilary Hinds, Elaine Hobby and Helen Wilcox (eds). *Her Own Life: Autobiographical Writings by Seventeenth-Century Englishwomen*. London: Routledge, 1989.

Greenblatt, Stephen. 'Psychoanalysis and Renaissance Culture.' In *Literary Theory / Renaissance Texts*. Ed. Patricia Parker and David Quint. Baltimore: Johns Hopkins University Press, 1986. 210–224.

Greene, Robert. *Mamilia. A mirrour or looking-glasse for the ladies of Englande*. London, 1583.

——. *Penelopes web. Where, in a christall myrror of feminine perfection represents to the viewe of every one those vertues and graces, which more curiously beautifies the mynd of women* ... London, 1587.

Greer, Germaine et al. (eds). *Kissing the Rod: An Anthology of 17th-Century Women's Verse*. London: Virago, 1988.

Grieco, Sara. *Ange ou diablesse: La representation de la femme au XVIe siecle*. Paris: Flammarion, 1991.

Grossman, Marshall (ed.). *Aemilia Lanyer: Gender, Genre, and the Canon*. University Press of Kentucky, 1998.

Grosz, Elizabeth. 'Bodies and Knowledges: Feminism and the Crisis of Reason.' In *Feminist Epistemologies*. Ed. Linda Alcoff and Elizabeth Potter. London, Routledge, 1993. 187–215.

——. *Sexual Subversions*. Sydney: Allen and Unwin, 1989.

Grundy, Isobel. 'Women's History? Writings by English Nuns.' In *Women, Writing, History: 1640–1740*. Ed. Isobel Grundy and Susan Wiseman. Athens, GA: University of Georgia Press, 1992. 126–138.

Grymeston, Elizabeth. *Miscelanea, Meditations, Memoratives*. London, 1604.

Guillemeau, Jacques. *Child-Birth*. London, 1612.

Guillen, Claudio. 'Notes Toward the Study of the Renaissance Letter.' In *Renaissance Genres: Essays on Theory, History, and Interpretation*. Ed. Barbara Kiefer Lewalski. Cambridge: Harvard University Press, 1986. 70–101.

Gunn, Alan. *The Mirror of Love: A Reinterpretation of 'The Romance of the Rose.'* Lubbock: Texas Technology Press, 1952.

Gutierrez, Nancy. 'Valuing *Mariam*: Genre Study and Feminist Analysis.' *TSWL* 10 (1991): 233–251.

Hackett, Helen. '"A book, and solitariness": Melancholia, Gender and Literary Subjectivity in Mary Wroth's *Urania*.' In *Renaissance Configurations: Voices/ Bodies/Spaces, 1580–1690*. Ed. Gordon McMullan. New York: St Martin's, 1998. 64–85.

Hageman, Elizabeth. 'Women's Poetry in Early Modern Britain.' In *Women and Literature in Britain 1500–1700*. Ed. Helen Wilcox. Cambridge: Cambridge University Press, 1996. 190–208.

——— and Sara Jayne Steen. 'From the Editors.' *Shakespeare Quarterly* 47.4 (Winter 1996): v–viii. Special issue: *Teaching Judith Shakespeare*.

Hake, Edward. *A Touchestone for this Time Present*. London, 1574.

Hall, David. 'The Uses of Literacy in New England, 1600–1850.' In *Printing and Society in Early America*. Eds William L. Joyce et al. Worcester: American Antiquarian Society, 1983. 1–47.

A Handful of Pleasant Delights (1584). Ed. Hyder Rollins. New York: Dover, 1965.

Hannay, Margaret. *Philip's Phoenix: Mary Sidney, Countess of Pembroke*. New York: Oxford University Press, 1990.

Harington, John. *Nugae Antiquae*. Ed. Henry Harington. London: Vernon and Hood, 1804.

Hartsock, Nancy. 'The Feminist Standpoint: Developing the Ground for a Specifically Feminist Historical Materialism.' In *Discovering Reality*. Ed. S. Harding and M.M. Hintikka. Dondrecai, Holland; Boston; London: D. Reidel, 1983. 283–310.

———. 'Re-Thinking Modernism: Minority vs. Majority Theories.' *Cultural Critique* 7 (Fall, 1987): 187–206.

Harvey, Elizabeth. *Ventriloquized Voices: Feminist Theory and English Renaissance Texts*. London and New York: Routledge, 1992.

Haselkorn, Anne and Betty Travitsky (eds). *The Renaissance Englishwoman in Print*. Amherst: University of Masschusetts Press, 1990.

Haug, Frigga. *Female Sexualization*. Trans. Erika Carter. London: Verso, 1987.

Heale, William. *An Apology for Women*. Oxford, 1609.

Heilbrun, Carolyn. *Writing a Woman's Life*. New York: Ballantine, 1988.

Henderson, Katherine Usher and Barbara F. McManus (eds). *Half Humankind: Contexts and Texts of the Controversy about Women in England 1540–1640*. Urbana: University of Illinois Press, 1988.

Her Own Life: Autobiographical Writings by Seventeenth-Century Englishwomen. Ed. Elspeth Graham, Hilary Hinds, Elaine Hobby and Helen Wilcox. London: Routledge, 1989.

Herrup, Cynthia. *A House in Gross Disorder: Sex, Law, and the Second Earl of Castlehaven*. Oxford: Oxford University Press, 1998.

Herz, Judith Scherer. 'Aemilia Lanyer and the Pathos of Literary History.' In *Representing Women in Renaissance England*. Ed. Claude Summers and Ted-Larry Pebworth. Kansas City: University of Missouri Press, 1997. 121–135.

Hester, Marianne. *Lewd Women and Wicked Witches*. London and New York: Routledge, 1992.

Heywood, Thomas. *Nine Books of Various History Concerning Women*. London, 1624.

Hic Mulier; or The Man-Woman. London, 1620.

Hildegarde von Bingen. *Causae et Curae*. Ed. Paul Kaiser. Leipzig: B. G. Teuliner, 1903.

Hill, Christopher. *The World Turned Upside Down*. London: Temple Smith, 1972.

Hincks, Elizabeth. *The Poor Widows Mite*. London, 1671.

Hobby, Elaine. '"Discourse so Unsavory": Women's Published Writings of the 1650s.' In *Women, Writing, History: 1640–1740*. Ed. Isobel Grundy and Susan Wiseman. Athens: University of Georgia Press, 1992. 16–32.

———. *Virtue of Necessity: English Women's Writing 1649–88*. Anne Arbor: Michigan University Press, 1989.

Hoby, Margaret. *Diary of Lady Margaret Hoby*. Ed. Dorothy M. Meads. London: Routledge, 1930.

Hogrefe, Pearl. *Tudor Women: Commoners and Queens*. Ames, Iowa: Iowa State University Press, 1975.

Hollander, Anne. *Seeing Through Clothes*. Berkeley: University of California Press, 1993.

Holm, Janis Butler. 'Struggling with the Letter: Vives' Preface to the *Instruction of a Christen Woman*.' In *Contending Kingdoms*. Ed. Marie-Rose Logan and Peter L. Rudnytsky. Detroit: Wayne State University Press, 1991. 265–297.

Holmes, Martin. *Proud Northern Lady: Lady Anne Clifford, 1590–1676*. London: Phillimore, 1975.

Horne, Robert. *Christian Governour*. London, 1614.

Hufton, Olwen. *The Prospect Before Her: History of Women in Western Europe 1500–1800*. New York: Knopf, 1996.

———. 'Women, Work, and the Family.' In *History of Women in the West: Renaissance and Enlightenment Paradoxes*. Ed. Arlette Farge and Natalie Zemon Davis. Vol 3. Cambridge, MA: Harvard University Press, 1993. 15–45.

Hughey, Ruth. *Cultural Interests of Women in England from 1524 to 1640 Indicated in the Writings of Women*. Unpublished dissertation. Cornell University, 1932.

Hull, Suzanne. *Chaste, Silent, and Obedient: English Books for Women 1475–1640*. San Marino, CA: Huntington Library, 1982.

Hutchinson, Lucy. 'The Life of Mrs Lucy Hutchinson, By Herself, A Fragment.' In *Memoirs Of the Life of Colonel Hutchinson*. Ed. James Sutherland. London: Oxford University Press, 1973.

Hutson, Lorna. 'Why the Lady's Eyes are Nothing Like the Sun.' In *New Feminist Discourses*. Ed. Isobel Armstrong. London: Routledge, 1992. 154–175.

Hyrde, Richard. See Desiderius Erasmus. Preface to the *Devout Paternoster*.
Irigaray, Luce. *Elemental Passions*. Trans. Joanne Collie and Judith Still. New York: Routledge, 1992.
———. *An Ethics of Sexual Difference*. Ithaca: Cornell University Press, 1984.
———. 'Interviews.' In *Les Femmes, la pornographie et l'érotisme*. Ed. Marie-Francoise Hans and Gilles Lapouge. Paris: Seuil, 1978. 43–58; 302–304.
———. *Marine Lover of Friedrich Nietzsche*. Trans. Gillian C. Gill. New York: Columbia University Press, 1991.
———. *Sexes and Genealogies*. Trans. Gillian C. Gill. New York: Columbia Press, 1993.
———. *Speculum of the Other Woman*. Trans. Gillian Gill. Ithaca, NY: Cornell University Press, 1985.
———. *This Sex Which Is Not One*. Trans. Catherine Porter. Ithaca, NY: Cornell University Press, 1985.
Jankowski, Theodora. '"Where there can be no cause of affection": Redefining Virgins, their Desires, and their Pleasures in John Lyly's *Gallathea*.' In *Feminist Readings of Early Modern Culture: Emerging Subjects*. Cambridge: Cambridge University Press, 1996. 253–274.
Jardine, Lisa. 'Isotta Nogarola: Women Humanists – Education for What?' *History of Education* 12 (1983): 231–244.
Jeamson, Thomas. *Artificiall Embellishments*. Oxford, 1665.
Jed, Stephanie. *Chaste Thinking*. Bloomington: Indiana University Press, 1989.
Jinner, Sarah. See Sarah Ginnor.
Joceline, Elizabeth Brooke. *The Mothers Legacie to her Unborne Childe*. London, 1624.
Johnson, Barbara. 'Metaphor, Metonymy, and Voice in *Their Eyes Were Watching God*.' In *Black Literature and Literary Theory*. Ed. Henry Louis Gates. New York: Methuen, 1984. 205–219.
Jones, Ann Rosalind. *The Currency of Eros: Women's Love Lyric in Europe, 1540–1620*. Bloomington: Indiana University Press, 1990.
———. 'Nets and Bridles: Early Modern Conduct Books and Sixteenth-Century Women's Lyrics.' In *Ideology of Conduct: Essays on Literature and the History of Sexuality*. Ed. Nancy Armstrong and Leonard Tennenhouse. New York: Methuen, 1987. 39–72.
———. 'New Songs for the Swallow: Ovid's Philomela in Tullia d'Aragona and Gaspara Stampa.' In *Refiguring Women: Perspectives on Gender and the Italian Renaissance*. Ed. Marilyn Migiel and Juliana Schiesari. Ithaca: Cornell UP, 1991. 263–277.
———. 'Surprising Fame: Renaissance Gender Ideologies and Women's Lyric.' In *The Poetics of Gender*. Ed. Nancy Miller. New York: Columbia University Press, 1986. 74–95.
——— and Peter Stallybras. 'Fetishizing Gender: Constructing the Hermaphrodite in Renaissance Europe.' In *Body Guards: The Cultural Politics of Gender Ambiguity*.

Ed. Julia Epstein and Kristina Straub. London and New York: Routledge, 1992. 80–111.

Jordan, Constance. *Renaissance Feminism*. Ithaca, NY: Cornell University Press, 1990.

Josephus, Flavius. *The Complete Works of Josephus*. Trans. William Whiston. Grand Rapids, MI: Kregel Publications, 1981.

Josselin, Ralph. *The Diary of Ralph Josselin: 1616–1683*. Ed. Alan Macfarlane. Oxford: Oxford University Press, 1976.

Julian of Norwich. *A Book of Showings to the Anchoress Julian of Norwich*. Ed. Edmund Colledge and James Walsh. Studies and Texts, no. 35. 2 vols. Toronto: Pontifical Institute of Medieval Studies, 1978.

Keeble, N. H. *The Cultural Identity of Seventeenth-Century Woman: A Reader*. New York and London: Routledge, 1994.

Kelly-Gadol, Joan. 'Did Women Have a Renaissance?' In *Becoming Visible: Women in European History*. Ed. Renate Bridenthal and Claudia Koonz. Boston: Houghton Mifflin, 1977. 139–164.

———. *Women, History, and Theory*. Chicago: Chicago University Press, 1984.

Kelso, Ruth. *Doctrine for the Lady of the Renaissance*. Urbana: University of Illinois Press, 1956.

Kennedy, Gwynne. 'Lessons of the "Schoole of wisedome",' In *Sexuality and Politics in Renaissance Drama*. Ed. Carole Levin and Karen Robertson. *Studies in Renaissance Literature*. Vol. 10. Lewiston/Queenston, Lampeter: Edwin Mellen Press, 1991. 113–136.

King, Kathryn. 'Jane Barker: *Poetical Recreations* and the Sociable Text.' *ELH* 61 (1994): 551–570.

King, Margaret L. 'Book-Lined Cells: Women and Humanism in the Early Italian Renaissance.' In *Beyond Their Sex: Learned Women in the European Past*. Ed. Patricia Labalme. New York: New York University Press, 1980. 66–90.

———. *Women of the Renaissance*. Chicago: University of Chicago Press, 1991.

Kinnaird, Joan. 'Mary Astell and the Conservative Contribution to English Feminism.' *Journal of British Studies* 19 (1979): 53–75.

———. 'Mary Astell: Inspired by Ideas.' In *Feminist Theorists*. Ed. Dale Spender. New York: Pantheon, 1983. 28–39.

Kipnis, Laura. 'Feminism: The Political Conscience of Postmodernism?' In *Universal Abandon*. Ed. Andrew Ross. Minneapolis: University of Minnesota Press, 1988. 149–166.

Kirkham, Victoria. 'The Book and the Idea of the Book.' Conference paper. University of Pennsylvania, 27 October 1989.

Kristeva, Julia. *Desire in Language: A Semiotic Approach to Literature and Art*. Ed. Leon S. Roudiez. Trans. Thomas Gora, Alice Jardine and Leon S. Roudiez. New York: Columbia University Press, 1980.

———. *The Revolution of Poetic Language*. Trans. Margaret Waller. New York: Columbia University Press, 1984.

———. 'Stabat Mater.' *Tales of Love*. Trans. Leon S. Roudiez. New York: Columbia, 1987. 234–264.

Krontiris, Tina. *Oppositional Voices: Women as Writers and Translators of Literature in the English Renaissance*. London: Routledge, 1992.

Kussmaul, Ann. *Servants in Husbandry in Early Modern England*. Cambridge: Cambridge University Press, 1981.

Kusunoki, Akiko. 'Their Testament at their Apron-Strings: The Representation of Puritan Women in Early Seventeenth-Century England.' In *Gloriana's Face: Women, Public and Private in the English Renaissance*. Ed. S.P. Ceresano and Marion Wynne-Davies. Detroit: Wayne State University Press, 1992. 185–204.

Labalme, Patricia (ed.). *Beyond Their Sex: Learned Women of the European Past*. New York: New York: New York University Press, 1980.

Lacan, Jacques. *Ecrits: A Selection*. Trans. Alan Sheridan. New York: W.W. Norton, 1977.

———. 'The Insistence of the Letter in the Unconscious.' In *Modern Criticism and Theory*. Ed. David Lodge. London: Longman, 1988. 80–106.

The Ladies Dictionary. London, 1694.

The Ladies Remonstrance. London, 1659.

The Lady Falkland Her Life By One of Her Daughters. In *The Tragedy of Mariam Fair Queen of Jewry*. Ed. Barry Weller and Margaret Ferguson. Berkeley: University of California Press, 1994.

The Lady Falkland: Her Life. From a MS in the Imperial Archives at Lille. Also, A Memoir of Father Francis Slingsby. From MSS in the Royal Library, Brussels. London: Catholic Publishing and Bookselling Company, 1861.

Lamb, Mary Ellen. *Gender and Authorship in the Sidney Circle*. Madison: University of Wisconsin Press, 1990.

———. 'Patronage and Class in Aemilia Lanyer's *Salve Deus Rex Judaeorum*.' In *Women, Writing, and the Reproduction of Culture in Tudor and Stuart Britain*. Syracuse: Syracuse University Press, 2000. 38–57.

Lanyer, Aemilia. *Salve Deus Rex Judaeorum*. London, 1611.

———. *Salve Deus Rex Judaeorum*. Ed. Susanne Woods. New York and Oxford: Oxford University Press, 1993.

Laqueur, Thomas. *Making Sex*. Cambridge, MA: Harvard University Press, 1990.

Laurence, Anne. *Women in England 1500–1760: A Social History*. New York: St Martin's Press, 1994.

———. 'Women's Psychological Disorders in 17th-Century Britain.' In *Current Issues in Women's History*. Ed. Arina Angerman, Geerte Binnema, Annemieke Keunen, Vefie Poels and Jacqueline Zirkzee. London: Routledge, 1990. 203–219.

The Lawes Resolution of Womens Rights: or the Lawes Provision for Women. London, 1632.

Lead, Jane. *The revelation of revelations, particularly as an essay towards the unsealing, opening and discovering the seven seals*. London, 1683.

Leicester, H. Marshall. *The Disenchanted Self: Representing the Subject in the Canterbury Tales*. Berkeley: University of California Press, 1990.

Leigh, Dorothy. *The Mothers Blessing*. London, 1616.

Levi-Strauss, Claude. *Tristes Tropiques*. Trans. John and Doreen Weightman. New York: Atheneum, 1974.

Levine, Laura. 'Men in Women's Clothing: Anti-Theatricality and Effeminization from 1579–1642.' *Criticism* 28 (1986): 121–143.

Lewalski, Barbara. 'Of God and Good Women: The Poems of Aemilia Lanyer.' In *Silent But for the Word*. Ed. Margaret Hannay. Kent: Kent State University Press, 1985. 203–224.

———. 'Seizing Discourses and Reinventing Genres.' In *Aemilia Lanyer: Gender, Genre, and the Canon*. Ed. Marshall Grossman. Lexington: University Press of Kentucky, 1998. 49–59.

———. *Writing Women in Jacobean England*. Cambridge, MA: Harvard University Press, 1993.

Lilley, Kate. 'True State Within: Women's Elegy 1640–1700.' In *Women, Writing, History 1640–1740*. Ed. Isobel Grundy and Susan Wiseman. Athens: University of Georgia Press, 1992. 72–92.

Lipovetsky, Gilles. *The Empire of Fashion: Dressing Modern Democracy*. Trans. Catherine Porter. Princeton: Princeton University Press, 1994.

Lives of Lady Anne Clifford ... and of her Parents. Ed. J.P. Gilson. London: Roxburghe Club, 1916.

Love, Harold. 'Manuscript versus Print in the Transmission of English Literature, 1600–1700.' *Bibliographical Society of Australia and New Zealand* 9 (1985): 130–154.

Luecke, Marilyn. 'The Reproduction of Culture and the Culture of Reproduction in Elizabeth Clinton's *The Countesse of Lincolnes Nurserie*.' In *Women, Writing, and the Reproduction of Culture in Tudor and Stuart Britain*. Ed. Mary E. Burke et al. Syracuse: Syracuse University Press, 2000. 238–252.

Lucas, Caroline. *Writing for Women: The Example of Woman as Reader in Elizabethan Romance*. Milton Keynes: Open University Press, 1989.

M.R. *The Mother's Counsell*. London, 163[0].

Macdonald, Michael. *Mystical Bedlam: Madness, Anxiety, and Healing in 17th-Century England*. Cambridge: Cambridge University Press, 1981.

Macfarlane, Alan. *Marriage and Love in England 1300–1840*. Oxford: Blackwell, 1986.

Mack, Phyllis. *Visionary Women: Ecstatic Prophecy in 17th-Century England*. Berkeley: University of California Press, 1992.

Maclean, Ian. *The Renaissance Notion of Woman*. Cambridge: Cambridge University Press, 1980.

Mahl, Mary and Helen Koon (eds). *The Female Spectator: English Women Writers Before 1800*. Bloomington: Indiana University Press, 1977.

Makin, Bathsua. *An Essay to Revive the Antient Education of Gentlewomen, in Religion, Maners, Art, and Tongues*. London, 1674.

Manning, Roger. *Village Revolts: Social Protest and Popular Disturbances in England, 1509–1640*. Oxford: Clarendon Press, 1988.

Marcus, Leah. 'Shakespeare's Comic Heroines, Elizabeth I, and the Political Uses of Androgyny.' In *Women in the Middle Ages and the Renaissance*. Ed. Mary Beth Rose. Syracuse: Syracuse University Press, 1986. 135–153

Markham, Gervase. *Country Contentment in Two Books. The English Huswife*. London, 1615.

Marotti, Arthur. *Manuscript, Print, and the English Renaissance*. Ithaca: Cornell University Press, 1995.

Marquis, Paul A. 'Oppositional Ideologies of Gender in Isabella Whitney's *Copy of a letter*.' *MLR* 90 (1995): 314–324.

Masham, Damaris. *Occasional Thoughts in reference to a Vertuous or Christian Life*. London, 1705.

Massey, Doreen. *Space, Place, and Gender*. Minneapolis: University of Minnesota Press, 1994.

Masten, Jeffrey. '"Shall I Turne Blabb?": Circulation, Gender, and Subjectivity in Mary Wroth's Sonnets.' In *Reading Mary Wroth: Representing Alternatives in Early Modern England*. Ed. Naomi J. Miller and Gary Waller. Knoxville: University of Tennessee Press, 1991. 67–87.

———. *Textual Intercourse: Collaboration, Authorship, and Sexualities in Renaissance Drama*. Cambridge: Cambridge University Press, 1997.

McDonald, Diane L. *Transgressive Corporeality: The Body, Poststructuralism, and the Theoretical Imagination*. Albany: SUNY Press, 1995.

McGrath, Lynette. 'John Donne's Apology for Poetry.' *SEL* 20 (1980): 73–89.

———. 'Isabella Whitney and the Ideologies of Writing and Publication.' *Options for Teaching Early Modern British Women Writers*. Ed. Susanne Woods and Margaret Hannay. New York: MLA, 2000. 283–288.

———. '"Let Us Have Our Libertie Againe": Amelia Lanier's 17th-Century Feminist Voice.' *Women's Studies* 20 (1992): 331–348.

———. 'Metaphoric Subversions: Feasts and Mirrors in Amelia Lanier's *Salve Deus Rex Judaeorum*.' *LIT* 3 (1991): 101–113.

McLaren, Angus. *A History of Contraception: Fertility Control in Early Modern Europe*. Oxford: Blackwell, 1990.

McLaren, Dorothy. 'Marital Fertility and Lactation, 1570–1720.' In *Women in English Society*. Ed. Mary Prior. London: Methuen, 1985. 22–53.

McLaughlin, Eleanor Como. 'Equality of Souls, Inequality of Sexes: Woman in Medieval Theology.' In *Religion and Sexism*. Ed. Rosemary Radford Ruether. New York: Simon and Schuster, 1974. 213–266.

Mendelson, Sara Heller. *The Mental World of Stuart Women: Three Studies*. Amherst: University of Massachusetts Press, 1987.

———. 'Stuart Women's Diaries and Occasional Memoirs.' In *Women in English Society, 1500–1800*. Ed. Mary Prior. London: Methuen, 1985. 181–210.

Merleau-Ponty, Maurice. *The Phenomenology of Perception*. Trans. Colin Smith. New York: Humanities Press, 1962.

Mildmay, Grace. 'Journal.' Ed. Rachel Weigall, 'An Elizabethan Gentlewoman.' *Quarterly Review* 215 (1911): 119–138.

Miles, Margaret. *Carnal Knowing: Female Nakedness and Religious Meaning in the Christian West*. Boston: Beacon, 1989.

Miller, Edwin. *The Professional Writer in England*. Cambridge: Harvard University Press, 1959.

Miller, Jacqueline. 'Mother Tongues: Language and Lactation in Early Modern Literature.' Paper read at Renaissance Society of America annual meeting. New York, 31 March 1995.

Miller, Naomi. 'Domestic Politics in Elizabeth Cary's *The Tragedy of Mariam*.' *SEL* 37 (1997): 353–369.

———. '(M)other Tongues: Maternity and Subjectivity.' In *Aemilia Lanyer: Gender, Genre, and the Canon*. Ed. Marshall Grossman. Lexington: University Press of Kentucky, 1998. 143–166.

Mintz, Sidney. *Tasting Food, Tasting Freedom: Excursions into Eating, Culture, and the Past*. Boston: Beacon, 1996.

More, St. Thomas. *Selected Letters*. Ed. Frances Rogers. New Haven: Yale University Press, 1961.

Moulsworth, Martha. *'My Name Was Martha': A Renaissance Woman's Autobiographical Poem*. Ed. Robert C. Evans and Barbara Wiedemann. West Cornwall, CT: Locust Hill Press, 1993.

Mueller, Janel. 'The Feminist Poetics of Aemilia Lanyer's *Salve Deus Rex Judaeorum*.' In *Feminist Measures*. Ed. Lynn Keller and Christianne Miller. Ann Arbor: University of Michigan Press, 1994. 208–236. Reprinted in *Aemilia Lanyer: Gender, Genre, and the Canon*. Ed. Marshall Grossman. Lexington: University of Kentucky Press, 1998. 99–127.

Mulcaster, Richard. *Positions necessarie for the training up of children* ... London, 1581.

Murrell, John. *A Daily Exercise for Ladies and Gentlewomen*. London, 1617.

Myers, Mitzi. 'Fictions of the Self.' *Women's Review of Books*. 8:4 (1991): 20–22.

Neely, Carol Thomas. 'Considering the Subject: Feminist Practice and the New Renaissance Discourses.' *ELR* 18 (1988): 5–18.

Nelson, Karen. 'Elizabeth Cary's *Edward II*: Advice to Women at the Court of Charles I.' In *Women, Writing, and the Reproduction of Culture in Tudor and Stuart Britain*. Ed. Mary E. Burke et al. Syracuse, NY: Syracuse University Press, 2000. 157–173.

Newman, Karen. *Fashioning Femininity and English Renaissance Drama*. Chicago: Chicago University Press, 1991.

Newton, Judith Lowder. 'History as Usual? Feminism and the "New Historicism".' In *The New Historicism*. Ed. H. Aram Veeser. New York: Routledge, 1989. 152–167.

———. 'Making – and Remaking – History.' In *Feminist Issues in Literary Scholarship*. Ed. Shari Benstock. Bloomington: Indiana University Press, 1987. 124–140.

Nichols, John. *The Progresses and Public Processions of Queen Elizabeth*. London: John Nichols, 1823. Rpt. New York: AMS Press, 1969.

Nolan, Edward Peter. *Now Through a Glass Darkly: Specular Images of Being and Knowing from Virgil to Chaucer*. Ann Arbor: University of Michigan Press, 1990.

Norton Anthology of English Literature. Gen. ed. M.H. Abrams. 5th edn. Vol. 1. New York: Norton, 1986.

Oates, Mary I. '*Fowre Hymnes*: Retractions of Paradise.' *Spenser Studies* 4 (1983): 143–169.

Offen, Karen. 'Defining Feminism: A Comparative Historical Approach.' *Signs* (1988): 119–157.

Oliver, Kelly. *Reading Kristeva: Unraveling the Double-Bind*. Bloomington: Indiana University Press, 1993.

Ong, Walter. 'Commonplace Rhapsody: Ravisius Testor, Zwingler, and Shakespeare.' In *Classical Influences on European Culture. A.D. 1500–1700*. Cambridge: Cambridge University Press, 1971. 91–126.

———. *Orality and Literacy: The Technologizing of the Word*. London: Methuen, 1982.

Orgel, Stephen. 'Nobody's Perfect, Or: Why Did the English Stage Take Boys for Women?' *South Atlantic Quarterly* 88 (1989): 7–29.

Orlin, Lena Cowen. *Elizabethan Households: An Anthology*. Washington, DC: Folger Shakespeare Library, 1995.

Otten, Charlotte F. (ed.). *English Women's Voices 1540–1700*. Miami: Florida International University Press, 1992.

Overbury, Thomas. *The Overburian Characters*. Ed. W.J. Paylor. Oxford: Blackwell, The Percy Reprints 13, 1936.

Owen, Jane. *An Antidote against Purgatory*. London, 1634.

Oxlie, Mary, of Morpeth. 'To William Drummond of Hawthornden.' Prefatory commendatory poem, *Poems of William Drummond of Hawthornden*. London, 1656.

Ozment, Steven. 'The Family in Reformation Germany: The Bearing and Rearing of Children.' *Journal of Family History* 8 (1983): 159–176.

Pagels, Elaine. *The Gnostic Gospels*. New York: Random House, 1979.

Pantzer, Katherine F. (Comp). 'Printers' and Publishers' Index.' In *A Short Title Catalogue of Books Printed in England, Scotland, and Ireland and of Books Printed Abroad*. London: Bibliographical Society, 1991.

Park, Katherine. 'The Rediscovery of the Clitoris: French Medicine and the Tribade, 1570–1620.' In *The Body in Parts*. Ed. David Hillman and Carla Mazzio. New York and London: Routledge, 1997. 171–193.

Parker, Patricia. *Literary Fat Ladies: Rhetoric, Gender, Property*. London: Methuen, 1987.
Parr, Susanna. *Susanna's Apology Against the Elders*. London, 1659.
Paster, Gail Kern. *The Body Embarrassed: Drama and the Disciplines of Shame in Early Modern England*. Ithaca: Cornell University Press, 1993.
Paul, Henry N. *The Royal Play of Macbeth*. New York: Macmillan, 1950.
Pearse, Nancy Cotton. 'Elizabeth Cary, Renaissance Playwright.' *TSLL* 18 (1977): 601–608.
Pearson, Jacqueline. 'Women Reading, Reading Women.' In *Women and Literature in Britain 1500–1700*. Ed. Helen Wilcox. Cambridge: Cambridge University Press, 1996. 80–99.
———. 'Women Writers and Women Readers: The Case of Aemilia Lanyer.' In *Voicing Women: Gender and Sexuality in Early Modern Writing*. Ed. Kate Chedzgoy, Melanie Hansen and Suzanne Trill. Keele, Staffs: Keele University Press, 1996. 45–54.
Pearson, Lu Emily. *Elizabethans at Home*. Stanford: Stanford University Press, 1957.
Pepys, Samuel. *The Diary of Samuel Pepys*. Ed. Robert Latham and William Matthews. London: Bell and Sons, 1976.
Pequigney, Joseph. *Such is My Love: A Study of Shakespeare's Sonnets*. Chicago: Chicago University Press, 1985.
Perry, Ruth. *The Celebrated Mary Astell*. Chicago: University of Chicago Press, 1986.
Philips, Joan. *Female Poems on Several Occasions*. London, 1679.
Philips, Katherine. *Poems*. London, 1664.
Phillips, Roderick. *Putting Asunder: A History of Divorce in Western Society*. Cambridge: Cambridge University Press, 1988.
Plat, Hugh. *Delights for Ladies to Adorn their Persons*. London, 1602.
———. *Floraes Paradise, beautified and adorned*. London, 1608.
———. *The Floures of Philosophie*. London, 1572.
The Political Works of James I: Reprinted from the Edition of 1616. Ed. Charles Howard McIlwain. New York: Russell and Russell, 1965.
Pollock, Linda. 'Embarking on a Rough Passage: The Experience of Pregnancy in Early Modern Society.' In *Women as Mothers in Pre-Industrial England*. Ed. Valerie Fildes. London: Routledge, 1990. 39–67.
Poovey, Mary. 'Cultural Criticism: Past and Present.' *College English* 52 (1990): 615–625.
———. *Uneven Developments: The Ideological Work of Gender in Mid-Victorian England*. Chicago: Chicago University Press, 1988.
Powell, Thomas. *Tom of All Trades. Or the Plaine Pathway to Preferment*. London, 1631.
Prescott, Anne Lake. Paper read at conference on 'Attending to Women in Early Modern England.' University of Maryland, 9 November 1990.

Prior, Mary (ed). *Women in English Society 1500–1800*. London: Methuen, 1985.

Purkiss, Diane. 'Producing the Voice, Consuming the Body.' In *Women, Writing History 1640–1740*. Ed. Isobel Grundy and Susan Wiseman. Athens: University of Georgia Press, 1992. 139–158.

Puttenham, George. *The Arte of English Poesie*. Ed. Gladys Doidge Willcock and Alice Walker. Cambridge: Cambridge University Press, 1970.

Quilligan, Maureen. '"Exit, Pursued by a Bear": Trivial Connections between the Epic and the Pastoral.' Paper read at MLA annual convention, 1989.

———. 'Staging Gender: William Shakespeare and Elizabeth Cary.' In *Sexuality and Gender in Early Modern Europe*. Ed. James Grantham Turner. Cambridge: Cambridge University Press, 1993. 208–232.

Quitslund, Jon A. 'Spenser and the Patronesses of the *Fowre Hymnes*: Ornaments of All True Love and Beautie.' In *Silent But For the Word*. Ed. Margaret Hannay. Kent, Ohio: Kent State University Press, 1985. 184–202.

Raber, Karen L. 'Gender and the Political Subject in *The Tragedy of Mariam*.' *SEL* 35 (1995): 321–343.

Raynalde, Thomas. *The Byrth of Mankynde*. London, 1545.

Regan, Mariann Sanders. *Love Words: The Self and the Text in Medieval and Renaissance Poetry*. Ithaca: Cornell University Press, 1982.

A Remonstrance of the Shee-Citizens of London. London, 1647.

Reynolds, Myra. *The Learned Lady in England 1650–1760*. Boston: Houghton Mifflin, 1920.

Riley, Denise. *'Am I That Name?' Feminism and the Category of 'Women' in History*. Minneapolis: University of Minnesota Press, 1988.

Roberts, Josephine (ed.). *The Poems of Lady Mary Wroth*. Baton Rouge: Louisiana State University Press, 1983.

Roberts, Sasha. 'Shakespeare "creepes into the womens closets about bedtime": Women Reading in a Room of Their Own.' In *Renaissance Configurations: Voices/Bodies/Spaces, 1580–1690*. Ed. Gordon McMullan. New York: St Martin's Press, 1998. 30–63.

Robertson, Elizabeth. 'The Rule of the Body. The Feminine Spirituality of the *Ancrene Wisse*.' In *Seeking the Woman in Late Medival and Renaissance Writings*. Ed. Sheila Fisher and Janet Halley. Knoxville: University of Tennessee Press, 1989: 109–134.

Roisin, Simone. *L'Hagiographie cistercienne dans le diocèse de Liège au XIIIe siècle*. Louvain, 1947.

Rose, Mary Beth (ed.). *Women in the Middle Ages and the Renaissance*. Syracuse: Syracuse University Press, 1986.

Rowlands, Samuel. *Uncollected Poems (1603–1617)*. Intro. F.O. Waage, Jr. Gainesville: Scholars Press, 1970.

Rowse, A.L. *The Poems of Shakespeare's Dark Lady: 'Salve Deus Rex Judaeorum' by Emilia Lanier*. New York: Clarkson N. Potter, 1978.

Ruether, Rosemary Radford. 'Misogynism and Virginal Feminism in the Fathers of the Church.' In *Religion and Sexism*. Ed. Rosemary Radford Ruether. New York: Simon and Schuster, 1974. 150–183.

Sadler, John. *The Sicke Womans Private Looking-Glasse wherein Methodically are handled all uterine affects, or diseases arising from the womb* ... London, 1636.

Salgado, Gamini. *The Elizabethan Underworld*. New York: St. Martin's Press, 1993.

Salter, Thomas. *A Mirror mete for all Mothers, Matrones, and Maids*. London, 1579.

Sankovitch, Tilde. 'Inventing Authority of Origin: The Difficult Enterprise.' In *Women in the Middle Ages and the Renaissance: Literary and Historical Perspectives*. Ed. Mary Beth Rose. Syracuse: Syracuse University Press, 1986. 227–243.

Saunders, J.W. 'The Stigma of Print: A Note on the Social Bases of Tudor Poetry.' *Essays on Criticism* 1 (1951): 139–164.

Sawday, Jonathan. *The Body Emblazoned: Dissection and the Human Body in Renaissance Culture*. London and New York: Routledge, 1995.

———. 'The Fate of Marsyas: Dissecting the Renaissance Body.' In *Renaissance Bodies: The Human Figure in English Culture c. 1540–1660*. Ed. Lucy Gent and Nigel Llewellyn. London: Reaktion Books, 1990. 111–135.

———. 'Self and Selfhood in the Seventeenth Century.' In *Rewriting the Self: Histories from the Renaissance to the Present*. London: Routledge, 1997. 29–48.

Scharfman, Ronnie. 'Mirroring and Mothering ...' *Yale French Studies* 62 (1981): 88–106.

Schiesari, Juliana. *The Gendering of Melancholia: Feminism, Psychoanalysis, and the Symbolics of Loss in Renaissance Literature*. Ithaca, NY: Cornell University Press, 1992.

Schleiner, Louise. *Tudor and Stuart Women Writers*. Bloomington: Indiana University Press, 1994.

Schleiner, Winfried. *Medical Ethics in the Renaissance*. Washington, DC: Georgetown University Press, 1995.

Schofield, R.S. 'Did the Mothers Really Die? Three Centuries of Maternal Mortality in "the World we have Lost."' In *The World We Have Gained*. Ed. L. Bonfield, R. Smith and K. Wrightson. Oxford: Oxford University Press, 1986. 231–260.

———. 'The Measurement of Literacy in Pre-Industrial England.' In *Literacy in Traditional Societies*. Ed. J.R. Goody. Cambridge: Cambridge University Press, 1968. 318–325.

Schwarz, Kathryn. 'Missing the Breast: Desire, Disease, and the Singular Effect of Amazons.' In *The Body in Parts*. Ed. David Hillman and Carla Mazzio. New York and London: Routledge, 1997. 147–169.

Schweikart, Patrocinio. 'Reading Ourselves: Toward a Feminist Theory of Reading.' In *Gender and Reading*. Ed. Elizabeth A. Flynn and Patrocinio Schweikart. Baltimore: Johns Hopkins University Press, 1986. 31–62.

Scott, Joan. 'Gender: A Useful Category of Historical Analysis.' *AHR* 91 (1986): 1053–1075.

———. 'The Evidence of Experience.' *Critical Inquiry* 17 (Summer 1991): 773–797.
Scott-Elliott, A.H. and Elspeth Yeo. 'Calligraphic Manuscripts of Esther Inglis (1571–1624): A Catalogue.' *PBSA* 84 (1990): 11–86.
Sedgwick, Eve Kokofsky. *Between Men: English Literature and Male Homosocial Desire*. New York: Columbia Press, 1985.
The severall places where you may hear news. London, c. 1640.
Sharp, Jane. *Midwives Book*. London, 1671.
Shawcross, John. ' "The Muses Females Are": Renaissance Women and Education.' In *The Muses Females Are: Martha Moulsworth and Other Women Writers of the English Renaissance*. Ed. Robert C. Evans and Anne C. Little. West Cornwall, CT: Locust Hill Press, 1995. 163–172.
Showalter, Elaine. 'Toward a Feminist Poetics.' In *The New Feminist Criticism*. Ed. Elaine Showalter. New York: Pantheon, 1985. 125–143.
———. *Speaking of Gender*. New York: Routledge, 1989.
Shuger, Deborah. 'The "I" of the Beholder: Renaissance Mirrors and the Reflexive Mind.' In *Renaissance Culture and the Everyday*. Philadelphia: University of Pennsylvania Press, 1999. 21–41.
———. *Habits of Thought in the English Renaissance*. Berkeley: University of California Press, 1990.
Sidney, Mary. *The Psalms of Sir Philip Sidney and the Countess of Pembroke*. Ed. J.C.A. Rathmell. New York: New York University Press, 1963.
Sidney, Philip. *An Apology for Poetry*. London: Nelson, 1965.
Siebert, Frederick Seaton. *Freedom of the Press in England 1476–1776*. Urbana: University of Illinois Press, 1965.
Silverman, Kaja. *Threshold of the Visible World*. New York and London: Routledge, 1996.
Simon, Joan. *Education and Society in Tudor England*. Cambridge: Cambridge University Press, 1967.
Skura, Meredith. 'The Reproduction of Mothering in *Mariam, Queen of Jewry*: A Defense of "Biographical" Criticism.' *TSWL* 16 (1997): 27–56.
Smith, Bruce. 'Premodern Sexualities.' *PMLA* 115.3 (May, 2000): 318–329.
Smith, Henry. *Preparative for Marriage*. London, 1591.
Smith, Hilda. 'Gynecology and Ideology in Seventeenth-Century England.' In *Liberating Women's History*. Ed. Berenice A. Carroll. Urbana: University of Illinois Press, 1976. 97–114.
———. 'Humanist Education and the Renaissance Concept of Woman.' In *Women and Literature in Britain 1500–1700*. Ed. Helen Wilcox. Cambridge: Cambridge University Press, 1996. 9–29.
———. *Reasons's Disciples: Seventeenth-Century English Feminists*. Urbana: University of Illinois Press, 1982.
——— and Susan Cardinale. *Women and the Literature of the Seventeenth Century*. New York: Greenwood Press, 1990.

Smith, Roger. 'Self-Reflection and the Self.' In *Rewriting the Self: Histories from the Renaissance to the Present*. Ed. Roy Porter. London and New York: Routledge, 1997. 49–57.

Smith-Rosenberg, Carol. 'The Female World of Love and Ritual: Relations Between Women in Nineteenth-Century America.' *Signs* 1 (1975): 1–29.

Souden, David and Peter Clark (eds). *Migration and Society in Early Modern England*. London: Unwin, 1988.

Southwell, Anne. '*Lady Southwell's Defense of Poetry*.' Ed. Jean C. Cavanaugh. In *Women in The Renaissance: Selections from ELR*. Ed. Kirby Farrell, Elizabeth Hageman and Arthur Kinney. Amherst: University of Massachusetts Press, 1988. 175–178.

Spain, Daphne. *Gendered Spaces*. Chapel Hill: University of North Carolina Press, 1992.

Straznicky, Marta. '"Profane Stoical Paradoxes': *The Tragedie of Mariam* and Sidneian Closet Drama.' *ELR* 24 (1994): 104–133.

Summit, Jennifer. *Lost Property: The Woman Writer and English Literary History 1380–1589*. Chicago: University of Chicago Press, 2000.

Speght, Rachel. *Mortalities Memorandum, with a Dreame Prefixed, imaginarie in manner; Reall in matter*. London, 1621.

Spivak, Gayatri. 'Subaltern Studies: Deconstructing Historiography.' In *Selected Subaltern Studies*. Ed. Ranajit Guha and Gayatri Spivak. New York: Oxford University Press, 1988. 3–32.

Spufford, Margaret. 'First Steps in Literacy: The Reading and Writing Experiences of the Humblest 17th-Century Spiritual Autobiographers.' *Social History* 4 (1979): 407–435.

———. *Small Books and Pleasant Histories: Popular Fiction and its Readership In Seventeenth-Century England*. Athens: University of Georgia Press, 1981.

Stallybras, Peter. 'Patriarchal Territories: The Body Enclosed.' In *Rewriting the Renaissance*. Ed. Margaret Ferguson, Maureen Quilligan and Nancy Vickers. Chicago: University of Chicago Press, 1986. 123–142.

Steen, Sara Jayne. 'Fashioning an Acceptable Self: Arbella Stuart.' In *Women in the Renaissance: Selections from ELR*. Ed Kirby Farrell, Elizabeth Hageman and Arthur Kinney. Amherst: University of Massachusetts Press, 1988. 136–153.

Stock, Phyllis. *Better than Rubies: A History of Women's Education*. New York: Putnam, 1978.

Stone, Lawrence. *The Family, Sex, and Marriage in England 1500–1800*. New York: Harper, 1977.

———. 'The Education Revolution in England 1560–1640.' *Past and Present* 28 (1964): 41–80.

———. 'Literacy and Education in England 1640–1900.' *Past and Present* 42 (1969): 69–139.

Stubbes, Philip. *Anatomie of Abuses*. London, 1583.

———. *A Christal Glasse for Christian Women*. London, 1591.

Stuckey, Elspeth. *The Violence of Literacy*. Portsmouth, NH: Boynton/Cook, 1991.

Sutcliffe, Alice. *Meditations of Man's Mortalitie or, A Way to true Blessednesse*. London, 1633.

Tattlewell, Mary and Joan Hit-Him-Home. *The Women's Sharpe Revenge*. In *Half Humankind*. 306–325.

Teague, Frances. *Bathsua Makin: Woman of Learning*. Lewisburg, PA: Bucknell University Press, 1998.

———. 'Judith Shakespeare Reading.' *Shakespeare Quarterly* 47 (1996): 361–373.

Thickstun, Margaret Olofson. *Fictions of the Feminine*. Ithaca, NY: Cornell University Press, 1988.

Thomas, Keith. 'The Meaning of Literacy in Early Modern England.' In *The Written Word: Literacy in Transition*. Ed. Gerd Baumann. Oxford: Oxford University Press, 1986. 97–131.

Thornton, Alicc. *The Autobiography of Mrs Alice Thornton of East Newton, County York*. Durham: Surtees Society, 1875. Vol. 65.

Thrupp, Sylvia. *The Merchant Class of Medieval London*. Ann Arbor: University of Michigan Press, 1976.

Tilney, Edmund. *A Briefe and Pleasant Discourse of Duties in Mariage, called the Flower of Friendship*. London, 1586.

Tittle-tattle; or the severall branches of gossipping. B.M. Satires no. 61.

The Tragedy of Mariam: The Fair Queen of Jewry with The Lady Falkland Her Life By One of her Daughters. Ed. Barry Weller and Margaret W. Ferguson. Berkeley: University of California Press, 1994.

Trapnel, Anna. *Anna Trapnel's Report and Plea*. London, 1654.

Traub, Valerie. 'Gendering Mortality in Early Modern Anatomies.' In *Feminist Readings of Early Modern Culture*. Ed. Valerie Traub, M. Lindsay Kaplan and Dympna Callaghan. Cambridge: Cambridge University Press, 1996. 44–92.

———. 'The (In)Signficance of "Lesbian" Desire in Early Modern England.' In *Queering the Renaissance*. Ed. Jonathan Goldberg. Durham: Duke University Press, 1994. 62–83.

———, M.L. Kaplan and Dympna Callaghan (eds). 'Introduction.' In *Feminist Readings of early Modern Culture: Emerging Subjects*. Cambridge: Cambridge University Press, 1996. 1–15.

Travitsky, Betty. 'The *Feme Covert* in Elizabeth Cary's *Mariam*.' In *Ambiguous Realities: Women in the Middle Ages and Renaissance*. Ed. Carole Levin and Jeanie Watson. Detroit: Wayne University Press, 1987. 184–196.

———. 'The Lady Doth Protest: Protest in the Popular Writings of Renaissance Englishwomen.' *ELR* 14 (1984): 255–283.

———. 'The New Mother of the English Renaissance (1489–1659): A Descriptive Catalogue.' *BHR* 82 (1979): 63–89.

———. 'The New Mother of the English Renaissance: Her Writings on Motherhood.' In *The Lost Tradition: Mothers and Daughters in Literature*. Ed. Catherine N. Davidson and E.M. Broner. New York: Ungar, 1980. 33–43.

———. *The Paradise of Women*. New York: Columbia University Press, 1981.

———. 'Placing Women in the Renaissance.' In *The Renaissance Englishwoman in Print*. Ed. Anne Haselkorn and Betty Travitsky. Amherst: University of Massachusetts Press, 1990. 3–41.

The Trial of the Lord Audley, Earl of Castlehaven for Inhumanely Causing His Own Wife to be Ravished, and for Buggery. London, 1679.

Trill, Suzanne. 'Spectres and Sisters: Mary Sidney and the 'Perennial Puzzle' of Renaissance Women's Writing.' In *Renaissance Configurations: Voices, Bodies, Spaces 1580–1690*. Ed. Gordon McMullan. London: MacMillan, 1998. 191–211.

Triumph of Female Wit. London, 1683.

Trousdale, Marion. *Shakespeare and the Rhetoricians*. Aldershot: Scolar Press, 1982.

Trumbach, Randolph. 'London's Sapphists: From Three Sexes to Four Genders in the Making of Modern Culture.' In *Body Guards: The Cultural Politics of Gender Ambiguity*. New York: Routlcdgc, 1992. 112–141.

Trye, Mary. *Medicatrix or the Woman-Physician*. London, 1675.

Tuke, Thomas. *A Treatise against Painting and Tincturing of Men and Women*. London, 1616.

Turner, James Grantham. *One Flesh: Paradisial Marriage and Sexual Relations in the Age of Milton*. Oxford: Clarendon University Press, 1987.

Tyler, Margaret (trans.). *The First Part of the Mirrour of Princely Deeds and Knighthood*. London: 1578.

Van Meteren, Emanuel. *Pictures of the English in Queen Elizabeth's Reign. England as Seen by Foreigners in the Days of Elizabeth and James the First*. Ed. William Brenchley Rye. London: Benjamin Blom, 1865; 1967.

Van Schurman, Anna Maria. *The Learned Maid*. London, 1659.

Varchi, Benedetto. *The Blazon of Jealousie*. Trans. R. Toste. London, 1615.

Verney, Ralph. 'Letter, 27 July, 1652.' *Memoirs of the Verney Family*. Vol. 3. Ed. Frances Parthenope Verney. 4 vols. London: Longmans Green, 1892–1899

Vicary, Thomas. *The English Mans Treasurie*. London, 1641.

Vickers, Nancy. 'Diana Described: Scattered Woman and Scattered Rhyme.' *Critical Inquiry* (Winter 1981): 265–279.

———. 'Members Only.' In *The Body in Parts*. Ed. David Hillman and Carla Mazzio. New York and London: Routledge, 1997. 3–22.

Vives, Juan Luis. *Instruction of a Christian Woman*. In *Vives and the Renascence Education of Women*. Ed. Foster Watson. London: Edward Arnold, 1912.

———. *A very frutefull and pleasant boke called the Instruction of a Christen Woman*. Trans. Richard Hyrde. London, 1529.

Vokins, Joan. *Gods Mighty Powere Magnified*. London, 1691.

Vosevich, Kathi. 'The Education of a Prince(ss).' In *Women, Writing, and the Reproduction of Culture in Tudor and Stuart Britain*. Ed. Mary E. Burke et al. Syracuse: Syracuse University Press, 2000. 61–76.

Wack, Mary Frances. *Lovesickness in the Middle Ages: The Viaticum and its Commentaries*. Philadelphia: University of Pennsylvania Press, 1990.

Walker, Anthony. *The Holy Life of Mrs Elizabeth Walker*. London, 1690.
Walker, Kim. *Women Writers of the English Renaissance*. New York: Twayne, 1996.
Wall, Wendy. 'Disclosures in Print: The "Violent Enlargement" of the Renaissance Voyeuristic Text.' *SEL* 29 (1989): 35–59.
———. *The Imprint of Gender: Authorship and Publication in the English Renaissance*. Ithaca: Cornell University Press, 1993.
Waller, Gary. 'Struggling into Discourse: The Emergence of Renaissance Women's Writing.' In *Silent But for the Word*. Ed. Margaret Hannay. Kent, Ohio: Kent State University Press, 1985. 238–256.
Warnicke, Retha. 'Private and Public: The Boundaries of Women's Lives in Early Stuart England.' In *Privileging Gender in Early Modern England*. Ed. Jean R. Brink. Kirksville, MO: Northeast Missouri State University Press, 1993. 123–140.
———. *Women of the English Renaissance and Reformation*. Westport, CT: Greenwood Press, 1983.
Watson, Foster, ed. *Vives and the Renaissance Education of Women*. New York: Longmans, 1912.
Wayne, Valerie. 'Advice for Women from Mothers and Patriarchs.' In *Women and Literature In Britain 1500–1700*. Ed. Helen Wilcox. Cambridge: Cambridge University Press, 1996. 56–79.
———. 'Some Sad Sentence: Vives' *Instruction of a Christian Woman*.' In *Silent But for the Word*. Ed. Margaret Hannay. Kent, Ohio: Kent State University Press, 1985. 15–29.
Wecker, John. *Cosmeticks, Or The Beautifying Part of Physick*. London, 1660.
Weigall, Rachel. 'An Elizabethan Gentlewoman: The Journal of lady Mildmay, circa 1570–1617.' *Quarterly Review* 215 (1911): 119–138.
Weimann, Robert. *Structure and Society in Literary History: Studies in the History and Theory Of Historical Criticism*. Charlottesville: University Press of Virginia, 1976.
Wentworth, Anne. *A Vindication of Anne Wentworth*. London, 1677.
Wetherill, Lorna. 'The Meaning of Consumer Behaviour in Late Seventeenth- and Early Eighteenth-Century England.' In *Consumption and the World of Goods*. Ed. John Brewer and Roy Porter. London: Routledge, 1993. 206–227.
———. 'A Possession of One's Own: Women and Consumer Behavior in England, 1660–1740.' *Journal of British Studies* 25 (1986): 131–156.
Whalen, Molly Kirsten. 'The Public Currency of the Private Letter: Gender, Class, and Epistolarity in England, 1568–1671.' Unpublished dissertation. University of California, Santa Cruz, 1994.
Whateley, William. *A Bride Bush or Wedding Sermon*. London, 1617. Also *A Bride-Bush or a Direction for Married Persons*. London, 1619.
Whitehead, Anne. *An Epistle for the True Love, Unity, and Order in the Church of Christ*. London, 1620.
Whitney, Geffrey. *A Choice of Emblemes*. Ed. Henry Green. New York: Benjamin Blom, 1967.

Whitney, Isabella. *The copy of a letter, lately written in meeter, by a yonge gentilwoman: to her unconstant lover.* London, 1567.

———. *A sweet nosgay, or a pleasant posye: contayning a hundred and ten phylosophicall flowers*. London, 1573.

Wight, Sarah. *A Wonderful Pleasant and Profitable Letter Written by Mrs Sarah Wight*. London, 1656.

Wilcox, Helen. 'Private Writing and Public Function: Autobiographical Texts by Renaissance Englishwomen.' In *Gloriana's Face: Women, Public and Private in the English Renaissance*. Ed. S.P. Ceresano and Marion Wynne-Davies. Detroit: Wayne State University Press, 1992. 47–62.

Williamson, George. *George, Third Earl of Cumberland (1558–1605). His Life and Voyages*. Cambridge: Cambridge University Press, 1920.

Wilson, Adrian. 'The Ceremony of Childbirth and Its Interpretation.' In *Women as Mothers in Pre-Industrial England*. Ed. Valerie Fildes. London: Routledge, 1990. 68–107.

Wiltenburg, Joy. *Disorderly Women and Female Power in the Street Literature of Early Modern England and Germany*. Charlottesville and London: University Press of Virginia, 1993.

Woodbridge, Linda. *Women and the English Renaissance: Literature and the Nature of Womankind 1540–1620*. Urbana: University of Illinois Press, 1986.

Woods, Susanne. *Lanyer: A Renaissance Woman Poet*. Oxford: Oxford University Press, 1999.

——— (ed.). *The Poems of Aemilia Lanyer: Salve Deus Rex Judaeorum*. New York: Oxford University Press, 1993.

———. 'Vocation and Authority: Born to Write.' In *Aemilia Lanyer: Gender, Genre, and the Canon*. Ed. Marshall Grossman. Lexington: University Press of Kentucky, 1998. 83–98.

Woolf, Virginia. *A Room of One's Own*. London: Harcourt Brace Jovanovich, 1929.

Wright, Louis. *Middle Class Culture in Elizabethan England*. Chapel Hill: University of North Carolina Press, 1935.

Wright, Stephanie. 'The Canonization of Elizabeth Cary.' In *Voicing Women: Gender and Sexuality in Early Modern Writing*. Keele, Staffordshire: Keele University Press, 1996. 55–68.

Wroth, Mary. *Pamphilia to Amphilanthus*. London, 1621.

Wynne-Davies, Marion (ed.). *Women Poets of the Renaissance*. New York: Routledge, 1999.

Yates, James. *A glasse for amorouse maydens to looke in ...* London, 1582.

Yeager, Patricia. *Honey-Mad Women: Emancipatory Strategies in Women's Writing*. New York: Columbia University Press, 1988.

Zimmerman, Bonnie. *The Safe Sea of Women*. Boston: Beacon, 1990.

Zimmerman, Shari. 'Disaffection, Dissimulation, and the Uncertain Ground of Silent Dismission: Juxtaposing John Milton and Elizabeth Cary.' *ELH* 66 (1999): 553–589.

Index